The Sex Radicals

The Sex Radicals

Free Love in
High Victorian
America

Hal D. Sears

The Regents Press of Kansas
Lawrence

© 1977 by Hal D. Sears
All rights reserved
Reissued 2021.

Display initials are from the human alphabet by
Jo. Theodor and Jo. Israel De Bry, Frankfort O. M., 1596,
which was much used in the Victorian period.

The text of this book is licensed under a Creative Commons Attribution-
NonCommercial-NoDerivatives 4.0 International Public License
(https://creativecommons.org/licenses/by-nc-nd/4.0).

Published by the University Press of Kansas (Lawrence, Kansas 66045),
which was organized by the Kansas Board of Regents and is operated and
funded by Emporia State University, Fort Hays State University, Kansas
State University, Pittsburg State University, the University of Kansas,
and Wichita State University

Open access edition funded by the National Endowment for Humanities and
the Andrew W. Mellon Foundation Humanities Open Book Program.

Typographical errors may have been introduced in the digitization process.

Library of Congress Cataloging-in-Publication Data
Sears, Hal D. 1942–
The sex radicals : free love in high Victorian America / Hal D. Sears
Bibliography: p.
Includes index.
  ISBN 978-0-7006-0148-6 (hardback)
  ISBN 978-0-7006-3169-8 (paperback)
  ISBN 978-0-7006-3119-3 (ebook)
1. Free love—History. 2. Sexual ethics.
3. Feminism—United States. 4. Radicalism—United
States. I. Title.
HQ961.S4   301.417 76-49946

The paper used in this publication meets the minimum requirements of
the American National Standard for Permanence of Paper for Printed Library
Materials Z39.48-1992.

This work is lovingly dedicated to
Davida Moore Sears

Acknowledgments

A reading by Gilman M. Ostrander of some early chapters of this work convinced me to undertake a broader study of sex radicalism. A later draft benefited from Professor Ostrander's crisp editing, and in a number of ways his advice and encouragement have been most helpful. An invitation to a symposium on sexual thought in St. Louis in May 1971 allowed me to return to the Midwest to complete my research, and I am grateful to the history faculty of the University of Missouri–St. Louis.

My thanks to Carl Degler for reading portions of the manuscript and to David Danbom and Page Smith for their readings of complete versions. Correspondence with James C. Malin clarified and gave direction to some thoughts on various reform affairs. Although I did not always follow the astute suggestions of these scholars, I feel that the book has been improved greatly by their interest in it. I am beholden to John S. McCormick for his help in contacting the present Harman heirs; to George H. O'Brien for a helpful interview concerning the Harman family; to Jerome Harman, commissioner of the Kansas Supreme Court, for information and for a copy of Justice William A. Smith's paper on Moses Harman; and to Marvin Liebling, whose work on the Heywoods aided my own researches.

Those institutions which helped at a distance in supplying crucial or rare material include the New York Public Library, the Library of Congress, the Institute for Sex Research, Inc., at Indiana University, the University of Wyoming Library, the Archives of Brown University, and the University of California–Berkeley library. My work is much indebted to the resources and the resourceful librarians of the Kansas State Historical Society, the State Historical Society of Missouri, the Labadie Collection and the University Library of the University of Michigan, the

University of California–Santa Cruz library, and, particularly, the main, medical, and law libraries at Stanford University.

Moses Harman's experiences in Valley Falls, Kansas, suggest that the people of that town were probably more long-suffering and civilized toward his eccentricities than those of many other small American towns of that era would have been. The help I received from Arthur Strawn and the Valley Falls Historical Society demonstrated that tradition of civilization; my thanks to them. The editor of the *Virginia Quarterly Review* has kindly given me permission to use material that originally appeared in an article in that publication. I am grateful to Val Faulkenburg for her typing and other attentions to the manuscript.

In the realm of subtle debts, I would like to acknowledge one to John Chandler, formerly of the Danforth Foundation; he encouraged a spirit of worthiness to undertake large tasks. And I owe something to the anonymous microform librarian who, in 1970, phoned to tell me that the microfilm of *Lucifer* had arrived —some time after I had taken leave from Stanford and was working as an editor. I began taking notes on *Lucifer* at nights, with no expectation of writing a book, but with a desire to find out more about this free-love business in Kansas and perhaps to put together an article. This "not writing a book" effectively got me into writing one.

My gratitude to my mate, Davida Moore Sears—my patroness and refuge while writing this book—extends to all realms.

Contents

Acknowledgments — vii
List of Illustrations — xi

Part 1: The Ties That Bind — 1

1. Love Worketh No Ill: Free Love and Spiritualism — 3
2. Moses Harman — 28
3. Organized Free Thought: The National Liberal League — 34
4. *Lucifer, the Light Bearer* — 53

Part 2: Unrespectable Reform — 65

5. Awful Letters: Part 1 — 67
6. Children of Progress — 81
7. Public Opinion, the Satan Paper, and the Kansas Free Lovers — 97
8. Awful Letters: Part 2 — 107
9. The Prairie Cauldron: Reform and Regeneration, 1885–1895 — 118

Part 3: The Sex Radical Circle — 151

10. Comstock's Yokes — 153
11. The Doctors Foote — 183
12. Handmaidens of Diana: Superwomen vs. "Cumberers of the Ground" — 204
13. Handmaidens of Diana: From the Horse Penis Affair to Modernity — 229
14. The Last Chapter — 254

Appendix — 275
Notes — 281
Bibliographic Essay — 321
Index — 331

List of Illustrations

Moses Harman	31
Ezra Heywood	31
E. B. Foote, Sr.	31
E. B. Foote, Jr.	31
Excerpt from the front page of *Lucifer*	56
Classified page, *Lucifer*	56
Masthead, *Lucifer*	57
Lillian Harman	84
Edwin C. Walker	84
Moses Harman and grandson	84
George Harman	84

Part 1
The Ties That Bind

1/ Love Worketh No Ill: Free Love and Spiritualism

AMERICAN reformers of the nineteenth century, straining their imaginations to match the sprawling destiny of a rich young nation, considered no institution immune from questioning or improvement. Conventional marriage, always a provocative subject, sustained attacks from several directions.

Christians, freethinkers, Mormons, and infidels—all announced new dispensations of love and matrimony. Communitarian experiments following the doctrines of Robert Owen or Charles Fourier sought rational sexual alignments, while the Perfectionists of Oneida turned radical Christianity into a radical sociology that abjured sexual exclusiveness and enjoined the free commerce of love among the heavenly host who yet dwelled on earth, near Oneida Creek. Frances Wright, notorious because she dared the unwomanly deed of public speaking, increased her notoriety in the 1820s by arguing that free unions should replace legal marriage. Nearly a half-century later, the first woman candidate for president, Victoria Woodhull, boldly proclaimed herself a free lover from the lectern, thus creating a predictable sensation.

In the period between the proclamations of these two women, questions of sex and marriage drew a remarkable share of intellectual attention. The discussion reached its greatest intensity around the 1850s as printing presses churned out a spate of works on the subject. The founder of the Oneida Community, John Humphrey Noyes, believed that this interest in the so-called free-love question had been spawned in the religious revivalism of his own "burned-over district" of New York State. "Religious love is very near neighbor to sexual love," he wrote, "and they always get mixed in the intimacies and social excitements of Revivals. The next thing a man wants, after he has found the salvation of his soul, is to find his Eve and his Paradise."[1]

Indeed, sex radicalism was a leading product of the burned-over district. The early Mormons advocated polygamy; the Shakers preached radical celibacy; the Oneidans enjoyed complex marriage; and for those who were not interested in these sects, spiritualism offered liberation in temporal as well as ethereal spheres. In fact, the spiritualist movement, with its emphasis on personal revelation and "spiritual affinities," soon became a bastion of marital experiment. The mid-nineteenth-century quest for conjugal fulfillment rested upon a strong religious basis.

As an important effect, this interest in marriage created the myth of the "free lover," a label that was likely to be received by any who criticized or offered alternatives to prevailing domestic arrangements. But nineteenth-century free love, early or late, could seldom be characterized as libertinism; and however it varied in practice, free love always invoked an ethical justification to counter detractors who correctly argued that free love sought to subvert conventional marriage. Free love simply allowed no coercion in sexual relations, whether from the legally prescribed duties of marriage or from the unrestricted urgings of libido.

The banner of Memnonia, the Ohio free-love community of Thomas L. and Mary G. Nichols, proclaimed "FREEDOM, FRATERNITY, CHASTITY," and their doctrines justified coition between any man and woman only when they felt intense spiritual affinity, only in total absence of coercion, and then only for the sake of procreation. *Marriage and Parentage,* written by Henry C. Wright and publicized by the "American Swedenborg," Andrew Jackson Davis, summarized important principles of free love, among them the priority of female control in the sexual and generative relations, the irrelevancy of positive law to the attractions, the justification of seminal expenditure only for reproduction, and the attractional definition of marriage, which held that those who were joined by transcendental affinities were automatically and truly mated and that those who were not were divorced, regardless of legalities. Less conservative free lovers of later periods—such as Ezra Heywood, Victoria Woodhull, and Moses Hull in the 1870s, and the Moses Harman circle still later in the century—would add agitation for birth control and "free motherhood" to these principles and would disagree that coition could only be justified for procreation; but these early principles stood substantially as the basis of sex radicalism into the twentieth century.[2]

The slavery of blacks in the South provided the sex radicals of the 1850s with a great living metaphor for the sex slavery of women. It was no accident that free-love agitation emerged as a current in the same reform stream that included abolition of slavery; after all, women and slaves suffered from the same oppressor—the white male. But abolition became a Northern cause aimed at freeing the slaves in the South, whereas free love, also a Northern cause, aimed at freeing the "sex slaves" at home. Contrary to the claims of Southern critics, free love did not characterize the abolition movement. In fact, a good case can be made that the opposite sensibility prevailed: to such reformers as Theodore Dwight Weld, Angelina Grimké, and James G. Birney, civilization depended upon the personal and institutional restraint of sexual and emotional forces.[3]

Free lovers, however, did tend to be abolitionists, and in fact, many later sex radicals gravitated to the free-love cause after an apprenticeship in antislavery work. An important number became individualist anarchists in accordance with the teachings of Josiah Warren which held the individual to be sovereign in all relations so that one is "at liberty to dispose of his or her person, and time, and property in any manner in which his or her feelings or judgment may dictate, WITHOUT INVOLVING THE PERSONS OR INTERESTS OF OTHERS."[4]

Thomas L. Nichols, an exceptional free lover who decried "any rash change" in the South's peculiar institution, fled to England to escape what he considered a useless and illegal war. There he wrote a book for English readers which ranged widely over American topics and spoke knowledgeably of free love. "It is scarcely known . . . in England," he began, "to what extent the antimarriage theory has been maintained in the Northern States of America." This fortunate lack of awareness allowed Thomas and Mary Nichols to be unharried in England about their past as free-love experimenters in America; in fact they became such paragons of respectability that one present-day student of Victorian sexual respectability, Peter Cominos, used them as exemplars, apparently unaware of their free-love history. Their transition from free love to respectability did not entail a startling change in outlook, considering the ascetic element in their free-love scheme, although the two did convert to Catholicism before they left for England.[5]

Limited government and broad religious freedom contributed to the prevalence of free love in America, wrote Nichols: "If marriage was held to be a sacrament, as among Roman Catholics, then it was an affair of religion, with which American governments had nothing to do. Religious liberty required that people should be left in freedom to follow the dictates of their own consciences." Stephen Pearl Andrews, less piously inclined than his friend Nichols, never implied that free love had sanction from God. This abolitionist drew the logical secular implication from the right of private judgment: love itself, not the blessings of any religious body, sanctified sexual relations. "Man and Woman who do love," he wrote in 1853, "can live together in Purity without any mummery at all."[6]

Dr. and Mrs. Nichols had early been guided on their free-love journey by Andrews, who, as one of the first to apply Josiah Warren's doctrine of individual sovereignty to the "Realm of the Affections," helped establish the Modern Times community on Long Island, which the Nicholses joined. "Individual Sovereignty begat Modern Times; Modern Times was the mother of Free Love, the Grand Pantarchy, and the American branch of French Positivism," wrote John Humphrey Noyes, referring to the contributions of the Nicholses, Andrews, and Henry Edger. Dr. Nichols published *Esoteric Anthropology* from Modern Times, and according to Noyes, he also issued a directory containing names of affinity seekers from all over the country.[7]

Those with traditional social and religious views gasped at such ideas and goings on. One historian of Methodism characterized mid-century America by its "systems of infidelity, and infidelity without system, [which] sprang up in every direction and found supporters amongst those that were least suspected."[8] Those who were least suspected included the humble, the mighty, women, and ministers. Among many causes, three great "infidelisms" did appear in Northern society: feminism—the infidelity to male supremacy—officially began as an organized movement at Seneca

Falls, New York, in 1848; spiritualism—the direct communication with the spirit world, which profoundly subverted organized religion—began with the Fox family rappings at Hydesville, New York, in 1848; and free love—the infidelity to the primary social institution, the family—began in the same general area and time.

These three enthusiasms mutually supported one another; a true social radical of the time often worked simultaneously for all three causes and, perhaps, leavened the mixture with abolition, phrenology, and hydropathy. Such faith in a new trinity of salvations suggests that reformers of the new industrial age sought a revolution in the humanistic realm to match the revolution that they believed was occurring in the material realm. At least the appeal of spiritualism suggests this. "There can be no question that an undoubting faith in the genuineness of communications from deceased friends has been to vast numbers a source of consolation and happiness," wrote Nichols on the attractions of spiritualism. It filled the needs of those who considered themselves too sophisticated for literal heavens and hells but who still craved eternal existence and could not face the "doom of annihilation" of finite life.

As science and industry revealed their new truths and as Americans felt a need for a compensating spiritual revelation, why could not the spirit of optimism, progress, limitless expansion, and individual opportunity foster a victory over death? And if the sting of death itself could be thwarted through spiritualist communication, then—taking a page from John Humphrey Noyes of the Oneida Community—why could not the full glories of heaven (where the "marriage supper of the Lamb is a feast at which *every dish is free to every guest*") be realized on the earth? Perhaps, as Emma Hardinge asserted in her credulous but valuable documentary history of the movement, spiritualism did serve as the glorious capstone of all the sciences; at least such an interpretation comforted those who, underneath their optimism, sometimes wondered what material progress was doing to spiritual values.[9]

This modern resurgence of spiritualism began in the United States, took the country with epidemic force, then quickly spread to other parts of the world. It ascribed the wave of inexplicable phenomena—apparitions, noises, kinesis, clairvoyance—to the power of departed spirits; and although it is easy to say that its essence was hope and its evidence was credulity, spiritualism possessed tremendous appeal for a multitude of people. "Men neglected their fields, women their homes and children their schools, and for whole days and nights hung with bated breath upon the supposed communications from departed spirits," noted a head-shaking report from the Midwest. "Judging from its rapid extension and widespread effects, it seems to be the new Mahomet, or the social Antichrist, overrunning the world," lamented the *New York Times.* From his vantage in 1864, Dr. Nichols reported that nothing within his memory had had so great an influence on so many as spiritualism. By conservative estimate, spiritualism attracted some two million adherents out of a national population of twenty-five million in its heyday in the early 1850s.[10]

But of the three infidelisms, free love appeared as the most extreme, the one least likely to be countenanced by society at large. Those who most successfully broke down the conventional "wall of partition" between the sexes did so by partitioning themselves, spiritually and physically, from the outside world. Apart from these detached communities, free love existed as a ward of the other two infidelisms. The feminist movement in the main, however, opted for conventional morality and discrete political goals and forsook the revolutionizing of domestic relations. Free love, then, came to lodge most solidly with the spiritualists.

In an early editorial countering spiritualism, Henry Raymond of the *New York Times* disparaged the trivial concerns of spiritualist manifestations—the thumping walls, the floating tables, and the secondhand philosophical ramblings of the entranced. "When they [the spirits] will come with any message of consequence—with any revelation of new spiritual truths—any novel declaration of duty for our guidance in life, it may be worth while then to scrutinize their pretensions more closely," announced the editor. As if the spirits themselves read the *Times,* they very soon bore to their disciples a revelation of some consequence, indeed a novel declaration of duty: social bonds should be assumed or abolished according to individual spiritual revelation.[11]

This doctrine, called "spiritual affinity," swept the ranks of spiritualism in the early 1850s. Founded on Charles Fourier's theory of passional attraction and on the harmonial philosophy of Andrew Jackson Davis, the doctrine claimed that certain individuals had an attraction for one another that was based on complementary spiritual auras, and this made them "natural mates." This affinity superseded the bond of legal marriage, allowing an escape from what Fourier and some Americans considered the brutality and dullness of marriage and family life. As sages of this world and the next one announced new possibilities for the affections, the spiritualist and free-love causes merged their identities in the popular mind.[12]

The *New York Times* believed free love to be a systematic and subversive movement, and it dedicated some effort in the mid fifties to agitation against it. Editor Raymond admitted that the three-quarter-page review panning Mary Gove Nichols's *Mary Lyndon* was unusual, but he thought her defense of free love and passional attraction "a book of very bad tendencies." A few weeks later the *Times* carried a long editorial essay which sought to demonstrate the connections between the free-love movement and spiritualism, women's rights, Fourierism, and the various doctrines of John Humphrey Noyes, Josiah Warren, Stephen Pearl Andrews, Henry C. Wright, the Nicholses, and others. In addition, the editorial referred darkly to a free-love "Secret Society, or League" operating in New York.

Shortly thereafter, the *Times* featured an insider's report exposing the New York Free Love League. Begun in 1853 by an important thinker, whom the article described but did not immediately name (Stephen Pearl Andrews), the private club held regular twice-weekly meetings which were attended by about one hundred fifty members; its total membership numbered one thousand, the story claimed. Surprisingly, the writer admitted that the free-love meetings were refined and entirely social: "Whatever there may be in the theory which binds these people together, there is, it must be said, nothing to the outward view which differs from the scenes of an ordinary family party." Henry Raymond apparently did not read the complete details in the story, since his editorials continued to fume at the "orgies" supposedly occurring at the club at Number 555 Broadway.

The exposé of the club, as well as the *Times*'s insinuation of Fourierist influences, riled the Fourierist publisher of the *New York Tribune*, Horace Greeley. Worried that libertinism might sully the image of his own philosophy, he reacted with his own muckraking investigation, which jogged authorities into making a raid of the club. Police interrupted a regular meeting and, after a scuffle, arrested four persons, including the Fourierist leader Albert Brisbane (the "Chief of the League," Stephen Pearl Andrews, was ill at the time, however). The unwarranted arrests, with no evidence of wrongdoing, caused the case to be thrown out of court. Even the *Times* chided the police's bungling. The club continued to exist as a part of "The Pantarchy" circle surrounding Stephen Pearl Andrews. The *Times,* meanwhile, sought other special targets, such as the Berlin Heights, Ohio, free-love community. The spiritualist movement continued to be a *bête noire* of the newspaper. "The spirits, besides being unmistakable blockheads, are as prurient as Peter Dens himself," commented the *Times.* "They were not in the field five years till they sought a 'fusion' with the Free-Lovers, began to assail the marriage relation, invent new causes of difference between man and wife, and find excuses to satisfy the consciences of bigamists, and adulterers and fornicators."[13]

In 1844, only four years before the Hydesville knockings, Karl Marx, in the *Philosophico-economic Manuscripts,* developed Hegel's concept of alienation to describe the distintegration of organic society and the estrangement of persons from their work and their fellows in the capitalist industrial order. This concept of alienation—which has been summarized as the substitution of imaginary relations between, or worship of, inanimate objects or ideas for real relations between, or respect for, persons—appeared in American reflections on this period. "Instead of the social existence which all shared," Emerson wrote, "was now separation." In 1847 he wrote his famous lines "Things are in the saddle,/ And ride mankind./ There are two laws discrete,/ Not reconciled,—/ Law for man, and law for thing;/ The last builds town and fleet,/ But it runs wild,/ And doth the man unking."[14]

It was a timely response. About 1843/1844, the United States economy entered what some economists see as the "takeoff" stage, the brief period of decisive and radical structural change in which the economy and the society themselves became transformed into a sort of machine which produced continued growth as well as goods. Barriers to modernization were eradicated, and steady development became the normal condition. The "take-off" stage signaled an alteration of culture by machine so profound that, as Samuel Butler wrote in the 1860s, "it is the machines which act upon man and make him man, as much as man who has acted upon and made the machines."[15] To reassert his specialness and his individuality in the face of the new order, man summoned spirituality.

As railroads, steam mills, and the telegraph changed the wild face of America into a tame landscape laden with "improvements," one area epitomized both the impact of technology and the new quest for spiritual answers—the "burned-over district" of western New York, so called because of the waves of religious revivals that swept the area. Here, possibly more than anywhere else in America, change had worked faster and more dramatically. In 1812 western New York could still be termed the frontier, but by 1820 the mass of New Englanders who had moved into the area made New York the nation's most populous state. The completion of the Erie Canal in 1825 assured the initial industrial and commercial development of the area, which intensified with the coming of the railroad and telegraph in the early 1840s.

Although such rapid development through the incursion of the machine exacerbated social anxieties, it was less the nature of Americans to find fault with progress itself than to mask misgivings in exultation. Utopians and Whigs harmonized in paeans to the miraculous "progress of the age," which seemed characteristically American. And their bombast was not without justification, as Leo Marx has written: "Consider how the spectacle of the machine in a virgin land must have struck the mind. Like nothing ever seen under the sun, it appears when needed most: when the great west finally is open to massive settlement, when democracy is triumphant and gold is discovered in California." But the dogged insistence, particularly by spiritualists, that "life, whether here or hereafter, is *progress*, not violent and unnatural change" had a defensive ring, as if they were aware that less optimistic people might use no other two words to describe the industrialization of America.[16]

These sensitive Americans who wanted to believe the best about the new technology found a rationale in the core of the technology itself—in electricity, the nonmaterial, mystical force that amazed the learned and ignorant alike. A democratic ignorance of the nature of this force generated speculations that repealed old notions in the public mind about the limits of matter and mitigated the social tensions that were caused by increasing technology. Not just visionaries but figures such as John C. Calhoun believed that the force signaled the very apex of progress itself; "the subjugation of electricity to the mechanical necessities of man," he said, "would mark the last era in human civilization."[17]

In the decade before the Hydesville knockings, Americans became widely exposed to mesmerism or animal magnetism through numerous itinerant "magnetizers" and lecturers. They popularized the seemingly astounding discoveries of the Austrian physician Anton Mesmer, who had created a stir in Paris in the 1780s with his demonstrations of hypnotism. Mesmerism was explained in terms of theories of magnetism which held that a subtle and invisible fluid permeated every portion of the universe; inanimate objects, such as a lodestone, and animate ones, such as a mesmerist's body, provided a reservoir or channel for the force. Animal magnetism, with its attendant trances and clairvoyance, not only prepared the public mind for later spiritualist manifestations but also helped to provide a holistic explanation of all apparently supernatural phenomena. One German student, Johann Jung-Stilling, theorized that light, electricity, ether, and magnetic and galvanic "matter" were all the same force or substance, but under different modifications. This matter connected soul and body and the spiritual and material world together.[18]

The possibilities of electricity, magnetism, and the first significant application of these invisible forces—the telegraph—seemed limitless. So limitless did they seem, in fact, that the language used to describe the telegraph conjured up the spiritual, while the parlance of spiritualism fastened on the metaphor of the telegraph. A straightforward engineering history of early telegraphy, *The Story of the Telegraph* (1858), shifted into grandiloquence when describing electricity and the telegraph:

Of all the marvelous achievements of modern science, the Electric Telegraph is transcendently the greatest and most serviceable to mankind. It is a perpetual miracle, which no familiarity can render commonplace. This character it deserves from the nature of the agent employed [i.e., electricity] and the end subserved. *For what is the end to be accomplished, but the most spiritual ever possible? Not the modification or transportation of matter, but the transmission of thought.* To effect this an agent is employed so subtle in its nature, *that it may more properly be called a spiritual than a material force.* The mighty power of electricity, sleeping latent in all forms of matter, in the earth, the air, the water; permeating every part and particle of the universe, carrying creation in its arms, it is yet invisible and too subtle to be analysed.

. . . .

The telegraph has more than a mechanical meaning; it has an ideal, a religious, and a prospective significance, far-reaching and incalculable in its influences.[19] [Emphasis supplied]

The Hydesville rappings occurred at the dawning of the telegraph age. In 1844 the first American telegraph line joined two cities, Washington and Baltimore; by 1846 New York, Boston, Buffalo, Philadelphia, and Washington had been connected. Is not the telegraph "*the* feature of the age?" exulted a New York paper that year, as it boasted of the 1,269 miles of telegraph line in the United States. As the spirits descended in 1848 the phenomenon of the telegraph was becoming widespread; the South, the upper reaches of New England, and the Mississippi Valley had been reached by the circuit. Additional lines were going up through the burned-over district.[20]

American spiritualists did more than use the electromagnetic telegraph as a convenient analogy to describe their invisible communications. The spirits themselves, in fact, claimed that spiritualist intercourse depended upon electricity. "From the first working of the spiritual telegraph by which invisible beings were enabled to spell out consecutive messages," wrote Emma Hardinge, "they ['the spirits'] claimed that this method of communion was organized by scientific minds in the spirit spheres; that it depended mainly upon the conditions of human and atmospheric magnetisms." The spirits disclosed that the house at Hydesville had a peculiar suitability for their purposes, "from the fact of its being *charged with the aura requisite to make it a battery for the working of the telegraph*"; the Fox family possessed similar electrical propensities. The spirits called the aura the "life principle," continued Hardinge, and the person or place that contained it in abundance became a medium through which spirits could communicate.[21]

Spiritualists believed that the similar nature of terrestrial and spiritual telegraphy demonstrated a scientific, and hence respectable, basis for their cause. Commonly, the shades communicated with mortals by coded tappings on tables or walls; usually these signals were referred to as "spiritual telegraphy" or simply "telegraphy." The first important spiritualist journal, published in New York from 1852 to 1860, bore the name *Spiritual Telegraph*. Emma Hardinge, wife of the copublisher of the paper, dedicated her history of American spiritualism, not to the rank and file of the spirit world, but to the Samuel Morses and Henry O'Riellys of the spheres—"To the Wise and Mighty Beings through Whose Instrumentality the Spiritual Telegraph of the Nineteenth Century Has Been Constructed."[22]

If spiritualists appeared to be confused about the physics of electricity, they were in good company. When Congress acted on the bill appropriating $30,000 for Samuel F. B. Morse to construct the Washington-Baltimore telegraph, Congressman Cave Johnson attempted to defeat the bill by adding an amendment granting one-half the appropriation to the study of mesmerism. Another suggested that Millerism, a millenialist sect, should also be included. Twenty-two members of Congress then voted to include mesmerism in the bill. That mesmerism should be adduced to ridicule electromagnetism demonstrated the degree of public confusion surrounding both electromagnetism and "animal" magnetism. "It would require a scientific analysis to determine how far the magnetism of mesmerism was analogous to that to be employed in telegraphs," said the chairman, amidst laughter as he ruled the amendments in order. Morse's bill, minus amendments, later passed the House by a margin of six votes.[23]

A few creditable scientists, such as Robert Hare of the University of Pennsylvania, became spiritualists; a number of important personages also expressed belief, among them present and former congressmen, governors, and judges, such as Nathaniel P. Tallmadge of Wisconsin, Robert Dale Owen of Indiana, and John Worth Edmonds of the New York Supreme Court. Edmonds, in fact, resigned from the bench in a controversy about the spiritualist influences upon his decisions. Horace Greeley, editor of the *New York Tribune*, publicized spiritualism; and other literary men and reformers, among them James Fenimore Cooper, William Cullen

Bryant, and William Lloyd Garrison, became interested in the movement. Three dedicated materialists from the University of Buffalo raised the ire of dedicated spiritualists when their investigation into the Rochester rappings concluded that the noises came from the snappings of the knee joints of the Fox sisters. In 1857 a Harvard College investigating committee, which included Louis Agassiz, came out against spiritualism as a "contaminating influence," a threat to the "truth of man and the purity of woman," after spirits failed to make any demonstration of their existence in a monitored seance; some suggested that the aggressive style of the investigators had scared away the spirits. Spiritualists had a point when they claimed that the optimum conditions for spiritual manifestations, such as darkness and the willingness to believe, were not met by the nineteenth-century laboratory, but most of them refused to accept the implications of this reasoning and thus admit the essentially religious nature of spiritualism.[24]

One reason for this reluctance was the secular bias of spiritualism; as a consummation of two primary forces in American life—Protestantism and individualism—it allowed every man to be in touch with the hereafter without the benefit of clergy or dogma. In the 1850s, Christianity and spiritualism were demarked as opposing doctrines. Although a few ministers—Adin Ballou, for instance—saw the Christian possibilities of spiritualism, most of the clergy regarded the age of miracles as past, and viewed spiritualism either as fakery or the work of the devil. Many spiritualists, holding "advanced ideas" and freethinking tendencies, likewise disdained Christianity. Alarmists reported that spiritualism attracted the faithful from the fold, and while some spiritualist leaders came from liberal sects such as Universalism, a recent study reiterated the claims of nineteenth-century spiritualist writers—the rank and file of spiritualism came from those with no close connections to organized religion. It should be remembered that in 1850 only 15.5 percent of Americans were church members.[25]

The claims of spiritualism to erase the annihilation of death through some sort of scientific force had great attraction—it provided the eternal life benefits of old-time religion without any of the naïve theology. More importantly, spiritualism offered "empirical proof" of the reality of spiritual existence, something that Christianity could not do. An example of one who needed this sort of proof is provided by Moses Hull. An orthodox minister whose fear of death drove him to embrace and reject several denominations, Hull finally found fulfillment in spiritualism. Outside of spiritualism, he argued, there existed no evidence that man continued his life after the death of the body: "While the Bible is a book to conjure by, it is a poor book to die by. It points to the tomb as a deep and dark cavern, and it doubtfully hints at an impossible resurrection of the old body. It leaves so little for a dying man, for although professedly without doubt of its integrity, he finds himself in despair."

After the Civil War, Hull set out both to recruit Christians to spiritualism and to reconcile spiritualists to the Bible. Since many who embraced spiritualism had not studied the Bible, they naturally assumed from the arguments of their Christian opponents that the Bible itself opposed spiritualism. Not so, former preacher Hull argued; although the Bible was not divinely inspired, it was indeed a voluminous account of spiritualist phenomena: "The Bible was a Spiritualist book, no more, no less. If Spiritualism was the work of the devil, then the Bible was also, and vice versa, if the Bible was the gift of God, then was also Spiritualism the gift of God." The orthodox, of course, abhorred Hull all the more for this line of argument, and in the mid seventies a Christian organization in New Jersey had him arrested for his "free marriage" alliance to fellow lecturer Mattie Sawyer.[26]

Besides departed relatives, one of the favorite shades that communicated with spiritualists was Dr. Benjamin Franklin. Emma Hardinge gave the apparent reason for this: as one of those spirits who had helped to construct the spiritual telegraph of the nineteenth century, he had a particular interest in imposing some sort of orderly system of telegraphy upon the jumble of spiritual communications. But although Franklin dropped gems of wisdom about electricity to many mediums, once even appearing in a vision with a galvanic battery under his arm, the venerable symbol of American science and democracy perhaps served another function. Of all the nation's patriarchs, he alone would be most able to guide Americans through the political and technological hazards which they faced head-on.[27]

Since the machine had caused man's phenomenal "progress" as well as his alienation, it is not surprising that the spiritualist response to the machine contained an overt attempt to redeem the promise of the machine and to integrate mankind with his creature in the new environment. By the revelation of the spirits, John M. Spear attempted to construct a New Motor, the humanistic machine. This Universalist minister had worked in the causes of abolition, peace, temperance, and prison reform before becoming a spiritualist medium in 1852. From the outset, his spiritual ministry had seemed rather odd even to other eccentrics. Hardinge reported that Spear seemed to be a passive tool of the spirits, "to whom he professed himself willing to tender a child-like and unquestioning obedience," as he journeyed about the country at their behest. Andrew Jackson Davis corroborated Spear's passiveness, noting his "extremely beautiful simplicity, his teachable and therefore receptive nature"; Davis, however, considered that Spear was in large measure a prey to his own impulses disguised as spiritual forces. The Boston correspondent for the *New York Times* described Spear as "either a wonderful knave or a lunatic," reporting that "he spoke with such a vague, hazy periphrasis of words, that you did not well know whether he spoke figuratively or literally."[28]

At any rate, Spear knew the anxieties of the age and appeared ripe for a grand scheme. In Utica in 1853 he revealed to readers of the spiritualist *New Era* (Boston) that the spirit world had organized seven associations—Electrizers, Healthfulizers, Educationizers, Agriculturalizers, Elementizers, Governmentizers, and Beneficents —and that these associations would soon select earthly agents to execute their schemes. Shortly, the spiritual Electrizers informed Spear of their readiness to unfold to man a more perfect knowledge "of electrical, magnetic, and ethereal laws, that a new motive power might be exhibited," and they selected Spear as their agent. He had been known to tinker about in public with zinc and copper batteries, in hopes of combining mineral with vital electricity to achieve a breakthrough in spirit communication. But even according to sympathetic reports, he was ignorant, at least of electricity.

The editor of the *New Era*, an important supporter of Spear, broke the story in the spring of 1854, heralding the "New Motive Power, or Electrical Motor" as the "Great Spiritual Revelation of the Age." Based on some two hundred revelations, Spear and a few helpers had erected a machine at High Rock in Lynn, Massachusetts, which, they claimed, not only harnessed the power of spiritual electricity but also had a living soul. The components of the machine corresponded to the parts of the human body, "the most superior, natural, efficient type of mechanism known on the earth." It took nine months of "incessant labor" to build, and Spear and the *New Era* trumpeted it as the birth of a new messiah. The New Motor "is to be the physical Savior of the race. The history of its inception, its various stages of progress, and its completion, will show the world a most beautiful and significant analogy to the advent of Jesus as the spiritual Savior of the race."

Unbeknownst to the builders, they claimed, a woman spiritualist in Boston had contracted a pregnancy much like that of the Virgin Mary. "Mrs. ———," as she came to be delicately identified, remained with her symptoms in Boston until the spirits bade Spear to call her to the machine. She came, and in the presence of the machine reached "a crisis" in which she supposedly gave birth to the "living principle" of the machine. "At precisely the time designated, and at the point expected, motion appeared corresponding to embryotic life," announced Spear. Andrew Jackson Davis, who interviewed the Boston "mother," reported her symptoms to be very good imitations and psychologically produced.

The reported motion did not appear in the drive wheel of the machine, however, but in some little balls suspended within the apparatus. Detractors pointed out that such movement could hardly be considered miraculous, particularly since the balls were in the presence of electrical current. Davis wrote a detached but not unsympathetic description of the Electrizers and their wood, zinc, and copper contraption:

They invest the very materialism of the mechanism with principles of interpretation which give out an emanation of religious feeling altogether new in the development of scientific truth. Each wire is precious, sacred, as a spiritual verse. Each plate of zinc and copper is clothed with symbolized meanings, corresponding throughout with the principles and parts involved in the living human organism.

Spear announced that there existed a universal electricity which had never been "naturally incorporated" with mineral and other forms of matter; the present "merely scientific" application of electricity to motive power was superficial and mostly useless. The construction of the New Motor followed the laws of man's material physiology and utilized "atmospheric electricity obtained by absorption and condensation, and not by friction or galvanic action." The builders planned the New Motor to replace, not to supplement, all other sources of power. It brought the practical, physical salvation of humanity, cried the *New Era,* a revolution that the world had deeply longed for and had "agonized and groaned away its life because it did not come sooner."

As Emma Hardinge pointed out, the New Motor (or "Wonderful Infant") excited the same sort of expectations as Frankenstein's monster did in the novel by Mrs. Shelley. She did not extend her comparison, but she could have. As press and pulpit barraged him with ridicule, Spear moved his machine to Randolph, New York, in order to take advantage of its "lofty electrical position." By night a mob broke into the shed that housed the machine and, in Spear's terms, "tore out the heart of the mechanism, trampled it beneath their feet, and scattered it to the four winds." It never rose again.

John M. Spear had one more bit part in the playing out of spiritualism in America. After the New Motor debacle he and some followers established a community near the mineral springs at Kiantone, New York, which came to espouse free love as a concomitant of spiritualism. Emma Hardinge and some other conservative spiritualists considered free love the Great Heresy of spiritualism, and they traced its genesis to the Kiantone community. But although Kiantone helped to precipitate the free-love/spiritualist discussion, the possibilities of sexual liberation that it demonstrated had been obvious for some time, notably in the spiritualist/ free-love community at Berlin Heights, Ohio, and at the Modern Times settlement on Long Island.[29]

Despite its romantic content, spiritualism considered itself scientific, not only because of its avowed electrical nature, but also because of democratic misunderstandings about the nature of science: whatever a numerous public experienced or witnessed, with no careful regard for conditions, had fulfilled the test of democratic empiricism and hence could be considered scientifically "true." Behind this assumption can be discerned a heritage from Jacksonian America: scientific technology not only should distribute its benefits democratically, but science itself should be understandable to all the people; after all, a force that held such implications for the future of the republic should be comprehensible to all its citizenry, not merely to an elite.

Just as spiritualism demonstrated that anyone could grasp, apply, and benefit from the unseen force of electricity, it reasserted that the source of the most important sorts of knowledge remained in the hands of the people—the humble and unlearned, not the mighty, made the most effective mediums. These aspects of spiritualism suggest a deeper function: spiritualism acted as a device to accommodate Americans to the exigencies of technological change; it promised that the same forces that caused upheaval in their lives (symbolized, for instance, by electricity), allowed them benefits, two in particular—victory over the ultimate alienation called death, and liberation from sexual and familial constrictions.

On the surface, free love appeared to be a resurgence of the kind of individualism that was intimately connected with the circumstances of America. "The doctrine of free love," wrote an early-twentieth-century family sociologist, "was bound to develop as an ethical counterpart of laissez-faire economics; both are anarchism; both were stimulated by the spacious freedom of the new world." But private judgment in morals held dangers that private enterprise had not. Worried Victorians condemned a perverse individualism for the increased divorce rates and for other evidence of "laxity," which they believed heralded the dissolution of the family. "We know that to subdue the beast that is in us, and to suppress the individual for the sake of the community is the higher law. This cry for making divorce so easy as to destroy all sacredness in marriage, is a step backward," lamented a typical critic.[30] Even John Humphrey Noyes had traced non-Christian free love back to the individualistic economic theories of Josiah Warren.

Most students of the family believe that, despite appearances, the turmoil within the nineteenth-century family represented adaptation rather than breakdown as the atomistic family, rather than the individual, became the unit of social accommodation to the changing realities of the industrial state.[31] And free love served as a romantic critique of the family as much as it functioned as a social force of rampant individualism. The belief that marriage contravened love had wide currency among free lovers; it reflected the "omnipotence of love" theme in the novels and romantic poetry of the eighteenth and nineteenth centuries and recalled the myths of courtly and precious love which traditionally disesteemed marriage. The notion of "affinity" in spiritualism offered a romantic freedom from the constriction of familism, a freedom which eagerly pitted the morality of ethereal spheres against that of the mundane family and conventional religion.

Because spiritualism freed the individual from the authority of organized religion, it also freed him from recognized social authority. J. W. Towler of Cleveland, in a publicized "confession," explained that he had come to be a free lover ("one who holds that the individual has the right to make and remake his or her connubial relations without consulting any authority, religious or legal") as a "legitimate result of the doctrine of individual sovereignty which Spiritualism unquestionably teaches." Many individualists, however, had not been schooled by spiritualism; indeed numerous individualist anarchists, also called "scientific anarchists," prided themselves on their rationalism, and if they disapproved of conventional marriage, they did so on rationalistic grounds. Early in his career, the American anarchist Dyer D. Lum wrote a book denouncing spiritualism as an anti-intellectual reaction against modern scientific progress.[32]

Contributing to the acknowledged identity between spiritualism and free love were the many leading spiritualists who taught or practiced the doctrine of spiritual affinity, such as Andrew Jackson Davis, Henry C. Wright, Cora L. V. Hatch, Thomas L. Nichols, and Mary Gove Nichols. After the Civil War, when some spiritualists attempted to remove the stigma of free-lovism from their cause, they encountered difficulties. In 1867 Towler wrote that it could still be said that all free lovers, with rare exceptions, were spiritualists, and that there remained "an abundance of Free Lovers amongst Spiritualists."

In the 1870s the split between free-loving and conservative spiritualists widened as the leading spiritualist paper, *Banner of Light,* attacked free love and urged spiritualists away from social radicalism. The dissenters, meanwhile, gathered around Moses Hull's paper, *Hull's Crucible.* This spiritualist split coincided with a rift between the two factions of free lovers—the exclusivists and the varietists; the exclusivists followed Victoria Woodhull's new canon in her *Weekly,* and the varietists following *Hull's Crucible.* Although both factions generally held that, for sexual purposes, true love created true marriage, the exclusivists argued that such love could exist only between two people; whereas the varietists held that love, like lust, was general rather than specific in its objects, and therefore it naturally sought plurality and variety in its arrangements.[33]

Both spiritualist and free-love causes offered a needed model of female power and leadership which many feminists appreciated and many traditionalists deplored. To some critics, the role of women in earlier reform efforts paled beside their spiritualist activity. "The first female lecturers and public speakers were spiritualists," recalled a Methodist writer, "and in the spiritualists' church, so-called, women are the high-priests; and the scriptural teachings in regard to the relation of men and women and their duties are reversed." Stephen Pearl Andrew's call for the dominion of woman over the whole sphere of the affections sounded entirely in place to the spiritualists who were also free lovers. The sex radicalism associated with spiritualism explains much of the heated general criticism of the spiritualist movement that has puzzled some historians.[34]

Conventional marriage and moral standards already allowed men a practical degree of sexual freedom. What most distinguished the new free-love impetus from acceptable philandering, then, was its demand that woman have the sexual autonomy customarily enjoyed only by the male. For woman to attain these rights against the traditionally assertive force of man, free lovers felt that she needed final authority in the sex question: coition should take place only at the will of the woman. The word "free" in free love held two meanings for woman: the freedom not to surrender her vagina to anybody, regardless of their relationship or supposed duty, and the freedom to offer it at will.

Both male and female sex radicals of the free-love cause idealized women as a repository of sexual virtue, reflecting Western civilization's veneration of woman transposed into Victorian terms. Among free lovers and others, this Victorian idealization resulted in the belief that coition must have a higher purpose than mere physical pleasure. The most conservative free lovers, such as the Nicholses, believed that coition and its delights could be justified only for the purpose of procreation, while the most liberal ones agreed that *some* worthier motive than pleasure must sanctify intercourse, most likely love. "Copulation without love," wrote Victoria Woodhull, "is prostitution." Regarding the matter of pleasure, any contradiction in being a free lover and a sexual conservative was more apparent than real.

Victoria Woodhull's free-love agitation in the early seventies marked the end of the serious and widespread discussion of sexual alternatives in nineteenth-century America. The Civil War had shattered dreams of utopia, and Victorian culture decreed a consensus of prudery. In 1872 Victoria Woodhull and her sister, Tennessee Claflin, shocked—and entertained—much of the country with their open agitation for sexual freedom, unleashing the Beecher-Tilton scandal, which revealed beyond reasonable doubt that one of the foremost men of God in the nation, Henry Ward Beecher, had regularly and carnally known his close friend's wife, Elizabeth (Mrs. Theodore) Tilton. In 1877, "The Woodhull" left America for England, denied her earlier work, and married into respectability, leaving behind her a string of adventures which several biographers have delighted to tell. Her mentor of sexual liberation, Stephen Pearl Andrews, continued his influence on those sex radicals who did not desert the cause. "Free love," however, increasingly became only an epithet used to discredit anything that smacked of social aberration.

Nevertheless, American sex radicalism, as a movement to revolutionize the institutions and conventions regulating sexual intercourse, remained alive and well—if quarantined—from the Gilded Age to the eve of World War I, when a newer movement for sexual liberation appeared. Amid repression, obloquy, and the outer darkness of unrespectability this small group of sex radicals dared society with their outspoken campaigns and iconoclastic ideas. These radicals were partially abetted by moderates in respectable society who argued for reformed divorce laws. Easier divorce probably confounded the sex radicals, however, by providing a safety valve that ensured the perpetuation of conventional marriage and domesticity.[35]

24   The Sex Radicals

Even today the century-old ban on the sex radicals has persisted in obscuring their history. Historians who have considered sex radicalism at all, apart from its communitarian and sectarian aspects, have viewed it as a subsidiary of the more respectable nineteenth-century feminist movement.[36] The sex radicals were indeed feminists in that they believed in a feminist solution to the sex question, ascribing all contemporary sex problems to the denial of sexual rights to the female. But to group these activists with those who simply sought votes for women is to misplace them historically. Among the pioneers of woman suffrage in America, only exceptions like Elizabeth Cady Stanton and Ernestine Rose flouted respectability to advocate divorce reform and an end to the churches' obstructions of women's rights. Many later sex radicals denied the suffragist argument that the franchise would appreciably raise woman's status. To these sex militants, the woman question centered in the bed, not in the polling booth.

The difference in political attitudes of these two groups was evident in their contrasting responses to the Comstock Act of 1873. When the Claflin sisters aired the Beecher scandal, they also helped to launch Anthony Comstock's career as a prominent vice hunter; this Connecticut Yankee prosecuted *Woodhull & Claflin's Weekly* for its "obscene" exposé, but the obscenity law of 1872 proved inadequate for his purposes, a situation that was remedied the next year when he encouraged Congress to pass the far-reaching postal law that came to bear his name. Conventional feminists bowed before the statute which, without bothering to define obscenity, prohibited it from the mails along with other such "indecent" and "immoral" items as contraceptives and birth-control information. The sex radicals, on libertarian principles, broke this law in order to raise the questions of government censorship and individual self-ownership.

Although nineteenth-century feminists, particularly early ones, had often identified feminism with sex reform, sex radicalism in its *fin de siècle* stage had developed as a separate movement, parallel to and somewhat overshadowed by the popular feminist movement. These sex radicals bore close ties to earlier marriage critics; when Moses Harman and his circle condemned marriage in the 1890s they used many of the arguments voiced forty years earlier by Thomas L. and Mary G. Nichols, Stephen Pearl Andrews, Henry

C. Wright, and Andrew Jackson Davis. In fact, a line of direct, personal influence can be traced from Andrews and the Nicholses to postwar sex radicals such as Victoria Woodhull and Ezra Heywood.

The "sex cranks" of the Comstock era, however, drew ideas from a surprising range of thinkers. One essayist in 1905 acknowledged not only Mary Wollstonecraft, William Godwin, and the poet Shelley but also the obscure and important work of William Thompson, whose *Appeal of One-Half the Human Race* (1825) offered a challenge to Wollstonecraft on the question of domestic values. Thompson saw the home as a "prison-house of the wife," an institution "chiefly for the drillings of a superstition to render her more submissive." The house, along with everything in it, was the husband's property, "and of all fixtures the most abjectly his is his breeding machine, the wife."[37]

John Humphrey Noyes's analysis of the propagative and amative functions of the sexual organs in *The Bible Argument* (1848) influenced sex radicals fully as much as his arguments against exclusive love did. Freethinking sex rationalists turned Noyes's theological arguments to the task of building the new sexual science. Despite its avowed scriptural basis, Noyes's Oneida Community became a symbol to sex radicals of the practicality of their own secular ideas. Sex radicals drew more than birth-control information from George Drysdale's *The Elements of Social Science* (1854); they used it to argue the evils of celibacy, the good of sexual satisfaction, and the logic of varied sexual arrangements. This work inspired Ezra Heywood's *Cupid's Yokes* (1876), a pamphlet that sought to bring sex within the realm of reason but instead mostly brought sex radicals into the snares of Anthony Comstock; Heywood and D. M. Bennett both served prison terms for circulating it.[38]

Karl Heinzen, the feminist editor of Boston's *Der Pionier*, influenced a select few in Europe and America with *The Rights of Women and the Sexual Relation*, which was published in German in 1852. The English editions of the 1890s, prefaced by a tribute from abolitionist hero Wendell Phillips, made Heinzen's work directly available to sex radicals. He argued for a formalized variety of free love known as free marriage. "The agreement of the lovers and a notice concerning their union must suffice for the forming of marriage," he wrote. Couples would be free to marry or divorce at will, according to love's transient attractions; and parental obligations would be eased by voluntary state nurseries. John Stuart Mill, another critic of marriage and a theorist of free expression, widely influenced the sex reformers. His repudiation of the legal rights that he had acquired over his partner, Harriet Taylor, echoed in some provocative free-marriage cases in America. Jane Cunningham Croly won the respect of radicals for the anonymous 1872 work that was commonly attributed to her, *The Truth about Love*. The book argued that present sexual institutions "do not correspond with the facts of that relation; the test of truth is not observed and our institutions are organized lies. Society only recognizes one form of the relation; there are many." Croly, America's first newspaper woman, also founded the earliest important woman's club, Sorosis.[39]

The singularity of the late-Victorian sex radicals rests not merely in their adherence to a dissenting undercurrent of thought, but in their application of this thought in the new context of Comstockian America. The concerns of free lovers as secular perfectionists were mirrored in an ironic way by a coexisting corps of sex reformers, the Comstockish "Social Purity" group. Prostitution in the northern cities had replaced southern slavery as the reigning symbol of immorality and enslavement, and the forces of Social Purity aimed to purge society of prostitution. Mostly WCTU feminists, the Social Puritans and the sex radicals shared transcendentalist and abolitionist roots as well as a common quest for social perfection. Free love, in fact, may be viewed as a version of Social Purity, one that sought amelioration through rationalist, libertarian means rather than through restriction. Although postwar sex radicals held more liberal attitudes toward sexual pleasure than their mid-century forbears had, they still largely agreed that a higher morality, not hedonism, was the goal of free love.[40]

Of course the differences between the two groups overshadowed the similarities; primarily they disagreed on the foundations of society. Advocates of purity saw conventional marriage, home, and the family as the moral and organizational bases of society. They agreed with Gamaliel Bailey's earlier affirmation that "the *Family* is the great primal institution, established by the Creator himself, as the first and best school for training man for all social relations and duties." In extreme contrast to this Victorian domestic ideal stood anarchist free lovers, such as Stephen Pearl Andrews and Ezra Heywood, who saw the individual, not the conventional family, as the natural basis of society. Andrews even went so far as to provide an alternative plan for rearing and educating children.[41]

Comparing the standards of sex radicalism to those of Victorian puritanism, one female radical explained: "[We] endorse the puritan principle of self-control, but not that of abstinence and social coercion. [We] admit the ideal of constancy, but not of enforced exclusiveness. [We] reject compulsory maternity and persecution of unmarried mothers, and reject bonded sex service [i.e., conventional marriage], asceticism and ignorance, for either men or women."[42]

Resemblances that did exist between the Puritans and free lovers, however, caused interesting confusion. Since free love always connoted the freedom not to make love, as well as the positive freedom, some free lovers and some Social Puritans both held the doctrine that there should be no coitus except for reproduction.

Some far-reaching implications of the free-love doctrine did not become obvious until after the Civil War, when the new generation of radicals, having seen a moral cause triumph over obstinate institutions, confidently set themselves against the increased constraints of the postwar era. To its traditional interests in sexual liberty and women's rights, the free-love cause now added the struggles for a free press, birth control, and sex education. These radicals, moreover, usually held a cluster of antigovernment and antireligion ideas that made them more than fair game for prudish district attorneys. Hence their pioneering work in sex reform was often accompanied by contributions to political thought and civil liberty, usually refined in the heat of court battles or aged in the damp of jail cells.

The marriage of radical action and philosophy, in fact, characterized the lives of the late-Victorian sex radicals, and if utter fearlessness in defense of simple axioms is a virtue, they were very virtuous individuals. But this history does not aim to recount the virtue of individuals; rather it seeks to record what they thought and did about sex, guided, as they were, by their own ideas of sexual virtue.

2/ Moses Harman

FROM Gilded Age to Progressive Era, *Lucifer, the Light Bearer* (1883–1907) carried the torch in the Midwest for American sex radicalism. The outstanding—and virtually the only—journal of sexual liberty in these times, *Lucifer* forms the middle link between pioneering sex-reform efforts and today's liberationists, and to a great degree it defines the limits of social dissent in the late nineteenth century. Its closest relative, *The Word*, edited in Massachusetts by the anarchists Ezra and Angela Heywood, antedated *Lucifer* by a decade but expired in the early nineties. So iconoclastic a paper as *Lucifer* could not have survived without an indomitable editor and, perhaps, enough official persecution to ensure a following. The story of *Lucifer*, a personal but not a private journal, is the story of its editor-publisher, Moses Harman.

Born in western Virginia in 1830, Moses Harman grew up in the mammoth spring backwoods of southern Missouri. His parents, Job and Nancy Harman, moved the family from Virginia to Springfield, Ohio, in 1835. A year later they moved again, this time to a malarial site in Mercer County near the St. Mary's River. Tales of gushing pure springs and fertile land in the hills of southern Missouri enticed the family to move once again, in 1838.

The zigzag 600-mile trek from Ohio to Missouri took nearly two months. Job settled the family near Leasburg in Crawford County, and, besides farming, he tried his hand at mining, land investing, and other schemes. A frontier bust wiped out his "little accumulation," and the spring of 1840 found the Harmans settled on a squatter's claim in the woods, a mile from their nearest neighbor, without a team for plowing, and with no prospects of getting one. To survive, they made baskets of white-oak splints and traded them for corn.

Although he had only a few months of formal schooling during boyhood, Moses learned to read well. "Before reaching my tenth year . . . I read everything readable that I could get hold of in that back-woods settlement," he recalled. His bookishness, which was enforced by an accidental fall that made him a lifelong cripple, provided him the chance, at age sixteen, to teach school. Two years later it enabled him to enroll at Arcadia College in nearby Iron County, which, if only a high school, was the most advanced one around. "Father sent him to college because of his crippled condition, though poor and illy able to do so," wrote Joseph of his older brother Moses. The whole family sacrificed for Moses' education. Moses found most of his fellow students well-to-do, many of them the sons of slaveholders. He helped pay his way by doing odd jobs and by tutoring other students.[1]

Moses, who by age twenty had been licensed to preach by the Methodist Church (South), repaid the family well, in terms of respectability, for its sacrifices. As an advanced student and circuit-riding preacher, Moses became, in Joseph's words, the "pride" of Crawford County. Joseph himself followed Moses' early example of piety and eventually became an important figure in the Seventh Day Adventist Church, helping to found the Loma Linda colony in California.

At twenty-one the new graduate of Arcadia took charge of the high school at Warsaw, Missouri. Outside of classes he made the acquaintance of local sharp-witted Universalists, who, before his stay was out, argued him out of his Methodist dogma and into the broader paths of their doctrine. Universalism became the midpoint on Moses' journey to rationalism. His increasing unease over the proslavery position of the southern branch of Methodism hastened his apostasy. Moses left Missouri in the mid fifties to travel, and probably to teach, in Indiana. About 1860 he returned to Missouri to enroll—and starve—for a term at the St. Louis Normal School. Afterward the schoolteacher returned full circle to Crawford County.[2]

In the hills of the border state in the 1860s a man could express his opinion on the way to town and be hanged by a grapevine on the way back; the outbreak of national civil strife only pitched the much-divided state into its own consuming civil war. Although Crawford and surrounding counties had a relatively small slave population in 1860—Crawford's population numbered 5,640 whites to 182 black slaves—the area was predominantly proslavery and Democratic. The split between Southern (Breckinridge) Democrats and Northern (Douglas) Democrats in the presidential election of 1860 degenerated into outright conflict between Secessionists and Unionists by the onset of the war. The conflict had a highly explosive, even theatrical quality. Before federal troops occupied Rolla in 1861, correspondents reported the ritual of struggle in Crawford County: roving bands of Secessionists galloped from settlement to settlement; at each place their leader made a stump speech while the others clapped and cheered. Local Secessionists would then be encouraged to help as they raised the Confederate flag. On this cue, Unionists would begin their counterdemonstration, parading, speaking, and cheering the village housewives who bore the stars and stripes to the public square. One Unionist correspondent tried to cheer up his St. Louis readers: in Washington and in Crawford County, things looked better than ever for the Unionist cause, he enthused, and Secessionists were making little headway anywhere in the area except, he added, in St. François, Iron, Madison, and Wayne counties.[3]

In short order after his return to Crawford County, Moses Harman earned notoriety for his abolitionist views. In democratic fashion the community met and voted to run him and a fellow abolitionist, Dr. Stephan S. Briggs, out of the county. Moses did eventually leave in order to try to enlist as a soldier, and Briggs later became a lecturer-in-residence at a communist colony not far away. Prevented from enlisting because of his lameness, Moses helped to recruit the regiment that came to be stationed in Rolla. He tried once more to serve, this time as a nurse, but again he was rejected.[4]

Although in 1863 Moses Harman resigned himself to teaching and, in fact, became Leasburg's first school teacher, the war was not over for him. Directly in the path of Price's raid of 1864, he witnessed the dumb fury of war as straggling soldiers shot straggling prisoners and routed local Union sympathizers. A raiding party captured him as he lay ill in bed. They threatened to shoot him

Moses Harman
From *Pioneers of Birth Control in England and America*

Ezra Heywood
From *Pioneers of Birth Control in England and America*

E. B. Foote, Sr.
From *Pioneers of Birth Control in England and America*

E. B. Foote, Jr.
From *Pioneers of Birth Control in England and America*

but, considering his illness and lameness, let him go free. A neighbor, Amos Scheuck, aged eighty and an invalid, was "shot in cold blood by these raiders within a few rods of his home and in hearing of his family," Moses remembered. The old man had been a Union sympathizer.

After the war, Moses married Susan Scheuck, daughter of the executed man. Even at that time he may have had questions about conventional marriage, since before their marriage the couple made a personal contract that pledged certain voluntary standards of conduct based on love rather than duty. They settled on a farm and had two children, George and Lillian, and Moses continued to teach and to read whenever he had the time. In 1877 Susan died with her infant in childbirth.[5]

On a hot June Sunday in 1879 Moses Harman and his two children stepped from the train at Valley Falls, in eastern Kansas. Halfway between Atchison and Topeka, this town, once called Grasshopper Falls, did not appear particularly promising as the launching place for sexual reform. And Moses almost certainly entertained no grand visions of the future as he first surveyed the village. The settlement, which was carved out of a walnut grove above the Delaware River, was the standard attempt at civilization —stone and sunbaked mud and whitewash and planking. The lines of the buildings were not plumb, somehow, and the doorways looked low. The streets, like those of all western towns that expected to become St. Louises of the steppe, could accommodate five wagons abreast.

He knew that he could always get on by teaching school, anywhere that he moved. He would of course have to do that here in Valley Falls, although it did not quite satisfy his hunger for intellectual engagement. Maybe something else would develop—after all, was this not Kansas, the home of freedom, the household of abolition, of enlightenment? Moses' cousin Noah, who was almost a prosperous farmer by local standards, welcomed them at the train.

As teacher at the district school, Moses became known, if not immediately liked, as a quiet but direct man. His tendency to follow his intellectual lights rather than community pressure perhaps suggested a private superiority that was somewhat out of place in a state just entering its settlement boom period. Perhaps Valley Falls, with its small-town atmosphere punctuated by "perpetual Spiritual disputes," was not unlike the characterization in *The Story of a Country Town* (1883), written by a young, overworked editor in nearby Atchison, Edgar Howe. Like Howe, Harman rebelled against the smugness of the American village, but in a way that rather savored of spiritual contentiousness. Harman's reform zeal found a home, for awhile, in the postwar free-thought movement, a spurt of rationalist enthusiasm that was begun by militant anticlericalists, Boston Unitarians, and religious liberals.

Valley Falls's Republican paper, the *New Era,* grew quite lively as the churchgoers and the freethinkers exchanged volleys in its pages. Out of the local Free Religious Society, freethinkers organized a chapter of the National Liberal League and elected Noah Harman president. When the *New Era* became overburdened with the disputation, the league, fifty members strong, began a monthly of its own. The first issue of the *Valley Falls Liberal* appeared in August 1880; at first it had no formal editors, all league members being free to lend a hand in its publication. Moses Harman and another school teacher, A. J. Searl, however, directed the early issues.[6]

Harman had eagerly entered the debate. Writing as "Rustic" in the *New Era* and the *Liberal,* he assailed the local spokesmen of "popular theology." His journey from the ministry to free thought provided him with powerful arguments and insights into his clerical opponents. He used a common free-thought tactic, presenting his cause as that of Science, of rational deduction from natural phenomenon; the foes of progress were the forces of superstition and enslavement—namely, dogmatic religion.

He had found new work, new friends, a new paper, and even a new wife during his first year in Valley Falls. At the age of fifty, Moses Harman launched on a new career as a free-thought publicist.

3/ Organized Free Thought: The National Liberal League

No, Liberals! the morals of children first.
—Anthony Comstock

ISBELIEVERS were to be met with in America, but there was no public organ of infidelity, Tocqueville reported after his 1831 sojourn in the United States. The unofficial sway of the "empire of the majority" over popular thought, he believed, accounted for the absence of antireligious or licentious publishing in America. Yet during the decade of the 1830s a significant free-thought movement arose in the United States, and the editor of its most important journal, Abner Kneeland of the *Boston Investigator,* underwent a trial for blasphemy. Some thirty free-thought journals appeared between 1825 and 1850, but most of them were ephemeral and, perhaps because of the unliterary nature of this free thought, none developed sufficient scope to be considered the national voice of infidelity.[1]

This free-thought movement paralleled what has been considered the rise of the common man in America and has been labeled Jacksonian Democracy. Unlike the aristocratic Deism of the eighteenth century or the middle-class free thought that followed the Civil War, antebellum free thought attached to working-class radicalism and became a part of the working man's attempt to improve his material status. Materialism, in this case, connoted rationalism as well as concern for physical welfare. Tocqueville early predicted that the pervasive materialism of the Jacksonian era would bring a spiritualistic reaction, and in fact, the rise of mediumistic spiritualism about 1850 did coincide with the decline of antebellum free thought. Antislavery agitation, of course, became at the same time an important focus for radical energies.[2]

After the Civil War a small group of Boston Unitarians, who had made unsuccessful attempts to excise "every implication of a creed" from their denomination, founded the Free Religious Association. A new chapter in American free thought had begun. A sort of religious fellowship for those who considered themselves beyond the theological pale of liberal Christianity, the association claimed the leadership of such men as Francis Abbot and Octavius B. Frothingham and the support of such figures as Ralph Waldo Emerson. Its leaders shared an overriding reverence for progress, evolution, and the transcendency of science; but as ministers would, they retained a sentimental attachment to the idea of religion. Believing that "the creed of the Future is to be settled by science, not by theology," they accorded highest spiritual value to the scientific method of discerning Truth. Subordinate values included brotherhood, the unity of man, and the performance of good works. Their transcendentalist backgrounds never allowed them to be very clear about the superiority of concrete science over mystical religion, but they sensed that even "free" religion needed the validation of science more than science needed the validation of religion.[3]

It is not surprising that Francis Abbot sought to enroll Charles Darwin in the Free Religious Association. Darwin's evolutionary theory provided a useful plank, if not the full foundation, for many free-thought arguments against the "superstitious creeds" of religion in postwar America. Darwin's work corroborated rather than initiated basic tenets of free thought, but more importantly, it confirmed freethinkers in their equation of science with anticlericalism. The freethinkers only capitalized on an already popular connotation of the word "science"; as the *Dublin Review* noted in 1867, the word had commonly come to express an exclusion of the theological and metaphysical realms of knowledge. If Darwin became a minor saint to freethinkers, he worked his miracles for the churchmen, forcing them to accommodate "Genesis creation" to evolution by natural selection, thereby giving Christianity a new, a scientifically certified, lease on life.[4]

The Free Religious Association did not develop into a national organization, but rather remained a loose fellowship, which was in keeping with its vague program. Local societies, such as the one in Valley Falls, were founded around the country, but these had no administrative connections to the Boston Association. The *Index*, founded in 1870 by Francis Abbot, became the unifying agent of these societies. The idea of a national pressure group of secularists and religious liberals had strong appeal among Free Religionists, however, and in the mid 1870s the *Index* proposed a national convention of freethinkers. Inspired to patriotism, perhaps, by President Grant's encouraging proposal to tax church property, the interested ones gathered on the Centennial Independence Day in Philadelphia and formed the National Liberal League. To members the word "Liberal" had a simple meaning: belief in the radical separation of church and state. But from association, "Liberal" came to be used by Liberal Leaguers themselves as a synonym for freethinker, particularly one who questioned the supernatural aspects of Christianity. The presence of denominational progressives or "religious liberals" in the league further confused the meaning; the churchman-on-the-street had no problem labeling unbelievers—he called them infidels.[5]

In the beginning, conservative Free Religion advocates such as President Francis Abbot dominated the leadership of the league. For the mostly honorary office of vice-president, Liberal Leaguers chose a collection of persons, some well known; early ones included James Parton, the biographer; Robert Dale Owen, the congressman; and Elizabeth Cady Stanton, the feminist. The league aspired to be an active national force dedicated to the secularization of the United States. It charged that national and state governments maintained "numerous practical connections of the State with the church," which violated the spirit of the Constitution and the best American tradition. Consequently, it pledged an energetic campaign for a constitutional amendment to enforce the secularization of all levels of government. The league promised legal support for appropriate cases, established a lecture bureau, and began to organize local chapters.[6]

The Nine Demands of Liberalism, which were first published in the *Index* in 1872, served as the league's statement of principles. Besides urging taxation of church property and the abolition of government chaplaincies, the "Demands" attacked all public appropriations for sectarian educational and charitable institutions, as well as all religious services and uses of religious artifacts in government procedures. They urged that religious days and occasions not be recognized by the government; that "Sunday laws" be repealed; that oaths be replaced by simple affirmation; that laws enforcing "Christian morality" be abrogated in favor of the criteria of natural morality, equal rights, and liberty; and that governmental favoritism to any religion be stopped.

The federal postal obscenity law of 1873, the Comstock Act, caused trouble in the league almost from the beginning. Initiated through the efforts of vice-suppression societies and their knight errant, Anthony Comstock, the law prohibited obscenity from the mails, without defining it. Moreover, the statute came to be energetically and selectively applied by the government's own Special Agent, also Anthony Comstock. He not only influenced decisively the course of sex radicalism, as detailed in chapter 5, but he helped to discourage organized free thought as well. Comstock, it has been said, equated "Liberal" with "libertine"; at any rate he viewed agnosticism as blasphemy and, with his considerable powers, sought to rout out the blasphemers along with other vice-mongers. Freethinkers understandably viewed Comstock with alarm; as a minority, the infidel fringe, they expected and received special harassment.[7]

Three factions formed within the league over the Comstock issue. A majority—led by the important free-thought publisher De Robigne Mortimer Bennett and by Thaddeus B. Wakeman, a leading Liberal League organizer and attorney—favored repeal of the act. A minority led by E. P. Hurlbut clearly supported Comstock's efforts at censorship and suppression. A larger minority—led by league president Francis Abbot and the famous agnostic Robert G. Ingersoll—feared adverse public opinion and urged the league to go on record as opposing obscenity rather than as opposing Comstock. Abbot's *Index* vacillated momentarily before reaching this position; at first Abbot decried the obscenity laws and supported outright the two freethinkers recently indicted by Comstock—Ezra Heywood and De Robigne Mortimer Bennett. In short order, however, Abbot proclaimed support for obscenity laws, urged Liberal Leaguers not to sully their reputations in an anti-Comstock-Law fight, and, for good measure, chided Comstock for abusing his power.[8]

In February 1878 the Liberal League presented to Congress a petition 2,100-feet long, bearing 70,000 names protesting the Comstock Act. By involving the federal government in moral and religious persecution, claimed the petitioners, the statute had fundamentally "reversed the policy and practice of our Government since its foundation." The protest included the spectrum of Liberal League opposition to the Comstock laws; although the majority of Liberal Leaguers favored full repeal, the first signatory, Robert Ingersoll, expressly favored only modification of the laws. Introduced in the House by the capricious reformer Ben Butler of Massachusetts and supported in committee by Dr. Edward Bond Foote and others, the petition quickly provoked the opposition of Anthony Comstock and his supporters, notably Samuel Colgate, the soap magnate. They successfully foiled the petitioners' attempts, and on May 31 Congressman George Bicknell of Indiana tabled the measure. This cavalier treatment by Congress of a mass protest affirmed many sex radicals in their contempt for the state.

In the wake of the protest to Congress a majority of the league voted for full repeal of the Comstock measures at the league's national convention in Syracuse later that year. Comstock's arrests of De Robigne Bennett and Ezra Heywood in 1877, as well as his attempts to portray the free-thought efforts of Bennett as blasphemy and the sex-reform efforts of Heywood as obscenity, did not sit well with liberty-conscious Liberal Leaguers. The outvoted element of the league, led by Francis Abbot, objected that Bennett's plan to mobilize the league in order to expunge the Comstock laws would involve the league in extraneous matters and would divert it from its main purpose of separating the church from the state; Abbot, like Ingersoll, advocated precise construction of obscenity legislation so that immorality might be punished with minimum impairment to personal liberty. Abbot lost his presidency of the league over the matter and, with some ill feeling, considered starting a rival organization of liberals.[9]

The Comstock issue surfaced at the next national meeting of the league in 1879 at Cincinnati, and the group passed a resolution on the matter that was sufficiently broad to encompass most shades of opinion. One section of the measure called for the application of the Comstock laws to the earthy tales in the Bible. This convention also founded what proved to be a stillborn political party. Although a majority of those present favored the idea of a political party as a method of achieving their goals, poor leadership and internal bickering kept the party from becoming operable. The newly elected president turned out to be under indictment for forgery and bigamy. Later attempts at organizing a national party similarly failed. Some intimated that Robert Ingersoll, the Great Infidel and the popular leader of American freethinkers, could have saved the party. Ingersoll had a limited view of such a party, however; he wanted it to be only a lobbying auxiliary to the major parties. Moreover, Ingersoll wanted a genteel, respectable party that would be free of free lovers and of those who sought total repeal of the Comstock laws. Differences on these issues caused "Fighting Bob" to resign as a vice-president of the league at its 1880 convention. He "went right out," remarked Thaddeus Wakeman, "and was rebaptized into the Republican party, and has been the hewer of wood and the drawer of water for it ever since."[10]

At the St. Louis convention in 1882 the Committee on Political Action drafted a platform covering an array of social issues in a new attempt to form a party. Edwin C. Walker, who was soon to join Moses Harman as his coeditor in Valley Falls, sat on this committee; and as it reported at the subsequent convention in Milwaukee, he presented the minority report. As an anarchist, he opposed, among other things, involvement in conventional ballot politics. Eugene MacDonald commented in the *Truth Seeker* that "had the platform been entirely anarchistic, anti-prohibitory, and radical on the marriage question," Walker would have loved it. The party never jelled, members being persuaded by its president, Thaddeus B. Wakeman, that under any circumstances they lacked the necessary financial resources for success.[11]

Because the league—which included capitalists and anarchists, unitarians and atheists, materialists and spiritualists—could agree on little else save secularism, it gave up all attempts to unite on other social issues and confined itself to the Nine Demands. Signifying this change of policy, the league changed its name in 1884 to the American Secular Union, and Samuel P. Putnam, its secretary, assumed leadership. This incapacity for political organization persuaded some freethinkers that secularism alone was too limited and ineffective an issue to compel much vital involvement. This political impotence, moreover, may have indicated a tacit recognition by Liberal Leaguers that the union of Protestantism with

American politics was so deep and unofficial as to be out of range of legislation—an ironic effect of the doctrine of separation of church and state in America.

The thought of the late-nineteenth-century Liberal League movement offered nothing particularly new nor uniquely stimulating; indeed, its anticlerical ideas and doctrines had been expounded by European thinkers for several centuries. The movement gained its limited momentum in the late nineteenth century as adherents claimed free thought to be the necessary basis for advanced ideas or scientific thought. D. M. Bennett named his paper *Truth Seeker,* and its logo pictured the editor seated at his desk, engrossed in scientific pursuit; shelves of books, chemistry apparatus, a globe, and a telescope completed the tableau. Underneath was the motto: "Devoted to Science, Morals, Freethought and Human Happiness." Bennett's "scientific" credentials did not depend on his pharmaceutical skill—he had once vended patent medicine—but rather on the antireligion that he now promoted. That some mistook the figure in the engraving for Benjamin Franklin was not surprising—for in their conception of science, many freethinkers were closer to the age of Franklin than to that of Darwin.

The positivism of Auguste Comte and John Stuart Mill influenced the freethinkers, but they were nevertheless more akin to the extreme rationalists of the eighteenth century; they conceived of science in terms of religion, and they believed that the primary work of science was to confute "sectarian superstitions"; they saw scientific research as an exercise of logic and of simple observation which rested ultimately and intuitively on "natural law." Comte's stress on positive phenomenon, on the other hand, disregarded rather than opposed theological cause. The notions of an elitist order in Comte's social science, moreover, conflicted with the libertarian disposition of many Liberal Leaguers. Comte's American disciple Henry Edger miserably failed to convert to positivism the libertarian Modern Times community, some veterans of which, notably Stephen Pearl Andrews, later became patriarchs of radical free thought.

In the post–Civil War era, which witnessed the professionalization of knowledge in America, free-thought organizations offered a convenient way for many nonprofessionalized "free-lance" intellectuals to relate to the scientific and intellectual advances of the day. The increasing centralization of intellectual life around the university excluded many of these individuals whose intellectual preparation had assumed the continuing antebellum style of intellectual discourse, with its open journalistic debates and its emphasis on egalitarianism and humanitarian reform. Most of the postwar generation of professional scientists were secularists, but they felt no compunction to join a free-thought movement in order to prove or protect their scientific standing. Indeed, the active attempt of the free-thought movement to popularize, democratize, and worship science had little outward support from important scientists. Significantly, the one outstanding scientist who was connected at all with activist free thought, Lester Frank Ward, gave up free-thought journalism early in life in order to devote his career to scientific vistas that were broader than anticlericalism.[12]

The freethinkers' largest journal, which was dedicated to popular scientific truth-seeking and was edited by the former Shaker medicine man D. M. Bennett, actually represented a reaction to the new professionalization of thought and to the elitism of modern science. Meanwhile the *Index* and its quest for the "scientific study of theology" attracted a coterie of religionists rather than a symposium of scientists.

If free-thought editors did not attract many scientists, they did attract some radicals by crusading for significant issues such as free speech, women's rights, sex education, and, to some extent, radical political systems. The important element of Liberal Leaguers who defined liberalism in libertarian and anti-Comstockian terms attracted sex radicals to the cause and nurtured others who would eventually become sex radicals. The movement's anti-Christian, "scientific" cast drew both spiritualists, who were intent upon empirically demonstrating the possibilities of the soul, and materialists, who were intent upon proving the absence of one. In the eighties, spiritualists made up one-quarter of the *Truth Seeker*'s readership; and according to Bennett's successor, nine-tenths of America's spiritualists supported Bennett's anti-Comstock effort.[13]

The movement fostered some full-scale attempts at social regeneration. In the eighties, G. H. Walser founded the town of Liberal, Missouri, as a city-on-a-hill in order to demonstrate the superior virtues of churchlessness. The community split when a free-love couple, Georgia and Henry Replogle, began promoting their sexual doctrines in their paper, *Equity*. Walser, who had dedicated the town to "universal mental liberty," led a mob of Liberal Leaguers against the Replogles and forced them out of town. Apart from this irony, the experiment produced a Liberal University and an interesting plan by Edwin C. Walker for an anarchistic economic system that would free the community from the "ranks of capital's dependents." The Liberal University never quite worked out in practice, although it made another attempt in 1899 when it adjourned to Silverton, Oregon; Walker's ambitious plan did not weather the free-love storm at Liberal, Missouri.[14]

The predominant, if slightly off-brand, intellectual tone of the Liberal League kept it from falling prey to the anti-Catholicism that surfaced most noticeably during the 1890s in the American Protective Association (A.P.A.). A strong temptation to crusade against Catholics existed, however well checked it was. Staid Free Religionists could be depended upon to offer a sort of high-toned nativism, as when Henry Blackwell argued in the *Index* that woman suffrage in Massachusetts could once more "thoroughly Americanize" (and Republicanize) its politics by enfranchising native American women and by neutralizing the heavily Democratic immigrant vote. Later, the *Truth Seeker*, in its rambunctious dislike for popery, gave limited support to some A.P.A. declarations. As a rule, however, the Liberal Leaguers steered surprisingly clear of overt anti-Catholicism. Edwin Walker, who was bitterly critical of the A.P.A., appeared to speak for many throughout the league when he suggested that the greatest danger to liberty in America came from the "machinations" of the Protestants; "the Catholics are dangerous only as the Protestants prepare the way for them," he believed. Liberal Jews, or Israelites as the *Yahudim* preferred to be called, occupied prominent positions of leadership in both the Free Religious Association and the Liberal League. Isaac M. Wise, of the *American Israelite*, helped to found the Free Religious Association; and in 1879 both Wise and Moritz Ellinger, of the *Jewish Times*, served as national vice-presidents of the Liberal League.[15]

The *Truth Seeker*, which was founded in 1873, came as near to being what Tocqueville called the "public organ of infidelity" as any publication ever did in America. Its well-drawn cartoons, humerous jabs (Mark Twain subscribed to it), and iconoclastic approach bolstered its popularity among militant freethinkers. The *Index*, with its audience of "scholars, ex-ministers, and polite society," was succeeded by the *Open Court* in 1887. Under the editorship of Paul Carus the journal devoted itself to the Religion of Science. The *Truth Seeker*'s long-lived career—it is still being published—followed the example of the veteran free-thought journal the *Boston Investigator*. Founded by Abner Kneeland in 1831 and merged with the *Truth Seeker* in 1904, the *Investigator* provided the earliest platform for many brilliant freethinkers. Robert Ingersoll once credited the success of his national lecture tours to the wide distribution of the journal. The American free-thought press numbered from six to twelve regular journals in any one year between 1880 and 1895.[16]

The popularity of Robert Ingersoll and the active free-thought press no doubt had an effect on the creation and growth of the postwar Liberal League movement. Fear of an American theocratic government served as an additional spur to Liberal League organizing. In the dark days of the Union in 1863, a group called the National Reform Association organized to bring about the official juncture of church and state in America. This association sought to amend the Constitution to recognize "the authority of God, Christ, and His law." The theocrats, who had a precedent in Ezra S. Ely's antebellum attempts to form a Christian political party, viewed the Christian God as the creator of the nation and believed that government leaders should serve as His delegates. The earlier founding date of the National Reform Association and the copying by Liberal Leaguers of some of its tactics suggest that the Liberal League in some degree was a reaction to the Reform Association, although fear of organized "infidelism" may have urged the theocrats to subsequent organizational efforts. The freethinkers especially feared the counter organization because men of great public prominence served as its officers; its president in 1872 was Justice William Strong of the United States Supreme Court, and its vice-presidents included three state governors, one former governor, a justice of the New York Supreme Court, and Rhode Island's commissioner of public schools.[17]

By the mid eighties, the Liberal League, or Secular Union, numbered about three hundred chapters throughout the country. The great majority of these, however, existed as one-man clubs or as mere local debating societies; the Union had no real organizational power.[18] "Freethought organization is difficult," admitted Samuel P. Putnam in his book *Four Hundred Years of Freethought*. The individualist tendency of free thought worked against attempts at organization, while, in contrast, the unifying tendency of religion favored organization, he believed. Only the issue of self-defense in the face of religious tyranny forced free thinkers to organize.

The Liberal League of Kansas proved to be a spirited exception to the national experience; here, it seemed for a while that organized free thought might transcend its defensiveness and get on with the task of freeing the provincial culture from some of the pervasive strictures of Protestantism, particularly the crippling literalness that Bob Ingersoll twitted with effect. In September 1879, Kansas freethinkers organized a national meeting of the Liberal League at the Bismarck Grove camp-meeting area near Lawrence. The convention enjoyed the support and leadership of individuals who figured prominently in Kansas history, among them Charles Robinson, Annie L. Diggs, and Frank Doster. During this national meeting, Kansas Liberal Leaguers formed a state organization.[19]

After the camp meeting, a good deal of organizing took place on the local level in Kansas. One man claimed that he had organized nearly forty separate chapters. Several Liberal League newspapers cropped up in 1879 and 1880, among them the *National Monitor,* at Wichita; the *Liberal Advocate,* at Topeka; the *Western Reformer,* at Salina; the *Cloud County Blade,* at Concordia; and the *Valley Falls Liberal*. The *Blade* and the *Liberal* were the only ones to last for a substantial period.[20]

Several factors spurred interest in organized free thought in Kansas. The outstanding Kansas minds who identified with the movement attracted many to the league, while the specter of a theocratized government drew others. The theological threat had special meaning for Kansans. Two of the vice-presidents of the God-in-the-Constitution National Reform Association had been

Kansas governors. The former Republican governor John P. St. John headed the Prohibition ticket for president of the United States in 1884; contrary to the Constitution, the Prohibition platform "acknowledged almighty God as the rightful sovereign of all men, from whom the just powers of government are derived." In alliance, the Woman's Christian Temperance Union sought to bring about Christian reform in government through woman suffrage. Adding to the reform ambiguities, the initial state platform of the People's party recognized "Almighty God as the rightful sovereign of nations, and from whom all just powers of government are derived, and to whose will all human enactments ought to conform."[21] Free-thought reformers, many of whom had been abolitionists, were learning that the doctrine of a higher law than the Constitution could be a two-edged sword.

Radical ideas and reform politics often colored the annual meetings of the Kansas Liberal Leaguers. The *Topeka State Journal* denounced in advance one such mass affair at Ottawa in 1891 as a "Free Love" fest, not an unusual charge against the admitted infidels and unorthodox thinkers, but misleading when applied to rank-and-file Liberal Leaguers. The press commonly mistook toleration of free-love viewpoints for advocacy of them. This time the meeting at Ottawa did boast some notable opponents of convention. Its entirely female slate featured feminist editor Lois Waisbrooker, young Voltairine de Cleyre, and Kansas freethinkers Lillie D. White and Etta Semple. Waisbrooker and White had long supported the principle of free love, while de Cleyre, romantically draped in a Roman toga, would one day rival Emma Goldman as a popular anarchist speaker in America. Etta Semple, creator of the event, must have fed the fantasies of staid Kansans when she urged those coming to "bring your trunks with blankets and luncheon and live in the Park" during the three-day event.[22]

The 1894 annual meeting in Topeka attracted notice with the resolutions it addressed to President Grover Cleveland, one of which demanded that "you take off your crown, vacate your throne, lay down your sceptre and take yourself away from the sight of human eyes forever." Moses Harman's paper later commented that the freethinkers' demands had been more in jest than in earnest, but major Chicago and Kansas City papers accepted at face value the telegraphed accounts of the event. The *Topeka*

Capital responded with a terrified article about the "Populist 'Free Thinkers,'" revealing the twin fears of the state's official Republican paper. The freethinkers had been addressed by Populist spokesmen who supported the initiative and referendum.[23]

The resolutions brought censure from the national director of the Secular Union, Samuel Putnam; Etta Semple demurred, accusing the national voice of the Liberal League, the *Truth Seeker,* of contempt for Kansas Liberal Leaguers and suggesting that Putnam mind his own business. Under Putnam's direction, the American Secular Union had indeed become what it had decided it had to be in 1884 in order to continue existing: a loose congregation of those who agreed on the one issue of separation of church and state, an issue so basic that it was perhaps irrelevant in itself to other reforms. Any assessment of the secularists after the mid eighties must focus on local organizations such as the Kansas one, since the national Secular Union had become primarily a lecture bureau.

In the earliest years of the decade, when liberalism alone seemed a sufficient radical cause, Valley Falls teemed with free-thought activity. On the first Sunday of each month the local Liberal League held spirited and well-attended meetings, and during one of these, they elected Moses Harman as secretary. Under Harman the *Valley Falls Liberal* became the ascendant voice of liberalism in Kansas; A. J. Searl, who helped to start the paper, soon moved away to the University of Kansas and dropped out of the movement. In September 1881 the journal became the *Kansas Liberal.*

The next spring, as the organ of the Kansas Liberal Union, the *Kansas Liberal* moved for a short time to Lawrence, a move occasioned by an offer that Harman had made at the union's executive committee meeting in March. The committee decided that the paper should be published weekly, that it should be enlarged, and that its columns should be equally open to each "interest" within the ranks of Kansas liberalism. These interests—or, more appropriately, factions—included spiritualism, materialism, and Unitarianism.

In Lawrence, Annie L. Diggs, the secretary of the Kansas Secular Union, assisted Harman in editing the paper. At twenty-eight, the energetic woman already held high office in the Boston-based Free Religious Association. She would later become a prominent Populist editor and perhaps the most outstanding woman in that movement, Mary Elizabeth Lease's platform popularity notwithstanding. Other interests of "Little Annie" included the Woman's Christian Temperance Union, woman suffrage, and Fabian-type socialism. An example of her utilitarian reform style was her 1883 manual on silk culture, which was written in order to help farm women make some money of their own while they were engaged in their ordinary duties.[24]

With Harman and Diggs at the helm, the paper enjoyed an enthusiastic beginning. Within two months, however, the paper changed from a weekly to a fortnightly; finally, in October, a clash over the prohibition question caused Harman to assume his original control of the paper, and after six months in Lawrence, he returned with it to Valley Falls.

Harman opposed prohibition laws as arbitrary infringements upon personal freedom. Support of prohibition was, however, prevalent among free-thought activists, as it was among woman-suffragists. Reestablished in Valley Falls, the *Liberal* became a forum for the minority element that opposed prohibition. Lucien V. Pinney, editor of the *Winsted* (Connecticut) *Press*, praised the *Liberal's* antiprohibition stand as the "first sign of fellowship" that he had found in ten years as a liberal, antiprohibition editor laboring against the criticism of the church and antichurch alike.[25]

From 1880 to 1883 Moses Harman's paper reflected an aggressively anticlerical brand of free thought. Taking a cue from the *Truth Seeker,* the *Liberal* used ridicule as well as reason in order to persuade, devoting ample space to jokes and light matter about the Christian religions. Poetry having a rationalist or anticlerical slant often appeared on the front page. In its Prospectus of August 1880, the *Liberal* had added to the National Liberal League platform its own intention to "champion the rights of the poor, laboring man as against monopolists of every class." In the second number the paper added support of temperance, which the editor later carefully distinguished from legal prohibition.

Besides the standard free-thought fare—"Col. Ingersoll on Sunday Law," "The Church and Slavery," and so forth—articles dealing with local or political themes appeared, although the *Liberal* did not concentrate on these issues. The editor's attitude on such matters leaned emphatically toward the libertarian and, as promised, against monopoly, with a hazy indication of a socialist analysis of capitalism. When it became the *Kansas Liberal* the journal carried slightly more than a full column of advertising per issue. After the short stint as the official paper of the Kansas Liberal Leaguers, the paper increased its advertising, principally offering more books, pamphlets, and such periodicals as the *Radical Review* (Chicago), *The Word* (Princeton, Massachusetts), the *Liberal* (Nashville), the *Boston Investigator, Man* (the National Liberal League's official semimonthly), and of course, Bennett's *Truth Seeker.*

In addition to the works of Proudhon, Paine, Darwin, and Haekel, Harman's paper offered studies on subjects ranging from sexual relations to Russian nihilism; in the potpourri could be found Ezra Heywood's *Cupid's Yokes,* Annie Besant's *Marriage,* and Whitman's *Leaves of Grass.* Elmina Slenker, who supported her radicalism through the sale of radical literature, regularly ran a competing ad, offering some of the same selections as well as her own *Private Physiology for Girls, Crimes of Preachers,* and *Diana,* a pamphlet that applied her belief in prohibition to the realm of sex, but which shocked prudes by its directness and alienated sex radicals with its asceticism. Harman offered Dr. E. B. Foote's countering pamphlet on the same page: *Dr. Foote's Reply to Alphites—Crushes Diana and All Such.* Prices ranged from ten cents for pamphlets to two dollars for books. In the mid eighties the paper expanded its literary offerings to include works by Bakunin, Stepniak, Josiah Warren, Lysander Spooner, J. K. Ingalls, Dostoyevsky, and Chernyshevsky. From 1881 on, the mail-order sale of radical literature would help to meet the expenses of publishing the paper.

Although a paper could be published quite cheaply in the late nineteenth century, the winning of men's minds in Kansas could still be a difficult job ideologically and financially. In 1881 Harman wrote to William Denton, a Massachusetts state geologist who had lectured at the Bismarck Grove convention, that local Liberal League debaters were "sadly in need of some good authorities to quote from." A recent lecture in Valley Falls by a Chicago Jesuit on the topic "Religion and Science" had shaken the freethinkers: "From the Church Standpoint it was certainly an able effort," Harman admitted. He asked for a free copy of Denton's *Is Darwin*

Right? Harman added: "You will no doubt think it Strange that I do not Send you the dollar with this request; but the fact is I am dunning everybody I think is favorable to our cause for money to pay the printing bills for our little paper. We have been publishing very cheaply, & giving away Something like half our edition. Consequently the enterprise has been a heavy one to carry for some of us, & those few by no means able to do much financially."[26]

Distinct eccentricities characterized Liberal League journals; instead of A.D., they used the chronology E.M., for Era of Man. This chronology had been adopted at the St. Louis Liberal convention in 1882 in recognition of one of science's first martyrs, Giordano Bruno, who was burned at the stake in 1600 for teaching that other solar systems, plural worlds, existed. In this chronology the year 1882 became 282 E.M. Harman began using the chronology in January 1883, and he continued to use it throughout his life. Earlier his paper had experimentally used a chronology A.N. (American Nation), dating from the Declaration of Independence, an established date that had no theological implications.

From the eighteenth century and into the twentieth, American communities loved the blend of entertainment and edification that was offered by the camp meeting. Organized religion had no monopoly on this form of convention; indeed, freethinkers, spiritualists, and politicians welcomed any excuse to congregate under brush arbors or open skies to spout their remedies. In 1883 the town of Valley Falls offered the people of Kansas two noteworthy conventions: one a meeting of theocrats, the other a meeting of freethinkers.

The freethinkers met in true camp-meeting style. In early fall, after crops had been laid by, those who sought fellowship and the promotion of their special cause flocked from all over Kansas to the fairgrounds outside of Valley Falls. Here for several days they created a communal city of wagons and tents and people bound by common beliefs; a roster of speakers, entertainers, and special sessions filled the hours from ten in the morning to midnight. Such free-thought conventions in Kansas, when they occurred, modeled themselves upon the large national meet at Bismarck Grove in 1879. By contrast, the other Valley Falls meeting, that of the

National Reform Association, took place in winter, indoors, and was a creature of the church. Moses Harman figured in both.

The National Reform Association (N.R.A.), which sought formally to Christianize the United States government, arranged a two-day convention at the Valley Falls Methodist Church in mid February 1883. M. A. Gault, who had been having some success promoting such conventions throughout the Midwest, invited Harman as a representative opponent to make a presentation at the convention.[27]

Harman appeared on the first night of the meeting and duly read his objections to the N.R.A. An emotional scene ensued, and Harman found himself being ardently exhorted by an excited Christian woman. Even winter storms did not keep people at home for the second meeting; Harman sat in the packed church and listened as a clergyman from Tippinville lambasted him and his free-thought arguments. Denied a chance to reply (even the editor of the *New Era* later wrote that Harman was treated unfairly), Harman, incensed, slogged away from the church. His irritation grew when the proceedings of the meeting omitted his dissenting contribution. Gault did report, however, the following comment in the National Reform Association's *Christian Statesman*:

> Our Convention in Valley Falls was a gratifying success, considering that it was the hardest field we have yet found. . . . It has three or four weak struggling churches, most of whose members reside in the country. It is the headquarters of Liberalism. A radical infidel sheet called the "Kansas Liberalist," is published there, and the town is noted as a godless place, a center of immorality. Several murders have recently been committed in and around the town.[28]

Such a report on Valley Falls did not deter the Liberal League camp meeting. The idea of holding such a meeting stemmed from an editorial suggestion by Harman in April, possibly in response to the earlier N.R.A. meeting. On the morning of the last day of August, Liberal Leaguers spread out on the Valley Falls fairgrounds under banners that proclaimed such mottos as "No Mental Popery on This Platform" and "Individual Sovereignty and Social Order Are Parent and Child." Edwin C. Walker, Harman's publishing partner, convened the four days of camp-meeting rhetoric and music, from which emerged a new state liberal organization to replace the Kansas Liberal Union. The old organization had been shaken not only by the issue of prohibition but also by disputes between spiritualist and materialist factions. The newly elected president, James M. Hagaman, a materialist who was the self-taught editor of the *Concordia Blade,* claimed that under the new leadership and revised constitution both factions would enjoy nearly equal representation in affairs of the league. The group elected five delegates, among them E. C. Walker, to attend the national Liberal League congress, which was scheduled to meet on September 21 in Milwaukee.[29]

Business matters aside, the camp meeting offered a mixture of homiletic, anticlerical, and evolutionist fare. The Tippinville minister who had denounced Harman at the N.R.A. meeting came and registered his dissent, but the assembled "professors"—as many of the lecturers styled themselves—overmatched the parson. Representative presentations from the event included: "Hold the Flag of Freedom Flying," sung by Prof. W. F. Peck; "Orthodox Religion a Fraud upon Humanity and a Slander on God," a lecture by O. Olney of the McPherson *Thinker*; "There is no Hell," a talk by Professor Peck; and "The Love of the Beautiful," a lecture by Prof. C. W. Stewart. The appearance of Professor Peck's wife in "free marriage" highlighted the meeting. Known as Mrs. H. S. Lake, she delivered a lecture on "The Effect upon Morality of a Decline in Religious Belief" and an exposition on the subject of woman suffrage, which a partisan reporter called "radical and brilliant."

The first governor of Kansas, Charles Robinson, spoke on "The Fallacy of Prohibition" and on "God in the Constitution" to large crowds. An influential supporter of the Liberal League cause, Robinson criticized as "absurd" and "mischievous" the attempt to base government on a theological scheme. "What arrogance and presumption for one man or sect of men to claim that they only have the true conception of God and that all who differ from them shall be classed as heretics and infidels to be punished by disenfranchisement if not by torture and death," said Robinson. He tempered his pronouncements with waggish humor: If God is to be head of government, "Will he want a salary & if so how much? Will taxes be higher or lower?"[30]

On the last day of the camp meeting the Liberal Leaguers approved a resolution extending sympathy to Ezra and Angela Heywood, publishers of *The Word* in Princeton, Massachusetts, for their prosecution under the Comstock obscenity laws. Mrs. H. S. Lake gave the final talk, "Individualism"; and her husband, apparently as adept a singer as a lecturer, sang his "Laughing Man," which, reportedly, ended the meeting on a good-humored note.

4/ Lucifer, the Light Bearer

ALMOST a year before the Kansas Liberal Leaguers held their camp meeting at Valley Falls, Moses Harman had made the acquaintance of one of the most energetic young men in the National Liberal League, Edwin Cox Walker of Norway, Iowa. As secretary of the Iowa Liberal League, Walker had probably organized more local leagues over a wider area than anyone else in the country. Born in Lancaster, New York, in 1849, Walker had grown up on a farm in Iowa. Like Harman, he became a schoolteacher as well as a farmer, and for a time, he was active in the Universalist religion. At the age of twenty-six, Walker discarded these pursuits for radical journalism and the free-thought lecture circuit.

In the late 1870s Walker's articles began to appear in the free-religious *Index* and in the *Truth Seeker*. They ranged in topic from support of the beleaguered Oneida Community to criticism of the cautious policies of the Liberal League's president. He initiated a national debate among freethinkers on prohibition, arguing that "prohibition involves a principle which, if carried to its logical conclusion, would stop every press in the country, and close the lips of every Freethinker." Many reform-minded people and Liberal Leaguers supported prohibition as a matter of course, because they viewed alcohol as a primary cause of social ills.

In 1882 Walker began contributing articles to Benjamin Tucker's new anarchistic journal, *Liberty*, published in Boston. Walker's incisive style and "plumb line" antistatism quickly won him Tucker's respect, as well as regular space in *Liberty*'s columns.

As his name became familiar to readers of *Truth Seeker* and *Liberty*, he began to write for Harman's *Kansas Liberal*. His reputation did not go unnoticed by the conventional press. Edgar Howe, who edited the *Atchison Globe* by day and struggled over his novel *The Story of a Country Town* by night, characterized Walker as "a fellow so intensely liberal that he opposes the law against indecent exposure."[1]

Harman's acquaintance with Walker grew from friendship into partnership. They joined forces on the *Kansas Liberal* just before the beginning of the new year of 1883, or, as they would have it, E.M. 283. The *Liberal* gained an energetic polemicist, whose tours could help finance and publicize the paper; while Walker, as an editor, gained a paper of his own.

Walker's first article as coeditor expressed his journalistic philosophy. Editorials in the *Liberal* would not cater to the prejudices of the "presumably hostile majority," he wrote, nor would the paper follow the lead of metropolitan journals that "gather the news, and reflect popular prejudices by seeking to conserve that which *is*, instead of prophesying that which should be"; however unpopular or unprofitable it might be, the reform paper must "point to the evils existing in individual life, society and government, and labor for their elimination."[2]

In the next issue, Walker wrote a flowery eulogy to D. M. Bennett, the recently deceased editor of *Truth Seeker*. Bennett was no anarchist nor even a consistent supporter of sexual liberty or free speech, but his iconoclastic style as a free-thought editor and publisher set an example for the Kansas journalists. Besides distributing much of the free-thought literature in the country, Bennett's publishing house had introduced American readers to such important works as George Drysdale's *The Elements of Social Science*, a book that encouraged contraception as a means of increasing the amount of love and sexual happiness in the world, particularly for women. Bennett, one of the most famous objects of Comstock's harassment, held an important place as a near-martyr in the crusade against the Comstock laws.

Almost immediately, Walker began to make lecture tours on behalf of the paper. He stopped at settlements along the railway lines, sometimes with invitations, sometimes with only the name of a local Liberal Leaguer, and sometimes with no lead at all. The money earned from these lectures and from the sale of radical materials—"many of the works of our most advanced English, French and American thinkers"—soon became a major source of support for the Valley Falls journal.

There were enough willing listeners to his lectures to support the paper as a weekly. Most of them wanted to hear the free-thought message; of the thirty lecture topics advertised—including "Eden and Evolution," "The New Sexual Morality," and "Medical Laws and Obscenity Legislation"—about two-thirds directly dealt with free thought. This list may be considered reflective of his hearers' tastes, since it appeared after Walker's first successful year on the road. His first lecture tour lasted a year and a half, December 1882 to June 1884. His return from the lecture circuit, combined with general hard times, forced Harman in his turn to take to the road, not to lecture, but to visit the paper's subscribers in search of funds.[3]

The *Kansas Liberal* became *Lucifer, the Light Bearer* on August 24, 1883. According to Harman, correspondents and patrons in other states objected to the local flavor of the name *Kansas Liberal*; moreover, "Liberal" was overused, Harman felt, in the names of periodicals. *Lucifer* made a compelling and fitting short title. As the herald of dawn after the black night of the Age of the Gods, the morning star, *Lucifer,* would appropriately shine forth from the Kansas plains. Benjamin Tucker exulted in *Liberty* over the name change: "A very happy thought! Quite the best name we know of, after Liberty!"[4]

Of course a certain calculated perversity figured in taking a name that had, in addition to luminary connotations, a diabolical one. Harman wrote that

> while we do not adopt the reputed character of any man, god, demigod or demon, as our model, yet there is one phase of the character of *their* Lucifer that is also appropriate to our paper, viz: that of an Educator. The god of the Bible had doomed mankind to perpetual ignorance—they would never have known Good from Evil if Lucifer had not told them how to become wise as the gods themselves. Hence, according to theology, Lucifer was the first teacher of science.

Henceforth the paper received many comments about its name from earnest freethinkers as well as from choleric clerics. Harman

56 The Sex Radicals

Price 2 Cents.

LUCIFER.
THE LIGHT-BEARER.

THIRD SERIES, VOL. V., No. 26.   CHICAGO, ILLINOIS, JULY 13, E. M. 301. [C. E. 1901.]   WHOLE No. 87

TRUE FREEDOM.

Is true Freedom but to break fetters for our own dear sake,
And, with leather hearts, forget that we owe mankind a debt?
No! true freedom is to share all the chains our brothers wear,
And, with heart and hand, to be earnest to make others free!

They are slaves who fear to speak for the fallen and the weak;
They are slaves who will not choose hatred, scoffing, and abuse,
Rather than in silence shrink from the truth they needs must think;
They are slaves who dare not be in the right with two or three.
—Lowell.

telepathists, let me say that I found the Earthites living very material lives, very sensuous lives; that their bodily senses are six in number, namely

1. Sight;
2. Hearing;
3. Taste, or the gustatory sense;
4. Smell;
5. Touch, or the sense of feeling;
6. Gender, or the sense that finds its use and manifestation in the differentiation called sex.

Excerpt from front page of *Lucifer,* 13 July 1901
Courtesy Kenneth Spencer Research Library, University of Kansas Libraries

Lucifer's specialty is freedom of women from sex slavery but under our present system how is a mother to support her self and child when there are millions of able-bodied men who can't make a living for themselves? I'm ready to admit that, all things considered, marriage is no protection to a woman, but is often an extra burden. Both reforms must be brought about together. The laborers of the country should unite and contend for one *thing*, viz.: *The referendum.* When they get that, they can take the lines in their own hands and do the driving, but until they get it they may expect to be driven.

Wishing you success, I am yours for the rights of humanity, peaceably if possible, forcibly if necessary.

A COUNTRY GENTLEMAN. 34 years young; owner of a beautiful country seat in the mountains; 1,500 feet altitude, 5,00 fruit trees, choicest and best acclimated varieties—wants correspondence with a lady, healthy, well formed, dark eyes and hair, not over 35 nor under 20 years, who either understands or is interested to learn and put into practice the art of Vegetarian and Fruitarian living and care for a pleasant home. One who is a good, clean, honest thinker a lover of nature, freedom and mental growth—and musical preferred. Address X, care Lucifer.

A PHYSICIAN IN THE HOUSE.
A New Family Medical Work, by Dr. J. H. Greer.

This book is up-to-date in every particular.
It will save you hundreds of dollars in doctors' bills.
It tells you how to cure yourself by simple and harmless home remedies.
It recommends no poisonous or dangerous drugs.
It teaches how to save health and life by safe methods.
It teaches prevention—that it is better to know how to live and avoid disease than to take any medicine as a cure.
It is not an advertisement and has no medicine to sell.
It has hundreds of excellent recipes for the cure of the various diseases.
It has 18 colored plates, showing different parts of the human body.
The chapter on Painless Midwifery is worth its weight in gold to women.
The "Care of Children" is something every mother ought to read.
It teaches the value of Air, Sunshine, and Water as medicines.
It contains valuable information for the married.
This book cannot fail to please you. If you are looking for health by the safest and easiest means, do not delay getting it. It has eight hundred pages, is neatly bound in cloth with gold letters, and will be sent by mail or express prepaid to any address for $2.75. Address M. Harman, 1394 Congress St., Chicago, Ill.

Mystic Science Menos, occult initiate, gives lessons in mystic science, casts horoscopes and may be consulted on all questions. Fee .$1.00 Address him in care of this office.

WANTED. A friend of mine wants a life companion. A woman not over 35, not yet too young to appreciate a good, clean,

Send us twenty-five cents for a thirteen weeks' trial subscription to Lucifer and we will present to you your choice of the following books, to the value of 25 cents. Read the list carefully. Every book is interesting and thought-inspiring.

John's Way; a domestic radical story, by Elmina D. Slenker, .20
Vital Force, Magnetic Exchange and Magnetation; Albert Chavannes, .25
Human Rights; J. Madison Rook, .10
Prohibition and Self-Government; E. C. Walker, .10
Practical Co-operation; " " .10
The Revival of Puritanism; " " .10
Love and the Law; " " .10
Sexual Enslavement of Woman; " " .05
Digging for Bedrock, by Moses Harman, .10
In Hell and the Way Out; H. E. Allen, 10

THE BLICKENSDERFER TYPEWRITER

The Only High-Grade
Writing Machine
Sold at Low Price.

No.5, $35; No.7, $50

Interchangeable Type;
No ribbons; Permanent alignment; Unlimited speed; Durability guaranteed; 30,000 in use. For full particulars address W. J. Blickensderfer & Co., 195 LaSalle street, Chicago.

C. S. Wood, M. D. Radical Physician and Surgeon. Successful treatment of all chronic and special diseases, by new and correct methods. Satisfaction guaranteed, as we will undertake no case that we cannot cure or permanently benefit. Especial facilities for the care of women suffering from any disease or irregularity peculiar to their sex. Consultation free. If by mail, inclose stamp. C. S. Wood, Department O, 121 LaSalle st., Chicago, Ill. Suite 64. Office hours 10 A. M. to 4 P. M.

A Private Home with the best care and treatment for women and unfortunate girls, before and during confinement; securing an absolutely safe and easy delivery. A home provided for the child if the mother cannot keep it. For full particulars call on or write to, Dr. Wood, 121 La Salle St., Chicago, Ill. Office suite 64. Hours 10 A. M. to 4 P. M.

ELMINA'S REQUEST. Women who would like gentlemen for correspondents, and who feel free to discuss all reforms, will send name and address and two two-cent stamps to ELMINA DRAKE SLENKER, Snowville, Pul. Co. Va.

Classified page, *Lucifer,* 2 July 1898
Courtesy Kenneth Spencer Research Library, University of Kansas Libraries

LUCIFER, THE LIGHT-BEARER

PUBLISHED AT 507 CARROLL AVE., CHICAGO, ILLINOIS.

M. HARMAN, EDITOR AND PUBLISHER.

Entered at the Chicago Post Office as Second-class Mail Matter.

Eastern Representative, B. C. Walker, 244 W. 143d st., N. Y.
European Representative, William Duff, 9 Carfin St., Glasgow Scotland.

The name LUCIFER means LIGHT-BRINGING or LIGHT-BEARING and the paper as t has adopted this name stands for Light against Darkness—for Reason against Superstition—for Science against Tradition—for Investigation and Enlightenment against Credulity and Ignorance—for Liberty against Slavery—or Justice against Privilege.
Published weekly. One dollar per year. Three months twenty-five cents

Marriage by Compulsion.

It is not often that Lucifer publishes a cartoon, but the one printed in this issue, which appeared in the Chicago "Inter Ocean" of last Sunday, is so suggestive of one of the striking eatures of our present imperialistic government that it deserves

wide circulation. The "Inter Ocean" is a staunch republican newspaper, but, in explanation of this cartoon, it gives the following account of some of the doings of Captain Richard Leary of the United States navy, who was appointed governor of the little island of Guam, one of Uncle Sam's new possessions out in the Pacific ocean:

"Captain Leary found plenty to do in Guam. He was priest doctor, judge, and emperor in that little isle. He found the natives gentle, slothful, dirty, and living in a state of Arcadian simplicity which did not call for clothes for the body or the blessing of church or state on affairs matrimonial. The innocent islanders explained to the astonished Governor that their fathers and mothers did the same way, but Captain Leary said those days were past, and made the men and women who were living together march up in droves and get married, at the same time issuing a ruling that no more of these promiscuous unions should take place."

Continuing to describe the "reforms" introduced by Governor Leary, the writer for the "Inter Ocean" lapses into verse and says:

Out among the coral islands of the sandy beached Ladrones,
There lies Captain Leary's kingdom, where the broad Pacific means,
All the land is clad in verdure, but the people of the isle
Think they're amply dressed for dinner if they only wear a smile.
There came Captain Richard Leary, less than one short year ago,
And it made his Boston bosom pant with grief to see things so;
But the pants his bosom panted were the only "pants" in sight—
Twould have dazed a Watch and Ward man down in Guam that summer night
Divorce courts held no daily sessions, social students to alarm;
For heavenly rule existed, when first Leary came to Guam;
"There's no wedlock up in heaven!" But the Yankee despot's power

Soon set native clergy sailing fifty knots each quarter hour.
And poor Roberts—he of Utah—as a Guamite soon would cease,
For the king from cultured Boston gave but one plump bride apiece.

When Captain Cook first landed on the Sandwich Islands he found them populated far more densely than they now are. The people seemed happy, peaceful, contented, and healthy. They knew nothing of the white man's religion, his morals nor his vices. After a century or two of Learyism a prime minister of King Kalakua testified that "wherever the missionaries come, in the Sandwich Islands, depopulation ensues." The white man's vices that go with the white man's religion destroy these simple-minded children of nature.

The same thing occurred in the West India Islands when the Spaniards undertook to teach marriage morality and the Catholic religion to the nakednatives. When Columbus came to the Islands he found them densely inhabited by a friendly and hospitable people. In about forty years, says the historian, the original inhabitants of these islands had disappeared completely, not by emigration but by extermination.

Much the same thing happened to the numerous and powerful "Six Nations," of New York and Pennsylvania. The attempt to make them moral and religious according to the Puritanic ideas, destroyed them.

Will the Anglo-Saxon invaders and meddlers ever learn a lesson from experience ? Will they learn that climate, environment and racial peculiarities have much to do with what we call morality? and that nature must not be forced through rapid gradations if we would secure beneficent results?

Home Again.

After another winter's outing, of some five months duration, I find myself once more in Lucifer's office trying to settle down again to the usual routine work.

Thinking it due to those of our friends who kindly helped in various ways to make this outing possible I will try to make a brief statement or summary of results thereof, so far as results can now be seen or estimated.

Of the things accomplished by or during my vacation it is perhaps not amiss to mention the writing and sending home to the office about fifty-five columns of editorial correspondence, which if printed in book form would make a book of more than one hundred pages the size of " Hilda's Home," or " Cityless and Countryless World." Whether this correspondence has worthily filled the space it has occupied is a question for the reader rather than the editor to decide.

2. I might perhaps mention also the writing of about two thousand letters, in the interest of Lucifer and its work, a goodly portion of which letters have already brought answers more or less satisfactory to those whose business it is to see that the weekly bills are duly paid.

3. Several weeks were spent in canvassing, lecturing and visiting—making new friendships and renewing old ones—the immediate and tangible results of which efforts are not yet large, but may in time bring forth fruits a thousand fold.

4. Health. On careful examination of the patient and comparing stock in trade with what was visible last fall, the comparison seems fairly satisfactory. While no one could reasonably expect a chronic invalid—whose years are nearly three score and ten, and whose ailments are of more than forty years' standing—to recover the vigor and elasticity of youth in a few short months of vacation and relaxation, even though giving himself up wholly to the business of recuperation, nevertheless the balance in my favor, on casting up the account, seems quite encouraging. My gain in weight is about eight pounds since last November, while my muscular strength has increased to a degree quite beyond expectation; also my ability to sleep soundly at night and to digest a comfortable amount of food.

Last but not least in this inventory I am glad to be able to report substantial progress in writing the long promised autobiography. Although this progress is not what I could wish it to be—partly because of distance from office and delays in getting the mechanical work done, yet if no further delays occur always seemed to enjoy printing their letters and replying to them. Those who considered liberalism the work of the devil very soon had a suitably named periodical to attack. When the editors later became involved in affairs that were even more shocking to the orthodox than liberalism was, the name of the paper appeared as a burning prophetic vision.

Sometime before the change in name, Harman seemed to have tired of publishing large amounts of the standard liberal line about the evils of religion. After all, the Nine Points of Liberalism did not call for much complex elucidation, particularly since the National Liberal League had given up attempts at political organization. Deeper issues attracted Harman, who had written a criticism of conventional marriage in the paper's second issue of September 1880. He seemed ready to be influenced by E. C. Walker's anarchism and nonconformist views of social institutions.

Walker's beliefs represented the indigenous strain of American anarchism—individualist anarchism—which traced its origins to Josiah Warren and the first quarter of the nineteenth century. Characterized by its emphasis upon individual sovereignty, it opposed any agency, such as the state, that either limited individual autonomy or compelled acceptance. Individualist anarchism contrasted to communist anarchism, which, in the very year that Walker teamed up with Harman, moved to the forefront as a radical cause under the leadership of the German immigrant Johann Most. Both strains of anarchism enjoyed growth in America during the eighties; anarchism rivaled socialism as an activist movement. Yet the boundaries of individualist anarchism, communist anarchism, and revolutionary socialism were not always obvious to participants or spectators. Indeed, both capitalist and anarchist laid claim to common elements in Herbert Spencer's thought, particularly his individualism and his early antistatism. Individualist anarchism, in fact, restated in radical fashion many tenets that were identified with political conservatism—belief in private property, emphasis on natural law, and opposition to majority rule. Later on in the eighties the Haymarket violence created in the popular mind the idea of the anarchist as terrorist pure and simple.[5]

The two anarchisms held in common a rejection of constituted authority; both saw that society and its institutions must be based upon other relationships that did not coerce; both sought workable noncoercive institutions; and both refused to work within the system in order to achieve partial or reformist ends. The communist anarchists, rejecting private property, sought to revolutionize society through the institution of collective communes; some of them advocated the violent overthrow of the existing state. The individualist anarchists rejected the idea of collectivism, holding that such a scheme necessarily implied authoritarianism, which would inevitably lead to totalitarianism. In short, to the individualist, collectivism ensured the continued life of the state.[6]

Individualist anarchists believed in cooperating for mutual economic or social purposes, but only in a framework of strict voluntarism. An individual's sovereignty extended only to himself, of course, and he could not infringe upon another's rights. These anarchists believed in rights to private property so long as such property represented only the amount of one's labor. They strictly abjured capitalism and the exploitation of a fellow's work for one's own profit. As opposed to the communist anarchist, the individualist anarchist sought no equalitarian society, but only one that would be free from arbitrary restriction and systematic inequality such as discriminations based on sex or race. True individual autonomy was their standard; anything more ornate or specific they left for the future to decide. In order to achieve their ends, most individualists favored passive resistance, although many did not necessarily condemn violence, particularly in extreme cases involving self-protection. Harman, writing in later years, effectively summed up the egoistic implications of this anarchism:

> No outsider, unitary or collective, can rightfully interfere to prevent the sovereign individual from indulging his appetites in his own way so long as he does so at his own cost. Contingent and remote consequences to others cannot be considered when estimating the civil right of the individual to gratify his appetites.[7]

In the eighties, Benjamin R. Tucker became an important spokesman for individual anarchism. In his journal, *Liberty*, he synthesized the doctrines of individualist forerunners and contemporaries such as Josiah Warren, Lysander Spooner, and Ezra Heywood, while at the same time he reflected the European influence of Proudhon, Spencer, and Bakunin. During this period,

Liberty, Lucifer, and, to some extent, *The Word* of Ezra and Angela Heywood provided the national forum for individualist anarchists. Tucker's "philosophical anarchism," however, increasingly shunned practical action, and he eventually attained a sort of bourgeois respectability. The editors of *Lucifer,* however, followed the example of the Heywoods, who backed up their libertarian doctrines of "love and labor" with practical action.

Tucker's urban, continental orientation led him to declare that anarchists should focus their efforts in the cities, the fulcrum of modern civilization. As an arena for social change, the countryside was a "desert." In contrast, the agrarian wing of individualist anarchism—E. C. Walker, John William Lloyd of Florida, and Marx Edgeworth Lazarus of Alabama—argued for rural colonization, after the manner of Josiah Warren. Walker warned that "the industrial and social emancipation of the rural and village populations cannot safely be permitted to lag behind that of the cities." Although he voiced the common argument that the farmer's role as food producer made him essentially important to society and its reform, he did not accept the "agrarian myth" that held that those close to the soil were morally and politically superior to others. In fact he deromanticized the farmer:

We are accustomed to boast of the purity and devotion to liberty of the country populace, but never was boasting more inappropriate and misplaced. If ignorance and mis-education regarding natural law are purity, then indeed are the masses of the farming population pure; while their conception of liberty is that embodied in a majority despotism which lays its hand upon and controls every private concern of the individual.

Walker's boyhood on the lonesome prairies of Iowa, as well as the thousands of miles that he logged as a village lecturer, colored his portrayal of agrarian life: "Necessarily scattered and isolated, farmers have not been able to co-operate to any extent worthy of mention, and the work of production is carried on in a most laborious and wasteful manner." The farmer's work day, twelve to sixteen hours long, surpassed that of any wage worker, to say nothing of the natural rigors that the farmer endured. Since the farmer had little time or inclination to read, was cut off from other sources of knowledge, and was mostly dependent upon church or schoolhouse meetings for "recreation(?)," Walker did not wonder that the "farmer is old before his time, that he is away behind the age, and that the condition of his wife is still more deplorable than his."

Indeed the woman's plight drew Walker's special attention:

> With *her* it is a ceaseless round of drudgery from morning until night, and it may with absolute literalness be said of her that her work is never done. She has no time to read, no time for recreation, and her nearest neighbor may be a half-mile or a mile away. Who shall wonder, then, that she often knows nothing outside of the details of her housework and the latest neighborhood gossip? Who shall wonder that the statistics of our insane asylums show a larger relative proportion of demented from the class of farmer's wives than from any other?

Walker saw both the isolated farm and the overgrown city as doomed social institutions, and he believed that the "cooperative township" must replace them. These communities would provide economic liberation through shared labor, mutual banks, and "labor exchange" money, but more importantly, they would provide a haven from pressures that society at large brought upon radicals and their loved ones, particularly those who practiced free love. Walker recognized that public opinion could be more insidious and coercive than government; vast numbers of radicals, in fact, "are lost to us in a short time because the pressure brought to bear upon them through their families is too great to be endured." In cooperative townships, radicals and the "noncombatants" in their families would receive the social support necessary for effecting "the industrial and sexual emancipation of the race." In the city, many people accepted economic radicalism, Walker conceded, but generally these activists were "as blind as moles" to the same arguments applied to the sexual sphere. Since Walker believed that social revolution must be sexual as well as economic, he saw the rural cooperative, rather than the city, as the vanguard of the new society.

Walker and Tucker debated other important questions in the mid eighties. Walker, a neo-Malthusian, argued that a decline in family size would reduce economic pressures on the workingman, whereas Tucker argued the "iron law of wages"—that a decrease in family size would cause a reduction in the subsistence wages of the worker. They also disagreed sharply on marriage: Walker held that a couple could freely join themselves in an autonomistic marriage, with duties and duration dictated only by mutual love; Tucker believed free marriage to be a contradiction in terms, as well as a compromise with public opinion.[8]

With new editorial assistance, Moses Harman gave increasing play in *Lucifer* to anarchism, as well as to labor problems, the property question, and women's rights. In "Our Object," an ebullient piece in the first issue after forming the partnership, Harman extrapolated his free-thought principles to include the liberation of virtually everything that was currently being regulated by society or government—"free press, free rostrum, free mails . . . , free land, free homes, free food, free drink, free medicine, free Sunday, free marriage and free divorce." "In short," he wrote, "we advocate the *Sovereignty of the Individual* or Self Government. We would have every man and every woman to be the proprietor of himself or herself!" Harman's rhetoric and his insistence on the pending emancipation of man from external government could have come from Josiah Warren or Stephen Pearl Andrews a generation earlier. But the problems of postwar capitalism invested the words with new urgency. Many felt, Harman asserted, that no government at all—anarchism—would at least be an improvement over the present government, which seemed "to be chiefly employed in protecting the strong against the *weak*—the rich against the *poor*." Harman promised that the editors of *Lucifer* would use direct methods to obtain their objects; they would aim straight at the face and eyes of the opponent, rather than attacking deviously.[9]

A month later the paper helped to promote a movement to eliminate the word "male" from the laws of Kansas, thus granting the franchise to women. This proposal accorded with Harman's belief in using the framework of government as it existed in order to phase it out, allowing the individual legally to repossess his rights from the government. Later he and Walker would disagree on this question. Walker saw participation in government as sanctioning its coercion, while Harman believed that an anarchist could vote to repeal laws.

Regarding the land question, Harman believed, after John

Locke, that an individual had the right to only so much land as he could use for his own food and lodging; man had no more proprietary right in land than he did in air or ocean; hence monopoly was wrong. Since man had no exclusive land rights, he added, no government created by him could have such either; therefore the property necessary to his existence should not be taxed. To prevent and to do away with existing monopolies, increasingly heavy taxes should be levied until this land was forfeited back to the people.[10] Harman advocated a tentative sort of anarchistic cooperation, and he left *Lucifer*'s correspondents to fight the ideological battles of communism, socialism, Single-Taxism, and Bellamy Nationalism. After Walker joined the paper, editorial critiques of these positions became more pointed; Walker particularly criticized state socialism and the rising Social Revolutionary press, which encompassed the communist anarchists.

At the same time, ironically, Harman reflected the inflammatory rhetoric of the Social Revolutionaries in his long "Dynamite Column," which appeared in the summer of 1883. He believed in gradual anarchism; but under the probable influence of Johann Most and Albert R. Parsons, he felt that if tyranny compelled the use of force, dynamite should be used. Dynamite would be the great equalizer, leveling the social classes and obliging the upper classes to share their education with the ignorant masses whom they formerly exploited:

Then welcome the Age of Dynamite! . . . This latter age promises to be one of fierce convulsions . . . it will be marked by sudden, and, for the time being, disastrous changes. . . . The law of force against force, or the gospel of dynamite will not usher in the millenium of anarchy, but it will help prepare the way for that blessed era.[11]

It was in such an expansive and reckless mood that the *Kansas Liberal* became *Lucifer*.

In the years 1883 to 1886 *Lucifer* established itself nationally as a radical and somewhat notorious journal, despite lean finances in 1884. Benjamin Tucker, who had recommended the *Kansas Liberal* to his own readers in *Liberty*, heaped praise upon its successor, *Lucifer*. In one of his columns he glowingly claimed that *Lucifer* was "so good and true and live and keen and consistently radical" that he feared its light would eclipse *Liberty*'s. Despite disagreements between himself and Walker, he considered Walker a radical of "rare consistency," and he followed his writings "with the greatest care, interest, and admiration." These anarchist journalists reserved their flattery, as well as their toughest criticism, for their own kind.[12]

Consciously or not, the foundations were being laid in *Lucifer*'s composing room for a period of great experimentation. Harman busied himself with the day-to-day editorial chores, while Walker's tours, extending into Nebraska and Iowa, helped to pay the bills. Under these conditions, Walker contributed less to the paper's columns than did Harman, and much of Walker's material concerned Liberal League quibbles. Walker, however, continued to contribute articles to the eastern papers and to Henry Seymour's the *Anarchist* in London, a journal of individualist anarchism that seemed to be particularly influenced by *Lucifer*.[13]

In 1885, after a break of some months during which *Lucifer* appeared monthly, Walker went back on the road, and *Lucifer* took on new life as a "weekly Anarchist-Freethought Journal." It retained a New York agency to accept eastern advertising, and it began a campaign for new readers. By fall the editors of *Lucifer* had obtained pledges of $550 ($143 had been paid) toward the purchase of a $600 seven-column Prouty Press. Although at this time *Lucifer*'s circulation numbered only about six or seven hundred, only a few more than Tucker's *Liberty*, it would soon more than double its readership.

Spreading the anarchist word, raising money, and sparring with editors from Maine to Oskaloosa, the light bearers of Valley Falls (population 1,335) had to illuminate the most important radical questions. The editor of the *Kansas City Sun*, writing in *Liberty*, commented: "*Liberty* attacks the State, the *Truth Seeker* attacks the Church, the *Word* attacks Madam Grundy, but *Lucifer* is not content, in its own way, without attacking all three." Three Harmans now helped on the paper: Moses' son George served as copublisher, while his daughter Lillian—pretty, golden-haired, and sixteen—worked as compositor.[14]

Part 2
Unrespectable Reform

5/ Awful Letters: Part I

SINCE his antislavery days, Moses Harman had been involved in reform politics. Like many other abolitionists, he had joined the Republican party, believing it to be "the party of Liberty and Justice." In the postwar era he grew disillusioned with the party, feeling that it had become the bastion of privilege rather than of equal rights. The Democrats attracted Harman even less—he could never forget that they had been the party of slavery. In 1880 Harman had supported the Prohibition Amendment to the Kansas Constitution, and in 1882 he had worked for the eminent Anti-Monopolist candidate for governor, Charles Robinson. Harman had also lent support to the Greenback party.[1]

Although the transformation of the *Kansas Liberal* to *Lucifer, the Light Bearer* marked Harman's own passage from reformism to anarchism, he did not become a doctrinaire revolutionary. He had little faith in the American people's receptivity to revolutionary political change. Great accumulations of wealth, which marked the age, represented prima facie evidence of moral wrongs committed against each worker, he believed, yet the workers did not fault the system: "Ask any man you meet whether he would like to stand in the shoes of Jay Gould, of Senator Stanford, or of Col. King. . . . Nine cases in ten he will eagerly answer, Yes! So then most poor men are simply undeveloped stock gamblers, railroad kings, or land monopolists."

The widespread hunger, joblessness, and industrial unrest of the mid eighties compounded the irony of this unrevolutionary consciousness. Closer to home, Harman noted, skyrocketing transportation costs forced farmers to feed their wheat to livestock and to burn their corn for fuel. The government appeared to be "a gigantic machine by which the many are robbed by the few." Financiers, railroad companies, cattle kings, land speculators, large manufacturers, and mining monopolists ran the country for their personal benefit.

It appeared difficult enough for anarchists to exist in such an environment, much less to try to alter it. No simple answers came to Harman in his attempts to apply anarchistic solutions to society's problems. At best, anarchism could offer only partial answers, and even then, to be effective, its individualist purity would most likely have to be diluted. He suggested that people must ignore, insofar as possible, the external government; they must peacefully organize a system of "self-protection" whereby natural rights would be secured and maintained against the encroachments of the state.

Methods for achieving this system eluded Harman, however, as he wrestled with the "Question of the Hour" throughout 1885. He theorized on several solutions, including the possibility of autonomous communities with strong, graduated income-tax schemes. Although the principles of anarchism strongly appealed to him, he found in anarchism no thoroughgoing solutions nor even any practical suggestions of methods. He would permanently retain a philosophy of anarchism as he retained his belief in free thought, but though he tried, he could not make anarchism his Great Cause.[2]

During these months of search, however, he did uncover the questions that were to engage him and his paper for the rest of their years. From free thought and anarchism, the quest of *Lucifer* turned toward freedom of expression, especially the freedom to discuss sexual questions openly. Much of the public discussion of sex in the nineteenth century dealt with sex in the gender sense, rather than the erotic—a lecture or editorial entitled "The Sex Question" was likely to deal with political discrimination against woman.[3] Harman and the sex radicals, however, were to base their discussion of the "sex question" on the coital relationship; their terms of discussion flouted the Victorian code of sexual respectability which, in its extremity, justified coitus only as a propagative duty, forbade erotic pleasure, and condemned discussions even of hygienic aspects of coital matters.

For enforcement, this code depended upon a powerful social consensus rather than upon legislation, although laws regulating the sexual sphere did appear with increasing frequency toward the end of the century. Legislators raised the age of consent, tried to regulate prostitution, regulated breeding in marriage, and struggled with the problem of divorce. America, of course, had no such national law as the English Criminal Law Amendment Act of 1885, which forbade certain sexual conduct such as homosexuality; but most states had statutes outlawing lewdness, sodomy, obscenity, and abortion. Moreover, such sexual "deviations" or "misconduct" were offenses under common law.[4]

The United States did acquire a counterpart to England's Obscene Publications Act—the "Comstock" Postal Act of 1873. This statute, enforced in arch-puritan spirit by Anthony Comstock himself, effectively banned sexual discussion and the exchange of information on matters ranging from abortion to criticism of Christianity. Sex radicals knew that Victorian respectability—what Lester Ward had termed the "conventional code"—was their real oppressor, but "St. Anthony" played the prude so wonderfully that he became the natural focus of attention. The vice-suppression societies that employed Comstock and lesser censors apotheosized an earlier, unambiguous morality that was associated with preindustrial America. These purity reformers sought to enforce a measure of social control on the increasingly disjointed and confused urban landscape.

Impressed by Comstock's free-lance efforts, the president of the New York YMCA, Morris K. Jesup, and a group of his eminent peers formed a YMCA Committee for the Suppression of Vice, which paid Comstock a salary to stamp out vice and underwrote efforts to bring about state and federal antiobscenity legislation. The organization eventually included such men as financier J. P. Morgan, copper baron William E. Dodge, and soap magnate Samuel Colgate. Because some YMCA leaders felt that Comstock's muck-stirring efforts were abhorrent to finer sensibilities, the committee divorced itself from the YMCA and became an independent Society for the Suppression of Vice in 1873. The state charter of the society enjoined the police to "aid this corporation . . . in the enforcement of all laws," and granted it the right to claim one-half of all fines levied against evildoers whom it brought to justice. The well-to-do members of the society provided Comstock with an expense account and an annual salary of $3,000; before taking action on any case, Comstock submitted details to the society for its approval. The young old man of vice-hunting—he was 29 in 1873—forsook his earlier career as a dry-goods clerk for full-time censorship and vice-suppression duties. Comstock believed himself divinely appointed to his task; his commissions from the Vice Society and the federal government were only ancillary.[5]

Although in 1836 President Andrew Jackson had tried but failed to obtain from Congress a law prohibiting "incendiary" abolitionist literature from the mails, Congress did step into the obscenity quagmire in 1842, apparently with little forethought. One section of the Tariff Act of that year empowered the Customs Office to confiscate and bring suit to destroy "obscene or immoral" prints and pictures within its purview. In 1857, the same year that the British government put the Obscene Publications Act into law, Congress added obscene "images," including photographs and daguerreotypes, and "obscene articles" to the prohibited list of the Tariff Act. In 1865, in response to reports that obscene materials were being mailed to soldiers, the Senate perfunctorily enacted the first law dealing with obscenity in the mails and in the printed word. This act prohibited obscene publications from the mails, giving the postmaster general the power to seize and destroy objectionable matter (leaving open whether by administrative prerogative or by due process); but it was so undetailed, complained Anthony Comstock, that only materials that were "obscene on their face" could be stopped. An amendment in 1872 strengthened the statute only a little.[6]

Supported by his influential backers in the YMCA committee, Comstock went to Washington in the early months of 1873 to lobby for a new, stronger bill to combat the "hydra-headed monster" of vice in the mails. Presented to a corrupt Congress, which was in the throes of the *Credit Mobilier* scandal, the vice society's bill finally passed at 2 A.M. in a rowdy early-morning session on Sunday, March 2. Perhaps, Comstock's traveling exhibit of pornography had suitably impressed the lawmakers. Senator William A. Buckingham of Connecticut and Congressman Clinton L. Merriam,

New York, served as sponsors of the bill. The Comstock Act, as it came to be called, policed a broader area than had the 1872 statute, and it provided stiffer penalties—up to ten years' imprisonment—for anyone who knowingly mailed or received "obscene, lewd, or lascivious" printed and graphic material. Significantly, one section of the act forbade the mailing of contraceptive and abortifacient materials and information, along with any "thing intended . . . for immoral use."[7]

On two crucial points the law was portentously silent: first, it offered no definition of obscenity, and second, it did not specify whether it intended to be solely a criminal statute (that is, concerned with seizing objectionable matter only as a contingency of the arrest of a violator) or whether it aimed to establish a civil post-office censorship separate from any criminal provisions of the law.

As it turned out, the *"Hicklin* Standard" for defining obscenity became federal law in 1879 with the case against D. M. Bennett for his sales of *Cupid's Yokes,* a small book written by Ezra Heywood. The *Hicklin* Standard, which was enunciated by Lord Chief Justice Cockburn in *Queen* v. *Hicklin* (1868), declared that the obscenity test "is this, whether the tendency of the matter charged as obscenity is to deprave and corrupt those whose minds are open to immoral influences, and into whose hands a publication of this sort may fall." As the terms of this decision became the standard in American courts, First Amendment arguments were regularly discounted, leaving "obscenists" with little but technical arguments for defense. Using methods that bordered on entrapment and with government authority and respectable public opinion behind them, Comstock and the vice societies won an impressive majority of their cases.

It also turned out that the Post Office Department assumed independent powers of censorship and confiscation based upon the Comstock Act. With no due process, postal officials prohibited, confiscated, and in some cases destroyed without remuneration any mails that they found to be objectionable. A mailer could either submit to expurgation or appeal to reluctant courts to enjoin the Post Office Department from interfering. But, as James Paul and Murray Schwartz have recently pointed out, the courts assumed that "the Postmaster General and his subordinates . . . were well equipped to decide what was 'obscene'; that was their job, and their judgment was only to be set aside in case of clear 'abuse.' Thus the plain fact was that by the simple act of seizing a publication, postal officials were able to throw a heavy burden of exculpation entirely upon the citizen who wanted to distribute it." An 1890 opinion of the United States attorney general validated this administrative censorship. Citing the Comstock laws, Attorney General Miller backed up a decision by Postmaster General Wanamaker to ban Tolstoy's *Kreutzer Sonata* from the mails "on the grounds of indecency." Sex radicals, some reform journals, and a few large dailies protested the ominous decision; some thought that Wanamaker was as great a threat as Comstock.[8]

The constitutionality of the Comstock Act itself rested on an obiter decision by the Supreme Court in *Ex Parte Jackson* (1877), in which the court affirmed a postal statute outlawing lottery materials from the mail. By invoking the Comstock Act to illustrate Congress's authority to police the mails, the Court implicitly confirmed the soundness of the act. When the first Comstock Act case, *Rosen* v. *United States,* came before the high court in 1896, it sustained the act and, with citations from the Bennett case, upheld the famous *Hicklin* Standard.

The effect of the Comstock Act intensified as state governments, influenced by efforts of vice societies, enacted laws prohibiting commerce in "obscene" items such as suggestive books and birth-control devices. The act had also created the position of post-office special agent, to inspect mail and to track down violators. Although it appears that Comstock did not lobby for his personal appointment, he was an obvious choice, and he expressed pleasure at being duly appointed. He declined to accept his government salary, however, until the year 1906.

The subtleties of art and of the First Amendment mostly eluded Comstock; therefore he not only created havoc for some publishers, booksellers, and museums, but he also wrecked the lives and reputations of a number of persons. In one famous case, Comstock hounded Ann Lohman, an abortionist and dispenser of birth-control methods and advice, until she committed suicide; hers was the fifteenth suicide that he personally credited to his account, and there were to be more. He cut a wide swath, mounting campaigns against quacks, lotteries, medical hoaxes, fraudulent advertising, and a number of swindles. He relied heavily on trickery in order to gain indictments, and his personal uncorroborated testimony dispatched many "evildoers" to confinement.

In a society that had few provisions for consumer protection, some good no doubt came from his scattershot assaults, but these effects must be weighed against the subjective and often contemptuous manner in which he wielded tremendous power. He was a sex reformer working for sexual purity, just as surely as Ezra Heywood or Moses Harman, despite a quite different approach. W. D. P. Bliss included him in his definitive *Encyclopedia of Social Reform* (1897), and even one of Comstock's prize catches, the contraceptives champion Edward Bliss Foote, M.D., considered Comstock to be engaged in a humanitarian reform. In tempered criticism of his "brother reformer," the doctor wrote in a letter to the *New York Times*: "He is trying to make people better by reformatory measures, and I by formatory processes." Foote became less temperate when a court fined him $3,500 for a violation of the Comstock Act.[9]

Comstock became confused in his attempts to define "suggestive" art works. He conceded that some works portraying the nude body were not obscene, provided that they fulfilled his notion of painterly art: the artist's technique must effectively divert attention from the nudity, which of itself is objectionable. Such a definition ruled out reproductions. In short, he felt that a direct link existed between the sight of a naked human body and the degradation of the viewer. The degradation, whether from a vision of nudity or an evil word, became all the more total if experienced by a child.[10]

He never quite explained how he himself escaped such degradation, even though he probably viewed more expositions of "evil" than most professional lechers were able to see. He allowed himself to sit through whole performances before making arrests, such as "Busy Fleas," which was enacted for him in 1878 by unwary prostitutes. On an 1881 occasion, a Philadelphia paper reported, he paid $14.50 for a specially ordered undressing act by three prostitutes; they performed for Comstock for one hour and twenty minutes before he arrested them.[11]

Comstock attacked weak and radical or nonconventional journals rather than the mighty dailies, although these large publications often criticized Comstock with more practical effect. The *New York Times,* however, served as a mouthpiece for Comstock and the Vice Society; its "news reports" of Comstock's efforts appeared to come verbatim from Comstock's own pen. By Comstock's definition, liberal or free-thought publications dispensed lies and impiety, and deserved no right to be mailed or sold. His personal assaults on Ezra Heywood and D. M. Bennett were examples that the western arm of the Society for the Suppression of Vice later followed in indicting Moses Harman, Elmina Slenker, and Lois Waisbrooker. Although Anthony Comstock died in 1915, not until the 1930s did the federal law that popularly bore his name become redefined. Some states still have lingering Comstock legislation on the books in the form of laws prohibiting or restricting birth-control devices.[12]

The sex radicals who took the libertarian approach to censorship focused on the Comstock laws as the major substantive obstacle to sexual reform and education. They saw freedom of speech and of the press as absolute. Taste and propriety did not enter into their considerations of free speech; speech was free only so long as no subject nor any word, however gross, was banned. Sex radicals pursued "social science" in the nineteenth-century understanding of the term, which meant social reform. Such a journal as *Lucifer* served as a forum where personal experience and acquired knowledge could be traded, argued, winnowed, and, it was hoped, be made to yield up maxims that would reform sexual relations. Censorial laws only restricted the march of science.

In the spring of 1886 Harman promised his readers that none of their correspondence submitted for publication would be altered because of their choice of words. On June 18 the first scandalous letter appeared in *Lucifer,* the "Markland letter," and after it came a half-dozen more. Printing this Markland correspondence—a letter from a Tennessee anarchist quoting a letter that *he* had received—engaged Harman in a simultaneous fight for women's liberation, sex education, and free speech:

Another "Awful Letter"
[Dudes, prudes and statute moralists had better not read this letter.—ED.]

Awful Letters: Part 1 75

EDS. LUCIFER: To-day's mail brought me a letter from a dear lady friend, from which I quote and query:

"About a year ago F—— gave birth to a babe, and was severely torn by the use of instruments in incompetent hands. She has gone through three operations and all failed. I brought her home and had Drs. ——— and ——— operate on her, and she was getting along nicely until last night, when her husband came down, forced himself into her bed and the stitches were torn from her healing flesh, leaving her in a worse condition than ever. I don't know what to do."

Now, Searlites; "Laws are made for the protection of life, person and property."

Will you point to a law that will punish this brute?

Was his conduct illegal? The marriage license was a permit of the people at large given by their agent for this man and woman—a mere child—to marry.

Marry for what? Business? That he may have a housekeeper? He could legally have hired her for that. Save one thing, is there anything a man and woman can do for each other which they may not legally do without marrying?

Is not that one thing copulation? Does the law interfere in any other relations of service between the sexes?

What is rape? Is it not coition with a woman by force, not having a legal right?

Can there be legal rape? Did this man rape his wife? Would it have been rape had he not been married to her?

Does the law protect the person of woman in marriage? Does it protect her person out of marriage?

Does not the question of rape turn on the pivot of legal right regardless of consequences!

If a man stabs his wife to death with a knife, does not the law hold him for murder?

If he murders her with his penis, what does the law do?

If the wife, to protect her life, stabs her husband with a knife, does the law hold her guiltless?

Can a Czar have more absolute power over a subject than a man has over the genitals of his wife?

Is it not a fearful power? Would a kind, considerate husband feel robbed, feel his manhood emasculated, if deprived of this legal power?

Does the safety of society depend upon a legal right which none but the coarse, selfish, ignorant, brutal, will assert and exercise?

If "marriage is a civil contract," has the female partner a legal right to "twenty-five dollars" of the firm's money to purchase the civil consent of CIVILIZED law, to a civilized dissolution of said contract?

Why charge one dollar to get into the show and "twenty-five" to get out? Why not reverse it? . . .

Has freedom gender?

Will some archist, or semi-archist, please tell the mother quoted above, "what to do?"

Sherwood, Tenn.   W. G. Markland

Eight months after this letter appeared, a deputy United States marshal arrived in Valley Falls to arrest Moses Harman, George Harman, and E. C. Walker, the editors and publishers of *Lucifer*. They faced obscenity charges for the Markland letter and for three additional letters published in *Lucifer* during the intervening months. The second offending letter, "Mrs. [Celia B.] Whitehead to Elmina [Slenker]," had been a protest against contraceptives. With the availability of "contracepts," Mrs. Whitehead argued, women would lose "all excuse for not yielding to the sexual demands of their masters" and would increasingly become the playthings of men. The third indicted letter, "Family Secrets," retold an old anecdote about a Millerite couple who thought that the world was ending and therefore confessed their sexual improprieties to one another. Harman apparently printed the letter in order to demonstrate his belief that the right of free press should be unqualified by considerations of taste or propriety. The inclusion of this article in *Lucifer* suggested that Harman was intentionally building a comprehensive test case of obscenity laws. The final letter for which the editors faced prosecution, "Comments on Albert Chavanne's Article," appeared in January 1887, only weeks before the arrests. This contribution to *Lucifer*'s ongoing debate on sexual asceticism discussed the comparative virtues of two methods of sexual abstinence, "Alphaism" and "Dianaism." Alphaism prohibited coitus or erotic relations except for propagation; Dianaism similarly restricted coitus but, from a theory of sublimation, allowed some erotic expression.[13]

Before the publication of the Markland letter the issue of free speech received increasing attention in the columns of *Lucifer*. In a series of articles on the suppression of free speech in the Chicago Haymarket case, Harman set the stage for his own legal battle. In the weeks before the Markland letter appeared, he wrote that his own ideas of free expression stemmed not from the First Amendment—he was no governmentalist—but from natural law. He criticized a government that treated words as deeds and attempted to restrict their utterance because of possible consequences; words, however incendiary, should not be subject to government control.

In a variation on John Stuart Mill's philosophy, Harman saw a socially therapeutic use for unrestricted speech: it would serve as a vent to those who had evil in their hearts. Free utterance of such thoughts, he had observed, "has the effect of bringing about a reaction or revulsion of feeling in the thinker himself; besides putting others on their guard against him." In short he felt that freedom of expression never constituted a peril to society, but repression always did.[14]

Harman's declaration of a "free language" policy for *Lucifer*'s correspondents took the issue of free speech beyond the realm of theory. Harman, with Ezra and Angela Heywood of *The Word*, put into practice the plain-language ideas of Stephen Pearl Andrews. This pioneer sex radical had argued against the notion that words, in themselves, could be obscene. He urged that "dirty" words be reclaimed from disgrace and be put to unblushing use in society: "since there is no obscenity in Nature, no obscenity in Science, and no obscenity in Art," said Andrews, "there seems no place left for obscenity, but in the defilement of our own imaginations; and that, therefore when our thoughts and imaginations are freshened to the naturalness of nature, used to the clean-cut precision of science, and to the gracious sweetness of Artistic beauty, obscenity will cease to exist among us."[15]

In announcing that no contribution to *Lucifer* would be excluded simply because of words that it contained, Harman explained that he recognized no limits whatever in the realm of words—honest and natural expression must not be abridged in any way. Furthermore, he blasted obscenity laws as counterproductive, and he criticized as absurd the designation of some words as "coarse" and "scurrilous." He emphasized that this policy was his alone, and not that of E. C. Walker, his junior editor. The hundreds of radicals and scores of sex reformers who read *Lucifer* required no more obvious invitation than this.[16]

On the editorial page of the issue in which the Markland letter appeared, Harman devoted more than two full columns to an explanation of his decision to print the letter. First, the content of the letter illustrated the connection in Harman's mind between his hereditarian beliefs and the sexual liberation of women: an outrage on the mother affects the maternal mind, which transmits every thought and emotion to the "plastic form" of the unborn baby's mind and to its body. The baby born of such circumstances could be mentally and physically warped beyond repair.

In an age when the consequences of coitus were heavily exacted of the female, most acts of coitus, not to mention rape, represented a limited outrage against the woman. The Markland letter served as the extreme illustration of *all* women's situation. If Proudhon's philosophy could be aphorized to "Property is theft," then Harman's could be to "Marriage is rape." He wrote: "Maternity is more often forced upon her than desired. In other words, children are born *under protest* of the mother. She simply submits . . . because she thinks her duty to her husband requires obedience in the sex-relation." Children most often represented the fruit of exploitation and injustice rather than of love, and they, in turn, transmitted their defective inheritance.

Harman's own Victorianism should not be overlooked in this connection. *Lucifer*'s most respectable supporter, former governor Charles Robinson, pointed out that "every physician in his practice finds cases corroborative of the cases published by M. Harman, but he is dumb from necessity. . . . How often is a refined young lady wedded to an uncultured, uncouth brute, who conceals his real character until married, but as soon as revealed the wife loses all respect, to say nothing of love, for her husband. From that moment she is doomed to a life of terror and torture, which Madam Grundy compels her to bear in silence. It is for such as these that M. Harman has been speaking." The "War Governor" of Kansas expressed well the common feeling in the woman movement, that sex itself was mostly an insult to the more delicate sensibilities of Victorian womanhood, and the more uncouth the act, the greater the evil.[17]

Claiming a higher purity than puritanism, however, the martyr-on-the-make challenged the Victorian code of secrecy; exposure of evils, regardless of how "awful," constituted the first step in healing them. From the abolitionist crusade, Harman recalled that case examples of abuse brought more results than abstract moralizing.

The system itself must be changed or abolished if it be the cause of abuses, wrote Harman, in a favorite inference from slavery to marriage.

Finally, in printing the plain words of *Lucifer*'s correspondents, Harman tested his notion of absolute free speech. He had written earlier that "words are not deeds, and it is not the province of civil law to take preventive measures against remote or possible consequences of words, no matter how violent or 'incendiary.' " People needed no government to protect them from words, he believed. The justification of the Markland letter concluded with a note to the squeamish: "All words have their legitimate use . . . we wish to offend no one . . . but he or she who cannot bear the plain, scientific use of words and phrases is already lost to usefulness in the grand army of progress."[18]

The next week in *Lucifer,* Harman discussed the relationship of obscenity to Christian morality, pointing out that in a situation of equal rights, no man could rightfully by law compel another to conform to his own personal code of morals or, for that matter, to his own definition of obscenity. Developing his argument into an appeal for forthright sex education for children, Harman looked forward to a new generation which, presumably at least, would not be overwhelmed by the word "penis" in print.

Behind the explicit reasons for printing the awful letters lay a strategy of publicity, a force that Harman knew could not only unmask the subversion of the censors but could also turn *Lucifer* into a paying enterprise and assure Harman a hero's niche in history. Would not Ezra Heywood compare Harman to William Lloyd Garrison and John Brown, as well as to D. M. Bennett, whose trial and imprisonment "boomed his books, made his paper a paying, world-wide power, and himself immortal in history!"?[19]

The federal grand jury in Topeka first indicted the *Lucifer* staff on 270 counts of obscenity. This indictment, drawn up with the aid of the western agent of the Society for Suppression of Vice, R. W. McAfee, apparently took refuge in numbers because the jurymen could not bring themselves to specify exact instances of obscenity; the paper was "so obscene, lewd and lascivious as to dispense with the incorporation of the words and figures in this indictment." The jury simply picked nine subscribers, multiplied this number by five offensive issues of *Lucifer,* then separately and jointly charged the three journalists with an accumulated 270 counts.[20]

This awkward bill caved in before the arguments of *Lucifer*'s attorneys, David Overmeyer and Gaspar C. Clemens of Topeka. These reform lawyers opposed the entrenched Republican government of Kansas and welcomed the chance to debate radical questions with Republican prosecutors and judges. Both became stalwarts in *Lucifer*'s legal battles, a struggle that became very lengthy indeed. The grand jury filed a new specific indictment against the journalists, citing the four "awful letters" previously published in *Lucifer*. The court eventually dropped charges against George Harman and Edwin Walker, and Moses Harman faced the courts alone. Almost four years of delays and entanglement would elapse before his final trial for the Markland letter, however.[21]

6/ Children of Progress

I have never been able to find happiness in conformity.... A sure instinct told me that the majority was always wrong.... But whenever we do conform it is to endure the agony of humiliation, to drink the cup of degradation to the very last drop.... And [in] this mental torture, which the dull-thoughted persecutors of the Children of Progress can never feel—for they cognize not the subtle pains that torment the refined—we also charge up against the monkey-hyena Idol which is called "Society."

—Edwin C. Walker, from "Society," *Lucifer,* 10 September 1886

WHEN the marshal arrived in Valley Falls on a February day in 1887 to arrest the *Lucifer* staff, he knew that one of the editors, Edwin Walker, would not be found. Walker was already imprisoned; he occupied cell number two in the county jail at Oskaloosa. Cell number one held his wife by free marriage, Lillian Harman, the teen-age daughter of Moses Harman. *Lucifer* had opened another front in its crusade to dramatize woman's sexual bondage.

Although Walker did not share Moses Harman's enthusiasm for the plain-words crusade, both editors agreed on the issue of marriage reform. And Lillian Harman, her father's true daughter and *Lucifer*'s compositor, also agreed. On 19 September 1886, Moses Harman convened the "autonomistic marriage" ceremony in which Edwin, aged thirty-seven, and Lillian, aged sixteen, were joined; the word had become flesh for the *Lucifer* group.

Moses Harman had criticized both the church's and the state's involvement in marriage from the beginning of his Kansas career. In 1880, in the second issue of the *Valley Falls Liberal,* he replied to churchmen who disparaged freethinkers as free lovers; one had only to survey the mounting divorce statistics to see the true quality of their "God-made unions." From the evidence, he wondered "would it not be well . . . to let Jehovah go out of the business of marrying folks for a while and let them marry themselves?" Since marriage is an intensely personal thing, reasoned Harman, why recognize any authority greater than the self in performing it?

"Is a man who prefers to give his simple word of honor, any less likely to prove a faithful husband than he who must be bound up by an oath, or by his faith in Jehovah, that he will love his wife as long as they both shall live?" The belief that heaven created marriages and forgave partners for transgressions allowed an easy means to shirk personal responsibility for the union.[1]

Four years later he related his marriage stand to his position on temperance: he practiced abstention from liquor and he practiced monogamy in marriage, but he opposed state enforcement of his beliefs on anyone else; true morality, he believed, demanded liberty of choice in such matters. To outlaw plural marriages or to enforce monogamy, particularly in deference to religious forces, was "an unwarranted invasion of private and personal right." He noted ruefully that society banned the discussion of "sexual physiology and of social sciences, in its widest sense . . . this ignorance soon bears its legitimate fruit in inharmony and unhappiness whether outside or inside of the marriage pale." Children suffered most from this ignorance that was sanctioned by both the church and the state.[2]

Abruptly, in early September 1886, *Lucifer* began to publish a series of critical articles on social coercion. "Society," a scorching attack by Edwin Walker, revealed a firsthand acquaintance with social ostracism; the author, after all, was an anarchist, an infidel, and a divorcé whose former wife and two children lived in another part of Kansas. Together with this article appeared the first installment of a series on "Autonomy—Self Law," probably also written by Walker. These articles discussed the implications of the principle that sovereignty resides exclusively in the individual man and woman, rather than in the state. The writer noted the demands upon liberty that were made by the state, as a creation of the majority of society; and near the end of the second installment he speculated:

Now suppose two persons, a man and a woman, of mature age and sound minds, decide of their own free will and choice to live together in the sex-relation—they find this relationship mutually promotive of happiness—nature sanctions their union by giving healthy, well-formed and intelligent offspring. Now we ask, is the conduct of this man and woman—these autonomists—immoral and vicious?[3]

Posed in the abstract, such a debate between anarchists and "state paternalists" (almost everyone else) could be counted on to take up several more or less interesting columns of newsprint. Propriety would be outraged perhaps, and someone might become angry enough to suggest censorship. But, most likely, the effects of such a question, abstractly posed, would not be great. Well aware of the limits of abstraction, Edwin Walker and Lillian Harman married themselves at Moses Harman's house two days after the article appeared.

The ceremony began with the reading of a "Statement of Principles in Regard to Marriage" by the father of the bride. Based on Moses' previous writings on the subject, this statement pointed out that marriage, as it was generally enforced, existed preeminently as man's affair. According to Christian mythology, woman was made for man rather than man for woman or each for the other. Marriage created the family as an institution with the male member as its autocrat. Marriage merged woman's individuality as a legal person into that of her husband, "even to the surrender of her name, just as chattel slaves were required to take the name of their master."[4]

At this time, most states held that marriage could be solemnized by either civil or religious authority, although the laws of Maryland, Delaware, and the District of Columbia held that only a religious authority could legally join a couple.[5] Harman repudiated this prerogative of the church and the state in marriage; external regulation was not only impertinent but morally wrong and disastrous in practice. "We regard intelligent choice—untrammeled voluntaryism—coupled with responsibility to natural law for our acts, as the true and only basis of morality," he explained.

As to making promises on such an occasion—"to love and honor" by the male, "to love, honor and obey so long as both shall live" by the female—the first could not truthfully be promised, because it ignored the possibility that feelings could change over time; the second destroyed woman's being, making her the inferior and the vassal of her husband. If love ceased to exist between the two, that promise nevertheless continued to bind the woman to submit sexually, "to prostitute her sex-hood at the command of an . . . unloveable husband." No promises would be extracted, then, at this autonomistic wedding.

Lillian Harman
Courtesy Kansas State
Historical Society

Edwin C. Walker
From *Fifty Years
of Freethought*

Moses Harman and grandson
Courtesy Kansas State
Historical Society

George Harman
Courtesy Kansas State
Historical Society

After Harman had read his statement, Walker stood and announced to the assembled family that while he regarded public marital ceremonies as "essentially and ineradicably indelicate, a pandering to the morbid, vicious, and meddlesome element in human nature," he considered this form the least objectionable. He then abdicated in advance all conventional marital rights. "Lillian is and will continue to be as free to repulse any and all advances of mine as she has been heretofore. In joining with me in this love and labor union, she has not alienated a single natural right. She remains sovereign of herself, as I of myself and we . . . repudiate all powers legally conferred upon husbands and wives."

He acknowledged Lillian's right to the control of her own person, name, and property; he also specifically recognized her equality in the partnership, while recognizing his own "responsibility to her as regards the care of offspring, if any, and her paramount right to the custody thereof should any unfortunate fate dissolve this union." Then he explained to those present that "this wholly private compact is here announced not because I recognize that you or society at large, or the State have any right to enquire into or determine our relationship to each other, but simply as a guarantee to Lillian of my good faith toward her, and to this I pledge my honor."

Lillian then responded:

I do not care to say much: actions speak more clearly than words, often. I enter into this union with Mr. Walker of my own free will and choice, and I agree with the views of my father and Mr. Walker, as just expressed. I make no promises that it may become impossible or immoral for me to fulfill, but retain the right to act, always, as my conscience and best judgment shall dictate. I retain, also, my full maiden name, as I am sure it is my duty to do. With this understanding, I give to him my hand in token of my trust in him and of the fidelity to truth and honor of my intentions toward him.

The father concluded the ceremony, acknowledging that as the natural guardian of Lillian, he gave his consent to the union. "I do not 'give away the bride,' as I wish her to be always the owner of her person, and to be free always to act according to her truest and purest impulse, and as her highest judgment may dictate." Congratulations, as at most weddings, were then exchanged all around, the participants celebrating not only a personal union but also the wedding of two basic elements in *Lucifer*'s philosophy—extreme anticlericalism and individualist anarchism.

This outrage, which was compounded by the "awful letters" being printed in *Lucifer,* brought threats of mob violence in Valley Falls, and officials promised legal action against the "Lucifer Match" in order to head off the vigilantes. On the morning after their wedding night, the constable appeared at the *Lucifer* office with an arrest warrant for the couple, sworn out by Lillian's stepbrother, W. F. Hiser. The couple had flouted the peace and dignity of Kansas, read the warrant, by "unlawfully and feloniously" living together as man and wife without being married according to statute.[6]

The case promised to be sensational—at a time of growing concern about the frailty of marriage, the government's authority in the marriage contract was being challenged by an anarchistic, antichurch, free-love couple whose paper was named for the devil himself. The government's dramatic response assured that the Lucifer Match would be a cause célèbre among American social radicals for several seasons.[7] Such well-informed radicals as Lillian Harman and Edwin Walker did not view their marriage as a unique experiment, however, but rather as part of the radical tradition of "free marriage."

Communitarians and avant-garde individualists had traditionally focused the dissatisfaction with institutional marriage, but discontent surfaced even in the most respectable levels of nineteenth-century society. The efforts of moderate reformers were often personal and were confined to the ceremony itself; this narrow focus on the contract perhaps reflected the Victorian proclivity for seeking germinal causes. While the simple Quaker marriage pact frequently served as a model of form for reform ceremonies, the contract itself often voiced a protest against woman's subordination in conventional marriage and claimed her basic equality in the newly formed union. Such reform ceremonies, like that of Robert Dale Owen and Mary Robinson in 1832 and that of Lucy Stone and Henry Blackwell in 1855, wished to improve laws rather than flout or ignore them.[8]

"Free marriage" took the mild protests of the reform ceremonies to radical lengths. As a special definition of the amorphous term "free love," this union stressed freedom of the individual within an enlightened partnership in which neither partner would rule or be ruled. This definition had particular meaning for woman: it freed her from the subjugation to the sexual appetite of the male. Since free marriage left open the question of permanency, it was especially strong medicine for Victorian sensibilities, which, after all, viewed institutional marriage and its consequent, the family, as the basis of civilization. Victorians insisted on this view of the family with extreme defensiveness, even to the extent of justifying prostitution as the overflow valve for male sexuality that kept the family "pure."

The Lucifereans disagreed with the prevailing view of marriage as the regulator of base sexual instincts, an institution, as the senior Henry James put it, "to educate us out of our animal beginnings." The Markland letter demonstrated that marriage served as the refuge of sexual vileness; marriage, Lillian later wrote, "is the foe of true morality. Morality often exists in spite of, or regardless of, marriage, but I do not believe morality ever came into being because of marriage." Moses turned the Victorian theory of family primacy on its head: institutional marriage, as the basis of the family, was therefore the foundation of the coercive state; not only did marriage curb one's personal freedom, it was ultimately responsible for "most if not all the tyrannies."[9]

The new moralists of Valley Falls campaigned against conventional marriage in the name of "social science" in the nineteenth-century sense of the term, which equated sociology with social reform. Walker castigated the press for being ignorant of the larger meaning of the "autonomistic" marriage: "They speak of our marriage as 'novel,' 'strange,' 'queer,' 'anomalous,' " he wrote; one paper had even expressed surprise at the couple's respectable appearance. As a precedent, Walker cited the union of the Comtean positivist and critic George Henry Lewes with Mary Ann Evans ("George Eliot"); it was also well known that another positivist philosopher—John Stuart Mill, the author of *The Subjection of Women*—had joined Harriet Taylor in a ceremony that repudiated the usual legalities of wedlock.[10]

But the vision of society that was shared by Lucifereans reflected the doctrines of the pioneer sociologist Stephen Pearl

Andrews more than they did the influences of Comte's hierarchical order. "Men have sought for ages to discover the science of government; and lo!" proclaimed Andrews, "here it is, that men cease totally to attempt to govern each other at all! that they learn to know the consequences of their own acts, and that they arrange their relations with each other upon such a basis of science that the disagreeable consequences shall be assumed by the agent himself." John R. Kelso's pamphlet on the Lucifer Match defended the couple in Andrewsian terms; they had done no wrong since no one could show damage from the act. He further pointed out that the marriage had revealed the extent to which the state and the church still claimed property rights in woman, particularly in her sex organs:

The defendants in this case are charged with "illicit cohabitation";—that is, with illicitly using their own organs of sex. But what was it that rendered their cohabitation "illicit"? . . . You all admit that he [the marrying official] could convey to Mr. Walker a good title, as husband, to the sex-organs of the woman. And yet we all know that he could not convey to Mr. Walker, or to any one else, any title which is not vested in himself. In him, then, is still vested a husband's title to Lillian Harman's sex and to the sex of every other unmarried woman in his district.[11]

In Walker's criticism of the naïveté of the press, he also cited the legal struggles of two free-marriage couples a decade earlier, Mattie Sawyer and Moses Hull in New Jersey and Mattie Strickland and Leo Miller in Minnesota. Hull, the editor of *Hull's Crucible* (Boston) came out for free love in 1873 in *Woodhull & Claflin's Weekly*. Just as people needed changes of scenery, he believed, so did they need changes of sex partners. Monogamy had chafed so cruelly that he finally yielded "humbly and prayerfully" to the "diviner impulses." Elvira, his wife, concurred in the experiment and publicly judged Moses a better companion for it. When Moses and Elvira dissolved their marriage by a single announcement, claiming that a law higher than man's had divorced them, they aroused a torrent of public criticism. When Moses and his lecture mate, Mattie Sawyer, announced their free marriage, similarly without benefit of church or state, criticism became intense and enduring. Four years later a Christian organization in New

Jersey filed a complaint against the two and had them arrested for their unconventional union. The couple expected to fight their case in court, but it never came to trial; a judge dismissed the action after a hearing.[12]

At the same time, however, the law moved against another notable spiritualist lecturer and free lover, Leo Miller, and his wife in spiritual affinity, Mattie Strickland. An angry crowd rioted at his lecture on "Social Freedom" in Waterford, Minnesota, in June 1876. The cry "Put him down! He's come here to break up families!" touched off the scuffle, and in a hail of rotten eggs and rocks, Miller scurried off the stage and made for his carriage. Officers arrested Miller and Strickland a short time later at the home of a friend in Castle Rock. The friend was W. G. Markland, later of "Markland letter" fame. The grand jury charged the couple with "lewd and lascivious cohabitation" as a result of their nonlicensed union. They also cited Miller for obscenity because he had distributed copies of Ezra Heywood's paper, *The Word*.

The couple, who had joined themselves by a written agreement, knew beforehand of plans to arraign them; they planned to plead guilty to the technical charge and then go to jail as the first American couple to be martyrized by the marriage laws. A lawyer and a gifted speaker, Miller relished the prospect of carrying the case to the Supreme Court, arguing it on the ground of the constitutional right to liberty of conscience. As it turned out, Miller alone went to jail for the marriage; his wife's health kept her from being tried. Although the district court found him innocent of the obscenity charge, it judged him guilty of the illegal union and sentenced him to ten days in jail or a $25 fine; the state supreme court later upheld the decision. Miller served his time in the Dakota County jail, a milder martyrdom than the young man would have preferred.[13] Social radicals had to wait another ten years for a full-fledged hero and heroine of free marriage to emerge.

Even the Liberals of Valley Falls would not post the $1,000 bond for Lillian and Edwin. Noah Harman, an older cousin of Lillian's, later offered to post bail for her, but R. D. Simpson, the justice of the peace, refused to allow a separate bond to be made. The couple spent the second night of their marriage under guard at the Cataract House in Valley Falls. With no bond, they traveled the eighteen miles to the county jail at Oskaloosa the next day.

The jail had no facilities for a woman, so Moses persuaded Sheriff Housh to allow Lillian to return under guard to Valley Falls. Lillian at first refused to return, declaring that she would share equally the responsibility for the marriage. Her father finally convinced her, however, that she was needed in the press office at home. The three male prisoners who were already occupying the two-celled jail added a vigorous protest against jailing Lillian.

A week later in Valley Falls, Moses Harman appeared as the single witness at a preliminary examination into the marriage. David Overmeyer and G. C. Clemens had been hired by Harman to defend the "Lucifer lovers." Overmeyer argued that the marriage constituted a legal civil contract and suggested that charges were being pressed in an attempt to ruin *Lucifer* and the Kansas radicals. The county attorneys argued that society had rights in the matter of marriage, that these rights had been ignored, and that the authority of the state had been defied. Punishment must therefore be exacted, urged the prosecution. Justice Simpson concurred and ordered the couple bound over to district court for trial on charges of violating Section 12 of the Marriage Act, which deemed "any persons, living together as man and wife, within this state, without being married," guilty of a misdemeanor and subject to a fine of from $500 to $1,000 and a jail sentence of from thirty days to three months. The crowd at the hearing, which was all male except for Lillian Harman and Edwin Walker's mother, received the decision with boisterous applause.[14]

Lillian remained out of jail until October 6, when officials brought her and Walker to the Shawnee County jail in Topeka to await trial. Walker described the underground jail as a horror: filth everywhere; the spectacle of young boys thrown in with the hardened tenants; a sadistic keeper; rats; loud sounds of cursing; dirty bedclothes too flimsy for warmth; and, worst of all, the pervasive degradation of spirit, "the unfortunate prisoner made to feel he has no rights, that the very fact of being there is proof positive that he deserves to be there."

The presence of Lillian sent the prisoners scurrying to bars and cracks in order to gawk. No privacy existed. When the caged men found out that this was a "free-love couple," they taunted and jeered and made "vulgar sounds." Outraged that his young wife should have to endure such degradation at the hands of the state, Walker remembered blackly the free-thought "friends" who had refused to post bail for them. What Lillian felt is not recorded.

On October 14 the Walker-Harman marriage case came before the district court at Oskaloosa, Judge Robert Crozier presiding. As a first move, attorneys Overmeyer and Clemens presented a petition for a change of venue, charging that the great amount of local prejudice precluded a fair trial. They read extracts from five county papers, some of which had recommended mob violence against either *Lucifer* or the couple.

The judge overruled the motion, a jury was selected, and the trial proceeded quickly. W. F. Hiser, Moses' step-son who had sworn the original complaint, provided important testimony. Hiser reported that he was present the day before the marriage and that he knew about the plans and proceedings for the autonomistic wedding. At the prodding of the prosecuting attorney, Hiser said that he had heard Moser remark that "this marriage will take place regardless of law—in defiance of law."[15]

According to *Lucifer,* Hiser had sworn out the complaint against the two in order to avert mob violence, which had been openly threatened. But since it appeared that previously Moses Harman had intentionally set up a test case of obscenity laws, it is possible that the *Lucifer* group likewise planned the "Lucifer Match" as a test of state marital statutes. Very conveniently, an insider—one of the family—brought proceedings against the couple. It was also convenient that Hiser did not step in early enough to halt the wedding, but rather on the morning after consummation of it. Earlier issues of *Lucifer* had given plenty of warning of what was to occur. If the case had not been manufactured, it was at least modeled upon more or less exact specifications, Moses and the principals perhaps wishing to have some initial control in what would inevitably become a community affair.[16]

Following instructions from the judge, the jury found the couple guilty both of living together as man and wife without first having obtained a license and of being married by a legally prescribed officer. The judge then attempted to sum up the case and the situation of the guilty party. The case, early and late, revealed an amount of judicial confusion: in Judge Crozier's rambling remarks, for instance, he gratuitously admitted that if either of the two were now to marry a new partner, he would in fact be guilty of bigamy.

On the nineteenth, Judge Crozier refused motions for a new trial and for an arrest of judgment, being less than appreciative of attorney Clemens's argument based on the absurdity of some state marriage statutes; Clemens, for example, pointed out that the minimum fine for any incestuous marriage was $100, while the fine for being married without a license was $500. The couple was then called up for sentencing.

Following form, the court asked if either of them had anything to say regarding why sentence should not be passed.

"Nothing *now*, your honor," said Edwin.

"Nothing except that we have committed no crime," Lillian added. "But we are in your power, and you can, of course, do as you please."

"It is a melancholy sight to see a prisoner unconvinced of her guilt at such a time," remarked the judge. After determining if their financial status would allow them to pay a fine (the couple hardly intended to acknowledge their guilt by paying a fine, however), the judge sentenced Edwin to seventy-five days in the Jefferson County jail and Lillian to forty-five days. In addition, both were to remain in jail until court costs were paid. The couple's lawyers appealed to the state supreme court at once.[17]

"It would make a pretty good plot for a 'Hill Top' novel, this struggle between the ideal and the conventional," commented the *Star* (London) about the *Lucifer* lovers when its reporter interviewed Lillian while she was visiting England in 1898. More seriously the *Star* pointed out that the Lucifer Match gained fame as the only couple in the English-speaking world to be imprisoned for their act of marriage. Although this claim is difficult to verify, the imprisonment of both the man and the woman in the Kansas free-marriage alliance did constitute a legal rarity.

Locked up on October 25, Lillian and Edwin occupied adjacent cells in the Oskaloosa jail. The sheriff and the jailer, according to Moses, both attempted to persuade the judge to allow Lillian to stay in a room at the jailer's house instead of in jail. Crozier refused: "She must be punished," he ordered. Lillian's cell measured seven by ten feet, and its walls were covered with iron; it was a box with no windows. Although she had a lamp, the darkness was the worst thing about her cell, Lillian wrote in her first letter from jail.[18]

The case came before the high court in January 1887, presented by Overmeyer and Clemens. On the fourth of March the Kansas Supreme Court returned its opinion upholding the decision of the district court. The court treated the question as a test of the validity of common-law marriage, and as a test of the state marriage laws and of the legislature's power to regulate marriage and punish violators. In the principal decision, Justice Johnson affirmed the legislature's authority in marriage, ruled that the marriage laws were sound, and upheld the couple's punishment. This did not mean, however, that, according to Kansas law, common-law marriage was illegal; indeed the judge affirmed that "the mutual present assent to immediate marriage by persons capable of assuming that relation is sufficient to constitute marriage at common law." Such a marriage would be sustained as valid in the state of Kansas.

"The case was doubly notorious," a present-day official of the Kansas Supreme Court has noted, "in that for the first time the Supreme Court upheld the validity of a common-law marriage in Kansas through mandating a county jail honeymoon for violation of the marriage license statute." In essence the court had ruled that common-law marriage was legal but nevertheless punishable under law as noncompliance with the marriage statutes. Justice Johnson side-stepped the question of whether the Lucifer Match constituted a common-law marriage, while Chief Justice Horton purposely disregarded the issue of the couple's marital status: "The question, in my opinion, for consideration is, not whether Edwin Walker and Lillian Harman are married, but whether, in marrying, or rather in living together as man and wife, they have observed the statutory requirements." This construction infuriated Moses Harman, who wrote in *Lucifer* that the charge had effectively been changed by "a stroke of legerdemain" from that of living together without being married to that of "violation of regulations designed to secure a record of their marriage." The judge, wrote Harman, "seems utterly oblivious of the fact that if the parties are married they cannot lawfully be punished for living together without being married."

In contrast, Judge Valentine ruled on the union itself: "In my opinion, the union between E. C. Walker and Lillian Harman was no marriage, and they deserve all the punishment which has been inflicted upon them." According to common law, wrote the judge, "the mere living together as husband and wife of a man and woman competent to marry each other, with the honest intention of being husband and wife so long as they both shall live, will constitute them husband and wife, and create a valid marriage. But that is not this case. In the present case, the parties repudiated nearly everything essential to a valid marriage, and openly avowed this repudiation at the commencement of their union."[19]

The defense intentionally raised a women's rights issue in the trial, testing the degree to which marriage could legally subjugate the woman. In the mid nineteenth century many states had passed Married Women's Property Acts which allowed wives some basic rights in the ownership and negotiation of property which had been denied to them under common law. Interpreted by traditionalist judges, however, the laws did not immediately alter the status of women. Numerous cases in several states between 1853 and 1883, for instance, upheld that "the earnings of the wife still belong to her husband, as at common law. The married women's property acts have made no change in this respect." A Tennessee decision in 1877 held that the whole body of the common law on the subject of the domestic relationship "is the primary law of Tennessee." As late as 1893 a Nebraska court held that the earnings of the wife, made while she is living with her husband and is engaged in no separate business, are the property of the husband. An 1886 Indiana decision ruled that "while the statutes remove, as a general rule, the disabilities of a married woman, the common-law rule that a husband and wife are to be regarded as one person still prevails." Likewise, many decisions, even in the twentieth century, have denied the wife's right to be known by her maiden name. By about 1900 the interpretation of the property laws regarded wives with more favor, but the man clearly remained the legal head of the household, with special rights that his wife was bound to respect.[20]

Justice Horton responded to these issues in the Walker-Harman case by conceding that a married woman could legally retain her maiden name; that she had "the same control of her person and property as her husband," and that "the wife does not merge her individuality as a legal person in that of her husband." Compared to existent legal interpretations, this opinion of a high court represented a victory of sorts for the *Lucifer* lovers.

Horton enlarged upon the position of women in Kansas, which, in fact, was a comparatively advanced state in regard to women's rights. Besides enjoying equal property rights, women in Kansas could participate in municipal elections, for "here the burden of a common prejudice and a common ignorance against woman has been wholly removed," he effused, not bothering to explain the seeming contradiction of limited suffrage. Horton concluded with the suggestion that the couple unite themselves in an honest marriage ceremony, "then over their union there can be no contention. Then the wife may be to the husband in law and in deed, 'A guardian angel o'er his life presiding, Doubling his pleasures, and his cares dividing.' "

At the time of the high-court decision the couple were still in jail. They had legally served their sentences, but they had refused to pay court costs. Lillian, whose shorter sentence had been completed in December, had refused to allow the costs to be paid and had refused to leave jail, even though Moses had made a special trip to fetch her. This act forced the press to a grudging reversal of an earlier opinion that Lillian was a mere child, used as a pawn by her elders. "She's gritty, though misguided," commented the normally venomous *Oskaloosa Independent*.[21]

In a letter in *Lucifer,* Lillian had pointed out that it cost the county enough to keep a person in jail—sixty cents per day—and that the financial aspects of imprisonment cut both ways. Collecting her debt of $56.60 would *cost* the county, she promised. Some friends insisted that, for her health, she should pay the costs and go free; but she disagreed. To compromise on this point would be to admit that their relationship was merely a clandestine love affair. Furthermore, the girl, who had just turned seventeen, noted that clandestine love affairs historically had done nothing whatsoever for the emancipation of woman.[22]

Moses and George Harman, now forced to run *Lucifer* and the job shop by themselves, had little time to cheer the prisoners in

Oskaloosa. Then, on 23 February 1887, officials arrested the two journalists on charges of obscenity because of the "awful letters" in *Lucifer*. With Lillian and Edwin in jail and with Moses and George likely to be there soon, the future of the *Light Bearer* looked dim. Lillian and her husband acknowledged the peril:

We are willing to endure [imprisonment] in the cause of woman's sex emancipation. But we knew then, as now, that that was the paramount issue only so long as Pen, Paper, Tongue and Mail were free. When freedom of discussion and investigation is threatened there is no longer any question which can rightfully take precedence to that.[23]

After six months in prison the couple paid the costs and were set free, sacrificing a lesser principle for the greater one, as they saw it.

7/ Public Opinion, the Satan Paper, and the Kansas Free Lovers

THE radical abolitionist tradition in Kansas remained strong enough to raise doubts among *Lucifer*'s enemies (often reformers of another ilk who had a vested interest in free speech) that the paper could be effectively suppressed merely for what it printed. But *Lucifer* incited respectable sensibilities in manifold ways—infidelism, anarchism, free love, and inadmissible words—and it did so against the lowering clouds of America's first Red scare. Just before the marriage arrest there had been much discussion of the Chicago Haymarket affair in the pages of *Lucifer*. The editors had defended the Chicago Seven at length, while carefully pointing out the areas of ideological and tactical difference between themselves and the urban labor radicals.

The public made no distinctions in their condemnation of the Lucifereans, overlooking the opposition of Walker to Harman's free-word campaign. If the radicals might not be suppressed for their words, their actions offered different opportunities; the unfriendly press quickly seized upon free marriage as the excuse to shut down the dissenters for good. After all, everyone, at least all editors, knew that free speech rated an amendment to the Constitution, but free love?

R. E. Van Meter, editor of Valley Falls' Republican paper *New Era* and the Associated Press correspondent for the area, gave the story sensational treatment in his wire dispatches. To the eagerly receptive city dailies, his first highly colored account referred to Walker as "one of the free-love editors of *Lucifer*"; he erroneously stated that the couple had been charged with adultery and that

Walker had five children by another marriage. This assertion started a rumor that Walker was a bigamist who had fled his family in Iowa. Actually his divorced wife and two daughters resided in southern Kansas. Van Meter headlined his *New Era* account "A Disgraceful Affair," and his succeeding stories fulminated against *Lucifer* as a "social vampire" and a national menace. "It is breeding sentiment that will cost the nation dear some day.... Our advice is to seize it now and forever silence its rebellious, blasphemous and corrupting utterances." This first reaction honestly reflected the mounting national concern about the frailty of conventional marriage in the face of "free love," a term that for marital conservatives embraced divorce (seen as successive polygamy), emancipated womanhood, and even nonchurch marriage.[1]

Other area papers at once picked up the story and commented upon the goings on. The *Winchester* (Kans.) *Argus*, edited by A. W. Robinson, used the episode not only to suggest the suppression of *Lucifer* but also to criticize the rival town of Valley Falls as a whole. "Up at Valley Falls they do some queer things," he wrote, "in any other town almost, public sentiment would be so strong against the outfit, the *Lucifer* would suddenly close publication and the Walker-Harman crowd would evacuate the city." After libeling Walker as a bigamist, the *Argus* then expressed the bewildered sentiment of a great many non-Liberals in the area. *Lucifer* "is a fearfully demoralizing sheet, we have never seen anything like it before, and its publication should be suppressed."[2]

The Democratic paper in Valley Falls, the *Register*, allowed itself to be outdone by the Christian/Prohibitionist/Republican nexus, but it nevertheless called for a stiff punishment. The *Ozawkie* (Kans.) *Times* called Moses the "King Bee of the tribe" and advocated his arrest and the closing of the "rotten concern," while Senator Sol Miller's *Weekly Kansas Chief* (Troy) ridiculed as animalistic the idea of autonomous marriage. Miller further characterized Valley Falls as a scandal and a hotbed of "isms." The *Oskaloosa Independent*, voice of the county seat and rabid foe of the group, styled *Lucifer* "the Satan," a sobriquet that was picked up by several area editors.[3]

Harman responded to the editorialists by criticizing their journalistic philosophy: the angry editors had no conception of their responsibilities as teachers and defenders of free speech. "The question with them is *Dare* I publish this? not *Ought* I publish it. ... They do not express their own convictions, they simply register the opinion of their readers."[4]

The editors of the Winchester and Troy papers did raise a valid question regarding the extent of local support for the group. Generally speaking, only a limited audience for such a paper existed in the area. Earlier in 1884, while discovering its role as an iconoclast, *Lucifer* still served principally as the Liberal paper for Kansas and Valley Falls. At that time sixty-five local residents subscribed to the paper. This number dropped to fifty as *Lucifer* changed its focus from liberalism to anarchism and sexual reform. At the time of the marriage its total national subscription list numbered about seven hundred. The marriage forced *Lucifer* to develop this national constituency. In early 1887, pressing for publicity and income, *Lucifer* distributed as many as two thousand copies of each issue. By 1890, the subscription list stabilized at fifteen hundred. Fifty subscribers in a town of thirteen hundred is not poor by "underground" journalism standards, and Harman claimed some leading citizens of Jefferson County among these subscribers.[5]

Yet with this modicum of local support he had not been able to raise bail immediately for Lillian and Edwin. Judging from the comments of those whom he had solicited for bond money, Harman gave these reasons for their refusals: (1) Local freethinkers, oriented exclusively to fight theology, refused to follow the logic of freethought to other issues. (2) Fear of business and social boycott, compounded by "hard times," discouraged any display of support. (3) Finally, a strong fear of personal violence existed. Threats of lynching had been freely made against the couple, according to Harman, and those who might otherwise have provided bail feared that if local toughs should lynch Lillian and Edwin, they might also lynch their bondsmen. According to *Lucifer*, which admittedly would have preferred to trace its problems to a conspiracy rather than to widespread community dislike, a vigilance committee headed by a local churchman and a prominent businessman had instigated *Lucifer*'s persecution.[6]

The *Oskaloosa Independent* on September 25 raised the possibility of a vigilante "solution": "The common and emphatic expression is that the decent people up there ought to dump the outfit into the Delaware, and drive the gang who run it out of town." It emphasized that the last issue of the paper had defended the Chicago [Haymarket] anarchists, preached free love, and denounced Christianity. Even if this were not an oversimplification of *Lucifer*, it must be admitted that Harman *had* succeeded in some classic provocations of the American middle-class mind.[7]

The larger Kansas papers also attacked *Lucifer*. The *Topeka Commonwealth* reported that the *Lucifer* "free lovers" were average enough looking, "but in conversation they soon prove[d] themselves cranks." The *Leavenworth Times*, edited by D. R. Anthony, brother of Susan B. Anthony, called Edwin and Lillian "the infamous editor of *Lucifer* and his paramour." The *Topeka Daily Capital* surprisingly upheld the right of a couple to enter into marriage without the aid of a clergyman or officer of the law. If the two had followed the Quaker example, the *Capital* advised, and had excluded "all their talk about how long and under what circumstances they would live together, leaving all that for consideration when occasion for it should arise," they would not have been sentenced as criminals. The influential paper considered the pair "fools" and seekers after a "cheap notoriety." The chief motivation it could see for the couple's action was the money that the pair might make through funds sent to them for legal defense.[8]

The antilabor *Chicago Daily Times*, in a long column entitled "Devil in Kansas," used exceedingly strong language to condemn the *Lucifer* group, evidently believing that the whole town of Valley Falls was a free-love experiment. The writer drew the inevitable connection between the Kansas "disciples of Beelzebub" and the "dynamite butchers waiting to be hanged in Chicago."[9]

A *Kansas City Times* editorial, reprinted in *Lucifer,* explained that Harman had written to the *Times,* asking that his side of the marriage story be given. In the opinion of the *Times,* the editorialist wrote, "Mr. Harman's argument is simply not worth publishing." Their philosophy of breaking such laws as they happened to find personally disagreeable was "absurd, subversive and untenable." Affirming their right to persuade and preach in their attempt to change the world, he drew the line at action; if they wished to outrage the "moral sense of nine-tenths of the people who live in the prosperous commonwealth of Kansas," they would have to be willing "to take martyrs' chances." The editor of the

Democratic daily advised the misguided couple to conform to the law or to bear the consequences "with becoming patience." Pomposity gave way to frenzy in a later *Times* pronouncement: "That free-love abomination, the Valley Falls *Lucifer,* was a disgrace to the state of Kansas. Its permanent destruction will be a thing to be thankful for."[10]

The pair had few defenders until their case became widely known; then an assortment of radical editors rallied in support. The *Anti-Monopolist* of Enterprise, Kansas, suggested that the two were being persecuted because they made the mistake of believing that Kansas was free of Stone Age savages. The *Winsted* (Conn.) *Press,* in a long, praise-filled editorial by L. V. Pinney, supported the rights of the two and suggested financial aid in the form of mail orders for *Lucifer's* books. Pinney concluded that every freethinker would at least support the Lucifereans' first contention protesting the necessary church sanction (in some states) of the marriage ceremony; the second, protesting state sanction, represented an anarchist opinion, but the right to hold it should nevertheless be supported by freethinkers.[11]

Lucifer printed many letters of support during the weeks following the news of the marriage arrest. Twenty letters from friends filled an October 22 supplementary sheet of the paper, and yet several dozen had been left over. Letters came from Kansas, Massachusetts, Alabama, Connecticut, Illinois, Delaware, Dakota Territory, Nebraska, Minnesota, and New York. Supporters started a Defense Fund in order to raise money for legal expenses, and fifty contributors sent several hundred dollars within the month. Kansans and Iowans dominated the list, but virtually every state was represented. The letters written by contributors indicated that *Lucifer's* support came from resident radicals in communities throughout the country. Some heard of the group's plight through a sympathetic area editor. One such, Alfred Cridge of the *San Jose* (Calif.) *Times,* solicited California support.[12]

Two Iowa reform journals, both edited by spiritualists who had been active in the free-marriage–free-love cause in Boston in the seventies, defended the couple's marriage and urged support. Moses Hull, who published Lillian's correspondence in his *Des Moines New Thought,* pointed out that the couple had surely harmed no one in their exercise of a rightful liberty. Rather, they were in jail "for being anarchists, agnostics, atheists and everything bad that begins with an A." He suggested that readers make up a purse that would not only cover legal costs but would also reimburse the couple two dollars per day for each day that they were imprisoned. In less than a month, Hull himself was in jail, arrested for libel on another matter.[13]

Lois Waisbrooker, editor of the *Clinton* (Iowa) *Foundation Principles* influenced the *Lucifer* group by her argument that woman's true freedom lay in sexual and maternal liberation from male domination. Illness cut short her editorial support of the couple's marriage struggle, however, and she wrote to express sorrow that she could not presently do more for the pair. She was particularly concerned that a test case be made of prison officials' practice of restricting and censoring prisoners' mail, as the sheriff had done in the case of the jailed couple.[14]

The *Topeka Daily Capital*, on November 18, printed a long interview with the pair's attorney, David Overmeyer. Overmeyer took the opportunity to correct the erroneous stories about Walker's bigamy and about the couple's general licentiousness. He vouched for their integrity, wholesomeness, and dedication to ideals—and of course he held them to be legally married. This aura of respectability and legality in which Overmeyer sought to clothe his clients was not entirely appreciated by the principals. In fact the question of legality and the *Lucifer* wedding became a point that split the radical press.

Liberty, edited by the Boston anarchist Benjamin R. Tucker, devoted most of its editorial space in the October, November, and December numbers to arguments and criticisms of the marriage. This "scientific anarchist" paper, to which Walker frequently contributed articles, charged that the couple had betrayed anarchism by trying to establish autonomistic marriage as legal. Tucker saw free *marriage* as a contradiction in terms, although the free-love principles of the Lucifer Match were clearly ones that Tucker supported; in addition, he charged *Lucifer* with soliciting for the Defense Fund under false pretenses.[15]

Lucifer carefully responded to the *Liberty* attack, taking pains to clarify its position. To begin with, the couple had not appealed to the law in order to decide the rightness of their deed. "On the contrary," Walker wrote to Tucker, "we ignored all the statutes, and proceeded to exercise our natural right to associate, without asking the permission of any person or aggregation of persons." They conceded that attorney Overmeyer's attempts to prove them "legally married" could be misleading from an anarchistic point of view, but lawyers' tactics aside, they maintained that they were seeking only to reclaim their individual rights which the state had assumed. If they did win recognition of legality, were they not affirming anarchism and individualism?

Furthermore, they felt that their act had affirmed the "superior right of woman to control in all matters pertaining to sex," a point that did not much interest Tucker. "We have maintained her right to own and control her sex-hood, her maternal functions as against ALL assumed rights of man, as her husband, or of governments whether of church or state." As autonomists, they also did "claim and demand" the right of woman to the sort of marriage that she wished, whether religious, civil, or autonomistic; woman's right "to sex-association with a man without ANY public acknowledgement" was equally upheld.[16]

A perennial and intemperate critic, Tucker did not show much discrimination in his analysis of the Lucifer Match; he drew no distinction between the statute law of instituted governments and the "natural" social rights, protected in the concept of common law, to which the Luciferans explicitly appealed. His position was a surprising one since he admired the anarchistic legal philosophy of Lysander Spooner, which carefully examined these distinctions. Tucker berated defenders of the Lucifer Match, particularly the anti-Comstock physician E. B. Foote and the editors of the leading free-thought paper, *Truth Seeker*. Support by these nonanarchists, argued Tucker, demonstrated the compromise nature of the autonomistic union. While Walker had been disappointed at the lack of official support by his friends in the American Secular Union, he regarded Tucker's influential diatribes as the unkindest cut.[17]

A reader of both journals, W. G. Markland, whose name figured significantly in *Lucifer*'s history, commented: "A true Anarchist will fly to the aid of Infidel, Christian or Pagan, when his rights are invaded. The question of Walker's toe being on the line, has nothing to do with the case. The hounds are after the hares, they have caught two of them; how to get them out of the bloody jaws alive is the only question worthy of attention." He added, "You do not voice my views on some points as exactly as does *Liberty* but I had much rather sail in your boat just now."[18]

St. Louis's most peculiar radical, the communist Alcander Longley, gruffly criticized the Valley Falls marriage; it chafed against his bourgeois legalism: "A little more of the same sort of defiance of law may teach him [Walker] that other folks sometimes have some rights and opinions which he is bound to respect or suffer the consequences." Longley, a communitarian who dreamed of eventual state socialism (he had earlier advertised his communities in *Lucifer*), had once run afoul of both radical and redneck opinion on the issue of marriage in one of his experimental communities in eastern Missouri. That experience had caused him to add the advocacy of conventional marriage to his particular reform brew, whose various other elements included a nostalgic Fourierism and a rabid hatred of anarchists.[19]

Ezra and Angela Heywood's *Word* staunchly supported the Kansas radicals. Hailing *Lucifer* as "the flag of Liberty, West," and the imprisoned couple as "brave exponents of Progress," the Heywoods besought their readers to send financial aid to the group.[20] The *Anarchist* (London), setting aside an argument with *Lucifer* on the advisability of the present use of dynamite (*Lucifer* now felt that the time was not right for such violence), found the marriage case indicative of the corruption of law and republican rule. The law encouraged secrecy and hypocrisy: "It is because of their honesty of purpose in making known to the world this autonomistic marriage and nothing else, that has secured their punishment." Again it was proved, the editor remarked, that jails are for those who do right.[21]

Friends of *Lucifer* were often far away—whether in London, Massachusetts, or Des Moines—while the danger lay close at hand. The public sentiment never became actively violent, although local editors did their best to encourage direct action. In January 1887 the *Oskaloosa Independent* attempted to ignite the tinder by publishing an anonymous letter from a supposed Iowa supporter of *Lucifer*. Warning that there would be bloody consequences if the letter were not heeded, it ordered Justice of the Peace Simpson, Sheriff Housh, and Judge Crozier to release Lillian and Edwin, or "your old carcasses will be more liable to be in the dissecting room than anywhere else." Harman denounced the letter as a clumsy fraud and an intentional provocation, while a friend of *Lucifer*, probably Noah Harman, acted quickly to quell an angry reaction by offering a $50 reward for information about the writer of the letter. From internal evidence in the letter, Harman believed that it had been written in Valley Falls and sent to Iowa to be mailed.[22]

As the sixteen-year-old female party to the marriage, Lillian Harman elicited much curiosity from the press. Early newspaper reports either dismissed her as a loose woman or treated her as an average girl who had been misled by wrong-thinking adults. She emphatically replied that she had not been led at all except by her own moral principles, a shocking statement from a freethinking—and free-living—sixteen-year-old girl, in the view of many mature Kansans. Compared to Edwin and Moses, Lillian had kept silent about her views in the columns of *Lucifer*. Sympathetic readers suggested that her silence, however, tended to prove the accusation that, in her own words, she was only "a nonentity; simply a child having no will of my own and going blindly where my father and Mr. Walker lead me." She explained that, being young and often busy as a compositor, she did not feel prepared for writing for publication. Perhaps, she conceded, she had been wrong to keep silent.

Launching into print with the enthusiasm of youth, Lillian thus began her long career as a feminist journalist. The marriage seemed a simple act of anarchistic choice to her: "The canvasser and a compositor concluded to marry in their own way without asking leave of Judge Mosher [*sic*] and going through a certain form prescribed by the paternal state legislature for its children who are unable to draw up their own marriage contracts." The officialdom of Kansas, she believed, hoped to "crush the Radical element which is springing up, by showing us as terrible examples." She ridiculed the attempt of prosecuting attorney Myers to co-opt the marriage issue when, at the preliminary examination, he suggested that the couple "can be legally married yet." The pair did not need the law, she emphasized, in order to love and honor one another. "I am married as truly as any one is, and if they want to prosecute they can just prosecute, and make the most of it," she concluded.[23]

Withstanding the harassment of the press and the government, as well as the barbs of reformers, *Lucifer* and its bearded old editor became a symbol of dedicated if misguided idealism to the people of Valley Falls. Most feared Moses' radical ideas and were slightly confounded by the rectitude of his personal life and his business dealings. A sense of frustration underlay the community's sufferance of Harman: "I don't like you, Mr. Harman, *I don't like you!*" exploded one of Harman's neighbors, a well-to-do farmer, on an August day in 1887. "The doctrines you teach in your paper if carried out in practice would take us back to feudalism, to barbarism . . . your opinions in regard to government are ridiculous in the extreme, to say the least of them. And then your religious views are worse yet."[24]

In 1942 William A. Smith, who grew up in Valley Falls and later became chief justice of the Kansas Supreme Court, recalled the ironic effects on the citizens of Valley Falls of Harman's ministry of free love and woman's emancipation. He remembered from earliest childhood his mother's references to Harman: "She always spoke of him as being a very wicked man, the teacher of free love as she saw it. His son [George Harman] was in my youth the publisher of a Democratic paper in Valley Falls. . . . Since this son was one of two or three Democrats in the city, for years I thought of all Democrats as people who believed in free love and who generally held in contempt most of the institutions I had been taught to revere." Although Harman "labored and suffered for the emancipation of women," continued the judge, "yet the two women I knew best—both poor[,] both mothers of large families, both having sunk their individuality in the task of bringing up a family[—]would have none of him."[25]

Although *Lucifer* answered the prayers of the local clergy and moved away from Valley Falls to the city of Topeka in 1890, Harman's decade of journalism left a lingering stamp on the character of the town. Even today in eastern Kansas, mention of the name Harman raises eyebrows and hushed references to free love; and throughout the state, one may still hear old-timers speak of Valley Falls as "that free-love town."

8/ Awful Letters: Part 2

HARMAN plunged with fervor into the role of martyr. Shortly after the grand jury issued a re-indictment against *Lucifer* for the four "awful letters," Moses Harman set about reprinting them in *Lucifer*. He republished the Markland letter side-by-side with Genesis 38, a chapter of the Old Testament which portrays incest, harlotry, and Onan's coitus interruptus. Publishing earthy portions of the Bible had been a favorite tactic of incorrigible freethinkers such as D. M. Bennett who hoped to embarrass puritans with their own contradictions. Although courts shied away from ruling upon the Bible's "obscenity," some determined efforts were made to call the question. In 1872 Anthony Comstock arrested the extraordinary eccentric George Francis Train on an obscenity charge for printing portions of the Old Testament in his journal, the *Train Ligue*. Train spent five months in Tombs prison awaiting his trial; but when it came, the judge ducked the issue of obscenity by pronouncing Train to be insane. In 1895 officials arrested J. B. Wise of Clay Center, Kansas, for mailing a postal card inscribed with Isaiah 12:36. Wise spent four weeks in a Leavenworth jail before his release on bond; in his obscenity trial a year later, Judge Caius G. Foster found him guilty and fined him fifty dollars. Friends of Wise's planned to appeal to the Supreme Court, but they never succeeded. Readers of the *Truth Seeker* raised money to pay the fine.[1]

Harman's free-language policy alienated radicals as well as conventional society. The editors of both the *Truth Seeker* and *Liberty* supported Harman's right of free press, but both considered his language tactics offensive; *Liberty* went so far as to pronounce Harman's efforts "superfluous and reactionary." The coeditor of *Lucifer* struck the most telling blow, however; Edwin Walker not only resigned from *Lucifer* to begin his own paper, *Fair Play*, but he used his new journal to lambaste Harman's word policy. Walker, who had recently finished his jail term for free marriage, felt that radical arguments would do the most good if they were pitched in conventional language: "If men are afraid of certain words, or if their use disgusts them, do not be so blindly stubborn as to persist in thrusting them into their eyes. The only possible effect of such perverse persistence is to get the truth you teach associated inseparably with the objectionable terms and, consequently, rejected."[2]

Walker did not care to acknowledge the libertarian issues raised by Harman's test of freedom of the press. Walker seemed to be increasingly influenced by Benjamin Tucker of *Liberty*, who not only spent a great deal of verbiage correcting radical comrades but also appeared to view social change as largely a matter of polemics rather than of action. Walker saw the radical journal as a platform for abstractions about a coming revolution, while Harman, in contrast, seemed to view the medium itself as the revolution.

As the Markland-letter trial drew near, a number of editors—some radical, some not—began to see a degree of professional self-interest at stake in the case. *American Liberty*, an antimonopoly quarterly published in Hampton, Virginia, saw danger in the government's effort to punish Harman's "breach of good taste"; it urged all editors everywhere to "stand shoulder to shoulder in defending the unrestricted rights of a free press." A convention of Kansas editors in Topeka discussed the case, and afterwards Harman reported that editors from the towns of Winchester, Oldsburg, Lancaster, and McLouth had supported, in principle, *Lucifer*'s right to publish its exposés. Although the Valley Falls radicals received publicity throughout the Midwest in the conventional press and across the country in reform papers, most newspaper editors—as town boomers, business promotors, or party spokesmen—were unenthusiastic about the civil-rights aspect of a Kansas obscenity case. In 1887 Harman had sent several hundred copies of a special anti-Comstock issue of *Lucifer* to editors throughout the western United States. Replies to the sampling were almost all negative; many editors suggested that *Lucifer* should be banned, and several expressed surprise that Kansas would allow such an irreverent sheet.[3]

Harman received only limited encouragement before his trial, and that mostly from extreme radicals, idealists, or nonconformist editors. In Massachusetts, Ezra Heywood of *The Word* championed Harman as a hero of "mental freedom" and advised his readers that "the more copies of *Lucifer*, the *Truth Seeker, Investigator, Liberty, The Word,* and other 'crazy' papers that can be showered in Kansas before the trial the more likely is acquittal or light sentence." The *Chicago Express* printed a praise-filled article about the *Lucifer* radicals, and its associate editor, E. C. Patterson, sent personal encouragements to Harman. Joseph Rodes Buchanan, a founder of the "eclectic" medical profession and a philosopher on education for *Arena* and other magazines, discussed the Lucifereans in his own *Journal of Man* (Boston). He compared their struggle with that of Walt Whitman; Whitman had been lucky, Buchanan allowed, for "if he had lived at Valley Falls he might have been consigned to prison by a pigheaded judge." In *Pomeroy's Advance Thought* (New York) the pungent journalist M. M. ("Brick") Pomeroy rallied to Harman's defense, praising him as one who "called the attention of thousands to the way some men who are husbands ruin the health of wives." The most distinguished of Kansas freethinkers, former governor Charles Robinson, reaffirmed his support of *Lucifer* as it faced the obscenity crisis; Harman was pleased that unrefined language had not alienated his respectable friend. From across the Atlantic, the *Revolutionary Review* (London) cheered *Lucifer's* efforts and pronounced Anthony Comstock a scoundrel.[4]

A "Remonstrance and Petition," coauthored by eleven women reformers from ten states, addressed itself to the Hon. Caius G. Foster, the judge handling the Markland-letter case. The women testified that the "awful letters" that Harman printed portrayed true conditions of womanhood, and they urged the judge not to ban *Lucifer's* efforts toward sexual education. This gesture initiated several petition efforts for Harman and also set off a mail campaign to Judge Foster. Harman encouraged this focus on the judge. Before his final trial, Harman printed numerous letters from *Lucifer* readers, advising and criticizing the magistrate for his previous handling of the Markland indictments. Two weeks before Harman faced the judge in 1890, the editor began printing in boldface on *Lucifer*'s front page the judicial oath of Judge Caius G. Foster. If the accompanying editorials did not exactly taunt the judge, they did broadly dare him to martyrize the editor.[5]

In this period immediately before the trial, Harman chose inalterably and finally to define his free-language policy. If twitting the judge and republishing indicted matter had caused some to believe that Harman craved confrontation, he now removed all doubt. On 14 February 1890 Harman published a letter from a proanarchist New York physician, Richard V. O'Neill, detailing the sex abuses he had seen and treated in his practice. To Harman it was a further opportunity to air the Victorian attic and to expose the abuses which, he believed, fed on darkness and ignorance.

In his letter the doctor affirmed that in his nineteen years of practice he had witnessed many cases of injury and even death caused by such abuses as the Markland letter described. Even normal intercourse could sometimes be considered abusive: "Many women are made sick by every act of coition. I know of several women who slowly perished from this cause," he asserted. And some men, whom he compared to elephants in intercourse, drove their wives to derangement or to early death by excessive coition. In a few cases, he added, husbands suffered from the immoderate passion of their wives:

> I often recall to mind the question I once saw discussed in a book for Catholic priests, on the Hearing of Confessions: viz, as to what penance should be imposed on a man for insisting on putting his private organ into his wife's mouth. A woman once came to me with her mouth and throat full of chancres (venereal ulcers) caused by *her husband's* doing as above intimated. There seems to be no limit to the brutality and bestiality of many men.

Mr. F. of Wyoming wrote me for advice concerning a disease resembling syphilis and scrofula, but he never had coition with a woman: always with sheep, pigs, mares, etc., all his life. He was aged 48.

Mr. P. C. of California wrote asking if I could cure him of an *insatiable* appetite for *human semen*; he is a rich man; all his family (grown up men and women) *suck* each other's *private parts* in the presence of each other. He himself goes roaming all over the country trying to find men to allow him to "suck them off" as he says. He wrote me about it two years ago. He says he inherited this fearful legacy from his father....

With regard to prevention of conception, there is not a physician who does not give advice how to do that every day in the week. Many medical journals contain full instructions as to use of sponges, injection, etc. See, for instance, the Columbus (Ohio) Medical *Journal* for February, 1889 (last year) and numerous others. Yet they are not prosecuted. Why?

I desire to enter my stern protest against the malicious persecutions of yourself and your associates by the enemies of freedom....

I hope to be able to be present at your trial (if it ever comes off, which I am inclined to think is doubtful). I am ready to verify upon oath and solemn affirmation all I say herein....

The letter remains significant as one of the few instances in nineteenth-century journalism of explicit discussion of oro-genital sex. Only the very recent sexual revolution has brought about attitudes that legitimize oro-genital sex acts, at least heterosexual ones, and justify them as another source of sexual pleasure. But the sensibility of Harman's time did not merely consider such acts perverted, it refused to consider them at all. Human sexuality, after all, was a questionable subject even in medical colleges. Harman also viewed oro-genitalism as an abuse, but as a Victorian heretic, he believed that the subject should be brought to public light. By the time the Markland-letter trial began in 1890, *Lucifer* had become a forum for discussion of oro-genital "abuses."[6]

On advice from supporters such as Ezra Heywood and Dr. E. B. Foote of New York, Harman decided to conduct his own court defense of the Markland letter on the constitutional issues of freedom of the press and freedom of the mails. Harman's lawyers, who had planned a technical defense, reluctantly accepted their dismissal. Being without an attorney as the trial opened, Harman allowed the court to appoint a "Colonel" Bradley to represent him. In agreeing to this, Harman believed that he would merely be getting a legal adviser to aid him in his own line of defense. He learned too late that the defense of his case was out of his hands. On such short notice, attorney Bradley decided that Harman's only chance of acquittal lay in convincing the jury that his client was insane. The hasty tactic failed to convince the court, however, and the trial for obscenity proceeded apace. With his defense badly compromised, Harman managed only a few words in support of *Lucifer*'s free-press tactics. The jury quickly found him guilty on four counts, based on the Markland and Whitehead letters.[7]

Harman refused to stand for sentencing before Judge Foster, but on the prodding of attorneys, he finally came to his feet. After allowing Harman to make a short speech, the judge lectured the prisoner, chiding him for a rebellious and defiant attitude throughout the trial. Referring to the editorial campaign that Harman had directed at him, the judge remarked, "[I have] seen circus performers stick their heads into lion's mouths, but [I have] never seen them have the temerity to twist the beasts' tails or kick them in the ribs while performing the risky act." There was laughter in the courtroom, and then the judge pronounced sentence: five years in the Kansas penitentiary and a fine of three hundred dollars on the single count of mailing the Markland letter in *Lucifer*.[8]

He served four months before attorney Overmeyer won his release on a technicality. While free, he was tried for the O'Neill letter, found guilty, and sentenced to one year. He served eight months for this offense before Overmeyer again obtained his release, this time on a deficiency in the sentencing procedure. After he had been released from prison, the court resentenced him to one year at hard labor for the Markland letter, and he returned to prison to serve out the time. When he finally left the Kansas prison in April 1896, his legal entanglement for publishing the "awful letters" had lasted almost a decade.[9]

The federal cases involving Moses Harman provided important precedents for significant twentieth-century decisions regarding obscenity. So forcefully did attorney Overmeyer argue that the Comstock Act contravened freedoms guaranteed by the First Amendment that Judge Philips felt compelled to address an opinion on the constitutionality of the postal act, apart from the Supreme Court's obiter decision in *Ex Parte Jackson*. It was a radical misconception of the scope of constitutional protection to believe that a person might print and publish, *ad libitum,* any matter that he might choose without accountability to law, said the judge: "Liberty in all its forms and assertions in this country is regulated by law. It is not an unbridled license. Where vituperation or licentiousness begins, the liberty of the press ends." He continued:

While the genius of our institutions of government accords the largest liberality in the utterance of private opinion, and the widest latitude in polemics, touching questions of social ethics, political and domestic economy, and the like, it must ever be kept in mind that this invaluable privilege is not paramount to the golden rule of every civilized society, *sic utere tuo ut non alienum laedas,*—"so exercise your own freedom as not to infringe the rights of others or the public peace and safety." While happily we have outlived the epoch of censors and licensors of the press, to whom the publisher must submit his matter in advance, responsibility yet attaches to him when he transcends the boundary line where he outrages the common sense of decency, or endangers the public safety. . . .

In a government of law the law-making power must be recognized as the proper authority to define the boundary line between license and licentiousness, and it must likewise remain the province of the jury—the constitutional triers of the fact—to determine when that boundary line has been crossed.

In the landmark *Roth-Alberts* decision of 1957, the United States Supreme Court reiterated the essential points of this argument, excluding obscenity from constitutional protection.[10]

But the most important portion of Harman's "O'Neill letter" case lay in the construction of obscenity. Judge Philips held that terms such as "obscene" and "indecent" could not be considered to have "acquired any technical significance . . . but are terms of popular use." And in the Markland-letter decision of 1889, the court ruled that "the question of obscenity in any particular article must depend largely on the place, manner, and object of its publication." The 1891 decision added a significant element to the determination of obscenity—the test of contemporary community standards—which would later be reflected in *Roth,* in Judge Manton's dissent in the *Ulysses* case (1934), and in a related case, *Parmelee* v. *U.S.* (1940). Judge Philips wrote that

laws of this character [obscenity laws] are made for society in the aggregate, and not in particular. So, while there may be individuals and societies of men and women of peculiar notions or idiosyncrasies, whose moral sense would neither be depraved nor offended by the publication now under consideration, yet the exceptional sensibility, or want of sensibility, of such cannot be allowed as a standard by which its obscenity or indecency is to be tested. *Rather is the test, what is the judgment of the aggregate sense of the community reached by it?* What is its probable, reasonable effect on the sense of decency, purity, and chastity of society, extending to the family, made up of men and women, young boys and girls,—the family, which is the common nursery of mankind, the foundation rock upon which the state reposes?[11] [Emphasis added.]

Moreover, it was the jury, wrote Judge Philips, which most nearly represented the average intelligence, the common experience, and sense of the vicinity, and the effect of questionable material upon their sensibilities should determine whether such material was obscene. In contrast the *Bennett-Hicklin* test had used the standard of the probable effect of obscenity upon the most susceptible element of society, rather than the predominant or average element. In explaining the *Hicklin* standard in the *Bennett* case, Judge Blatchford had cautioned the jurors that the question of obscenity "is not a question whether it would corrupt the morals, tend to deprave *your* minds or the minds of every person; it is a question whether it tends to deprave the minds of those open to such influences and into whose hands a publication of this character might come. It is within the law if it would suggest impure and libidinous thoughts *in the young and the inexperienced*" (emphasis added). Thus Judge Philips pointed the *Bennett-Hicklin* standard in a new direction which, again, would be incorporated in the *Roth* decision.[12] Ironically, the name of Harman, a man who tried to strike down obscenity laws in the United States, attached itself to three foundation stones in a new interpretation of obscenity law: his challenges affirmed the constitutionality of the Comstock laws, made community sensibility a determinant of obscenity, and placed the "mental sanitation" test on a broader segment of society.

Since Harman had spent a great deal of time fighting legal battles in Topeka, he moved *Lucifer* there in 1890. After his release from prison in 1896, he moved the journal to Chicago. This move freed him from government harassment for only a few years, however; he still had censorship battles and even another prison term in store.

By the early 1890s much of the reform press in America had become aware of Harman's effort to test the Comstock laws. Although most disagreed with his method of confrontation and his libertarian ideas on sex education, many journalists felt that Harman had received harsh punishment for what had been a well-intentioned stand. The *Twentieth Century,* in articles and editorials, lavished Harman with praise. Its editor, Hugh O. Pentecost, in "A Good Man Sent to Prison," classed Harman with "great reformers" in the tradition of Socrates, Jesus, and William Lloyd Garrison. Benjamin O. Flower, editor of *Arena,* called him a "venerable martyr" and chided the government for allowing pandering papers such as the *Police Gazette* to go unmolested while "poor old Moses Harman, who spends his money and life energies to secure what he believes to be a wider need of justice for women, and what he believes will lead to a higher and purer civilization, is made the victim of a postal bureaucracy essentially Russian in character and essence." Although Harman's reform efforts had seemed unwise at times, Flower wrote, the courts had committed an "outrage" against the Kansas editor by not considering his motives for publishing the letters. The Comstock law should be changed or annulled if such men as Harman could be victimized under it. "To imprison such a man," concluded Flower, "is to place a blister on the brow of the republic."[13]

Clara Bewick Colby's *Woman's Tribune* (Washington, D.C.) spoke up repeatedly for Harman:

The *Tribune* has always taken the ground that Mr. Harman was greatly misjudged and that the censorship of the press which could sentence him to five years imprisonment for publishing in a communication a physiological term and still allow the average daily paper to enter the homes, is straining at a gnat and swallowing a camel.... He has devoted himself to securing personal freedom for woman, and is striking many hard blows to accomplish this end.

The influential *Woman's Journal,* spokesman of the American Woman Suffrage Association, gave muted support to Harman: "No one can have less sympathy than the editors of the *Woman's Journal* with some of the views advocated in *Lucifer*; but on one point Mr. Harman's opinions are perfectly sound, and that is on the right of a wife to the control of her own person."[14]

As a moralist who pointed out the sexual impurities in society, Harman won support among some of the "Social Purity" reformers who also claimed Anthony Comstock as one of their own. This alliance of "free lovers" and "puritans" offered embarrassment to the Vice Hunter, however. In 1890 the organ of the National Purity Association, *Christian Life*, published a cover article on the Harman case which criticized the postal censor for thwarting Harman's efforts. Comstock's western agent, R. W. McAfee, forthwith arrested its conservative editor, J. B. Caldwell, for obscenity because he had published the Harman article and an earlier one on marital purity. As a case of the prude maligning the puritan, it represented a low point of discernment in Comstock's career. Even the *Woman's Journal*, which generally lauded the efforts of the vice societies, found it necessary to correct Comstock for this breach. To Harman it appeared "that there was much anxiety and tribulation on the part of government officials lest the prosecution of *Lucifer*'s editor should get an airing through the columns of a prominent Christian journal."[15]

A campaign got under way in 1890 which distributed four thousand petition forms to protest Harman's arrest and imprisonment. Virtually all freethought and several "social radical" papers in both the United States and Canada distributed the petitions. Dr. E. B. Foote, Jr., Secretary of the National Defense Association, which had been organized to defend free-speech cases, reported that "Brick" Pomeroy obtained an interview with President Harrison and Attorney General Miller on Harman's behalf on July 29. Pomeroy presented the case for Harman's pardon to the president, as well as a legal brief arguing the injustice of Harman's treatment. He also presented a petition for Harman's release, signed by 276 businessmen of Valley Falls who attested to Harman's moral character and to their belief that he "made the objectionable publication in good faith." On August 9 a petition of "over seven thousand names, two hundred feet long," was forwarded to the Justice Department. Others sent separate petitions direct to Washington on Harman's behalf; friends in Chattanooga, for instance, sent 535 names. Hugh O. Pentecost, of *Twentieth Century*, and his New York friends obtained the most names for Harman—1,500.[16]

Soon after Harman published the O'Neill letter, Ezra Heywood vowed to reprint it in his own paper, *The Word*. Comstock did not ignore this challenge from his veteran adversary Heywood; he immediately moved to confiscate *The Word* and to arrest its editor one final time. Other radicals shook their heads at the willfulness of Harman and Heywood, admiring their courage but not really understanding their passion to confront the government on the issue of "free words." The editor of *Truth Seeker* perhaps best explained the value of Harman and Heywood to the disparate reform elements of America in the 1890s. These two editors, wrote George Macdonald, served as buffers for the rest of the dissenting press; "their persecution marked the limits of safety for us."[17]

9/ The Prairie Cauldron: Reform and Regeneration, 1885-1895

KANSAS became the first state to enact municipal woman-suffrage laws, but that token victory came only after a twenty-year struggle. Kansas was one of the first states after the Civil War to put both the woman- and the black-suffrage questions to its voters, but its white males in 1867 voted down black suffrage, 19,421 to 10,483, and rejected woman suffrage, 19,857 to 9,070. Though women had contributed importantly in the struggle that brought constitutional amendments that freed the blacks from slavery and enfranchised the black male, the "weaker sex" could expect no such recognition of their own claims to citizenship.[1]

The 1887 enactment of a municipal woman-suffrage law in Kansas again brought wide attention to the "great experimental ground of the nation," as the *New York Times* called Kansas. In that year Argonia became the first town in the United States to have a woman mayor. Oskaloosa, the county-seat town near Valley Falls, also received a moment of notoriety in 1887 as news wires spread the story that it had become the first city in the United States to be entirely governed by women; it reelected the female slate in 1889. Cottonwood Falls and Rossville also elected completely female governments in 1889.[2]

Out of 1,406 women registered in Topeka in 1887, 1,200 went to the polls; three-fourths of them voted Republican. They almost held the balance of power, noted a contemporary observer, who reported that a wave of relief swept the drawing rooms of the city when the vote of the "degraded and ignorant class of women" did not "overbalance the vote of the respectable ladies," as had been predicted by opponents of woman suffrage.

Lighter moments, of course, occurred. In Wichita one-third of the 600 registered female voters listed their occupation as "Sports." The Sports drove en masse to the polls, where a throng of 5,000 greeted them with cheers and insults. The Sports voted solidly for the labor ticket, defeating the Republican candidate for mayor. In Leavenworth's 1887 election, women arrayed themselves against their own sex to the delight of the men and the Democratic party. A reported slur on the moral character of Leavenworth's "exclusive social set" by the WCTU organizer from Indiana provoked the ladies of the privileged class to reprisal. On election day the ladies "pressed into service carriages of all kinds, and ordered them driven hither and thither to pick up all classes of women, irrespective of social standing, to cast their ballots for their particular candidates." The retainer vote got the ladies their revenge, and the WCTU-Republican candidate was defeated.[3]

In 1889 a large turnout of women voters benefited the Democratic candidates in mayoralty races in Topeka, Leavenworth, and Atchison. Susan B. Anthony campaigned for her Republican brother in the Leavenworth race, but to no avail—the "notorious" Col. D. R. Anthony, editor of the *Leavenworth Times,* suffered defeat by seven hundred votes. One of the valuable lessons that the women seemed to have learned in two years was to get out the vote by providing transportation for registration and polling.[4]

Woman suffrage presented a dilemma to *Lucifer* and to its libertarian readership, because of their no-government bias. On the one hand, Harman and his paper strongly advocated women's rights, including all those enjoyed by man, yet according to its anarchistic analysis, voting was merely the affirmation of the state's coerciveness. *Lucifer* argued that so long as a woman has not the right to the control of her own person, "it is useless to give woman the ballot, to talk about social emancipation, to claim intellectual equality."[5] As a representative sex radical, Harman's view of the entire Woman Question sheds light on the subsidiary question of voting.

The Woman Question encompassed the whole problem of sexual relations—coital, social, personal, and political. Like his forerunner Stephen Pearl Andrews and his contemporaries Ezra and Angela Heywood, Harman sought a natural law of sexual relations to replace the prevailing discriminatory standards of sexual morality—one based on truth ("science") rather than on myth. The most debasing aspect of conventional morality, he felt, was not the differential of license between the sexes, but its cause, the differential of power.

Like conventional writers, he viewed motherhood as the highest function of woman. This office, he argued, required a well developed, vigorous sexual nature. But how, he asked, could woman "preserve the purity, the holiness, wholesomeness or healthfulness, of her sex-hood when that sex-hood is not under her control?" The utopian solution would be centralized control of mating guided by some ideal of quality, if only the state could be trusted with this responsibility. However, no state could be wise or responsible enough to do this, and so governments should completely remove their "meddling hands" from the regulation of sex and marriage. As it was, government sanctioned and protected an unjust system of sexual accommodation which obstructed man's destiny of greater freedom and, in Harman's opinion, also arrested man's genetic development.[6]

Harman voiced a theory of eugenics that was popular with free lovers. Moses Hull, Lois Waisbrooker, the Heywoods—all leaders of the free-love cause after the abdication of Victoria Woodhull—based their "Social Freedom movement" on an anarchistic eugenics. In their 1875 convention in Boston, the first resolution of the free-love votaries asserted that "the most important work to be done now for the present and future generations of humanity is to discover and *practice* the science of producing the most harmonious children." They agreed, as Ezra Heywood declared, that "since every human being has a clear right to be well-born, the marriage institution is a State Intrusion which destroys love, hinders intelligent reproduction, causes domestic discord, and enervates, corrupts and poisons the sources of life."[7]

This early eugenics reflected the basic premise of Francis Galton's *Hereditary Genius* (1869), that one's character and capabilities depended principally upon one's hereditary program and "that the improvement of the natural gifts of future generations of the human race is largely, though indirectly, under our [present] control." Although this brilliant Englishman exerted a wide if often oblique influence upon American thought (in the 1870s the *Popular Science Monthly* reprinted several of his essays), there was nothing new in his premise. The taproots of pre-Galtonian free-love eugenics lay in the stirpiculture experiments of John Humphrey Noyes and in the writings of such figures as Stephen Pearl Andrews and Henry C. Wright. A precept of this eugenics, that woman's superiority derived from her motherhood function, would be developed in more systematic fashion by Lester Frank Ward in the 1880s, but in the meantime this primitive eugenics found wide voice through the popular home medical books of Dr. Edward Bliss Foote, later one of Harman's most dedicated supporters. Harman himself published the first two periodicals devoted to eugenics in America—a quarterly in the nineties, called *Our New Humanity*, and, as successor to *Lucifer* in 1907, the *American Journal of Eugenics*.[8]

Not to be confused with the later prescriptive eugenics of the Progressive Era, anarchistic eugenics held that enslaved, male-dominated mothers could only perpetuate a race of slavish humans. This belief depended upon the prevalent notion that a child's character could be prenatally influenced; a mother's submission to sexist laws, it was believed, would affect the unborn child. In his justification of the Markland letter, Harman had explained that present laws exploited the difference between the sexual natures of male and female and thus contributed to the birth of deficient children. Harman shared the common belief that the male had a selfish and insatiable sexual appetite, whereas the female was prudently subdued or downright antipathetic toward coitus. This being the case, Harman argued, most instances of sexual intercourse and the consequent conception of offspring could be presumed to be initiated by the male against the will of the female. Children conceived under such conditions of coercion would naturally develop traits of inferiority and malevolence, he believed.

Sex radicals also utilized a theory of "natural selection" in order to justify their idea of free motherhood: a woman should be able to choose freely a father for her child from the best example of manhood available. Partly an application of Darwin's evolutionary theory, this idea had pre-Darwinian roots in Stephen Pearl Andrews's feminist thought. The dysgenics that Andrews believed was caused by legal marriage could be remedied, he wrote, by restoring "to outraged woman the right to choose freely, at all times, the father of her own child. Till that be granted, all the rest of your 'Woman's Rights' are not worth contending for."[9]

This idea surfaced in the 1890s in respectable as well as radical quarters. "In order to cleanse society of the unfit we must give to woman the power of selection in marriage," said Alfred Russel Wallace, the naturalist who discovered natural selection independently of Darwin. But Wallace added important qualifications to female selection—he had in mind educated, trained, and self-supporting women of a future reformed society. Women in such a society would not marry, as they now did, for reasons of a "bare living or a comfortable home." With rewarding alternatives to marriage available, woman, the less passionate sex, would be less inclined to marry, and those who did could take their pick from numerous eager suitors. "I think we may trust the cultivated minds and pure instincts of the women of the future in the choice of partners," Wallace said, for "the enlightened woman would know that she was committing an offence against society, against humanity at large, in choosing a husband who might be the means of transmitting disease of body or mind to his offspring."

Wallace took pains to distinguish his ideas from those of Grant Allen, the English biologist and popular writer who, despite his socialism, came very close to the *Lucifer* radicals on the subject of free marriage. Wallace thought that Allen's idea of replacing legal marriage with libertarian contracts for the purpose of breeding a better crop of children would be disastrous. It would not only impair the nurture function of the family, but, he believed, it would also favor "the increase of pure sensualism, the most degrading and most fatal of all the qualities that tend to the deterioration of races and the downfall of nations." The *Lucifer* radicals, of course, associated "pure sensualism" with legal marriage; their ideals of natural selection and free motherhood later became reality when Lillian Harman bore her daughter in bachelor motherhood, having made a contract with the father before birth for his share of support for the child.[10]

Although the work of the German zoologist August Weissman in the eighties and nineties helped to demonstrate that acquired characteristics could not be transmitted, the belief in inheritance of acquired characteristics remained in force, and it controlled hereditarian thought into the twentieth century. And for a still longer period the question of whether the character of the child could be affected through prenatal influence remained an open one to scientists, doctors, and laymen. In a letter to the editor of *Nature* in 1893 Alfred Russel Wallace wrote that while most current opinion rejected the idea that prenatal influences could physically mark the child, he was "not aware that the question of purely mental effects arising from prenatal mental influences on the mother has been separately studied. Our ignorance of the causes, or at least of the whole series of causes, that determine individual character is so great, that such transmission of mental influences will hardly be held to be impossible or even very improbable. It is one of those questions on which our minds should remain open."

In volume 5 (1906) of his *Studies in the Psychology of Sex,* Havelock Ellis traced the historical genesis of prenatal beliefs, reviewed current professional opinion, and cited reputable reports of apparent prenatal influence. He cautiously concluded that while definite effects of maternal influence upon the fetus had not been proven, neither had they been positively disproven. Later on he spoke with more assurance: "The mother is the child's supreme parent," he wrote in volume 6 (1910), "and during the period from conception to birth the hygiene of the future man can only be affected by influences which work through her."[11]

It was just this stress on characterological and psychic determinants that prompted the interest of the late Victorians in heredity. The first significant call by a "regular" physician for birth-control and sex education was, as well, a call to enlighten the masses about "the wonderful and almost unlimited extent of prenatal influence." If parents took advantage of the knowledge of this influence, wrote Sydney Barrington Elliott in the *Journal of the American Medical Association,* they "would have only those who were well born, free from all contamination, capable of almost unlimited attainment; and if those not fit to have children, whether from disease, vice or imperfection, were informed as to how to prevent conception in a proper, hygienic way, then all classes of unfortunates would soon be no more."[12]

In the nineties, Benjamin O. Flower's *Arena* did much to publicize heredity and prenatal influence as social issues. In muted form, this journal brought to a wide readership some of the reform notions of the free lovers, such as sexual autonomy, radical sex education, and free expression, but it became, ironically, an early platform for state eugenicists, who would later become an important component of Progressive reform. As opposed to the anarchistic eugenics of the Lucifereans, this Progressive eugenics of the first decade of the twentieth century stressed positive governmental measures to rid society of the insane, criminal, and pauper elements. These reformers worked intensively for permanent custodial care for the feeble-minded and for sterilization of defectives. At the same time a significant portion of these eugenicists urged the "fit" to reproduce as much as possible in order that the "unfit" might be eliminated.[13]

Although Francis Galton served as the patriarch of the Progressive eugenic movement, the document that called Americans to action was the 1875 study of the Juke family, written by Richard Dugdale, a New York merchant whose avocation was the study of social problems. On a tour of jails for the Prison Association of New York, Dugdale found six members of one family in the same jail, and he decided to look further into their backgrounds. The study that emerged, *The Jukes: A Study in Crime, Pauperism, Disease, and Heredity,* revealed that of 709 Jukes and those married to Jukes in seven generations, only 22 had acquired property, 128 had been prostitutes, 91 had been of illegitimate parentage, 67 had had syphillis, 76 had been convicted of crime, and over 200 had received some sort of public'relief. The total cost in "social damage" he estimated at $1,308,000, which included imprisonment, relief, medical care, and other items.

As present-day writers have pointed out, many of Dugdale's sources were faulty by today's standards, and he had no data on Jukes who had escaped the wretched ancestral environment. But the apparently scientific approach of the study and the dramatic results it derived from a simple genealogical methodology made the study appealing. Dugdale's own conclusion to part 1 suggested the uses to which the study would be put. Recounting the amount of social damage caused by the lone family in a relatively short span (without reckoning, he wrote, either the cash paid for whiskey or the crime, pauperism, and mental and physical disease caused to future generations), "it is getting to be time to ask, do our courts, our laws, our alms-houses and our jails deal with the question presented?"[14]

Dugdale did not, however, see heredity as the exclusive cause for the ills he chronicled; he carefully suggested that both hereditary and environmental elements worked upon the Jukes, and he labeled his important conclusions as tentative. His readers were not so careful. They misinterpreted the study as proof that crime, pauperism, and degeneracy were primarily problems of heredity. Other researchers turned out more studies of the ancestral type, proclaiming to corroborate the hereditarianism that, in fact, Dugdale did not assert. Those who read a eugenic "solution" into the study used it first to create a myth of the feeble-minded and then as a weapon to eradicate that element.[15] They saw prescriptive eugenics as an easy, economical, and encompassing social solution that could be effected with little threat to worthy elements of society, which, of course, contained the eugenicists. Put in other terms, this eugenics provided an apparent method for a conservative elite to adjust social problems without adjusting social conditions. From John Humphrey Noyes to William Shockley, this aspect of American eugenics has been a disturbing specter, which is profoundly at odds with democratic and equalitarian thought.

In the late eighties, anarchistic eugenics came to play a central role in the reform scheme of *Lucifer*'s editor. Commenting favorably upon the eugenical consciousness displayed by the International Woman's Council meeting in Washington in 1888, he observed that women were slowly coming to see that "the only rational hope for human improvement, and for the abolition of vice, crime, pauperism and misery, is through better conditions of heredity and maternity and that superlatively the most important of these conditions is the self-ownership of woman." Harman now affirmed that the right to be born well, free from avoidable physical or mental handicaps, was the most basic and transcendent of all rights. In the fall of 1889 he published a manifesto, "*Lucifer*'s Object," that called specifically for a revolution in the laws and customs of sex relations. Indeed *Lucifer*'s platform for the past three years—basic sex education, contraception, eugenics, sexual autonomy (free love, free marriage, free divorce, free motherhood)

—did have radical implications for American culture and politics. Long before Rosa Luxemburg and Margaret Sanger would do so, Harman saw the political potential of sex as he urged that birth control be used as a weapon against capitalism:

It matters little to the Parasitic Classes . . . what reforms are agitated so long as the supply of mental and moral *Imbeciles* is not cut off! And just so long as our present laws and customs in regard to Woman's Rights in the Sex-Relation remain in tact, just so long will the vast majority of children be born mental and moral imbeciles—fit for nothing else than to be ruled and exploited by the cunning, the capable, the narrowly selfish few.[16]

Readers of *Lucifer* on both ends of the spectrum dissented from Harman's special hereditarian views. The anarchist Voltairine de Cleyre and the sisters Lizzie M. Holmes and Lillie D. White insisted that reformers should focus on economic and social conditions rather than blame the victims of those conditions for some unclear hereditary deficiencies. Who really knew anything about how heredity or prenatal influence affected socialization? they asked; in practice, nothing conclusive enough to base a whole reform scheme upon had been discovered. White ridiculed Harman's notions that an ill-shaped head revealed a hereditary defect that would be reflected in crime or pauperism. "I have a good-shaped head and was well born [in Harman's terms]," she wrote, yet, "I feel myself very closely related to this hungry fellow in spite of his bad-shaped head, for I am nearly in the same fix"—she had no property, no land, and not "a week's security this side of starvation or his condition," she declared. She also questioned the bedrock assumptions of Harman's feminist eugenics:

But what is the process, what the conditions necessary for the well-born child? Mr. Harman talks of free motherhood, free women, free choice of fathers, and repeatedly quotes Ingersoll, "Woman the owner, the mistress of herself"—all of which I endorse, for I do not believe in the ownership or tyranny of any person over another—but is it "the solution of the whole question"? Is woman herself so powerful, so good, so scientific, so wise that she needs only to be let alone to produce perfect beings who cannot be made victims of the conspiracies of the ruling classes?[17]

On the other side of these critics and of Harman also, Joseph

Rodes Buchanan espoused race culture through widespread castration. Citing the Jukes study and believing in such concepts as "hereditary burglars," this forerunner of Progressive eugenics insisted that "castration is the supreme remedy for a diseased and bestialized race." Applied to criminals to begin with, it would become an adjunct to his "New Education" theories of practical and industrial training which made him well known to *Arena* readers and to educators. "But even with the New Education the surgeon's knife would be its most powerful aid and carry it still higher," he asserted. "What would our vineyards and orchards be without pruning?" He believed that the higher faculties of the mind—reverence, love, justice—were antagonized and, in weaker persons, overcome by the lower faculties of amativeness or animality. Those who exhibited the lower tendencies—such as rapists, other criminals, and paupers—could have the higher faculties enforced by disarming the lower faculties through castration.

As acting editor of *Lucifer,* Lillian Harman printed Buchanan's contribution but disclaimed it, reminding readers that suppression and mutilation were as ineffectual in literature as they were in the treatment of the criminal classes. She could not resist chiding Buchanan for his simple-minded correlation of crime with unfitness. After all, she, William Lloyd Garrison, Jr., and others were the offspring of apparently "habitual" criminals. George E. Macdonald of the *Truth Seeker* wrote a brilliant rejoinder, which demolished in most conceivable ways Buchanan's frightening propositions. Speaking for the majority of Lucifereans, he concluded that "congenital criminals have not as much to do with retarding the improvement of the race as that more influential class of offenders against mankind who pass laws and establish customs, and prescribe penalties for their violation."[18]

For one who saw progress in terms of individual amelioration rather than in governmental solutions, Harman's emerging position was consistent. Although he later tempered his extreme hereditarianism with the belief that early environment also affected the child, his eugenics revealed a deepening cynicism toward political solutions of social problems, a departure for the former abolitionist, radical Republican, Liberal Leaguer, and anarchist. Believing that progress could be determined by the advancement in individual freedom, Harman had at first been intensely attracted by the myth of individual freedom in the United States. Yet the American experiment, for all the rhetoric and good intentions of Paine or Jefferson, had to him obviously failed: he faced persecution, he believed, because he tried to be free and tried to help others to be free. If the United States represented, in terms of freedom, the highest attainment of organized government on earth, then surely politics could not be depended upon to bring man to his destiny of freedom. At least such a speculation seems to be a likely way to explain how Harman arrived at his eugenic "solution" for reforming society.

Concerned radically with individual choice, theories of free love and free motherhood naturally raised the issue of contraception. For feminist and eugenic reasons, sex radicals tried to make existing knowledge about birth control available to the public. Emma Goldman wrote that "neither my birth-control discussion nor Margaret Sanger's efforts were pioneer work. The trail was blazed in the United States by the grand old fighter Moses Harman, his daughter Lillian, Ezra Heywood, Dr. Foote and his son, E. C. Walker, and their collaborators of a previous generation."

The latest argument for contraception (and eugenics) in the eighties, E. B. Foote, Jr.'s, *Radical Remedy in Social Science* (1886), offered no improvement in technique over Robert Dale Owen's *Moral Physiology* (1830) or Charles Knowlton's *Fruits of Philosophy* (1832). Most of *Lucifer*'s readers knew that Owen's crude prescriptions could be fairly effective—withdrawal of the penis from the vagina before emission, use of a skin sheath for the penis, and the use of a vaginal sponge. Later editions of the work, however, omitted the last two methods. In a more thorough approach than Owen's, Knowlton recommended douching with various solutions as the best method of contraception. The contributions of Owen and Knowlton did not represent new scientific advances in the field but only publicized certain traditional methods. Recent scholarship suggests that these methods, particularly vaginal douching as described by Knowlton, were increasingly used in the nineteenth century among the middle and upper social strata. The thousands of "immoral" rubber articles confiscated by Anthony Comstock between 1873 and 1888 denoted the significant demand for contraceptives.[19]

Prevailing ignorance about contraception, however, compounded by Comstock statutes outlawing birth-control items and ideas, and Comstockish linguistics which regarded, for instance, a condom as an instrument of abortion, forced contraception to take on the aspects of an occult science. Quack remedies and ideas thrived. Poignant cries for relief from the despotism of nature prompted experiments based on little more than blind hope. One mother of five sounded just the right chord of desperation and propaganda for the *Lucifer* radicals. Overworked and married to a farmer who would not control his "lusts," she became frantic when she learned that she was pregnant again. She ran off into the countryside and by dangerous means aborted the fetus. "I know I am dreadful wicked," she wrote, "but I am sure to be in the condition again from which I risked my life to get free, and I cannot stand it. . . . How long will we poor wives have to bear so much? Is there no redress for us? Do you know any appliance that will prevent conception? I have heard of such things. If there is anything reliable you will save my life by telling me of it."[20]

Even mighty vice-fighters were directly involved in birth-control quackery. The "Colgate prescription case"—an anti-Comstock coup of the type that had supremely delighted D. M. Bennett— featured the famous soap magnate and president of the Society for Suppression of Vice, Samuel Colgate, as a promoter of contraceptives. Colgate's company, which was the agent for a product of the Cheeseborough Manufacturing Co.—Vaseline—began a promotion campaign for the petroleum jelly in 1878. In a pamphlet extolling the many uses of the product, one doctor's testimonial supplied the (erroneous) information "that Vaseline, charged with four or five grains of salicylic acid," made a satisfactory contraceptive agent. D. M. Bennett's *Truth Seeker* and *Dr. Foote's Health Monthly* ventilated the faux pas and energetically set about to undo the president of the Vice Society. The evidence for Colgate's promotion of contraceptives was even presented to President Hayes by Robert Ingersoll. Hasty withdrawal of the pamphlet and a plea of ignorance of its content cleared the blot on Colgate and the Vice Society, however.[21]

Another canard—which made the rounds and which *Lucifer*, with its marketplace-of-ideas approach toward discovering truth, reprinted—was something called the "Clough Circular." In a variation upon theories that electricity was the "vital force" and must therefore play a part in genesis, Clough asserted that conception could not occur unless the two sexes "connected in at least two places, thus allowing the electric current to make a complete circuit through the spinal column properly." This explained why people, birds, and animals sought to connect the top parts of their bodies as well as their reproductive organs in the act of intercourse. The lesson was simple: "If you do not want children keep your head away from your companion in sexual intercourse." Clough put forth his "Circular" expressly to "lengthen" sexual pleasure by allowing parents to control contraception.

Although *Lucifer's* national constituency barely noticed the "Circular," it sent shock waves through the Valley Falls area, which had only recently been jolted by "awful letters." The community was upset, it appeared, not because the information was erroneous—who would know for several months?—or outrageous to logic, but because it promised coition without toll. The crowning blow to the vigilant adult community was the sight of the *Lucifer* article in "the hands of the school children of Valley Falls."[22]

Besides eugenics, autonomy, and birth control, the Woman Question among the Lucifereans involved a particular analysis of woman's subjugation. Harman pointed out that the increasingly influential class analysis of social problems should be extended to include sex: woman should be viewed as an oppressed class much as the miner or factory worker. Of course, compared to men, women faced a physical handicap because they had to bear the burden of maternity, but such natural differences had been falsely extended to include a class denial (1) of a voice in making laws that governed her, (2) of the right to serve as judge or juror, (3) of the right to adopt rational dress, and (4) of the right to control "her own person, her sex-hood, her maternity."

In emphasizing the importance of the last item, Harman amended Robert Ingersoll's statement that woman merited all rights claimed by man, plus the additional right to be protected. Alert to the subtleties of exploitation, Harman suggested that a more just statement would be: "Woman is entitled to all the rights accorded to man, including the right *to protect herself against invasion by her so-called protectors.*" The parallels among chattel slavery, capitalist "wage slavery," and sex slavery were too obvious to Harman to be overlooked. The former abolitionist saw that the ignorance of the oppressed and the perversion of their natural aspirations in the interests of the master class were common to all of these relationships. Thus he asserted that "the most formidable difficulty lies in the apathy of woman herself. Besotted by countless generations of willing or enforced submission to the will of man[,] her slightest ambition is that she may have a good lord and master in the sex-relation. Man-made laws and customs, based upon and buttressed up by 'divine' laws, have made the sexhood of woman the property of man." Women themselves would have to play the central role in obtaining their own freedom; to do less—to allow men to assume the role of "liberator"—would only further the myth of woman's subservience to man; to be truly free, woman must free herself.

St. Paul's admonition to wives to "submit yourselves unto your own husbands" (Ephesians 5:22–24) not only illustrated woman's inferior place in Christian theology, but more importantly, it gave holy sanction to woman's subordination. Since marriage appeared to most women as preeminently a sacrament, the theological authority controlled to an extreme degree the other aspects of her life. Reiterating an earlier stand, Harman declared that as long as church teachings effectively controlled woman's moral education, just so long would woman refuse to protect herself and her children from the tyranny of her legal husband-master— whom she had taken forever for better or for worse. In the view of most *Lucifer* radicals, the church served as a prime enforcer and promoter of the sexual status quo, and thus it existed, together with the state, as a main agent of woman's enslavement. The right of woman to control her own person, Harman pointed out, was absolutely incompatible with the Christian view of wifely obedience.[23]

Harman excelled at pointing out subtle disabilities that men inflicted upon women. The trailing skirt, required dress for women, he termed a badge of immaturity. Men had made it a criminal offense for women to don the garments of maturity— short skirts or trouser-type clothing. Long dresses were a sort of swaddling clothes that played upon man's "protector" image of himself. Women's cumbersome dress, moreover, kept her limbs from vigorous exercise and thus perpetuated her weakness. "Man wants woman to be a timid, clinging, trustful, grateful creature.

He wants her to be the vine and he the oak that lifts her into sunshine and prosperity. Hence the most determined opposition to dress reform comes from men." Industry took advantage of this image of weakness in order to justify discrimination in jobs and wages. In practically every case, he pointed out, women received less wages than men for equal work. Again, psychological exploitation accompanied economic: those in positions of authority and those with particularly responsible jobs nearly always seemed to be the same self-perpetuating class—men.

The essential factor in the gross and subtle exploitation of women, the keystone of the whole structure of enslavement, in fact, was conventional marriage. In Harman's analysis, man had very cannily manipulated the unique child-bearing function of woman into a self-serving, exploitative relationship—marriage— "the most pitiable, most degrading of all dependencies." Man's law recognized no alternative to marriage for sex relations or childbirth. To be born outside the existent structure was to be, in fact, illegitimate. This seemed a particularly perverse manipulation of what Harman believed to be "the greatest want of woman . . . her greatest joy," that of maternity.[24]

The editor of *Lucifer* sought to heed his own doctrine that woman's liberation must be primarily her own doing. It was only through a series of events in 1889 that he resolved the disparity between his sex and his cause and found a viable place in the movement.

The columns of *Lucifer* had for some months been filled with a discussion of how often and under what conditions a man and woman should indulge in coitus. Alfred Cridge, a reform journalist from the San Francisco area, had begun the debate by attacking the idea of sexual asceticism, particularly the doctrine called Alphaism, which justified sexual intercourse only for the purpose of propagating children. Very quickly he drew the fire of several female writers in a debate which divided approximately along sexual lines, the women arguing the merits of continence and of exclusive sexual relations, while the men argued for indulgence and "varietism" of relations. Observing that he could publish only a portion of the letters that *Lucifer* received, Harman announced a policy "giv[ing] precedence to our lady contributors, compelling those of masculine persuasion to take back seats until the sisters and mothers could be heard."

"The sex question," he explained, "is pre-eminently woman's question," since she is the bearer of the natural result and burden of intercourse, children. She should be the final arbiter, then, on the questions of sex relations.[25] So saying, Harman devised his place in the movement: His *Lucifer* would not only be a medium for women's liberation, it would be a medium that gave priority to women contributors.

As the editor conscientiously attempted to rid himself of what one day would be termed "male chauvinism," he became increasingly aware of the anomaly of *Lucifer*'s being edited by a lone male. Moreover, since Lillian and Edwin Walker had left *Lucifer* to begin their own *Fair Play* in 1888, the heavy workload prompted Harman to look for a coeditor, preferably female. Harman sent a circular letter to friends, asking advice on the matter of a new editor and seeking names of likely candidates. He also sought suggestions about the future direction of *Lucifer*.

Of the responses published in *Lucifer*, most favored the idea of a woman editor. Juliet Severance of Milwaukee—a prominent physician, sex reformer, and radical feminist who was well known to *Lucifer* readers—received most mention as candidate for coeditor. Lucinda Chandler, who was a Christian socialist and reform author, Lois Waisbrooker, Celia B. Whitehead, and Elmina Slenker were also mentioned.[26]

Of some sixteen letters of advice about the matter printed in *Lucifer*, five were from women. Three of them favored a woman coeditor, and one, Celia B. Whitehead, perhaps out of modesty, opposed. Of the eleven male responses published, five opposed and five favored the idea. W. G. Markland, sender of the "Markland letter" three years earlier, most strongly favored a woman coeditor, specifically Lois Waisbrooker. "I think the appeal and arguments [of *Lucifer*] should be largely directed to the common people," he wrote. "Eminent scholarship is too frigid, selfish, unemotional. . . . There is a contagious disease among reform papers—'Respectability.' *Lucifer* has no symptoms yet, therefore I love it. Don't call a 'respectable' woman to your aid."

On the other hand, the advice of Edward W. Chamberlain, the New York free-thought lawyer who had successfully defended

Elmina Slenker in her recent obscenity trial, provided the most extreme opposing view. Other negative replies had been on the order of "paddle your own canoe," with no blatant antiwoman attitudes apparent. Chamberlain, however, advised: *"By No Means.* You can get all the earnest women you want without admitting to association as editors. Do you *hold the reins yourself.* ... The trouble is that many of these earnest women lack tact and management and policy and that kind of discretion which is needful to have." He suggested that *Lucifer* continue merely to print their articles.[27]

In early January 1890, Harman announced that current financial difficulties had necessitated postponement of the contemplated changes in *Lucifer*. Women would eventually edit *Lucifer*—Lois Waisbrooker, Lillie D. White, and Lillian Harman—but not until Harman's imprisonments.

In upholding the cause of women's liberation, the editor of *Lucifer* confronted other distinct problems. If he supported women in all their efforts for rights, particularly those of voting and office holding, then as an anarchist he would be working for goals that theoretically he considered irrelevant. He believed that ballots for women would not solve their fundamental problems, yet in the case of woman suffrage, he resolved his logical difficulty by arguing that females should enjoy the same chances that males did to work with existing governing tools, however inferior. He did not require liberated women to be anarchists, and in fact he professed respect for woman suffragists, particularly such feminists as Elizabeth Cady Stanton, even though he regarded their analyses as superficial. To him the injustice of the legal system was particularly glaring, perhaps because he suffered personally at its hands as he sought to challenge the laws. A man may have a jury of his peers, but a woman was forced to accept a jury of men; "the judge who passes sentence upon a woman culprit is always a *man!*" Neither ballots nor bullets, he sloganized, should be denied woman in her struggle for self-protection.[28]

But when the problem appeared in practical, specific terms Harman had an interesting response. In 1889, when the women of Valley Falls put up an all-female slate for municipal offices, Harman explained why he did not support the women's ticket.

The votes of women as demonstrated in Kansas, he argued, meant votes for prohibition and for increased power to the Church element. The WCTU, which Harman early criticized in the *Valley Falls Liberal*, appeared to him to be a particularly insidious organization. The Victorian female, as a repository of moral and Christian virtues, was nothing if not dangerous with the vote: "When we remember the well-known power of the clergy over the average woman, especially over the women who have enrolled themselves under the banner of the 'Woman's Christian Temperance Union,' we may well tremble for the immediate results of putting civil and political power in the hands of women."

The already potent force of the clergy in American politics would be strengthened to overwhelming proportions with the aid of women's votes, Harman felt. On a strictly local level, Harman noted that part of the platform of the women's ticket included a promise to "clean out" a local pastime club and then do the same to *Lucifer*. However, the women lost the election.[29]

Lucifer's editor chose not to dwell upon the problem of anti-*Lucifer* woman-suffragists. Harman's own opposition to voting, in fact, only dated from the anarchistic influence of Edwin Walker, who served as assistant editor of *Lucifer* from 1883 to 1887. As Harman and Walker became estranged in 1887, Harman became increasingly influenced by pre-Populist reform schemes which were attracting interest throughout the Midwest. Usually socialistic in some degree and advocating monetary reform and direct democracy in the interest of the farmer and the workingman, the groups went under the aegis of older organizations such as the Greenback party, or they formed new organizations such as the Union Labor party.

The lectures of Moses Hull—a veteran Greenbacker, influential spiritualist, and one-time crusading free lover—seemed to sway Harman on the voting issue at this time. Before his Greenback days, Hull had aided in the formation of the Equal Rights party of Victoria Woodhull and Stephen Pearl Andrews, which, in 1872, ran Woodhull as the first woman candidate for president. Hull placed the name of Frederick Douglass, the black abolitionist, in nomination for the party's vice-presidential slot. "We have had the oppressed sex represented by Woodhull, we must have the oppressed race represented by Douglass," announced Hull at the time. In the 1880s Hull had moved to the Midwest, where he continued to lecture on political reform and spiritualist topics and to publish his perennial journal, then called *New Thought*. He lived in Iowa for most of the eighties, and during that period he worked in the campaigns of the well-known Greenback Democrat congressman James B. Weaver. In the fall of 1887 Hull lectured in Kansas at enthusiastic rallies of the Union Labor party. After one such meeting in Wellington, he came to Valley Falls for a series of lectures.[30]

Hull preached a message of direct democracy as a cure for the ills of a corrupted society. According to his analysis, America had never been governed democratically; it had been a scantily disguised oligarchy from the outset. He offered several reform proposals, notably the abolition of obstructive political forms such as caucuses, nominating conventions, and law-making bodies. The people, he suggested, should directly propose and vote on issues and laws, with the House serving only as a recommending body. The Senate and all other appointive posts should be abolished, all officers of the government being directly elected. The presidency, not being necessary, should likewise be abolished.

Hull's programs intrigued *Lucifer*'s editor enough that the reform liberal in him overcame the anarchist. By voting on issues that would eliminate the despotic features of society, Harman reasoned, even the anarchist could support such "ballot-box" reform. He felt that although anarchistic demands for the abolition of governmental compulsion were just, most people would not accede to these demands. Meanwhile one could work through the ballot for the practical goal of eliminating *some* despotisms.[31]

Immediately, Walker called his senior editor to task for advocating such patchwork methods of reform. Pointing out that anarchists must direct people to a condition of autonomy rather than follow a majority, he faulted Harman for seeking reforms in law-making instead of advocating repeals of laws. The elimination of formal coercive governments, Walker stressed, would give rise to private noncoercive associations, while the advent of direct democracy would simply mean that the will of an ignorant majority would replace that of the present privileged minority.[32]

Though he shared Walker's elitism and had few illusions about the ability of the masses to govern themselves well, Harman nevertheless saw the problem in different terms than Walker did. At this period of his development, Harman was willing to gamble that man had progressed further than Walker believed he had; he could now begin to vote himself to freedom.

The conflict raged in the pages of *Lucifer*. Walker met head-on Harman's arguments that "ballot-boxism" served as a necessary crutch which could only slowly be discarded: "So long as the existing governmental machine is running, all who take a hand in operating it [by voting] *are enemies of the 'let-alone' principle* . . . voting for repeal is a tacit admission of the right of the majority to decide how much of the citizen's private concerns shall be under the control of said majority."

Walker cited the methods of reform that he thought they had both agreed upon: passive resistance to invasion, abstention from voting, and association for business and other purposes outside the state. The question finally developed of whether Harman had in the past regarded voting as he did now—as "distinctly and emphatically . . . one of the best methods of repeal." This argument on former positions began to have its hollow aspects, particularly since neither party claimed a great deal of respect for dogmatism. After five issues the editors dropped the argument.[33]

As a demonstration of some classical ironies within anarchism, the debate was of special interest, since it occurred as four of the famous Chicago Seven "anarchists" faced execution. *Lucifer* had devoted much space to the trial and to a critique of the Chicago police and the Chicago legal methods. Both Harman and Walker believed that the Seven were being punished for their unpopular socialist and free-thought ideas. Continued harassment and cruelty on the part of the Chicago police had spawned the protest meeting in Haymarket Square in the first place, and the subsequent case involving the Seven in bombing had been constructed, so it appeared to *Lucifer,* on specious evidence. "Four men were hung . . . for exercising their equal right of free speech. . . . The oligarchy can say what it pleases—they do and did counsel lawless violence and their paid retainers have often committed acts of lawless violence, and yet they go unpunished. . . . Freedom of speech is only for the oligarchy and their servants."[34]

While arguing for the absolute right to advocate such a position, *Lucifer* refused to endorse the violent methods of redress that were espoused by the Haymarket radicals. Its editors felt that conditions did not justify revolutionary violence, although the action of the Chicago police symbolized to *Lucifer* the increasing level of governmental violence toward citizens. *Lucifer* did not condemn force itself, but rather it defended the right of self-defense as necessary and absolute, especially against the police and other "public servants." But passive resistance, as a program for change, should be used so long as it remained practicable. When the freedom of dissent disappeared, it would then "be time to consider the expediency of meeting force with force."[35]

Walker and Harman both took pains to distinguish *Lucifer*'s anarchism from what they termed the "socialism" of the Chicago Seven. Walker, claiming solidarity with the general goals of the Chicago group in working for "labor's emancipation from ignorance, fear, authority and want," nevertheless could not fully support the ideology of the Chicago radicals because of its acceptance of state socialism. Yet the immediate duty in 1887, he felt, was not to split ideological hairs but to save the Seven from the hands of a wrathful state.[36]

Lucifer criticized the generally biased and slanted press coverage of the Haymarket affair, and it sought to publish the most objective accounts available. One of the best of these contemporary accounts—"Was It a Fair Trial? An Appeal to the Governor of Illinois" by Gen. M. M. Trumbull—appeared serially in *Lucifer*. Trumbull, a man with conventionally impressive credentials, hardly supported violent revolutionary ideology, but he was aghast at the mockery of justice that his close study of the trials revealed.[37]

In the issue of *Lucifer* memorializing the death of the five Haymarket prisoners, Walker resolved, as best he could, the argument with Harman on methods and voting. In view of the overwhelming catastrophe in Chicago, Walker admitted that he did not have the heart to continue the debate. In such times as this, he reflected, differences should be minimized and a "united phalanx toward the common enemy" should be presented.[38]

The following spring, Walker and his wife Lillian would launch their own journal, *Fair Play*. The conflict with Harman perhaps hastened such a move.

The years 1887 and 1888 were years of drouth and depression in Kansas, and the prevailing unrest encouraged a surge of Populist reform spirit which extended well into the nineties. This same unrest, however, gave rise to fear of extreme solutions, particularly among those in established positions of power, and to the consequent valuing of order over justice. The prospect of social upheaval, however, could be exploited and distorted to the benefit of those who sought no change. Panicky cries of "anarchism!" could help to obscure real problems whose solutions might require radical changes in the makeup of institutions.

In such a charged atmosphere as this, the issue of anarchism and violence raised by the Haymarket affair lived on in Kansas. As the 1888 election approached, antianarchist feelings agitated the eastern portion of the state. A diatribe against the *Lucifer* group constituted the main oration at Memorial Day services that year in Valley Falls. L. H. Gest, a former GAR post commander, launched a predictable list of criticisms against anarchists. Asserting that the "anarchical demon" was a foreign influence that America had no place for, he howled at home-grown *Lucifer*: "Government is wrong, laws are wrong, marriage is wrong, all is wrong [to the anarchists]." The crowd, Harman reported, showered the speaker with applause. The oratory of 4 July 1888 aimed with a particular fury at the anarchist "threat." At the Valley Falls ceremonies, a prominent Republican lawyer delivered the featured address. Directing his remarks to the young people present, he urged violent handling of all anarchists and other such traitors.[39]

The antianarchist unrest burgeoned into a full-blown panic in the autumn days before the election of 1888. A catalyzing Red scare, involving some reform editors, bomb explosions, and political conspiracy, gave rise to a hysteria which, in *Lucifer*'s view, rivaled that of the Civil War or of the Haymarket "Red scare." Although anarchism figured in the case only as a broad smear term, what occurred did demonstrate the popular identification of the terms with bombs, confusion, organized labor, conspiracy, and social change. Moreover, real-life anarchists, such as the well-known *Lucifer* editors, were not even involved. "Anarchism" seemed to have been injected into the affair because a prolabor paper named in the conspiracy accusations had once been sympathetic to the Haymarket radicals.[40]

The *Winfield* (Kans.) *Daily Courier,* a Republican paper edited by Edwin Greer, published exposés in October charging that the secret and paramilitary National Order of Videttes controlled the Union Labor party, a fresh reform party that was hopeful of its chances in the coming elections. Released simultaneously a few weeks before election to all the Republican papers in the state, the sensational *Courier* reports implicated, among others, the Vincent brothers, editors of the strongly prolabor *American Non-Conformist,* which was also published at Winfield. The crusading Vincents —Henry, Leo, and Cuthbert—urged that the Knights of Labor increase their involvement in radical politics and promoted a many-planked "Voice of the Farmer" platform, which was aimed at redistributing the benefits of capitalism from the hands of a corporate minority to those of the farmer and laborer.[41]

The Videttes of Greer's exposé were indeed a strange group; even a judiciously written account of their secret society would have raised some suspicions. A lurid account, however, presented in the atmosphere of the nation's first Red scare could, assuredly, raise irrational fears. Greer's exposés consisted of presumably authentic documentary materials larded with inflammatory interpretations of the Videttes as a revolutionary, anarchistic, and treasonable organization whose leaders had direct links to the Haymarket "anarchists."[42]

According to standard accounts, the National Order of Videttes began at the Union Labor party's national organization meeting in Cincinnati on 22 February 1887. The party itself, evidence suggests, came about as urban labor attempted to rescue itself after the discredit of the Haymarket affair.[43] A party of discontent, it attracted a variety of members ranging from the merely peeved to the militantly radical. Its platforms gave primary emphasis to opposing usury, monopoly, and trusts. Among other reforms, it urged a "national monetary system in the interest of the producer," free silver, a postal savings bank, and nationalization of communication and transportation systems; in addition it picked up the 1880 Greenback demand for a graduated income tax. The party's demands substantially foreshadowed the reform-party platforms of the next decade, while displaying the influence of such forerunners as the Prohibition, Greenback, and Antimonopoly parties.[44]

The short-lived party scored substantial victories, particularly in Chicago and Milwaukee, before internal dissension dissolved it in 1889. On the Kansas level, the 1888 Union Labor platform backed off from a nearly-proposed single-tax platform to advocate a thirteen-point program broadly aimed at helping the working man. It found its chief support among the farmers of Kansas, particularly those in the southern part of the state. Campaign rhetoric of all political parties in that depression year dealt with questions of mortgage, interest, and other monetary reforms.[45]

Apparently without the knowledge of the party rank and file, from the outset the Videttes programmed and controlled the Union Labor party, both on the national level and in Kansas. The Vidette organization, a combination of national-guard militarism and fraternal hocus-pocus, required members to swear a secret oath of absolute obedience. Organized as a military hierarchy, its ritual and constitution were in code. Only white men of superior intelligence who were not worth over $100,000 and who believed in God could join the Videttes.

The Kansas Videttes met as Brigade No. 34 in March 1888 at Yates Center to map a secret strategy for political victory. It directed thirteen members to infiltrate all other state parties and to work for the nominations of fellow Videttes. If this proved impossible, then the conspirators pledged "to work for the worst stick the party has, and thus weaken the party." In the Union Labor party, on the other hand, strategy called for the nomination of the best man, whether a fellow Vidette or not. At this meeting the Vincent brothers of Winfield, who were deeply involved in Vidette affairs, were chosen as the publishing house for the organization.[46]

The day before the state convention of the Union Labor party in August, the Kansas Videttes met at the convention site at Wichita and completed the party's platform. They allowed the rank and file to submit planks the next day, but under a Vidette management that protected the platform from substantial change. The Videttes controlled the state Union Labor party, but this did not necessarily make them powerful in state politics. Union Labor had yet to demonstrate a wide appeal.

After Greer's initial exposé the Republican State Central Committee met to consider the charge of conspiracy. From this meeting came the decision to have all Kansas Republican papers simultaneously feature the exposé. This lent credence to the charge that the Republicans had concocted the whole affair—a charge that, according to *Lucifer,* was widely accepted in the non-Republican state press. Although *Lucifer* reprinted several articles that were critical of the Republicans, it did not become directly involved in the fray.

The second and more comprehensive installment of Greer's revelations appeared on 18 October 1888, connecting the Vidette leadership—chief among them the Vincent clan—directly with the Chicago anarchists and painting a lurid picture of a violent Vidette revolutionary conspiracy. On the same day that this article appeared, a bomb disguised as an express parcel exploded while in the keeping of the express agent at Coffeyville. The agent escaped injury, but the explosion severely wounded his wife and daughter.

The parcel bore the address "L. Louden, Winfield, Kansas," from "P. Jason"—both apparently fictitious names. Accusations flew in all directions: some interpreted it as a deed of anarchist terror; others believed that the bomb had been meant for the Vincents at the *Non-Conformist.* Vidette sources identified P. Jason as C. A. Henrie, a printer for the Vincents who had helped to prepare an edition of the Vidette ritual and who had then given the documents to the Republicans. None of this was ever proved, and the bombing remained an unsolved mystery. *Lucifer* cautiously suggested that the explosion had been planned in order to discredit the Vincents and the whole of the Union Labor party, and it recommended the Vincent's "Dynamite Extra" edition of the *Non-Conformist* to those seeking more information.[47]

When several candidates of the People's party won election to the Kansas House in 1890, they mounted, true to their campaign promises, a legislative investigation of the affair.[48] The state Union Labor forces had by that time fused with the People's (Populist) party, and the charges lodged by the Populists included one against the Republican State Central Committee for "conspiracy to destroy the property, reputation, and possibly . . . people, for political effect." They also charged the Republicans with having rewarded C. A. Henrie for his alleged part in the explosion by securing him a clerkship in the Bureau of Labor. A magnificent noninvestigation followed, carried out by a joint committee composed of four Populists and one Republican from the House, and two Republicans and one Democrat from the Senate. The "findings" consisted of further magnification of earlier party positions on the affair. The joint report failed even to determine whether a dynamite explosion had actually occurred. Three separate reports were filed by the committee, one for each party.

In the 1888 election, the Republicans won overwhelming victories. Many believed that neither anti–Union Labor sentiment nor a Red scare could account for such a landslide. *Lucifer* speculated that the "party lash" had kept rank and file members from voting for the reform tickets. As evidence of this, Harman reported that in one county precinct where Union Labor had 75 registered voters, one-half either stayed home or voted with the old parties on election day. He speculated that the total Union Labor vote would be only about one-fourth of the 100,000 expected by the Union Labor papers. The actual outcome of the governor's race gave the Republican candidate, Lyman U. Humphrey, 180,841 votes, while Democrat John A. Martin received 107,480 and Peter P. Elder for Union Labor received 35,837. The similarly reform-oriented Prohibition party, which had, like Union Labor, an enthusiastic and well-supported campaign, produced its usual very small showing. To the chagrin of radicals, the anarchist-conspiracy charges did not backlash against the Republicans as some papers had predicted—and hoped—that they would.[49]

The poor showing of the Union Labor party disappointed the sex radicals at *Lucifer*, as well as most other Kansas radicals, not necessarily because of support for the party but because the results signaled a reactionary swing in the state. The prolabor *Ottawa Journal and Triumph* offered a thoughtful explanation of the Republican sweep. It had argued that the Union Labor party drew its strength from the Republican party, which had once been the party of reform in Kansas. However, the reform-minded had deserted the party in such great numbers that many came to regard the Republican party as deeply eroded and weakened. The Democrats had exploited this idea; its editors and politicians "loudly boasted in every quarter of the State that the Democrats would carry Kansas because the U[nion] L[abor] party was making fearful inroads on the strength of the Republicans." Reacting to this alarm on election day, Laborites stayed with the Republicans, fearing that to vote the Union Labor ticket would allow the Democrats to get into power.[50]

In addition to providing rhetoric for election campaigns and excuses for suppressing radicals in Kansas, the Haymarket affair caused other repercussions in the Midwest heartland. James Culverwell, a farmer from Jewell County, Kansas, organized a "National Army of Rescue" for the purpose of liberating the three remaining Chicago radicals from the Joliet prison. Culverwell's scheme did not receive effective support, but his ideas attracted interest. Culverwell, a self-educated Londoner who had immigrated to the Kansas farmlands, was something of an instinctual anarchist. His *History of the National Army of Rescue* (1888) described both his attempt to organize a liberating army and the opposition that his group met from local officialdom and the press. Harman, considered by many as no minor crank himself, looked with a degree of wonderment upon this crusading hayseed revolutionary. Although Harman had little faith in Culverwell's program of change through mass public demonstration, he printed his contributions in *Lucifer* and offered his *History* for sale alongside the works of Bakunin, Proudhon, and George Drysdale.[51]

In the early 1890s, out-of-state editors who saw copies of *Lucifer* often assumed that the radical paper, published in Topeka, was an organ of populism. This misconception revealed more about national confusions surrounding populism than about *Lucifer*'s relationship to populism.

In June 1890, members of the Farmers' Alliance, Knights of Labor, Farmers' Mutual Benefit Association, Patrons of Husbandry, and some single taxers met in the Kansas capitol to form a new political organization known as the People's party. It took as its platform the essential demands of the 1889 St. Louis convention of Farmers' Alliances and labor groups. Its most significant planks called for nationalization of transportation and communication, inflationary financial policies, and restrictions on land ownership that were aimed at large corporations and aliens. The party, called among kinder terms the Populist party, grew in strength in the first two years of the decade until it unseated the entrenched Republican establishment of Kansas with the election of a Populist governor and a majority in the state Senate. Conflict over the makeup of the House culminated in the "Kansas statehouse war" of 1893, in which Populist and Republican representatives and armed troops of both sides took turns seizing Representative Hall from one another.[52]

Lucifer was at one with the Populists in its sympathies for the laboring classes, and its editor read the tenor of the movement correctly when he saw it as an attempt to enlist government in the cause of neglected economic elements for a change, rather than in the cause of industrialists, financiers, and big capitalists. But writing from prison at the time of the much-heralded inauguration of the "first People's party government on earth," he expressed little hope that the Populist prescription for reform through more laws—"governmentalism"—would bring man to a greater realization of his freedom, particularly since the nation's basic law, in practice, did not even provide for free speech in support of sex education and reform.[53] Although in a state so traditionally dominated by Republican politics as Kansas it was not surprising that the justice meted out to *Lucifer* by judges, prosecutors, and elected officials was largely Republican justice, there is little evidence that any other representative party in power would have acted differently toward *Lucifer*. Populists and sex radicals shared a common Republican opponent, but this did not make them allies. The 1891 case of Clarence Lee Swartz, who had edited *Lucifer* during part of Harman's first imprisonment the year before, seemed to prove to the libertarians of *Lucifer* that the People's party was as repressive as any other.

Swartz, who formerly edited *Voice of the People* in Kingman, Kansas, gained an exposure as interim editor of *Lucifer* that gave him a push upward into the national circles of radicalism and anarchism. He would eventually write a notable study of anarchist economics, *What is Mutualism* (1927), edit a collection of Benjamin Tucker's writings, publish his own periodicals, and write the definitive article on "Anarchism Communism" in W. D. P. Bliss and R. M. Binder's *New Encyclopedia of Social Reform* (1908). With a Populist House and a Republican Senate, the Kansas legislature in 1891 investigated the Coffeyville bombings, defeated woman-suffrage attempts, passed some reform bills, and also whisked through an anti-sensational-literature bill which made it a felony, punishable by from two to five years imprisonment, to publish or distribute a paper "devoted largely to the publication of scandals." The lawmakers carefully included a provision that extended the bill to include papers that were published out of state and then sent into Kansas. This lent credence to those who claimed that the bill was aimed specifically at a Kansas City, Missouri, paper called the *Sunday Sun*, which Clarence Lee Swartz distributed in Topeka.[54]

Advocating "Reform and the Exposure of Frauds and Hypocrites," the *Sunday Sun* delighted in embarrassing the high panjandrums, of whatever political persuasion, with stories about their scandalous drinking bouts and sexual carousing. It aimed its blend of scandal, satire, and drollery at a national audience, and it attracted some brilliant writers, as well as more than one lawsuit. The legislature's anti-sensational-literature bill received the overwhelming support of both Populists and Republicans, and when the bill passed into law, its first fruit was the arrest of Swartz for circulating the *Sun* in Topeka. Identified in newspaper accounts as a printer for "Harmon's paper known as *Lucifer*," Swartz was placed under $4,000 bond, which was subsequently lowered to $2,000; and he languished in jail for thirty-six days before raising bail. When the Kansas Supreme Court met to hear the case in October 1891, the county attorney failed to appear to prosecute, and the charges against Swartz had to be dropped. In a later test, the court ruled that the law was constitutional and valid.[55]

This case of newspaper suppression by legislative action aroused comment in the East, from the *New York Recorder*, from Ezra Heywood at *The Word*, and from Benjamin Tucker's *Liberty*. Edwin Walker, who in his regular column in *Liberty* had once called the People's party "more paternalistic, therefore more dangerous to liberty, than the Republican and Democratic parties," now saw the Swartz case as a portent of what the Populists would do if they won national power. He censured those who privately professed support for libertarian goals yet continued to work as "active hustlers for the People's Party, chaplain-fenced and Comstock-blessed!" Addressing the Populists Annie Diggs, Moses Hull, and others, he wrote: "I exhort you to separate yourselves from the unclean thing and come over to help us. Have you noted the banner under which you serve? It is the ominous black cross of sacerdotalism, stained and clotted with blood."[56]

The radicals surrounding *Lucifer* also faulted the People's party for its failure to unite behind the women's-rights issue, particularly the issue of suffrage. The Populist Speaker of the House, in fact, led the fight against suffrage in the 1891 session. Speaker Peter P. Elder, an ardent antifeminist, warned against the danger of "ambitious and designing women" who would exploit the franchise and by feminine trickery add to the corruption of politics while debasing the moral standards of the female sex; the vote "hurls women out from their central orb fixed by their Creator to an external place in the order of things," pronounced the Populist leader.[57]

The theological appeal of the 1890 state Populist platform also alienated the freethinkers of *Lucifer*. The preamble asserted that the People's party of Kansas recognized Almighty God as the rightful sovereign of nations, "from whom all just powers of government are derived, and to whose will all human enactments ought to conform." Other radicals in the *Lucifer* orbit generally were drawn to the Populist party to a greater or lesser degree, depending upon whether their affinities lay toward socialism or anarchism. In the state of New York in 1894, for instance, Dr. Edward Bliss Foote, an important sex reformer and supporter of *Lucifer*, ran for congress as a Populist, while the energetic Liberal Leaguer Thaddeus B. Wakeman sought election to the court of appeals on the ticket. *Lucifer*'s faithful attorneys, David Overmeyer and Gaspar C. Clemens, both identified with populism. An outstanding figure in Kansas' weak Democratic party, Overmeyer aided in fusion attempts in 1892, and later in the decade he campaigned for the Populist ticket. Clemens played an important role as a left-wing propagandist for the Populists, eventually leaving the party for the Socialists in 1897; and in 1900 he headed the Socialist ticket in Kansas.[58]

George Harman, less extreme in his politics than his father, Moses, helped to edit one of the first Populist papers in Kansas, the *Farmers' Vindicator* of Valley Falls. Its publisher, Noah Harman, was himself a farmer and a relative of *Lucifer*'s editor. In less than a year of operation the Republican "ring" in Jefferson County filed two libel suits against the paper. The famous Populist speaker Mary Elizabeth Lease took time to praise *Lucifer* feminist Lois Waisbrooker for her *A Sex Revolution* (1893), although Lease's inconsistent positions on women's rights did not show much lasting influence from Waisbrooker.

Waisbrooker did not herself profess populism, but she came out in support of some of its planks in her paper in June 1894. Comstock's western agent, R. W. McAfee, arrested her shortly thereafter for an "indecent" letter published in her paper, leading Waisbrooker to wonder if the resurgent Republicans were enforcing an anti-Populist strategy against her. Ben Henderson, the strongest woman-suffrage man in the People's party, undertook Waisbrooker's legal defense.[59]

During the 1893 inauguration of the Populist government in Kansas, Lillie D. White edited *Lucifer*. Known as a left-wing Populist, she showed more concern in *Lucifer* for radical reform within the home and family than for party politics. During her six months' tenure as editor, *Lucifer* demonstrated a level of intellectual engagement with the question of women's rights which it never achieved under Moses Harman's sloppy and martyristic style of editing. When Harman returned from prison in the spring of 1893, White left *Lucifer* to work in the extreme antifusion wing of populism that was led by Cyrus Corning. She continued to write on women in feminist and Populist journals.[60]

Although several radicals who identified with populism also identified with *Lucifer*'s sex reform, the mainstream press of the People's party had few good words for *Lucifer*. Annie L. Diggs, editorialist for the party's main paper, the *Topeka Advocate*, once coedited the *Kansas Liberal* with Moses Harman, but she gave no support to the sexual efforts of her former colleague. Shortly before Diggs signed on as full-time editor, the *Advocate* aimed some hard words at *Lucifer*. Its liberality on social questions notwithstanding, said the *Advocate*, it considered sex education a delicate matter, to be broached only "within the sacred precincts of the home." *Lucifer*'s "constant parade of obscenity in a publication designed for miscellaneous distribution among the people, in our opinion oversteps the bounds of educational necessity and propriety, and panders to the passions of the vulgar instead of improving the morals of the masses." From its agrarian pedestal, the *Advocate* concluded its judgment of *Lucifer*: "It partakes too much of the character of an exponent of the literature of the slums of society."[61]

In the half-decade of populism's ascendency, *Lucifer* gave the party a relatively good press when it noted it at all, but Moses Harman did not consider the party as a serious means for social, economic, or sexual revolution; it was merely another brand of reformism. Judging from the past, Harman wrote in 1894, the only good that new parties seemed to do was to eliminate the old parties; if after killing off the old parties, the Pops "would have the grace to quietly commit suicide and leave mankind to live each his or her own life on the plane of equal freedom, then we might be safe in saying that the right party has at last been found."[62]

Part 3
The Sex Radical Circle

10/ Comstock's Yokes

IN the early 1870s, as Anthony Comstock consolidated his censoring power through state and national legislation, a journal of extreme dissent appeared in Massachusetts. Called simply *The Word*, this paper was a forerunner of *Lucifer, the Light Bearer*. Published by Ezra Hervey Heywood with the assistance of his wife, Angela Tilton Heywood, the paper at first concerned itself mostly with the anarchistic labor-reform ideas of Ezra Heywood, but in the late 1870s the question of sexual reform came to dominate its pages. Although different in style from Harman's *Lucifer*, *The Word* focused with an uncommon directness on primary issues of sexual freedom, and this helped to pave the way for *Lucifer*'s efforts. *Lucifer*'s "awful letters" and its exposés of oro-genital sex, coming as they did near the end of Heywood's career, marked the passing of the vanguard's torch from Heywood to Harman. In its candid and occasionally hedonistic treatment of sexuality, *The Word* achieved a liberation from the Victorian ethos that neither *Lucifer* nor any other American reform periodical could match.

Born in 1829, Ezra Heywood spent most of his life in the village of Princeton, Massachusetts. His scholarly interests developed at Brown University, where in 1856 he received a Master of Arts degree and, the same year, entered the Divinity School. He planned a career as a Congregational minister, and he preached at several Rhode Island churches during the period 1855 to 1858, but the rampant reform spirit of the times finally led him away from his youthful religious and political orthodoxy. The writings of Theodore Parker convinced Heywood that he should leave the church and devote himself to social reform, while William Lloyd Garrison's influence steered him toward abolition.[1] Heywood first heard Garrison speak when he was a student at Brown; later, in February 1858, at Garrison's home in Boston, Heywood pledged his full-time efforts to the abolition of slavery, and gave up the ministry.[2]

But Heywood's introduction to radicalism had come, not from Garrison, but from a woman—Phebe Jackson—whom he had met at his boardinghouse table near Brown. Heywood described her as "an adult, Baptist, maiden-lady" and a girlfriend of Garrison's wife, Helen Benson. Their discussions, he wrote, influenced him "more than all the books and learned Professors in College. . . . Till then I was conservative; she made me a radical, gave me to read Garrison's *Liberator*, the 'craziest' newspaper of that day, started me on the line of Anti-slavery, Woman's Rights and Peace." Another woman, a grammar-school teacher who attended the Sunday School class that Heywood taught at the Broad Street Church in Providence, started Heywood on his free-love quest. Anne Whitney, "an interrogative young lady, put questions that 'God's Word' did not answer; among others, this:—'If Love worketh no ill, why does human law interfere to hinder its evolution?' " For several sessions they searched for the answer through the New Testament and their "mutual wits," Heywood remembered, and "the result was that, *then*, I became a Free Lover, theoretically."

Twenty years later, Heywood claimed, her question led him to write his inquiry into marriage, *Cupid's Yokes*. He visited Miss Whitney in 1887 and good-naturedly asked her if she realized that her inquisitiveness had ultimately caused his term in Dedham jail.

"Do you know what a horrid conservative *you* were then?" she retorted, referring to his Sunday School days. "One Sunday when I quoted Mr. Garrison you put on a long face and solemnly said 'such infidels as he ought not to be mentioned here.' "[3] The initial mid-century flowering of the American free-love movement had touched Heywood directly.

Heywood left Brown to become a traveling lecturer for the Massachusetts Anti-Slavery Society. He and a few other radical abolitionists such as Adin Ballou and Parker Pillsbury stood firm as pacifists when the specter of the Civil War appeared. In contrast, Garrison and most former "peace men" gave at least limited support to the war as a method of ending slavery. Severely critical of the war stance of such "occasional" nonresisters as William Graham Sumner and Wendell Phillips, Heywood felt a greater shock when Garrison compromised his earlier positions toward the government, the war, and the draft.

Recalling the war days from his prison cell in 1891, Heywood wrote Moses Harman:

After Wendell Phillips surrendered to war and subjugation, April 16, 1861, the first Sunday I got leave to preach in Music Hall, I confronted the breakneck, furious frenzy of martial violence, and urged peace, States-rights, liberty by evolution, rather than by the sword. The nub of my speech was this: "It is a graver crime to kill a man than it is to enslave him; if you kill him you take life *and liberty*; if you enslave him, you allow life with the possibility that he may throw you over, and regain his liberty."

Boston papers carried Heywood's speech, and Garrison, with characteristic generosity toward Heywood, planned to print the text in *Liberator*. But first he brought the proof to Heywood, "calling my attention," Heywood wrote, "to the above, the main point of the sermon." Garrison asked if Heywood had not better leave that statement out.

"Is it not true, Mr. Garrison?" queried Heywood.

"Yes, but I guess I would not say it now," said Garrison.

Heywood was crushed: "I was amazed, astounded; this man whom I had revered as a god had lost his faith in truth and in human nature to example it! I replied, 'You can leave out all the rest but the passage!'" The *Liberator* published the article intact.[4]

As the war progressed, so did Heywood's denunciation of it. In time he stood largely alone among wartime abolitionists in his extreme adherence to earlier "Garrisonian" principles. He likened the draft law to the fugitive-slave law and said that such state coercion, "plainly in conflict with the divine law," should be "disobeyed and trod under foot." Not only did he reprimand Garrison for his double standard of judging violence and coercion, he later went so far as to blame the war on abolitionists who had bent their principles so that slavery was ended by government coercion and military necessity rather than by principle. Garrison,

Sumner, and their followers had lost faith in human nature, had ceased to be men, and had become "only Abolitionists." They "let slip the dogs of internecine conflict, pretending that 'the end justifies the means,' that evil can be overcome by evil, and sacrificed a million men to the bloody Moloch of 'philanthropic' violence." The blacks may have been freed, Heywood wrote, but "we are all negro slaves now," coerced by a government whose powers were increased and centralized by the war.[5]

For his determined antiwar role during the civil strife, Henry Richard, secretary of the London Peace Society, called Heywood the bravest man in the American Union. In his history of pacifism, Merle Curti judged Heywood the "most uncompromising" pacifist abolitionist because of his bold and tightly reasoned writings in the *Liberator*.[6] Like Moses Harman, Ezra Heywood retained the spirit of extreme abolition all his life, and when the war ceased, he applied himself to other areas of social reform. His no-government principles had prepared a fertile field for the individual anarchist doctrines of Josiah Warren, whom Heywood first met in 1863. This timely encounter with the originator of American anarchism influenced the rest of Heywood's life.

In 1877, looking back over twenty years of reform work, Heywood catalogued his reform interests as "negro emancipation, peace, woman's enfranchisement, temperance, labor and love reform."[7] If this list closely followed the chronological development of Heywood's career, it also revealed the interrelated roots. The last item, "love reform," came to be the most spectacular cause that he espoused and the one that brought down on him official repression—that ticket to reformers' glory which none of his other causes had fully furnished him. At first he appeared not to seek actively after martyrdom, hoping instead to achieve change through the rational arguments contained in his writings. Having martyrdom thrust upon him, however, he showed a talent for exploiting the new strategy of reform. His very life became a demonstration of the contradictions of a "free" nation; his adversary Comstock was no abstract paradigm of the evils of government, but a living villain, one that could stimulate people as no logical exercise could—or so Heywood hoped.

The Heywoods, who were married in 1865, began monthly publication of *The Word* in 1872. They dedicated the journal equally to the "abolition of speculative income, of Woman's slavery, and the war government." The direction that *The Word* was to take, however, was portended in an 1873 pamphlet, *Uncivil Liberty*, written by Ezra with Angela's help. This tract called for woman suffrage and argued that political enfranchisement of women would lead to the social emancipation of both sexes. The Heywoods distributed eighty thousand copies of the pamphlet from their press in Princeton.[8]

The Heywoods attracted enough interested radicals for them to establish the Mountain Home in Princeton as a lodge for these kindred spirits. The New England Free Love League began there in 1873 as a companion organization of the anarchistic New England Labor Reform League, which Heywood had begun when he lived briefly in Worcester. The Free Love League, which provided an audience for speakers such as Victoria Woodhull and Lois Waisbrooker, borrowed a calendar page from the freethinkers' Era of Man chronology; they regarded the year of the founding of their free-love league as Year One of the Year of Love, or Y.L., as it came to appear on the masthead of *The Word*.[9]

Fittingly, Heywood served as principal in both the Labor Reform and the Free Love leagues. He viewed the two causes as inseparable "twin brothers." Labor reform, to Heywood, rested on Josiah Warren's theory of labor value, which held that the cost of production alone should determine the selling price of goods and services, and on Warren's doctrine that the individual should be absolutely sovereign over his own person, time, and property. Like Warren, he believed that individual sovereignty required an amount of private property, but only that amount which represented the product of one's own labor. Since labor was the determinant of value, nothing had any value in exchange unless it had a person's "service impressed upon it." Natural resources and land, therefore, should be freely and commonly available. Heywood sought "the extinction of interest, rent, dividends, and profit, except as they represent work done."[10]

Heywood extended Warren's theories to include a new critique of rent and a theory of "free money," and he considerably surpassed Warren in the extremity of his social radicalism. Warren objected to some of Heywood's strong language in his attacks on government and on land ownership, but Warren most strongly objected to Heywood's involvement in the sex question. Warren felt that raising the question of sexual freedom and women's rights would only confuse efforts toward arriving at an equitable economy.[11]

At "Social Freedom Conventions," such as the one called by Moses Hull and Mattie Sawyer in 1875, the Heywoods set out a clear record of what they meant by love reform. The Boston affair took place on February 28 and March 1; and according to participants' reports, it enjoyed the attendance of "large numbers and animated interest throughout." Boston papers responded predictably. "A feast of madness and a flow of filth," grumped the *Boston Globe*. "The concentrated essence of distilled nastiness," wailed the *Boston News*. "They lie," shot back Heywood at the journals. He and Moses Hull dominated the six sessions of the convention with their separate but supporting sets of resolutions.

Heywood told the assembled free lovers that just as he had once left the church to save his soul, he now had come to the convention to find Christ. ("Christ is not here but is expected this afternoon—" piped a voice from the audience. Free lovers, fond of contention, appreciated the confounding power of wit.) Heywood explained that he sought the spirit of love and justice contained in the example of Christ. "As a reformer, a philosopher, a medium, a free-lover, Jesus Christ is of some use," Heywood continued, "but as a God he is not a success." In a more serious vein, he offered his seven resolutions. To the Jeffersonian enumeration of inalienable rights he added "the liberty of the sexes to cohabit, for reproduction, health, economy, pleasure or other purposes they deem proper." This liberty preceded all governments and religions and hence all the man-made ordinances that limited "the natural right of people to make and dissolve their own sexual contracts in obedience to reason, love and the best interests of themselves and their offspring."

A primary cause of prostitution and "secret vice" (the nineteenth century euphemism for masturbation), he claimed, was the denial by society of these natural rights of sexual relationship. He called for repeal of all marriage laws, asserting that the "nobility of sexual love, individual health, social purity and harmony" would be promoted thereby. He took to task those cultured Christians who sought to keep woman in her restricted domestic sphere by the "insinuating assertion that girls and women cannot associate and do business with men without having sexual intercourse with them." Women deserved all the rights of activity that men had; only the lewdness inherent in "conventional" morality could create such a myth of woman's unfitness.

The purpose of the free-love movement, according to Heywood, was to apply to domestic life those principles of liberty that Americans theoretically enjoyed in the political and religious spheres. He believed, as many free lovers did not, that the franchise for women would abolish male supremacy in the family. All agreed that the larger problem of emancipation of both sexes would only come through abolition of the institution of marriage. Heywood concluded with an appeal to all progressive minds to unite in the assault upon the nemesis of labor- and love-reformers, the state. His indictment was broad: the state was "that fruitful source of incontinence, usurpation, disorder and war."[12]

Although Ezra Heywood's voice had spoken the resolutions, Angela Heywood had provided much of the inspiration. Had it not been for his wife, he perhaps would never have been at the convention at all. Early in their marriage, Angela had apparently awakened Ezra to the immensity of the social discrimination against women. The Heywoods' first feminist tract, *Uncivil Liberty*, argued for woman's moral superiority and for the primacy of natural law over civic law. If women had the vote, their inherent morality would cause humane and libertarian reformers to be voted into office; as things presently stood, woman had no duty to obey any civic laws, since she had not made them. Marriage came under attack as a major institution which could not stand the test of reason, since it thwarted individual liberty.

This criticism of institutional marriage eventually became the main thrust of the Heywoods' feminist efforts. *Cupid's Yokes*, first published in January 1876, represented the grand marshaling of their antimarriage arguments. Subtitled "The Binding Forces of Conjugal Life: An Essay to Consider Some Moral and Physiological Phases of Love and Marriage, Wherein Is Asserted the Natural Right and Necessity of Sexual Self-Government," the twenty-three-page essay had a wide distribution, variously estimated from fifty thousand to two hundred thousand. It played an important role in promoting sex radicalism, in disseminating information about birth control, and in writing obscenity laws.[13]

As an attempt to rationalize the sexual relations, *Cupid's Yokes* has few peers. Heywood and, to a lesser degree, other sex radicals sought to remove sexuality from the thrall of instinct and to bring it under the control of reason, and perhaps in the process to sterilize the messy business connected with human sexuality. "My object in writing *Cupid's Yokes*," Heywood once said, "was to promote discretion and purity in love by bringing sexuality within the domain of reason and moral obligation." Of course partisans of free love knew how to assume an air of superior morality in their assault upon convention, but for Heywood such assertions were more than merely tactical. He believed his ideas to be the consummation of Enlightenment; through Reason he uncovered the Natural Law that purified and reformed a last institutional holdout of error—marriage and the social relationship between the sexes.[14]

He wished to end the confusions surrounding the subject of free love; popular distortion had it that free love was unbridled licentiousness which sought to "open the flood-gates of passion and remove all barriers in its desolating course." But free love meant just the opposite, he proclaimed: "It means the expulsion of animalism, and the entrance of reason, knowledge, and continence." It meant freedom *from* personal invasion, not freedom *to* give reign to sexual instincts. "The sexual instinct shall no longer be a savage, uncontrollable usurper," he continued, "but be subject to thought and civilization."[15]

Heywood's free love rested upon an integrated view of the nature of love. Love, "this mingled sense of esteem, benevolence, and passional attraction," necessarily involved the sexual association of men and women. This association could not be factored into spiritual and physical, aesthetic and passional elements; it existed whole, and as a unity, it naturally strived for some sort of genital expression. By its nature, love could not be exclusive, since "a man cannot love even one woman truly unless he is free to love what is lovable in all other women," an idea that he seemed to have picked up from Austin Kent's *Free Love* (1857). In practice, however, love did create a "natural privacy" which separated a couple from the rest of the world; in fact, a lovers' union created a gestalt, "a collective third personality, superior, in some respects, to either constituent factor." This "mystical confluence" did not, however, excuse the lovers from acting according to reason. With reason controlling mystery, practical monogamists such as the Heywoods could be consistent free lovers.[16]

The true "bonds of affection," therefore, or "Cupid's yokes" should be substituted for the enslaving statutes of marriage. One should not worry about the effect of free love upon the social cement, since, after all, the strongest bond of social union was love. Moreover, altruism—"the impulse to defer self and partial interests to the welfare of being loved"—characterized the bonds of Cupid, while selfishness characterized institutional marriage.[17] To Heywood the dragon tamer, the institution of marriage was a cage that provisionally held uncivilized sex at bay. But by imprisoning the sexual appetite, men and women had only imprisoned themselves. This confinement perverted the sexual relationship since, to mollify the imprisoned ones, a concession of license within marriage had to be made.

But Heywood did not believe, as pietists did, that the sexual impulse was depraved, nor like some freethinkers, did he believe that it was uncontrollable; indeed both views had sheltered sex from the illumination of reason and from the jurisdiction of moral obligation. Consequently the subject of sex existed as "an Ethiopia, an unexplored tract of human experience." No doubt existed in Heywood's mind that the "lovers' exchange" in all its phases could be subjected to rational choice, "entered upon, or refrained from, as the mutual interests of both, or the separated good of either, requires." This notion reflected the continence doctrines of John Humphrey Noyes, whom Heywood cited in support of his theses, although Heywood rejected the sectarian and communistic elements in Noyes's work. While Noyes sought a practical integration of two "mysteries," the physical and spiritual heaven, *Cupid's Yokes* undertook the more earthly task of reforming present marriage, an institution that was imperfect and unfinished, "a device to be amended, or abolished, as enlightened moral sense may require."[18]

The struggle of reason versus passion occurred on every page of *Cupid's Yokes*. "In entering the ecstatic state of love," Heywood wrote, "we cannot, if we would, leave reason, or the inevitable sequences of cause and effect, behind." In practical terms this meant that partners should "not allow themselves to gravitate to the propagative limit" even during the "safe" nonovulatory period that he carefully outlined. If, however, intercourse escaped control and went on to climax, compensating punishments occurred, which seemed to please Heywood's mechanistic concept of reason: climactic sex "exhausts both persons, admonishing them to keep within the associative limit, which is highly invigorating." If the weak-willed failed to cultivate habits of continence, nature would crash the fools' paradise: "she confronts them with a child, which effectually tames and matures both parents."[19]

In his vision of controlled sex, nonclimactic intercourse between lovers would occur often and be unrepressed within its limits, thereby relieving pressures that led to incontinence. In contrast to the moral and spiritual inclinations of the female, Heywood saw priapism as the male's ruling impulse. Through intelligent love, however, man's passional heat would be transformed into a force that would make him a "genial, civil, and serviceable being." Later enlarged by Henry M. Parkhurst and Elmina Slenker into a theory called Dianaism, Heywood's vision of continence looked forward to a perfect application, when "a lady and gentleman can as innocently and properly occupy one room at night as they can now dine together."[20]

Rational sex would cure the common sexual abuses of masturbation, celibate abstinence, involuntary emission, and illicit intercourse or prostitution. One might expect Heywood to decry prostitution, with its attendant venereal hazards, as the most dangerous of these abuses, but he considered the first three abuses, in combination, to "engender more disease and death than all other causes combined." Celibacy, intentional or not, caused self-destruction and outright suicide, while masturbation and involuntary emission presented the greatest dangers of all; he spoke of their culminations as a "fatal drain." Illicit intercourse could be "extremely hurtful," but only because it was usually "undisciplined and excessive." Since Heywood believed that venereal diseases could be spread by casual kissing, he considered that prostitution presented no singular health danger.[21]

When free lovers such as Heywood spoke of the prostitution problem they primarily had in mind the "prostitution" of the wife in conventional marriage. In Heywood's particular analysis, the male-dominated profit system had reduced woman to a dependent socioeconomic position, so that she faced the choice of selling her labor at a very cheap rate or selling her body (for a night as a whore, for a lifetime as a wife) in exchange for the necessities of life. *Cupid's Yokes* proclaimed a link between the prevailing economic and sexual frustrations: "The usury system enables capitalists to control and consume property which they never earned, laborers being defrauded to an equal extent; this injustice creates intemperate and reckless desires in both classes." The remedy, then, seemed obvious: "But when power to accumulate property without work is abolished, the habits of industry, which both men and women must acquire, will promote sexual temperance." But the Heywoods did not believe that an economic revolution must necessarily precede the sexual one, indeed so interrelated were the "twin relics of barbarism"—the marriage system and the profit system—that to destroy one would be to destroy the other. Just as their doctrine of free love encompassed the liberation of woman from the dominance of man in society, so would free love liberate the wage slaves. The delight and morality of free love was only the gilding on this powerful lever for social change.[22]

The new society could not be realized without sex education. When one discovered the true relationship of the sexes, then, "ideas [would] rule and bodies obey the brain"; this true relationship could be discovered, he believed, in "principles of Nature derived from a careful study of essential liberty and equity." As things presently existed, systematic miseducation prevailed: "We were all trained in the school of repression, and taught that, to love otherwise than by established rules, is sinful." With other sexual libertarians, the Heywoods were outraged that Comstock legislation should block their attempts to find and broadcast sexual truths. This "established ignorance" particularly hurt young people in their innocence and their susceptibility to error.[23]

Sex education to Heywood meant more than the imparting of information about the reproductive organs. When young people became pubescent they normally faced four alternatives, all unsatisfactory and, to Heywood, all "abuses": illicit intercourse, "secret Vice," conventional marriage, or celibacy. More than mere physiology lessons and a sexual outlet, they needed the "education of sexual desire and expression," the rational control of will that only the practice of free love could offer. *Cupid's Yokes* did not elaborate on the practical problems of applying free-love and sex education to young people, but the task would later be approached in *The Word*.[24]

In a very underplayed way the pamphlet included some important and concrete items of birth-control information. This aspect of *Cupid's Yokes* was overshadowed at the time, however, by the resurgence of interest in the work of an earlier Massachusetts physician and pamphleteer, Charles Knowlton. His *Fruits of Philosophy*, published in 1832, remained obscure until 1877, the very year that the legal furor arose over *Cupid's Yokes*. Two English reformers, Charles Bradlaugh and Annie Besant, went on trial in that year for promoting the birth-control pamphlet. The trial caused immense publicity and wide distribution for *Fruits of Philosophy*.[25]

Heywood did not know of Knowlton's book at the time that he wrote *Cupid's Yokes*, although he did cite Robert Dale Owen's *Moral Physiology* (1831). On the larger problem of regulating and improving human offspring, the scholarly Heywood consulted, among others, John Stuart Mill, Charles Darwin, Francis Galton, R. T. Trall, John Humphrey Noyes, Diocletian Lewis, Thomas L. Nichols, and George Drysdale. Heywood believed that economic, medical, and eugenic reasons required that married people be aware of contraceptive methods; he personally advocated male continence and what would today be called the rhythm method, and he explained how one could determine the safe period of intercourse.

George Drysdale's ideas on birth-control practices influenced Heywood greatly, and he eventually offered a vaginal-douche syringe for sale in his literature. Heywood disapproved of condoms and coitus interruptus as being "injurious," "disgusting," and "unnatural" contraceptive methods—an opinion adapted from Drysdale's *Elements of Social Science* (1854)—but in a footnote quotation from Drysdale he informed the readers of *Cupid's Yokes* about the practices:

Various unnatural means are employed to prevent the seminal fluid from entering the womb, thus preventing the union of the sperm and germ cell which is the essential part of impregnation; among these means are withdrawal before emission; the use of safes, or sheathes; the introduction of a piece of sponge so as to guard the mouth of the womb, and the injection of tepid water into the vagina immediately after coition. But these methods, except the latter, are injurious and disgusting.

In a later edition of his book, Drysdale sanctioned both douching and the vaginal sponge.[26]

Comstock could hardly allow such an affront to proper sensibilities and to the federal regulations that he had helped to institute. Under the false name of E. Edgewell, Squan Village, New Jersey, Comstock dispatched decoy letters to Heywood, requesting a copy of *Cupid's Yokes*. Ironically, In October 1877 Heywood printed as genuine one of the letters from "Edgewell" in *The Word*: "Press on [Comstock wrote] as you are going, and be sure in the end justice will be done you. It is a long lane that has no turn. You have labored hard, but many eyes have followed your efforts."

Comstock's double meaning became all too clear when, on a blustery Boston night in early November, the vice hound from New York surprised Heywood backstage at a convention of the New England Free Love Society. Heywood, chairman of the meeting, had gone backstage temporarily as his wife, Angela, held forth at the lectern. "A stranger sprang upon me," Heywood recalled, "and refusing to read a warrant or even give his name, hurried me into a hack, drove swiftly through the streets on a dark, rainy night, and lodged me in jail as a 'United States prisoner.'" Heywood learned the next morning that he had been arrested for mailing *Cupid's Yokes* and R. T. Trall's *Sexual Physiology* and that the "rude stranger" who had arrested him was Anthony Comstock.[27]

In a chapter devoted mostly to the Heywoods in his own *Traps for the Young*, Comstock also described the arrest. Armed with a warrant, Comstock attended the free-love meeting unrecognized. "I looked over the audience of about 250 men and boys. I could see lust in every face," he reported. Soon Angela took the lectern. She "delivered the foulest address I ever heard," Comstock wrote, "she seemed lost to all shame. The audience cheered and applauded. It was too vile; I had to go out." Once outside, and braced by the fresh air, he resolved anew to halt the "exhibition of nastiness." Unsuccessful in finding a policeman to help in the arrest, he called on God.

"I returned to the hall," he continued, where the "chieftain's wife continued her offensive tirade against common decency. Occasionally she referred to 'that Comstock.' Her husband presided with great self-complacency. You would have thought he was the champion of some majestic cause instead of a mob of free-lusters." When it seemed that Comstock could no longer endure "the stream of filth," Heywood went backstage, affording Comstock a chance for a discreet arrest. He collared Heywood, and as Angela raised the alarm to the crowd, Comstock sped off with his prey. "Thus, reader," chuckled the vice hunter, "the devil's trapper was trapped."[28]

Comstock may have been especially perturbed at *Cupid's Yokes* because it contained a scorching criticism of his work and tactics. In the pamphlet, Heywood pictured Comstock as a grand inquisitor, "a *religious monomaniac*, whom the mistaken will of Congress and the lascivious fanaticism of the Young Men's Christian Association have empowered to use the Federal Courts to suppress free inquiry."[29] At any rate, Comstock seemed determined to stop all distribution of *Cupid's Yokes*. The next year he moved determinedly against D. M. Bennett, an important free-thought publisher, and, with the aid of decoy letters, arrested him for mailing *Cupid's Yokes*. The Bennett and the Heywood cases brought *Cupid's Yokes* to national attention through the involvement of the famous infidel Robert Ingersoll and of the president of the United States. It split the National Liberal League, caused significant public outcry on both sides, and condemned Bennett and Heywood to agonizing prison terms. Most importantly, however, the *Cupid's Yokes* case wrote new obscenity law when for the first time in an important case the English "*Hicklin* standard" as a test for obscenity came to be applied in American law in *U.S. v. Bennett*, 1879.

The background of De Robigne Mortimer Bennett (1818–1882) makes an interesting contrast to that of Ezra Heywood. A former Shaker and "practical" physician, Bennett used his knowledge of botanicals to set himself up during the middle years of the century in a lucrative business in Cincinnati, selling such nostrums as Dr.

Bennett's Quick Cure, Golden Liniment, Worm Lozenges, and Root and Plant Pills. Thomas Paine's *Age of Reason* converted him to free thought, and he eventually dedicated himself full-time to anticlericalism. Like Moses Harman, he began his radical publishing endeavor late in life. In 1873, when he was in his mid fifties, he launched the *Truth Seeker* in Paris, Illinois, and in a matter of months he moved it to New York.

Being an experienced publicist, he eventually put the periodical on a solid financial footing. His techniques were openly and puckishly iconoclastic, confounding the clergy in their own contradictions and human failings, while at the same time devoting a fair amount of exposition to earthy portions of the Bible. The *Truth Seeker* provided free-thought ammunition for a widely scattered constituency. One biographer has called Bennett's journal "the organ of village infidels scattered far and wide." In contrast to Heywood the scholar, anarchist, and sex radical, Bennett worked principally as a crusading freethinker. He saw the Comstock laws as a threat to liberty of conscience, and he helped to mount the repeal effort that netted over fifty thousand signatures on a protest petition which was presented to Congress.[30] As a popularizer of free thought, he deserves to be ranked with Robert G. Ingersoll, whose books often appeared under Bennett's imprint.

If Heywood and Bennett held Comstock and his deeds in contempt, the vice hunter returned the sentiment with interest. Comstock labeled Heywood "the chief creature of this vile creed" of free love—a creed so offensive that "we must go to a sewer that has been closed, where the accumulations of filth have for years collected, to find a striking resemblance to its true character." Of Bennett, he wrote: "He is everything vile in Blasphemy and Infidelism." Comstock began his campaign against the two within a ten-day period in November 1877.[31]

After first arresting Heywood for *Cupid's Yokes* in Boston, Comstock descended upon Bennett's *Truth Seeker* offices in New York and arrested him on charges of blasphemy as well as obscenity for mailing a scientific pamphlet, *How Do Marsupials Propagate*, by H. B. Bradford, and a tract written by Bennett, *An Open Letter to Jesus Christ*. As usual, Comstock had used a decoy letter to create the charges. Dr. Edward Bliss Foote paid Bennett's bond of fifteen hundred dollars and put his influence to work to get the case dropped. Ingersoll's protest to the postmaster general and other Washington officials succeeded, and the government dismissed the charges against Bennett.[32]

Shortly after Bennett achieved this victory, Heywood went on trial for mailing *Cupid's Yokes.* Found guilty, Heywood received a fine and a two-year prison sentence. Comstock must have been cheered at the early outcome of the case; it appeared that *Cupid's Yokes* would surely be stamped out. Under state Comstock laws, local officials arrested some freethinkers who were selling *Cupid's Yokes* at a meeting of the New York State Freethinkers Association in Watkins Glen, New York. One of the sellers who were arrested happened to be D. M. Bennett. Seeing Comstock as the vile culprit behind this new trouble, Bennett threw down the gauntlet in *Truth Seeker,* pledging a crusade for his right to distribute *Cupid's Yokes.* Comstock responded with a decoy request; as "G. Brackett, Granville, New York," he wrote a semiliterate letter, ordering some pamphlets and "that Heywood book you advertise Cupid's something or other." Comstock again arrested Bennett, and this time he won a conviction against the editor. Judge Samuel Blatchford, who wrote the landmark decision, fined Bennett three hundred dollars and awarded him a thirteen-month sentence.[33]

For more than a half-century, Blatchford's decision on *Cupid's Yokes* would be the basis of obscenity law in the United States. Even before the 1879 decision, however, lower courts had been aware of the English "*Hicklin* standard" as a formula for determining obscenity. Lord Chief Justice Cockburn had announced in *Queen* v. *Hicklin* (1868) that "I think the test is this, whether the tendency of the matter charged as obscenity is to deprave and corrupt those whose minds are open to immoral influences, and into whose hands a publication of this sort may fall." The *Bennett* case in 1879 provided the first opportunity for an American appellate court to issue a studied application of this standard. Both the English and American courts erred in assuming that the *Hicklin* standard merely followed common law; common law had never defined obscenity.[34]

The *Hicklin* case carried other important terms which affected obscenity law. A work was to be judged according to certain isolated passages, not by its general import. If a jury found obscenity in any part, regardless of the nature of the work as a whole, the work must be judged illicit. The tendency "to deprave and corrupt," which was crucial to the standard, did not refer to entreatments to actual misconduct but only to the ability of the questionable matter to arouse sexual thoughts in those minds which comprised the lowest denominator of sophistication—the "young and inexperienced." The law considered that all works offered to the general public would fall into these susceptible hands.

Blatchford's decision affirmed the precedent that an indictment for obscenity did not have to set out *in haec verba*, or to put literally upon the court records, the alleged obscenity, provided that a claim of its offensiveness was made in the indictment and provided that the work was sufficiently identified that the defendant knew what it was. Blatchford answered the question of the constitutionality of the Comstock Act by referring to the Supreme Court's obiter opinion in *Ex parte Jackson* (1877), which sustained the power of Congress to regulate the content of the mails. Although the hasty decision concerned lottery materials in the mails, the *Jackson* opinion specifically referred to the Comstock Act as an example of congressional power over the mails, and it implied a confirmation of the obscenity statute. Blatchford also forbade as extraneous the comparison of indicted matter with similar passages from "standard literature," and he emphasized that the purposes for using obscene words were not to be considered.[35]

Blatchford's opinion drew substantially from Heywood's *Cupid's Yokes* trial a year earlier. Before Judge Daniel Clark of the United States Circuit Court in Boston, the prosecution had held *Cupid's Yokes* to be too obscene to be placed upon the records of the court. The judge allowed this, thus influencing the jury toward the prosecutor's opinion regarding the obscenity of *Cupid's Yokes* as a condition of the trial. The court prohibited Heywood from arguing the issues of obscenity—that was to be decided without defense argument by the jury in the jury room, when, for the first time, members of the jury would have access to the allegedly obscene passages. The court also forbade any explanation of the purposes of *Cupid's Yokes*, its possible merits, or the intent of its author. The ruling prevented the old free-thought tactic of comparing alleged obscenity with certain sections from the Bible; it also disallowed any discussion of the medical and scientific sources that Heywood had drawn upon in *Cupid's Yokes*. In short, the case for the defense was limited to whether *Cupid's Yokes* had been placed in the mail. The court even forbade Heywood to call character witnesses. In his charge to the jury, Judge Clark asserted that Heywood's ideas, if put into practice, would turn Massachusetts into a brothel. It was for this offense that Heywood drew a two-year sentence in the Dedham jail and a fine of $100.[36]

Friends rallied to help Heywood. Parker Pillsbury, using the copy of *Cupid's Yokes* that had been marked by the prosecuting attorney, issued a pamphlet comparing coarse passages in the Bible with the so-called obscene language of Heywood's pamphlet. Benjamin Tucker took over editorial duties at *The Word*, and he and the newly formed free-speech organization, the National Defense Association, called for a support rally for Heywood in Faneuil Hall. A surprising number, six thousand, turned out for the affair, which was chaired by Elizur Wright. As an outcome of the meeting, the National Defense Association sent the veteran female radical Laura Cuppy Kendrick to Washington with a request for Heywood's pardon. President Hayes granted the pardon in December 1878, after Heywood had served six months. Notably, United States Attorney General Charles Devins declared that *Cupid's Yokes* was not obscene and that it was not obscene to advocate the abolition of marriage. This decision caused embarrassment for President Hayes later when Ingersoll called upon him to pardon Bennett.[37]

Somewhat vindicated if not actually victorious in his bout over *Cupid's Yokes*, Heywood returned energetically to his sex-reform activities at Princeton, Massachusetts. Comstock seethed; the President had fouled his snares, and once more the menace of free love endangered the nation. His office blotter records his woe:

The Pres. pardons this man on the petition of Infidels and liberals, free lovers and Smutt dealers, in the face of a solemn protest signed by the officers of our Soc. and an affidavit setting forth the fact that Heywood was openly defying the law through his friends, and by their selling his book while he was in Jail. This action of Pres. Hayes practically licenses the sale of *Cupid's Yokes*, and is a strong encouragement for others to violate the law, as well as a great hindrance to the further enforcement of the law.[38]

Comstock's despair turned to jubilation when, in March after Heywood had been freed in December, Judge Blatchford announced his important decision in the *Cupid's Yokes* case of D. M. Bennett. Elderly and in ill health, Bennett faced a thirteen-month sentence. Bennett's supporters once more appealed to Robert Ingersoll for help. Ingersoll did not approve of the free-love contents of *Cupid's Yokes*, nor for that matter, Bennett claimed, did he; but both were convinced that Heywood's pamphlet was not obscene, and both believed that Comstock was using the issue in order to persecute Bennett for his anticlericalism.

Ingersoll took the case to President Hayes. In several audiences with the president, he pointed out the aspects of doubtful legality that were involved in Bennett's obscenity trial and asked for a pardon. Since Hayes had pardoned Heywood, the very author of *Cupid's Yokes*, Ingersoll appeared confident that Hayes would pardon Bennett. Moreover the orator felt certain that Hayes did not believe the tract to be obscene. Church and "purity" forces, who had strongly protested the pardon of Heywood, now brought a great deal of pressure to bear upon the president and his wife, a WCTU matron who eliminated liquor from White House functions, where, according to one report, during the Hayes Administration "the water flowed like wine." The prospect of the leading infidel and the leading infidel publisher being vindicated by the president did not sit well with the religionists. The president seemed inclined to make no move.

The situation reached the proportions of a tawdry melodrama as Comstock, at this crucial stage, produced some letters that Bennett had allegedly written to a woman who was not his wife. The letters made Bennett appear deceptive in his public attitude toward free love, a situation that effectively estranged Ingersoll from Bennett. Ingersoll withdrew from the case. Despite a petition campaign by the National Defense Association which claimed two hundred thousand signatures for a presidential pardon, the old man endured his term in prison. Following the initial reverse in his contest with Heywood, Anthony Comstock savored Bennett's punishment for *Cupid's Yokes*. After being released from prison in the spring of 1880, Bennett traveled around the world with money raised by his supporters and served as a delegate to an international free-thought convention in Brussels before his health finally gave way in December 1882.[39]

Encouraged by his victory over Bennett, Comstock continued to pursue Heywood. He arrested the sex reformer in 1882, again charging him with obscenity for mailing *Cupid's Yokes*; in addition, Comstock charged Heywood with distributing two of Whitman's poems from *Leaves of Grass*, and for advertising a vaginal douching syringe which Heywood had waggishly dubbed the "Comstock syringe." Before a judge who allowed him to argue the broad issues of the case—free speech, freedom of conscience, and the imperatives of a higher morality—Heywood convinced the jury of his innocence. Comstock, doggedly arrested him again a short time later on a state obscenity charge for distributing a tract written by Angela Heywood. The pamphlet advocated woman's right to prevent conception and spoke of the sexual organs in very direct language. Heywood's Princeton neighbors protested the arrest and induced local officials to drop charges. Comstock again collared Heywood in an 1887 arrest, charging him as usual with obscenity. But the case never was prosecuted; the United States district attorney, a Democrat, "vetoed the obscenist plot," in Heywood's terms. After four defeats, Comstock withdrew and lay in wait for some more opportune time to belay the "devil's trapper," a time that he must have felt would surely come.[40]

A singular woman among a remarkable group, Angela Heywood managed to transcend the Victorian consciousness of the period to a greater degree than any other sex radical. If Ezra sometimes intoned praises to the joys of love and sex, Angela exploded in melodies, filling *The Word* with flowing columns of impressionistic prose that enlisted the intellect to the service of the emotions. She did much to give *The Word* its characteristic style. One anarchist reader, comparing *The Word* to *Lucifer*, saw only a superficial similarity in the two journals which was based on a common preference for direct words: "Looking deeper, we find *The Word* phallic and angelically voluptous while *Lucifer* is rather ascetic and Malthusian," wrote M. "Edgeworth" Lazarus; continuing his play on words, he praised *The Word*'s "Angelic teacher" on the essential goodness of amative pleasure.[41]

The facts about Angela's life are more obscure than those about her husband's. Stephen Pearl Andrews and Lucien V. Pinney each wrote a short article in *The Word* on the Heywoods, and these articles shed some light on her history. Light-hearted but dedicated to radicalism, she probably produced her articles for *The Word* in spontaneous flurries. "She has visions," wrote Pinney, "hears voices, and dreams dreams, and she is at times a whirlpool of words, delivered with startling effect. She is naturally musical, and instinctively dramatic, loves the lights, colors and rythmic sounds of the theatre, loves Art in action . . . but she is in nothing frivolous."

Her husband sometimes edited her effusions to make them more readable, but he did not alter her directness of language, and he did not affect her style very much. Pinney said of this combination: "He is the sententious writer of resolutions, butchering her beauties of song to expose the bare bones of an idea." Those who knew them agreed that it was she who provided not only many of the ideas that Ezra worked for but also the psychic push, the energy that characterized his work. When Ezra died, *The Word* and the headline-grabbing radicalism of the pair died also, suggesting a gestalt of force which came only from a combination of the two.[42]

Her prose style was heavily larded with poetic personifications and was flavored with the rhetoric of New England transcendentalism. A romantic, she seemed to regard inspiration and intellect as one, and she identified herself with the common man rather than with upper-class intellectuals. Angela's extreme feminism viewed the liberation of men as an integral part of the liberation of women, a problem that required a basic readjustment of sexual expression in society. Sex and love could not be free—nor be freeing forces—until sexuality was first recognized with a level of candor and naturalness that befitted the "profoundest relation in Life."[43]

Society's debasement of sex completely astounded her: "Verily, how hath Natural Modesty forgotten herself if the Penis and Womb [her word for vagina] be not elegant organs of the Human Body, equal in ability to entertain us with eye and tongue." Entertainment figured importantly in her vision of sex, as did her enthrallment with the graphic aspects of sex. While others, including free lovers, assigned somber and homiletic purposes to coitus, she announced that physical fun was as important a function of sex as was the creation of new life. "Sexuality is a divine ordinance," she wrote, "elegantly natural from an eye-glance to the vital action of the penis and womb, in personal exhilaration or for reproductive uses." She elevated intercourse beyond the merely worthwhile: "The Penis and Womb, the Outer and Inner are sublimely worthy peers in body faculty; their attentions, purposes, capacities, demands, supplies,—moved by Brain and Heart are the pith and glory of Being."[44]

She abhorred prudishness and particularly the myths of femininity that deprived woman of sexual enjoyment. "We are related sexually; let us face the glad fact with all its ineffable joys." A woman might pretend that she wanted nothing of man, but "her lady-nature knows it is the very great *everything* she wants to do *with* man." If a woman "duly gives to man who cometh in unto her, as freely, as equally, as well as he gives her, how shall she be abashed or ashamed of the innermost?" And, she wrote in the same essay, "Lady Nature can put Madame Intellect behind the door, further than you can think while she revels with a man to her hearts content."[45]

Early in life, Angela came by her interests in physical sex. Her mother, Lucy M. Tilton, taught her children about sex in direct ways. Ezra, in one of his letters to Moses Harman, related how the Tilton children had once observed the mating of a stallion with a mare: "Mrs. Tilton arranged chairs at the window for all her little ones to witness the spectacle, and stood beside them explaining to them carefully what had occurred. So you see, Mrs. Heywood and her sisters went to school young in these matters."[46]

Her essay "The Ethics of Sexuality," an 1881 article in *The Word*, contained much of her thought and feeling about sex. Essentially, free love rested upon integrity. "One is not a Free Lover," she explained, "because she cohabits with one or more men, or with none at all, but rather by the import and tone of Association." Free love required "sincere thought and true action" and, above all, personal responsibility rather than "third party, arrogant intermeddlement" of what she termed "the physical force code of domestic, commercial, educational, church-and-state *heisms*." This personal, moral responsibility that each person had for his own actions must be the decisive factor in each sexual encounter. Lady Nature may take over in a frenzy from Madame Intellect, but Temperance and what was called "the balanced use of persons" must be considered before a sexual act is agreed to. She noted that women could have no respect for men who evaded the personal and moral implications of their sexual encounters through claiming a weakness-of-the-flesh defense. This popular theory of male sexual necessity, which justified prostitution and the double standard of sexual interaction, would be eliminated by the ethics of free love. But Angela reserved her special scorn for the man who claimed virtue through impotence, who piously "attempt[ed] to hide behind the inability of his penis to have an erection!"

Some passages in her writings collided with others, but often these oppositions could be taken as a statement of paradox about the human sexual condition rather than as simple contradiction. In drawing the line between love and passion, she recalled, "I used to think Passion was something *bad*, and was taught, by those who did not know, that Lust is the opposite of Love; I was mistaken, for the antithesis of Love is *hate*; while Lust means full, glowing, healthy animal heat." Passion, or lust, existed as a "source of beneficent power" that was quite different from love. A man might love a woman but have no passion for her, or he might feel passion for her but feel no love. In another place, however, she related that "when a man gives his Passion to a woman she feels he *must* love her; else he *could not* yield it to her. . . . Can he be otherwise than dear to her?"

Unintentionally she raised an important consideration in the question of sexual freedom—the fact of the interrelation of love with sexual connection. Although Angela represented a romantic, Western view of love, there is no denying the legitimacy of the connection that she pointed out between intimate physical union and the transcendent attraction called love. Sexual freedom, in asserting itself, called constraining forces into play. Voluntary sexual experimentation opened greater possibilities for exclusive love, or at least such was the case for women, Angela intimated. This effect, incidentally, seemed to be borne out by the experience of the Oneida Community, where, in theory, each member could enjoy the privileges of marriage with every other member of the opposite sex in the community. The fact that couples frequently fell in love—an act of "selfish love" that was specifically forbidden—presented one of the greatest problems of complex marriage.[47] In "The Ethics of Sexuality," all of Angela's references to the differences between passion and love are to these differences in man, not in woman. She seemed to imply, in fact, that passion and love are an identity in woman.

She reveled in the ideal of sexual difference and liked the idea of sex-determined cultural roles, although this did not mean that women should be passive or that they should be treated unequally. Sexual attraction, she believed, depended upon sexual differences: "Let truth now speak, we like men because they *are* men; you like us because we are *not* men," she told her male readers. The term "wife" had fallen into disfavor among some feminists who claimed it had a disgraceful etymology, but on this point Angela demurred. She felt that the term expressed a relationship "of the most candid order twixt a woman and a man." The words "husband" and "wife" simply designated the masculine and feminine sides of the "plural unity." She felt that the term and act of being a wife announced an "equality with man in the realm of Service; never did I feel demeaned by so accepting the term wife, or the fact wifehood." No doubt she felt that husband and wife should serve each other, and she had an appropriately Puritan concept of service as one's duty to human kind: "We . . . are *here* . . . with all our capacities for Work to transcend tragic evil in ecstatic good. 'The spirit of Culture does not exist/ Where thought of Service does not persist.' "

Her tone became more defensive as she discussed the service aspect of wifehood in greater detail. Some women might consider wifehood slavish rather than a "self-adjusted service," but Angela asserted that "such bondage is foreign to my girl and woman ideas; while Serving I always felt to be royally worthy." One may speculate about whether this idea of service became too concrete in her own home, especially since a friend once commented in a sketch of the Heywoods that Angela "dwells with rare fortitude in the 'cellar basement' of experience—a hard working housewife doing as an artist the work of a 'scrub.' " She bore four children—Psyche, Angelo, Vesta, and Hermes—and she and Ezra apparently shared a long, monogamous, and devoted relationship—a not uncommon circumstance among free lovers.[48]

Neither Angela Heywood nor her husband bridled at the word "fuck." In fact, their campaign for the use of the word in their aptly named *The Word* helped to put Ezra in prison a final time. The couple believed that speech could not be free until the direct, common words for things could be freely uttered. "In discussing ideas, doctrines, physiology, morals, names of body organs and actions were needed," Heywood recalled in later years. "Mrs. Heywood, coming on the lecture platform, in Boston, to talk to and tame male mobs . . . coined the term, 'generative sexual intercourse,' which was sufficiently roundabout, was it not? Three words, twenty-seven letters to define a given action commonly spoken in one word of four letters that everybody knows the meaning of."[49]

In 1880 the influence of Stephen Pearl Andrews and other radicals caused the Heywoods to make an important decision: "We came to see the utter stupidity, nonsense and villainy of evasion and cowardice in this serious business." The trouble, reasoned Heywood, did not inhere in words, "simply letters in line, sociated in sentences"; instead, the offense resided in "dirty thought, unclean habit, dishonest action relative to body forces." He could not help asking: "Is it obscene to be sired and born? Are judges and district attorneys immaculate conceptions?" He argued for a simple integrity of language: "The sex organs and their associative uses have fit, proper, explicit, expressive English names; why not have character enough to use them and no longer be ashamed of your own creative use and destiny?" Heywood seemed to believe that by naming the unnamable, as in some archetypal myth, the dark spell of ignorance would be broken. Then man's sexuality could finally be "brought under control, and within the jurisdiction of moral obligation."[50]

Angela defended direct language practically and ingenuously: "Such graceful terms as hearing, seeing, smelling, tasting, fucking, throbbing, kissing, and kin words, are telephone expressions, lighthouses of intercourse centrally immutable to the situation; their aptness, euphony and serviceable persistence make it as impossible and undesirable to put them out of pure use as it would be to take oxygen out of air."[51]

If the embroidery of such terms as "penis" and "fuck" in Angela's writings appeared natural and innocent, Ezra's use of such terms was often humorous and biting. He jabbed at the prudish, but he also kidded fellow radicals. His cryptic prose sometimes obscured his humor, however. In an 1889 issue of *The Word* there appeared, without introduction, a fantastic allegory by Ezra concerning something he half-seriously called the Fucking Trust. The piece was a marriage of the semantic and social consciousness of the Heywoods, compounded by zaniness. In earlier articles he had termed marriage a "penis trust," using "trust" in its economic sense as a legal, monopolistic form of exploitation. Now he sought to redeem the word from its negative connotations by proposing the Fucking Trust, a tongue-in-cheek "collective effort to bring the moral, social & physical uses of sex-meeting into the domain of reason and moral obligation." As a crowning touch, he deadpanned, Elmina Slenker had been made president of the trust. An elderly female sex reformer, Slenker had for years preached a method of sexual continence called Dianaism.[52]

One of the Heywood's most daring efforts came in a contribution to the letters column in the March 1890 number of *The Word*. "Letter from a Mother," by an anonymous New York mother, presented a straightforward approach to the question of childhood sex education. "The other day," related the mother, "my little girl who is in her twelfth year, came to me and said, 'Mama, what does "fuck" mean?'" The mother asked where she had heard the word. "Why, today at school, Willie ─── said to me, 'Mamie, won't you fuck me?'" replied the daughter. The mother took this as a cue to explain the sexual facts of life to her daughter. The mother herself, the letter revealed, had been initiated into sexual intercourse at age twelve ("in my inexperience, I was fascinated with it," she commented), but the writer cautioned that this age was generally too young. Intercourse for females should come only after transition of puberty had been completed. The mother advised parents to let a daughter "look forward to the time when she will become a woman as the time when she will taste of its pleasures." The writer never alluded to marriage. As Dora Forster would suggest some fourteen years later in her "Sex Radicalism" essays published in *Lucifer*, this mother urged that a youngster's first sexual experience be with a trusted adult who knew "what ought to be done and just how to do it."[53]

In the same issue of *The Word*, Ezra announced a crowning act of defiance against Comstock: he promised that the succeeding issue of *The Word* would reprint O'Neill's letter from *Lucifer*, the exposé of oro-genitalism for which Harman had recently been arrested while in the midst of his Markland-letter trial. "We will see what lewd official or citizen dare touch us," taunted Heywood. Ezra's old antagonist, Anthony Comstock, surprised no one when he took the bait.

The local postmaster at Princeton, who had recently been appointed by Postmaster General John Wanamaker, had been charged by his superiors in Washington to review each issue of *The Word* and to reject for mailing, or to pass on to Washington for judgment, any issues with opinions or style that he found offensive. Without informing Heywood, the Princeton official thus held up the March and April issues of *The Word*. In May a United States deputy marshal arrested Heywood, and within a week a federal grand jury in Boston returned a three-count indictment against Heywood for obscenity.[54]

The O'Neill letter, printed as announced in the April issue, constituted the first count; the "Letter from a Mother" the second; and "Natural Modesty," an 1889 reprint of an article that Angela had originally published in 1883, the final count. Besides some candid praises of the flesh, "Natural Modesty" contained a well-aimed slam at Comstock. Angela believed that the birth-control proscriptions of the 1873 law discriminated against women and had in effect installed Comstock as the policeman of the American woman's genitals. She satirized Comstock's powers in an interesting fantasy: every male would have his penis tied up by a length of wire and, upon occasion, would be inspected by a female Comstock; any offending males who had removed the constriction would be tried before a court of twelve women who would have the power to imprison a man for ten years. Understandably, Angela could not understand why Comstock never arrested her— only her husband.[55]

Two weeks after the grand jury's indictment, Heywood stood his final trial. There appeared to be a great unity of effort between Comstock, the Republican administration in Washington, and local officials to bring an end to Heywood's career. Heywood had at first been informed that he would have a number of weeks to prepare for the trial, but suddenly the prosecutor told him that he had "got orders from Washington to speed up the Heywood trial." Conveniently for Heywood's detractors, this order coincided with the illness of the district court judge, T. L. Nelson, in whose court Heywood had actually won an obscenity case in 1883. A less liberal judge from Rhode Island, George M. Carpenter, was brought in to hear the case in Nelson's absence.

Postmaster General John Wanamaker, the department-store magnate who became notorious for banning Tolstoy's *Kreutzer Sonata* from the United States mail, had appointed the new postmaster in Princeton, a sanctimonious man whom Heywood called "Deacon" Gregory. True to his instructions, Gregory took the important first step against Heywood by confiscating *The Word* and then informing Comstock about his action. Heywood protested both in *The Word* and at his trial against the confiscation, citing court cases which ruled that the post office had no further property nor moral jurisdiction over matter that had been refused admission to the mails. His objections did no good, however. Up to this time, local postmasters had always refused to interfere in Heywood's work, despite requests from Comstock. The previous postmaster, in fact, was a Democrat and a self-admitted infidel. Heywood believed that Comstock had directly influenced Wanamaker in his choice of the new postmaster at Princeton. Considering Comstock's seventeen years of service as an important "special" employee of the Post Office Department, Heywood's assertion did not seem far fetched.[56]

In the 1890 trial, as in Heywood's *Cupid's Yokes* trial of 1878, the court forbade all arguments exploring the nature of the "obscenity" for which Heywood faced charges: the defense was limited to the question of whether Heywood mailed the indicted material. Influenced by a court that considered the material to be too questionable to be read into the record, and untrammeled by distracting defense arguments or such niceties as character witnesses, the jury was to apply the *Hicklin* standard to the marked portions of the material when it finally got access to it. The jury heard Heywood testify that he had earlier been convicted, but the defendant was prohibited from saying that he had also been pardoned once and acquitted once. The charges against Heywood, in fact, were not read aloud to the jury at the beginning of the trial.

After the judge had lectured the jury on the evil of obscenity and had advised that only "proper fit and decent" speech had rights of protection, the jury retired to consider the material and the verdict. They pronounced Heywood guilty, and the judge sentenced him to two years at hard labor at Charlestown State Prison, and allowed no appeal. This time, petitions to the president for pardon went unheeded; the sixty-two-year-old editor served out his sentence, sewing prison uniforms.[57]

"It is something amusing that the world could have drifted on so long without being confronted with the sex question,—the whence, the what and the whither of us relative to each other as he's and she's," mused Heywood in one of his rambling letters to Moses Harman from his cell in the Charlestown prison. Although Lillian Harman and E. C. Walker visited Heywood in prison, Heywood and Moses Harman apparently never met. The feeling of partnership in finally confronting the world with the sex question pervaded Heywood's letters to Harman, however, particularly since both had, for a time, served concurrent prison sentences for what both considered to be the logical extension of their former abolitionist work. In vowing to publish *Lucifer*'s O'Neill letter, Heywood had drawn upon the antislavery era for images of martyrdom that would describe Harman: "As Sumner spoke for ravished Kansas, in the U.S. Senate, so Harman types the woes of raped wives." Now in prison, he wrote: "Woman is the negro of today, whom Mr. Harman and I are befriending; it is Massachusetts and Kansas over again." *Lucifer* became the mouthpiece for the imprisoned editor during the time that *The Word* was silent.[58]

The *Twentieth Century* published a pamphlet by Julian Hawthorne, "In Behalf of Personal Liberty" (1891), which protested the legal harassment and imprisonment of Heywood. The pamphlet also contained a letter from Moses Harman which described his similar treatment. The novelist disavowed Heywood's sexual theories, but he defended his right to free expression as being basic to American ideals and tradition. Heywood's honest if controversial work should not be confused with obscenity. "It would be better to have the country flooded with genuinely vicious and obscene literature, than to establish the precedent of imprisoning men for publishing their honest opinion," Hawthorne wrote.

When Heywood returned from prison, friends gave him a reception at Quincy House, Boston. Those who had visited him in prison noted his apparent poor health. Angela and the children had suffered too; as when Heywood went to jail for *Cupid's Yokes*, they again had to sell their house and goods in order to survive. And *The Word* had been silent for months.[59]

Unbent, and with his sense of humor still intact, Ezra Heywood began publishing *The Word* again. A year after his release he died of a cold that he had contracted at the annual convention of the American Labor Reform League, an organization that he had founded twenty-two years earlier. Edwin C. Walker wrote a long report of his funeral in *Lucifer*.[60]

11/ The Doctors Foote

BY some rickety principle of the law of excess, the tyranny of respectability called forth compensating forces. If in most cases these opposing responses did not countervail, they could nevertheless be implacable, as Harman and company demonstrated. Of this dogged number, few played such important roles as two medical doctors, Edward Bliss Foote and his son, Edward Bond Foote. A literary enterprise—home medical books—was the cause both of their fortune and of their vested interested in liberty of expression.

The elder Dr. Foote arrived at his career as everyman's health savant only after an apprenticeship in journalism. From childhood he had longed to be a physician, but opportunities for formal education were limited in the town of Cleveland, Ohio, where he was born in 1829. Consciously following the example of Benjamin Franklin, he became a printer in order to acquire an education. He flourished in the world of ideas which opened up to him in the composing room; at home, a stolid Presbyterianism had pervaded all intellectual discussion. But home had not seemed dull. His father had run the village store and post office, and the doctor recalled that their house had served literally as a free hotel for ministers, school teachers, and singing masters.

Along with the printer's trade, he also learned how to write. At nineteen he became editor of a weekly paper in New Britain, Connecticut, and according to his own unselfconscious account, his efforts soon turned the paper into the largest and most successful weekly in the state. Likewise, he claimed credit for the success of another paper which later enjoyed his editorial aid, the

Brooklyn Morning Journal. As a highlight of his early years in journalism, Foote liked to recall the stir over the "Rochester rappings" and the fact that he had called for a fair hearing for spiritualism while most papers ridiculed the phenomenon. During trips to Boston in these years he heard the preaching of Theodore Parker and became a liberal Unitarian.

True to his original ambition, he spent his spare time in devouring medical texts. After two years he quit the *Morning Journal* in order to study medicine full time under a botanical physician. He took a degree in 1860 from the Pennsylvania Medical University, but before he did so, he published, at age twenty-nine, a book destined to become a best seller, *Medical Common Sense*.[1]

Between 1858, when he first published his work, and 1870, when he incorporated it into a larger volume, *Medical Common Sense* sold 250,000 copies. The enlarged version of 1870, which was entitled *Plain Home Talk, Embracing Medical Common Sense*, enjoyed equal success; as his own publisher, Foote reported a steady demand of over 2,000 volumes a month at a selling price which ranged from $1.50 for the cheap edition to $5.00 for the calf-bound volume. Other works by the elder Dr. Foote included a periodical, *Dr. Foote's Health Monthly* (1876–1896); a children's book in five volumes, *Science in Story: or, Sammy Tubbs the Boy-Doctor, and Sponsie the Troublesome Monkey* (1874); and numerous pamphlets, two of which had more than passing significance: "Words in Pearl," which advocated and described contraceptive techniques, and "The Physical Improvement of Humanity," which pronounced his eugenical beliefs. Although his *Home Cyclopedia*, issued at the turn of the century, capped his own remunerative career in medicine and publishing, his son, a better-educated Dr. Foote, carried on the work. The historian of contraception, Norman E. Himes, believed that the enormous circulation of Dr. Foote's works was crucial in preparing the public mind for twentieth-century efforts concerning birth control.[2]

Foote looked upon the many editions of his medical books as a democratic medium for imparting a knowledge of therapeutics to the masses. With his popular bias, Foote opposed the efforts of the regular medical profession to make medical knowledge the domain of elite professionals. The agitation for "medical freedom," which encompassed good-hearted libertarians as well as greedy quacks, raised the specter of a medical monopoly which sought to keep the common man ignorant and dependent. It was charged that while the regular medical profession retained its autonomy and promoted its own interests, often at the expense of the public, it had allied itself with the state in order to gain police power over medical dissenters. For its motto, the *Health Monthly* chose a quote from Agassiz: "The time has come when scientific truth must cease to be the property of the few—when it must be woven into the common life of the world."

Foote liked to remark that popular problems had dictated the content of the revised editions of his book. His correspondence with the people, he wrote in 1870, often exceeded one hundred letters a day. The confidences of his correspondents, combined with his wide office practice, had enabled him to gauge the popular needs and to supply the physiological instruction that the public seemed to crave. Many of his letters came from young people who had gotten into trouble because of sexual ignorance and who often "charge[d] their parents with cruel neglect, in keeping from them knowledge of such vital importance."[3]

In fact, sex, in its physiological, social, and moral aspects, dominated the book and doubtless helped it to become a best seller, filling a gap that yawned wide in Victorian America. Using his physicians' privilege, he not only discussed taboo subjects but criticized the taboos as well—although he sometimes appeared to substitute a personal puritanism for the more conventional sort. In the 1881 edition of his 936-page book he devoted over 300 pages, the "Plain Talk" section, to his ideas on sex and marriage. About half of the rest of the book, the medical section, dwelt on sexual problems. The chapters in the "Plain Talk" part dealt with the sexual organs, the history of marriage, marriage in different cultures, common defects of marriage systems, and sexual immorality. A separate section offered suggestions for the "Improvement of Popular Marriage." From satyriasis to sexual indifference, from fallen uterus to seminal weakness, Foote attempted to cover the gamut of intimate problems.

His folksy prose style conveyed the impression of vast practical experience tempered by formal knowledge. He strove for a democratic voice, a "language strictly mundane, and comprehensible alike to the rustic inmate of a basement and the exquisite student of an attic studio." His style, like the content, sought to entertain as well as teach. Numerous illustrations, from an innocuous engraving of "The Old Oaken Bucket" to a drawing of the fallopian tubes, added to the compendious volume, offering the promise of hours of diversion on long winter nights.

Although Foote did advertise a few medications and other articles in the book, he carefully refrained from appearing to hawk nostrums. He seemed to be more interested in attracting new patients, to be treated either in person or through correspondence. He charged nothing for the first consultation in letter or in person, although if the correspondence was in the German language, he charged a dollar. A detailed questionnaire for patients appeared in the book, so that correspondents could more thoroughly inform the doctor about their problems.

With agents across the country busily letting Foote's book sell itself, the doctor had to develop some assembly-line methods for his mass practice. His Lexington Avenue office in New York, three stories with two basement levels, would do a present-day Los Angeles credit dentist proud. According to a description in the *New York Independent,* the top floor served as the factory for the doctor's botanical medicines. It included a fireproof furnace room, a storeroom with an expensive inventory of roots and plants, and a well-furnished laboratory where workers compounded Foote's concoctions. Stenographers and shorthand writers filled the second floor; they were all employed in answering correspondence under the doctor's dictation. "In no other way," volunteered the newspaper, "could one brain and one pair of hands attend to so many professional letters." The first floor, "elegantly furnished," contained the public offices. Here Foote and two assisting physicians attended their patients in person. The basement housed "smaller publications," a factory that made boxes for shipping the medicines, and a packing room. Foote's own publishing enterprise, the Murray Hill Co., operated at a separate location.[4]

Foote leaned toward the "eclectic school" in his medical practice. This persuasion accepted new methods of cure and diagnosis such as electricity, hypnotism, spiritualism, and physiognomy. Foote, himself a regularly registered physician in New York State, chose to define the difference between the regular and eclectic schools, not so much in terms of training, but in attitudes toward innovation, even though the eclectic school in its flowering had its own associations, schools, and journals, as well as, perhaps, more than its share of quacks. The conventional medical profession, said Foote in the first paragraph of his book, "proverbially ignores every thing that has not the mixed odor of incomprehensibility and antiquity. . . . Orthodoxy in medicine consists in walking in the beaten paths of Aesculapian ancestors, and looking with grave contempt on all who essay to cut out new paths for themselves." Foote also scouted the general-practice, jack-of-all-trades approach to medicine; he considered himself a physician of chronic diseases only. Foote's peculiarities included his use of phrenology as an aid in diagnosis and his use of botanical medicines only. Foote, in fact, was no patent-medicine charlatan, and he preached against the common tendency to consume bottles of questionable cure-alls. He particularly objected to a staple of the regular medical profession—mercury compounds—and he considered the reliance on mineral medicines to be another characteristic of the "old school." Foote, however, did have a weakness for electrical gadgetry and for mumbo jumbo about magnetism. In the portion of his book entitled "Philosophy of Sexual Intercourse" he showed that what he lacked in scientific depth he made up for in imagination.[5]

Foote based his theory of sexuality on the common nineteenth-century belief that individuals possessed distinctive magnetic auras. Since nervous impulses were electrical in nature and since the pubic area was supplied with many nerves, Foote postulated that sexual attraction was nothing more than an electric or magnetic force that varied between individuals according to the dissimilarity of their charges, much like the attraction of opposite poles of a magnet. He embellished this notion with a theory that intercourse itself was an electrical operation. First, chemical electricity was formed by the interaction of the alkaline vagina with the acidic mantle of the skin covering the penis shaft. This electricity pleasurably tingled the abundant nerves of the genital organs. In addition, sexual intercourse created "frictional," or static, electricity. Just as a glass rod becomes charged when rubbed vigorously with fur, so would parts of the body generate electricity when rubbed together; "but no part of the animal organization is so susceptible to this influence as the glans-penis of the male and the clitoris of the female," believed Foote.

Missing no opportunity to deplore masturbation, he revealed an electrical explanation for the danger of secret vice. Self-stimulation created only one kind of electricity, frictional electricity, and then drained it from one's own nervous system with no compensating draw from another body. Foote hypothesized an answer to a mystery that had baffled men of science for ages—the purpose of pubic hair. A nonconductor of electricity, the hair insulated the external parts of the sexual organs during coitus and confined to the nerve centers the charges that were generated and exchanged.[6]

Just as Foote mixed sexology and merchandising, he presented quack theories together with truly innovative ideas. He extended and made practical some ideas for sex education that had been proposed by earlier writers such as Andrew Jackson Davis. The study of the body and its sexual functions should be an integral part of school curriculum, wrote Foote, proposing that children be separated according to sex and age and that they be given instruction "in the *uses*, and consequences of the *abuses*, of the various organs of the body, not omitting those most sinned against—the organs of generation." Men teachers should instruct boys, and women should instruct girls, in a straightforward and graphic manner, using illustrations and manikins if possible. Particularly important was the instruction of girls at the onset of puberty, since they would eventually be responsible for the initial health of the oncoming generation. Foote saw in such sexual education of the young a deterrent to masturbation; in his mind, ignorance led to masturbation, and masturbation led to numerous later debilities, varieties of which depended upon the "idiosyncrasies of its slaves." Specifically, it caused seminal weakness or spermatorrhoea in men and leucorrhoea, or the "whites," in women, as well as mental depression, consumption, and insanity in both sexes.[7]

From his voluminous practice he drew an interesting observation on the incidence of masturbation among the sexes. Under sixteen or eighteen years of age, he wrote, girls seemed less addicted to the habit than did boys; but after that age and until marriage, females masturbated more than males. His explanation for the situation reflected his feminist critique of society. Society indulged its randy young men, while "the appearance of wildness among young ladies awakens the bitter tongue of slander, which only the most modest and retiring demeanor on their part can silence, while defiance to it banishes them from all good society. Thus the hot blood of budding man and womanhood . . . leads the young man to the embraces of the harlot, and the young woman to the vices of the secret chamber, so that the former sacrifices his moral sense, and the latter her physical bloom and health." Dr. Foote added that the dangers of venereal disease, which faced the whoring young man, were a lesser risk to health than the masturbatory destruction faced by the closeted young woman.[8]

He tried to do his part for the sex education of the young with his multivolume children's work, *Science in Story: or Sammy Tubbs the Boy-Doctor*, in which he sugar-coated various lessons in physiology and hygiene. It mixed "April-fool jokes, fantastics, monkey-tricks, etc.," with information on lacteal radicles, villi, and lymphatics. Volume 5 of the series, which Foote considered to be the most valuable, treated the reproductive organs. Never one to miss a sale, however, he sold the volumes separately, so that even prudish parents might buy the other four.

His book reminded women that "in the eyes of God, respectable prostitution, such as marrying for homes and wealth, is no better than that practised by abandoned women." Women should push themselves into all jobs in which they could physically do the work, not excepting the professions, particularly medicine. All means should be exploited in order "that women may become less dependent upon their 'legal protectors,' and be enabled to live lives of 'single blessedness,' rather than unite themselves to disagreeable masses of masculine blood and bones, for the mere sake of escaping from poverty and starvation." No justification existed for woman's economic dependence upon man; although woman's nature differed a great deal from man's, she was in all respects naturally his equal.

He advanced the idea that those who worked as housewives should be salaried by their husbands: one-half of the man's earnings should go directly to the wife. "Really, there is no position in social life where the wife's labors are not, valued in dollars and cents, worth just as much as those of her husband," he declared. Society should also allow women the same freedom that men enjoyed in procuring a marriage partner; that is, he wrote, ladies should be allowed to propose. It was ironic, he believed, that marriage served presently as the main method of woman's economic advancement, yet custom commanded her to a passive role while it allowed man the exclusive prerogative of choice. This demonstrated to him that social custom oppressed women more than did positive law in the practical matters of work and marriage.[9]

For both sexes, conventional marriage had proved somewhat less than successful, he believed, and he suggested very early that enlightened methods of divorce would actually work to save monogamic marriage. He devoted a large portion of his perennial book to a critical history of marriage, in an effort to show the cultural relativity of the institution. He included long descriptions of experimental arrangements, such as the Mormons' polygamy and Oneida's extended marriage. With certain caveats to placate conservative readers, he urged that marital experimentation and diversity be encouraged by positive government action. He proposed, in addition, that a national Department of Marriage, with a secretary of cabinet rank, be created. This office would supervise scientific investigation into all past and present marriage systems and would then present its findings and recommendations to the public. The national office would oversee local Licensing and Divorcing Boards, composed of an equal number of men and women, which would examine the mental and physical characteristics of candidates for marriage and would grant or refuse marriage licenses according to "the congenialites of the parties presenting themselves"; divorces would be granted to those who proved that they were miserably mated. Foote believed that phrenology could be an important tool in determining the compatibility of partners. "Monogamy, complex marriage, and polygamy should be tolerated expressly by national consent, and it should be the duty of the local boards and this national officer to see that no one of these institutions exercises tyrannical control over any individual," or even more restraint than was necessary for good order. This office, moreover, would oversee the national broadcast of scientific material regarding sex education.[10]

He developed the plan in greater detail in *Divorce: A Review of the Subject from the Scientific Standpoint* (1884), which at least two historians have cited as a forerunner of the twentieth-century "companionate marriage" ideas of Judge Ben Lindsey. Foote suggested that the board's approval would be necessary before a couple could have a child, if the man was under thirty and the woman under twenty-five. Before the birth of children, divorce would be easy; in fact, it would be encouraged until a couple was just entering mature family life. This formulation was eugenic in nature and demonstrated a leading cause for which both the elder and the younger Dr. Foote labored. Their eugenics, with its legal proscription of parenthood for those who suffered hereditary disorders and with its promotion of positive "race culture," did not exemplify the anarchist eugenics urged by Moses Harman, but rather portended state-controlled eugenics. Foote termed his eugenics "scientific propagation."[11]

Foote's promotion of contraception, his principal historical contribution, was of course a necessary part of this eugenical plan. But aside from eugenic arguments for birth control, his "Words in Pearl" pamphlet had advocated contraception for another important reason—the dangers of overpopulation, or as it was commonly termed, the Malthusian argument. Although Thomas Malthus, in his *Essay on the Principle of Population* (1798), was not the first to attempt to show the connection between population growth and food supply, and although Malthus categorically disapproved of "artificial and unnatural modes of checking population," the nineteenth-century advocates of contraception selectively utilized Malthus's argument that unchecked population would eventually outstrip the food supply and would cause lower wages, poverty, and, many added, the whole range of social calamities. The confusion about Malthus is compounded, since the British birth-control movement took on the label "Malthusianism" around 1860, which subsequently became "Neo-Malthusianism" about twenty years later.[12]

To eugenic, medical, and economic arguments for contraception, Foote added feminist and humanitarian ones. Children should not be the ones to suffer poverty and ill health for the sexual paroxysms of their parents. The wife should have contraceptives available to her so that only she, and not the husband or the chances of nature, would determine procreation. When the Comstock Act forbade Foote to include his essay on contraceptives in his book, he replaced it with a reprint of Noyes's argument for male continence, not because he approved of male continence, but because of Noyes's several arguments in favor of contraceptive measures. Foote scorned the "alphite" argument that abstinence should be the sole method of birth control; he considered such restraint unhealthy as well as unadaptable on a wide scale.

By today's standards it is a moot question whether the public faced greater danger of quackery from the eclectic or from the regular school of medicine. The conservative regulars, however, clearly tried to obstruct efforts to educate the public about contraceptives and sex. Writing in 1892, Foote noted a slight liberalizing trend in the regular profession over the past decade as medical journals gave more attention to sexual physiology. Unfortunately, the regulars seemed determined to restrict this information within the limits of the profession, he wrote, pointing to recent efforts of the profession to have state legislatures prohibit the printing and selling of all but the most "emasculated" physiology texts.[13]

A self-critical article by one of the regulars in the *Journal of the American Medical Association* that same year pointed out that most medical colleges and physiology textbooks did not teach or discuss human sexual hygiene and physiology. Worse yet, wrote Sydney Barrington Elliott, the author, "physicians are doing little to lift the veil of mock-modesty and hypocracy [sic] which keeps the masses in ignorance and vice." Elliott differed from most of his regular colleagues regarding birth control: he advocated it, on eugenic and other grounds, in almost the exact words used by Foote. In contrast, many regulars allied themselves with Comstock's Vice Society; and with the support of establishment bastions such as the *New York Times*, they not only succeeded in outlawing contraceptives but also slandered those doctors who advocated contraceptives by calling them abortionists and quacks.[14]

Foote thought that there was a fairly clear division between eclectics and regulars with regard to contraceptive- and sex-education issues. New York State law allowed abortion to be superinduced on the recommendation of physicians in consultation if they believed it necessary in order to save the life of a pregnant woman. At the same time, the law made it a crime to prescribe contraceptives, even for reasons of health. Thus the charge of being "abortionists," Foote felt, actually applied to the regulars. "It is a hard thing to say, but nevertheless true, that the professional abortionists are only to be found in the ranks of the old school, while the new schools in medicine are to a man preventionists." The recent attempts to modify the law that forbad prescription of contraceptives had been made by the eclectics and homeopaths, he reminded: "Few if any of the old school were included in it, while any number of them were ready to back up the Vice Society in its efforts to defeat the movement."[15]

Foote referred to the 1876 campaign, which he led, to amend the New York law prohibiting the manufacture and sale of contraceptives. Awaiting trial under obscenity charges at the time, however, Foote was at a disadvantage in his efforts. He managed to get a counter bill introduced in the legislature, but Comstock's efforts killed it. The *New York Times* report of the bill's demise perpetuated the Comstockian smear which purposely confused abortion with contraception. Headlined "A Blow to Quack Doctors," it reported that "an investigation showed that the bill was in the interests of abortionists, and that its introduction was caused by Dr. E. B. Foote, now under indictment in the U.S. Circuit Court on a charge of mailing improper articles." Anthony Comstock supplied the testimony regarding the "origin and tendency of the measure" and presented a protest signed by leading New York doctors, which stated that only quacks and frauds prescribed contraceptives. The committee that was hearing the bill then unanimously rejected it.[16]

Although 1876 marked a crucial year in Foote's anti-Comstock efforts, he had been battling since the outset of the censorship threat. In 1872 he fought practically alone against Comstock's New York State bill, which was the model for the later federal law. Though Foote had in reserve as powerful a weapon as the pen— namely money—he failed to stop the state law. The timing was poor; Governor Dix signed the state Comstock bill the same day that Foote sent his objections to it to the governor. A year later, Comstock's influence became national, when Congress ruled that the mails were off-limits to contraceptive devices and information; and in another year, 1874, Comstock bagged the well-known mail-order doctor who provided both. By arresting the doctor, Comstock unwittingly helped numerous radical causes, both present and future. Dr. Foote and his son eventually became principal bankrollers for those who opposed Comstock.[17]

A small ten-cent pamphlet caused Foote's arrest in 1874. Set in tiny pearl-sized type and specially printed to fit inside a letter-sized envelope, the pamphlet, "Words in Pearl," contained specific information about contraceptive methods and devices and about how they could be obtained through Foote. He only sent it to those who first requested such information, and he mailed it first class in a sealed envelope. To those who had read pre–Comstock Act versions of *Medical Common Sense,* the contents of "Words in Pearl" were no revelation; the book contained two essays on "preventions," which explained the use of several devices and offered them for sale. Times had changed in the fifteen years since the first edition of the book, and in 1873 Foote's contraceptive efforts became illegal.[18]

Foote had mailed Comstock a copy of "Words in Pearl" in response to a decoy request by the vice hunter. Charged with mailing an obscene pamphlet and "a notice giving information how an article designed for prevention of conception can be obtained," Foote came before the United States Circuit Court in New York in June 1876. In the classic and usually fruitless move to get the allegedly obscene matter on the public record, Foote's attorney argued that the indictment failed to give a definite description of the material in question. To get the material on record, either for public access or in order to raise the question of whether the indictment itself was obscene, would have constituted a victory for Foote. In what appeared to be a prejudgment, however, Judge Benedict ruled that "it is neither necessary nor proper to pollute the record by a detailed description of obscene matter, and, where the grand jury omit a definite description of the matter, by reason of its obscene and filthy character, such omission furnishes no ground of objection to the indictment."

More importantly, Benedict ruled on the question of the purview of sealed, first-class mail under the Comstock Act. At the time the law did not specifically proscribe the mailing of obscene material in letters, although one month later Congress revised the law, declaring every obscene publication to be nonmailable matter. The judge construed the Comstock Act to hold that letters were included. "It is not the form in which the matter is mailed," he wrote, "but the character of the matter itself, which fixes the criminality of the act." Foote stood before the magistrate for sentencing on 11 July 1876—a glorious centennial year, Foote noted ironically—and heard the court's lengthy opinion. The judge concluded that Foote had not distributed "Words in Pearl" in order to make profits from its sale but in order to obtain practice as a result of its circulation. The judge remarked that many people had expressed concern to him about Foote's prosecution and that he understood that many patients might suffer if the doctor were to be imprisoned. Under these circumstances he decided to levy a heavy fine of $3,500 for one count only and to suspend sentence on the others, reminding the doctor that he could have received as much as ten years' imprisonment. Total costs to Foote came to about $5,000, part of which was raised by his supporters. Had it not been for the general business depression, Foote believed, his friends would have raised the entire amount.[19]

Foote's *Medical Common Sense* had offered four types of contraceptives for sale, leading off with the "Membraneous Envelope." Foote explained the superiority of this device over the conventional condom in terms of his eccentric philosophy about sexual intercourse. The condom, or ordinary "French male safe" which was made from the intestines of sheep or hogs, was "more or less permeated with oleaginous or fatty matter, which is a non-conductor of electricity, and consequently a non-conductor of the magnetism of the sexes." More to the point, one imagines, the Membraneous Envelope was much thinner and more flexible than the condom, and thus, wrote the doctor, its use did not "in the least interfere with the pleasure of the act." Made from the bladder of a fish caught in the Rhine, this silky-textured sheath weighed only an average of ten grains, but Foote claimed that it surpassed the ordinary condom in strength. One could rely on the item to prevent conception as well as disease, a consideration of growing importance since "many married men are proverbially promiscuous, and do not attempt to hide their habits from their wives; and such persons, particularly, ought for humanity's sake to employ the Membraneous Envelope when having sexual connection with their wives—and the latter could not be blamed for rigidly insisting upon it." The mail-order price was high, five dollars a dozen, but a sample could be had for one dollar. As he did with all his contraceptive items, Foote allowed no agents and he warned against unreliable imitations.

He offered one other contraceptive for use by the male, the "Apex Envelope." This thin rubber device covered the head of the penis only; today it would be called a glans sheath. Foote did not hide its disadvantages. Made of rubber, it could not conduct chemical electricity in sexual intercourse, nor did it allow the alkali-acid interchange that was present in ideal coitus. However, it did have an advantage over the condom in that it did not insulate the whole phallus from the alleged exchange of electricity. He vouched for the safety of the sheath, and sold it at three dollars a dozen.

He offered two contraceptives for use by the female, the sex that should rightly control conception, since "she will become the mother, and the moral, religious, and physical instructress of offspring." The first device, sketchily described as an Electro-Magnetic Preventive Machine, conjures up grotesque images even though he assured his readers that it would not interfere with even unrestrained intercourse; and, he emphasized, "There *are no painful shocks or injurious results attending its use.*" Foote explained that the machine worked by exciting the womb electrically so that the sperm would not be retained. He did not explain in detail how the user applied the machine to her body, but only assured the ladies that it was not disagreeable. Whatever problems attended the contraption—and he referred darkly to one instance of failure, a fault that he chalked up to stupidity on the part of the operator—he claimed an eight-year record of success for everyone else who had used the device.

If the aspect of wired intercourse did not scare customers away, it seemed likely that the price of the machine would. It cost fifteen dollars, probably more than most people would pay for an experimental and possibly dangerous method of contraception.

It is characteristic of Foote that his inventions not only included a questionable electrical gadget but also a truly pioneer contribution to contraceptive technology, the rubber cervical cap. Although there is evidence that something like a cervical cap may have been used earlier in Germany, Foote probably did develop the idea independently and was probably justified in his claim that he invented it. He called the cap a Womb Veil, and as he described its function, it became clear that the device had several advantages over other methods. Easily fitted over the mouth of the uterus, even in the dark, it allowed "full enjoyment of the conjugal embrace," free from noticeable obstruction. It functioned simply and effectively as a mechanical sperm barrier; it could be used for years without replacement, and he added, it provided no barrier to the interchange of electricity and the interaction of acid and alkali. It sold for six dollars.[20]

Foote considered only these four means to be reliable for contraception. He notably excluded the syringe for water douching by the female after intercourse. This common practice, Foote believed, failed in eighty cases in a hundred. He warned of the flood of dangerous and quack contraceptives on the market, such as caustic douches and pills for men and women. He harshly criticized the practice of "withdrawal," or coitus interruptus, wherein the sexual act was not consummated nor was the sexual excitement diffused. Pent-up agitation from its regular practice created a progressive psychological and physical deterioration, and Foote considered it to be little more than masturbation or "self-pollution" for both sexes.[21]

Between 1858, when his book first appeared, and 1876, when he was obliged to expurgate the portions that dealt with means for contraception, he had sold, by his own estimate, about three hundred thousand copies of the book. There is no record of how many copies of "Words in Pearl" he distributed, but we may assume that he achieved his goal of demonstrating that contraceptives could be made widely available to married people through the medical profession. Foote replaced "Words in Pearl" with a pamphlet that was critical of the Comstock laws, "A Step Backwards"; and his expurgated *Medical Common Sense* now included a protest against the laws. Perhaps as a tactic to win repeal of the laws, he placed new stress on his eugenic argument for birth control, since it appealed to both social conservatives and progressives.

In the 1890s, *Dr. Foote's Health Monthly* included a regular department called Race Culture, in which he popularized the theories of important scientists such as Galton, Weismann, Darwin, and Lester Ward. It also reported the goings-on of such early organizations as the Institute of Heredity (New York), founded in 1881, and the Neo-Malthusians in Britain. Foote's works enjoyed great popularity on the Continent and in England, and Foote responded by taking an active interest in the English birth-control movement. He tried to create public support in the United States for Charles Bradlaugh and Annie Besant in their famous 1877 trial for selling Knowlton's *Fruits of Philosophy*. Besides publicizing their cause, he contributed money for their defense. Foote also gave financial aid to Edward Truelove, another English rationalist who stood trial about the same time as Bradlaugh and Besant for publishing another American pamphlet written in the 1830s, Robert Dale Owen's *Moral Physiology*. The elderly Truelove became the Malthusian League's first martyr when he suffered a short but cruel prison sentence.[22]

Foote's generosity and that of his son, who inherited his wealth, supported various reformers, radicals, and causes in times of need. Besides aiding English Malthusians and American social radicals such as Ezra Heywood, D. M. Bennett, and Moses Harman, the Footes contributed also in the wider political arena, helping Susan B. Anthony and the Populist party in New York, as well as giving funds to lobbying attempts against the Comstock laws.

Their interest in reform work often displayed a thorough commitment. Lillian Harman wrote that "both doctors were always very friendly to *Lucifer*, but after the cessation of the publication of the *Health Monthly* they seemed almost 'silent partners' in the publication of the paper—so warm was their interest, so ready their words of cheer and their financial assistance."[23]

The younger Dr. Foote received the elitist education that was denied to his father. Born in 1854, he attended the Charlier Institute in New York, studied science as an undergraduate at Columbia College, and later graduated from its College of Physicians and Surgeons. He and his father then founded the *Health Monthly*, which they edited together from the mid seventies to the mid nineties. In the words of Theodore Schroeder, an authority on free speech, this journal gave "an extraordinary number of reforms . . . their earliest publicity." Among other causes, it championed eugenics, women's property rights, free thought, contraception, abolition of interest, abolition of Comstockery, and Greenbackism. The paper also served as the unofficial organ for the free-speech efforts of the National Defense Association, and of course, it sought to popularize medical knowledge.[24]

The work of Edward Bond Foote can hardly be separated from that of his father. The younger Foote extended and developed some of the beliefs of the elder doctor and gave a respectably modern cast to many of the mid-nineteenth-century notions of his father. By his revisions of his father's books he literally made them his own, a friend noted. Despite his establishment credentials, the younger Foote chose to adopt his father's attitude toward the regular school of medical practice. At a time of increasing professionalization and of increasing state regulation of medicine, "Ned" Foote held that medical knowledge should be popularized and broadcast rather than mystified by elite professionals. The young man, of course, soon grew as unpopular with the established profession as his father was. In a literal sense, father and son were contemporaries—they died within six years of one another.

Ned Foote apparently showed a more direct interest in radical causes, and perhaps less interest in medicine, than did his father. An early radical speech on birth control that he made before the New York Liberal Club caused a furor that reportedly led to the dissolution of the club. Afterwards, Foote helped to organize the more radical members into a new club, the Manhattan Liberal Club, which attracted such personages as Stephen Pearl Andrews, Walt Whitman, and Horace Greeley. Foote held the office of president for many years, a position that was first held by Greeley. For a third of a century, wrote Theodore Schroeder, the Manhattan organization offered a platform for the most radical thinkers in the city.[25]

In 1878 Foote and eight others initiated the National Defense Association. Foote served as its first secretary; the Biblical scholar Albert Rawson served as president; and John P. Jewett, the publisher of Harriet Beecher Stowe and Margaret Fuller, was vice-president. The association proposed to investigate all questionable cases of prosecution under both federal and state Comstock laws and to defend those who were "unjustly assailed by the enemies of free speech and free press." The organization notably aided Ezra Heywood and D. M. Bennett in their legal battles. Besides soliciting defense funds and passing protest petitions, it staged the large meeting at Faneuil Hall on 1 August 1878 to protest against Heywood's imprisonment. Laura Kendrick, who was designated by the association to present the petition for Heywood's pardon to President Hayes, traveled to Washington and accomplished the feat by "infinite tact and persuasive tongue," according to Benjamin Tucker. When Hayes pardoned Heywood the following December and when his attorney general ruled that the advocacy of the abolition of marriage was not obscene, the N.D.A. had won its first big victory.

The association met the Vice Society on its home grounds, flooding their meetings with counter-Comstock propaganda. It aided such victims as Elmina Slenker in her 1886 arrest for mailing obscene letters, and it energetically defended Walt Whitman in the attempt to suppress his *Leaves of Grass* in Boston in 1882. It is doubtful whether Harman could have continued his anti-Comstock efforts beyond his first imprisonment except for the aid of the N.D.A. and the personal help of Foote. With some success, the association mounted lobbying campaigns in Washington and in state capitals against attempts to strengthen existing Comstock legislation. Along this line, it failed in its campaign to stay the Post Office Department from developing into an autonomous censoring agency, but the organization continued to agitate against what it saw as the increasing authoritarianism of the Harrison administration. Elizur Wright, who died in 1885 while he was president of the N.D.A., typified the old-line reform types such as Theron C. Leland, Thaddeus B. Wakeman, and Stephen Pearl Andrews, who provided the moral backbone of the organization.[26]

In 1902 Ned Foote's money and encouragement helped to found the Free Speech League, a spiritual forerunner of the present-day American Civil Liberties Union. The league grew out of proposals by the *Torch of Reason* (Silverton, Oreg.), *Discontent* (Home, Wash.), and the Manhattan Liberal Club that a committee be formed to "devise ways and means for a united and an effective movement in defense of that which is fundamental to all progress,—liberty of investigation and expression." Recent cases of government suppression spurred the creation of the league, particularly the harassment of the Home Community in Washington State and Comstock's hounding of Ida Craddock in New York for her booklets containing marital advice. Edwin C. Walker, president of the Manhattan Liberal Club, became provisional president of the league, and Foote served as treasurer. Besides Foote and Walker, others who helped to initiate the league included Moses Oppenheimer and Moncure D. Conway. Oppenheimer and Walker drafted the simple constitution. Foote later was credited as being the founder of the league, perhaps because of his financial aid and because he officially incorporated the league in 1911.

The Free Speech League concerned itself primarily with the defense of anarchists and sexual reformers—those who historically needed the most help in securing free speech in the United States. The league became the John Turner Defense Committee in 1903, when it mobilized to take the deportation case of an English anarchist, John Turner, to the Supreme Court. In these years the league attracted such figures in politics and journalism as Brand Whitlock and Lincoln Steffens. Much of the organization's efforts were channeled through an energetic attorney, Theodore Schroeder, who acted as a sort of one-man A.C.L.U. By means of testimony and an enormous amount of writing, he publicized numerous obscure cases of censorship, and he established himself as the nation's most prolific defender of free expression. He served for a time as associate editor of *Arena*, and he compiled the memorial biography of Ned Foote.[27]

In 1886 the younger Foote published *The Radical Remedy in Social Science: or Borning Better Babies through Regulating Reproduction by Controlling Conception*, which argued that present contraceptive knowledge could counter the recklessness of "natural" human propagation. In order to describe the basic social evils, he used the metaphor of a great tree, with ignorance as its roots and reckless propagation as the trunk "leading to one great branch called over-population, and to another called evil heredity tendencies, while in the entangled branches would be found the luxuriant crop of individual social evils." It was a plea to break the cruel chains of Malthus's "positive checks" on population— war, famine, disease—by enlightened, voluntary action:

We want a sufficient education in the science of private and public hygiene and morals, and especially in the direction of sex, reproduction and heredity, which shall be so general that every man and woman at the age of puberty shall know enough, and be religiously inclined, to guard against crippling himself or herself, the family or society, by indulging in vice of any kind, and particularly that of reckless propagation.[28]

A summation of his mature thought on birth control and eugenics appeared in a 1910 article in *Medical Critic and Guide*. Under all circumstances, he wrote, contraception was preferable to abortion and insofar as possible should be substituted for it. He felt that those who saw contraception as a "waste of seed" should consider the present "waste of the products of conception" that unchecked breeding brought about. If the physical health of either partner should be threatened by children, he advised contraception; in fact, if either parent believed it unwise to have children for any reason, then contraception was justified. Some persons, such as Theodore Roosevelt, felt that widespread birth control would cause extensive depopulation, particularly among the most "fit" classes and races. Foote believed that no such "race suicide" would occur, because "there is enough parental instinct, fatherly and motherly feeling, to insure the perpetuation of the race and the best specimens of it." To those who worried that contraceptives might destroy moral virtues by removing the obvious and traditional sanction to sexual intercourse (that is, children), he wrote that "the virtue worth preserving is not that which merely depends upon fear of consequences; where it [virtue] is lacking, fear does not save."

His hereditarian beliefs were no longer simplistic nor mechanistic. Instead of a direct relationship between overpopulation, heredity, and poverty, he now felt that "reckless reproduction and over-population are concomitants if not direct causes of poverty, pauperism, prostitution, drunkenness, crime, imbecility, insanity, infanticide, etc." He believed that regulation of reproduction through available contraceptives would be "one effective remedy" for these social ills, though not the panacea. He did not feel that certain government or social agencies should decide who should or should not propagate. The question, rather, should be a purely family affair, decided by "the only two persons directly interested." Foote's attitudes, which were essentially contemporary with those of the late twentieth century, led Norman E. Himes, the historian of contraception, to judge that Foote was "remarkably in advance" of his American medical colleagues in 1910.[29]

Ned Foote probably gave more generously to radical causes than did his philanthropic father. He took particular interest in Emma Goldman's *Mother Earth* and Harman's *Lucifer*. When he died, *Mother Earth* said of him: "He differed from the average liberal in that he was a firm and active believer in Free Speech even for those with whom he did not agree." It went on to praise him for his sympathy and concrete assistance to all who were persecuted for their utterances, from violent revolutionaries to benign idealists. He "*really* believed in freedom of speech," underscored the anarchist journal.

After his death, a memorial volume appeared, which celebrated the breadth of Foote's philanthropy. Unintentionally it pointed up the ironies of a capitalist social order that would allow its sex-reform entrepreneurs, the Drs. Foote, to inherit and accumulate great wealth while they in turn gave much of it back to those who would alter the system. Young Foote was extremely discreet in his giving, and one writer explained that "no organization received enough at one time to furnish spectacular headlines in the newspapers, but he probably gave most of his earnings."[30]

Ned Foote wrote *The Radical Remedy in Social Science* in the belief that he had only a few months to live. He actually lived for twenty-six more years—to the age of fifty-eight—with a progressively debilitating paralysis, which in his last years made him physically helpless. Like a true Malthusian and eugenicist, he married late and had no children.

12/ Handmaidens of Diana: Superwomen vs. "Cumberers of the Ground"

A DECADE after the arrests of Foote, Heywood, and Bennett, the hand of Comstockery began to work in earnest outside the Northeast. R. W. McAfee, western agent of the Society for Prevention of Vice, engineered one of the first important obscenity arrests in his bailiwick when he took into custody an old Quakerish lady, Elizabeth ("Elmina") Drake Slenker, in Virginia.

"She was probably more widely known than any other person of her peculiar 'faith,' " reported the *New York Times* in its account of her 1887 arrest. Since "a large number of letters and publications of the most obscene description were found in her possession," and since she refused to swear on a Bible at her preliminary hearing because she did not believe in the Bible, Christianity, God, heaven, hell, devils, angels, or ghosts, the *Times* allowed its readers only one conclusion about the nature of her peculiar faith—free thought *qua* free love. Indeed the whole cause of her arrest could be laid to the debilitations of libertinism: "Her belief in free love," wrote the correspondent, "has doubtless developed into a mania which has rendered her unguarded in her frequent violations of the postal laws."[1]

Born sixty years earlier into a Quaker household in Lagrange, New York, Elizabeth Drake grew up personally acquainted with a brilliant circle of reformers, which included the feminists Abby Kelley Foster and Ernestine Rose and the abolitionists Henry C. Wright and Parker Pillsbury. Her father, a Quaker minister who had been expelled by his congregation because of his freethinking tendencies, made their home into a sanctuary for abolitionists, feminists, and assorted dissenters. At age fourteen she began taking critical notes on the Bible which, years later in final form, appeared as a series of articles in the *Boston Investigator*. J. P. Mendum, publisher of the paper, also issued the lengthy series as a separate volume, *Studying the Bible: or, Brief Criticisms on Some of the Principal Scripture Texts* (1870). Although Slenker became most widely known as a free-thought publicist, over her lifetime she espoused the causes of temperance, free soil, water cure, phrenology, abolition, feminism, and sexual reform.

As the eldest of six sisters in her family, Elizabeth gained an early appreciation for feminine assertiveness. Wanting a husband at age twenty-six, she put into practice her ideas on woman's equality and advertised in the *Water-Cure Journal* for one. She received over sixty replies and soon married one of the respondents, Isaac Slenker, in a simple Quaker-style agreement.[2]

She adopted the pen name Elmina, and as she grew older she became "Aunt Elmina" to numerous reformers who knew her and had been addressed with her personal "thee." The *Times* portrait of Elmina seemed to bear out the dictum of the *Ladies' Companion* that "female irreligion is the most revolting feature in human character"; according to the news story, "Mrs. Slenker is an exceedingly homely woman. She can hardly be said to have a single attractive feature, and as if to render herself more unprepossessing, she wears her hair short, after the manner of women of 'advanced ideas.'"

Neither the disfigurement of irreligion or her cleft palate stifled her literary energy; her articles were regularly appearing in two dozen different journals at the time of her arrest. Although her arguments leaned toward the clever rather than the analytic, she seemed to be an instinctual reformer, with a well-read intelligence and a flair for raising issues. She wrote several didactic and romantic novels, which were usually published by the free-thought press: *John's Way* (1878); *The Clergyman's Victims* (18—); *Mary Jones, the Infidel School-Teacher* (1885); and *The Darwins* (1879). A discussion of her ideas in *Lucifer* provoked one of the obscenity indictments against Harman. Elmina often wrote for *Lucifer*; one of her more notable articles suggested that women should have access to free contraceptives as a starting point for freeing the sex.

She edited a special department in the *Investigator*, and for a time she served as an editor of the short-lived New York journal *Physiologist and Family Physician*. She published *Little Lessons for Little Folks* in 1886, and she conducted a children's column in *Lucifer*, telling stories in which the syrupy good guys were always infidels rather than Christians.

After editing the *Plaindealer* of Hastings, Michigan, in the early 1890s, she capped her children's crusade by starting a none-too-successful junior journal called the *Little Freethinker*. A talented teacher, she appeared to be well versed in Darwin, Spencer, and lesser theorists, whom she often cited to support her controversial stances.[3]

About 1880 she moved with her husband to the little village of Snowville, Virginia, where he operated the local woolen mills. During this period she directed a great deal of her energy toward the prohibition of alcohol. She viewed drink as the worst foe of the household, but her atheism kept her out of most temperance and prohibition leagues. Her increasing interest in sex reform, as well as her interest in free thought, alienated most of her neighbors in Virginia. Even her husband disapproved so much of her sex radicalism that he refused to post bail when she was eventually arrested.

Her approach to the sex question, as she came to deal with it in the 1880s, drew heavily upon her views on alcohol. In various forms she would preach sexual temperance for the next thirty years in many of the same terms that she had earlier preached alcoholic temperance. Although both sex and alcohol had positive if limited attributes, both were pleasures that were too easily indulged. Both gave temporary intoxication and pleasure to the senses but left the victim drained and exhausted. Both were habit-forming and, if continually indulged, would undermine spiritual and physical health. Any sexual activity or drinking that was solely for pleasure, in fact, was overindulgence. And since neither drink nor sex appealed to women as they did to men, both were masculine instruments for the destruction of the home and its queen, the wife. The unholy union of sex with drunkenness not only caused the degradation of womanhood; it also caused the conception of defective children. Woman's only apparent reward in this travail was the affirmation of her superiority over man. In Elmina's essay "Sexual Intemperance," she declared that

> we all know intemperance always grows out of temperate tippling, out of "enjoying" with the proviso of not overstepping the bounds of "moderation." But read the record and ask yourselves if there must not be bounds set and adhered to if safety is expected. And in this question of sexuality there is but one possible boundary, and that is, the legitimate and natural use of the function—propagation of our kind!

Elmina's essay reflected the influence of an early Swiss medical doctor and theorist of sexuality, Samuel Tissot, as well as the thought of two nineteenth-century Americans, Sylvester Graham and Thomas Low Nichols. Tissot argued that semen was the distillate vital force of the blood, so concentrated that its loss by ejaculation weakened the body more than did the loss of many ounces of blood. Graham and Nichols, on the other hand, argued that postclimactic exhaustion came, not from the loss of semen itself, but from the drainage of nervous energy. Countering the argument that moderate sexual indulgence was necessary in order to appease "natural desire," Elmina explained that every indulgence diverted "vital power from the brain and vital principle from the blood" and that continued excesses weakened the entire mental and physical system. Besides, she wrote on another occasion, "nature" was mostly what she was educated to be—a thesis that undermined most theories of sexual deportment. Only the pure and happy love that indulged in intercourse for the sake of procreation could afford to lose a little of the vital force.[4]

This doctrine of prohibiting coition except for propagation, which Elmina began to promote in the early 1880s, was known as Alphaism, and was part of the larger "Social Purity" movement which sought to cleanse society through the elimination of such evils as drinking, prostitution, and obscenity. Elmina's strictures on coitus did not appeal to most Lucifereans, and it may be said that she represented the "right wing" of the libertarian sex radicals. Many *Lucifer* essayists doubted that such sexual restraint could be applied to average households, and they criticized Elmina for deserting her earlier contraceptive principles in favor of abstinence.[5]

Elmina promoted the journal of the new puritans, the *Alpha* (Washington, D.C.), "a paper devoted to sexual purity and moral goodness—5¢," in her regular ads in *Lucifer*. She made her meager living, incidentally, by the sale of reformatory literature through such ads. These purity reformers, part of the general woman's movement of the late nineteenth century, dominated agencies of social feminism such as the WCTU, and they attempted, in short, to impose a traditional puritanism on an increasingly urbanized, industrial society.[6] In the main, their attitudes on marriage and the family conflicted with the antimarriage doctrines of free lovers.

On the surface it might have seemed incongruous that an elderly "obscenist," a regular contributor to the free-love *Lucifer*, would have identified herself with the Social Purity movement. But free lovers and Social Puritans both sought essential sexual reforms. The sex radicals of *Lucifer* could be considered the libertarian faction of sex reform, whereas the Social Puritans could be considered restrictionists. In contrast to the libertarians, this latter group plumped for traditional morality, sought the support of organized religion, viewed mankind as basically depraved, and sought to enforce "purity" through authoritarian means. At the heart of the matter was a divergence over the nature of morality: true morality required the operation of choice and could not be coerced, wrote Lillian Harman, speaking for the free lovers. Anthony Comstock's crusade against the obscenity of the sex radicals may be viewed as a conflict between reformers. In fact, B. O. Flower—the anti-Comstock editor of *Arena*, who sympathized with much of sex radicalism—sat on the executive board of the American Purity Alliance with Anthony Comstock. Even *Christian Life* (Morton Park, Ill.), the Social Purity journal which superseded the *Alpha*, once had kind words for Moses Harman and harsh ones for the postal censors—and subsequently Comstock arrested its editor. Although restrictionists and libertarians had differing notions about sexual purity and different ideas about implementing it, common interests also existed, one of which was the belief among some members of both groups that intercourse should be limited to propagative purposes. Free love, after all, implied freedom *from* sexual engagement, and hence was consistent with Alphaism. Elmina Slenker and another Luciferean, Lucinda

Chandler, served as visible links between Social Purity and sex radicalism.[7]

Although Alphaism found favor among dissimilar reformers, one can guess that the cause faced poorer prospects of success than did liquor prohibition. Never one to value theory over practical realities, Elmina eventually dropped Alphaism for its sister doctrine, Dianaism. This theory recognized that mankind was too "debased" for the high ideals of Alpha abstinence and conceded that sexual hunger must be satisfied in some way. Elmina seized on this revised theory as the true method of sexual temperance and set about to prove the doctrine to the world. Thereby she crossed the Comstock laws.

Diana: A Psycho-fyziological Essay on Sexual Relations for Married Men and Women, which was anonymously written by an obscure sociologist named Henry M. Parkhurst, printed by a phonetic publishing house, and championed by Elmina Slenker, owed much to the ideas of John Humphrey Noyes. Noyes taught that the genitals had two other functions besides the elimination of waste: the amative and the propagative function. This idea had extreme importance to those seeking the "natural law" of sexual relationships since it made possible the justification of sexual pleasure as a discrete function of the sex organs—thus coition purely for pleasure was validated.[8]

In theory, therefore, contraception could be justified by this argument, provided that there were suitable arguments against "wasting seed." No very good contraceptives were available in mid century, of course, and an alternative suggested itself to the spiritually minded leader of the Oneida Community—male continence.

"In intercourse the male inserted his penis into the vagina and retained it there for even an hour without emission, though orgasm took place in the woman. There was usually no emission in the case of the man, even after withdrawal, and he felt no need of emission," so one former member of Oneida, George Noyes Miller, described male continence in a study by Havelock Ellis. The method, first enunciated by Noyes in *The Bible Argument* (1848), is not to be confused with *coitus interruptus*, which describes the withdrawal of the phallus from the vagina at the onset of male orgasm so that ejaculation occurs outside the vagina. Male orgasm is avoided in male continence, but it is replaced, partisans claimed, by a high level of extended sensory and spiritual pleasure. The couple engages in the normal motions of intercourse, being careful to avoid male climax, and the phallus is retained in the vagina until detumescence occurs. With no strictures on her climax and with reduced fear of pregnancy, the woman may fully benefit from this generally unhurried, extended form of lovemaking.[9]

The idea of male continence had mythical and durable attractions: it offered the temporal delights of sex without the propagative cost, while at the same time conducting the participants to the higher realms of spirituality by overcoming the temptations of physical consummation—a patent case of man's "higher nature" conquering his "baser." Although Noyes arrived at the doctrine as a spiritually acceptable method of birth control which made complex marriage feasible, Alice B. Stockham's *Karezza: Ethics of Marriage* (1896) promoted the technique as a way to improve monogamous marriage, particularly the lot of the woman. Beneath her prosy tribute to spirituality in marriage lay the explicit details of the contraceptive method. The appendix of *Karezza* excerpted substantial portions of *Male Continence*, which in the 1890s was out of print.

The labels "Karezza" and "Zugassent's Discovery," from George Noyes Miller's 1895 book of that title, attached to the technique as Marie Stopes described it in *Married Love* (1918) and in *Contraception* (1926). In the latter she cited E. B. Foote and Margaret Sanger on the subject, but advised generally against experimenting with the practice. Recent editions of the perennial manual *Ideal Marriage: Its Physiology and Technique* (1926–1967), by T. H. van de Velde, still note the practice invidiously. Contraceptive technology has not completely outmoded variations on this technique. In the folklore of the contemporary counterculture, the practice of containing the ejaculate by muscular control during climax is described. The purpose of this is not contraceptive but epicurean, to prolong sexual intercourse and to avoid premature ejaculation.[10] And in the East, various yogic systems stress the retention of sperm and the cultivation of sexual energy, a purpose that, in its own way, the *Diana* essay attempted to promote.

By justifying pleasure as a separate and natural function of the genitals, Noyes provided an argument favoring sexual indulgence for those not connected with his Perfectionist community, or so the sexual "prohibitionists" believed, who wanted to restrict sex to purposes of propagation and alcohol to use as a remedy for flu. They believed that the spirituality of male continence should be raised another degree: this was the goal of *Diana*.

As Noyes had partitioned sexuality in *Male Continence*, Parkhurst divided sexual *desire* in *Diana*. All sexual feeling was physical in origin, deriving from the "sexual batteries" such as the ovaries of woman and the testes of man. From these batteries came the different identities and functions of the sexes and the two different kinds of sexual desire: affectional, or the general attraction between the genders, which might be analogized as the magnetic attraction of opposite polarity; and the generative, or the desire to create new life by the union of sperm and egg. The two components were independent, so the indulgence of affectional feelings did not necessarily tend to create generative desires, although in man's present brutish state, the two classes of feelings were generally confounded.[11]

In an early statement about sexual sublimation, *Diana* asserted that humans might be sexually satisfied by indulging the affectional feelings "without calling into action the special generative function of the sexual organs." But if "repression of this affectional activity" occurred, as was often the case in human relations, the desire for such activity became so intense that when opportunity for expression finally arose, "the activity becomes so great as to tend to call, under our present habits of the association of ideas, for the secretion and the emission of sperm." The true remedy for sexual intemperance, *Diana* stated, required the "full satisfaction of the affectional mode of activity by frequent and free sexual contact," which was chaste rather than amorous. Since the method and amount of sexual gratification depended upon the will, let the mind be convinced, urged *Diana*, that the highest gratification would be found in continence. To improve upon Noyes's theory, "full satisfaction may be reached without even approaching amorous excitement," which inhered in male continence. In *Diana*'s eyes, continence required more than nonejaculation.[12]

Dianaist gratification could take many forms, depending upon the individual: mere physical presence, conversation, a hand clasp, an embrace. Several times the pamphlet discussed the question of nudity. Since habits of association determined the erotic content in the sight or contact of the nude form, one should learn to associate nudity with affectional feelings by frequent nude contact "when the affectional action is all that is felt or thought of, in order to cultivate such habits and associations as will make the sight and contact of the nude form tend to repress passional desires." When man and wife learn "to be together, seeing each other, and embracing each other without the intervention of clothing, and to enjoy such caresses disassociated from passional feelings, there will be little danger . . . [of] sexual excess" which destroys mutual attraction. *Diana* unabashedly recommended nudity to its readers, yet because so much depended upon habit, it allowed that the pervasive urge for naked association might spring from "perverted passion" rather than from normal sexual feeling; only time and the correct channelization of sexual feeling would reveal the answer. In the individual's search for true satisfaction, *Diana* never doubted the necessity for both physical and spiritual contact, but of the two, the spiritual provided the greater portion of satisfaction.[13]

One popular argument-from-nature that *Diana* was forced to meet was that of "essential emission," which held that the body continuously and automatically manufactured sperm and ova and that these had to be excreted in some way, if not by coition or masturbation, then by nature's course of nocturnal or periodic emissions. This position could justify almost unlimited sexual activity. In the absence of much empirical study, dialectic still ruled in such "scientific" arguments. The author of *Diana* believed that man had simply cultivated the bad habit of manufacturing an abundance of sperm. After all, as one Dianaist colorfully put it, "some men will spit a pint a day, others seldom or never spit," depending upon their habituation. Parkhurst recognized that the overproduction of "germs" had ensured man's survival in the evolutionary past, but now, he asserted, "we have reached a period in the world's history when we need quality rather than quantity; and now the preservation of our full vigor by avoiding all useless expenditure, is equally a benefit to the individual and to the race." Germ production, also, depended upon the will.[14]

At heart *Diana* was a nun, an upholder of the venerable notion that abstinence augmented spirituality. *Diana* considered the enjoyment of affectional sex attraction a "chaste pleasure" which contrasted to the degradation of the "momentary paroxysm" of amorousness. Those who might wonder what was wrong with momentary paroxysm received an essentially religious argument for their answer. In fact, *Diana* seemed to be a replay of religious efforts to make sex into a religion—to glorify one facet of sexuality and to degrade another, to indulge platonic aspects and to make a virtue of denying orgasmic sex. Orgasm, *Diana* declared several times, had "evil effects" and was "injurious." *Diana* quoted in full Elmina Slenker's statement on the weakening effects of orgasm. For its suspicion that nothing as pleasurable as orgasm could be good and for its attempt to rationalize the irrational, *Diana* deserves a secure place in the literature of denial. At the same time it should be remembered that Dianaist methods of contact countenanced almost any degree of physical interaction short of orgasm. The pamphlet warned, however, that internal genital contact, such as that associated with male continence, clearly invited sexual excess. Individual experience alone would determine the sort and amount of physical contact that were necessary for satisfaction.[15]

Another aspect of *Diana*'s religiosity was the deification of the female. Quoting Elmina Slenker, the pamphlet stressed that a husband's chaste affection would convince a wife that he is "one friend who is ever fond and ever true, and is her very own to love and be loved, not in lust and passion, but with a higher and holier oneness of heart, mind, and soul." Orgasm could be justified only when it had the "high and holy purpose" of child-making. It was a logical step, then, to make the bed into an altar. Parkhurst argued that husband and wife should sleep together "with such degree of nude contact as may be adapted to each individual case," so that affectional feelings might be expressed and interchanged. Some sexual thinkers of the time, such as E. B. Foote, believed that sleeping together made people become less attractive to one another, and he advised against the practice. Parkhurst could see only one reason for following Dr. Foote's prescription of separate beds—if "the wife's bed be sacred to the higher law" of orgasmic denial. On such a sanctified mattress "association will be more free . . . from the knowledge that it will not be regarded as inviting ultimation."[16]

Arguments against orgasm often imply a religious theme, perhaps because in the Western dualistic tradition the supernatural seems to be the only force that is strong enough to contend with the passion-engorged animal. Such an argument may idealize the cloistered life as one that is free from the ups and downs of ordinary living. *Diana* voiced this desire for religious tranquility: "The maximum of enjoyment is not to be found in increasing the ecstasy of the scattered moments of pleasure, so much as in making more tolerable the hours of pain. We must fill up the valleys, taking the earth from the hilltops, to make the pathway more smooth." If life consisted of "exaltations, followed by corresponding depressions," added the writer, "the total of our happiness will be less."[17] *Diana* argued that people should savor the anticipatory joys of very infrequent orgasm and should cherish their memories of it from experiences long-past. In advancing orgasm to the category of the unordinary, *Diana* deified it. This romantic vision indicted coitions of normal married life as "fleeting sensations of the moment, unanticipated yesterday, experienced today, and forgotton tomorrow." Repetition, *Diana* taught, does not double the pleasure of an act.

With this line of argument, *Diana* broached a sensual justification for temperance, suggesting the gourmand's logic against that of the glutton. To strain nerves to their fullest in sexual climax soon ruined the entire affective palate and made one incapable of "real, quiet, satisfactory enjoyment of anything." In fact, the author justified the principle of orgasmic abstinence except for propagation solely in physical terms as bringing about "the greatest amount of physical pleasure" and, again, as giving the "most vivid pleasures." It appeared that *Diana* thus hedged its spiritual bet; if supernatural arguments could not convince the orgasm seekers, then perhaps the sensual arguments could.[18]

Diana's attempt to intensify the spiritual aspect of sexual relations emphasized the confusion arising from the assumption that the sensual opposes the spiritual. The dichotomy is hallowed in Western tradition, yet so is the confusion—the English language utilizes the word "feeling" to denote both phenomena. In its assertion that sexual intercourse encompassed more than orgasm,

Diana spoke wisdom to the durable tendency to make intercourse a purely climax-oriented act. Yet *Diana* appealed chiefly to those who sought to subdue the sensual, rather than those who sought an integration of the body and spirit through sex.

The pamphlet, in fact, won a partisan in Count Leo Tolstoy, who had been sent a copy in 1891 by the publishers. His essay "What 'Diana' Teaches" appeared in the Russian journal *Nedelya* ("the week"), and translated by N. H. Dole of Boston, it appeared in *Lucifer*.[19] The essay was later printed as a pamphlet and sold by *Lucifer*. Because of his importance as a writer and because of the apparent originality of his comment on the American pamphlet and the American scene, Tolstoy's essay is included in the Appendix.

In 1886, after Elmina had been advertising *Diana* in *Lucifer* for three years, the pamphlet went into its third edition. During this time she had promoted the pamphlet and publicized its arguments to such an extent that readers commonly assumed that she had written it. She encouraged the identification, adopting the persona of *Diana* and using "Diana" for a second pen name. The pamphlet, which had extensively cited Elmina's own writings, served in fact as a clarification of her beliefs: rather than *Diana* influencing Elmina, it seemed that Elmina had inspired *Diana*. In the inquiry following her arrest on obscenity charges, one of the crucial assumptions of the officials appeared to have been that Elmina was the author of *Diana*.

Elmina's efforts for Dianaist temperance did not follow a narrow dogmatism. In speaking of extracopulative sexual release, she and other Dianaists made clear that the diffusion of affectional feelings could be accomplished in a number of ways, "by direct external contact of the sexual organs, or by other contact which shall indirectly diffuse the magnetism." In any event, the question should be decided according to individual circumstances. Elmina stressed the double value of the Dianaist theory: it would effectively provide an outlet for sexual desire, and at the same time it would liberate the practicing parties from the consequences of conventional coitus—childbirth. The inscription "For Married Men and Women" appeared on the booklet mainly to thwart criticism, and Slenker logically saw the method as one answer to the problems of serious young lovers who could not yet afford the expense of marriage, but who suffered from the customary sexual impulses.[20]

Justifying her position in *Lucifer*, she wrote: "If a few outside of marriage find Dianaism a better and safer vent, is it not the more practicable of the two and less disastrous in its results?" Guilelessly she continued, "There are 64,000 more women than men in Massachusetts and an excess of females in twenty-two states. All of these are without sexual satisfaction of any kind save that of seeing, talking with and association in a brotherly way with men." She hastened to add that "free love and variety are no remedy for this, for passion grows by what it feeds upon, and sexual intemperance will only be increased by freedom and variety unless a true sexual education be given to all, and as I have before observed—Love be turned into other channels than coition." Presumably, Dianaism, with its nude association and noncoition, would do the latter. In the Victorian era, Elmina's recognition of female sexual passion was an exception, particularly among "sexual temperance" types. "Passion is not all confined to one sex," she once wrote, "and thousands of women are sexually intemperate from heredity and false training just as men are."[21]

As an effective method of birth control, Dianaism had eugenical applications. Elmina saw crime as a mere symptom of deeper social ills, ills that had roots in individual heredity, prenatal influence, and early training. By providing a sexual outlet for those who, eugenically speaking, should not produce children, Dianaism could aid in the perfection of mankind. *Lucifer* once pointed out that *Diana* expressed the "conservative viewpoint" toward sex, referring to its belief in the corrupting nature of sexual passion. Such conservatism notwithstanding, it is easy to see how *Diana*, with its admonitions to individual experimentation in nude relations, could be construed as upholding the virtue of sex play.[22]

As Elmina evolved into Diana, vice-society agent R. W. McAfee became aware of her. According to the *New York Times*, Elmina had distributed *Diana* and other examples of "free love" literature in large quantities all over the country. McAfee first noticed the pamphlets in Indiana. He contacted the Post Office Department, which had been working up a case against Elmina for several years and which at one time had assigned as many as four detectives to the case. McAfee teamed up with post-office inspector

W. A. Barclay from Richmond to work out a strategy for the arrest of Elmina.

While Elmina preached Dianaism in the radical press, she also promoted her brand of sex reform through a wide private correspondence. Using candid and direct language, she gave advice to and gathered data from those who applied to her in regard to matters of matrimony and sex. By this means she sought to "prove" the Diana theory. Using aliases, McAfee from St. Louis and Barclay from Richmond wrote decoy letters to her and, in return, received replies that they considered to be incriminating. Barclay made a further effort to obtain evidence by disguising himself and making a visit to Elmina, but his ruse only succeeded in arousing her suspicions. A few days later, on 27 April 1887, they arrested her, rifled her belongings, and seized "a number of letters relating to free love ideas" to use as additional evidence. In the indictment, which McAfee himself drew up, he charged Elmina with two separate counts of mailing obscene literature.[23]

Unlike sex radicals who were arrested for obscene articles in their public journals, Elmina was arrested and tried under the Comstock Act for mailing private material in sealed letters. The *Ex parte Jackson* decision of the Supreme Court prohibited the search, without a warrant, of sealed mail in order to enforce obscenity laws, but agents of vice societies overcame the obstacle by using decoy letters. In any case, the effect of the Comstock Act generally superseded the sanctity of sealed mail. The 1876 revision of the act had declared all obscene publications to be "nonmailable matter," while, the same year, a federal judge had pronounced in *United States* v. *Foote* that "to exclude from the [Comstock] statute all letters which, to the outward appearance, are harmless, would destroy its efficacy. . . . It is not the form in which the matter is mailed, but the character of the matter itself, which fixes the criminality of the act."[24]

"DEFIANT MRS. SLENKER. She Faces Court Alone and Defends Her Conduct," the *New York Times* headlined its report of her preliminary hearing. She refused to swear on the Bible, pronounced herself a "Materialist," and announced her unbelief in God and Christianity. She defended her work in sex education as a service to humanity and likened her allegedly obscene literature to serious articles on medicine or surgery. She sent materials only to private individuals who had requested it, she explained. Questioned about the authorship of *Diana*, she refused to say whether she had written it; the publishers' imprint appeared on the book, Elmina said, and her inquisitors could apply to them. She appeared without counsel, claiming that no Virginia lawyer could appreciate her case. The case went to the district court, and Elmina went back to the Wytheville jail to wait out the six months until her trial. She could not immediately raise bail money; even her husband refused to help.[25]

The New York free-thought lawyer Edward W. Chamberlain appeared on Elmina's behalf in the October trial. After hearing the case, Judge J. Paul instructed the jury to decide whether the material was obscene, using the *Hicklin* test, and whether, in fact, Elmina had mailed the material. The court once more affirmed the legality of decoy letters and the practice of not placing the indicted materials on the record of the court. After the jury found her guilty, Chamberlain charged that the indictment was faulty and asked the judge to arrest judgment and thereby free Elmina.

The Comstock Act charged that "any person who shall knowingly deposit" obscene matter in the mail "shall be deemed guilty." Chamberlain argued that McAfee's indictment alleged that Elmina knowingly performed the act of mailing, but it did not set out that she knew the mailed materials to be obscene. McAfee, in reply, argued that he had followed the example of the *Bennett* case, wherein Judge Blatchford had ruled that it was of no consequence that D. M. Bennett "may not have known or thought [*Cupid's Yokes*] to be obscene and so non-mailable, so long as it was, in fact, obscene, and he knew he was depositing the identical book complained of." Judge Paul, however, agreed with Chamberlain, and ruled that the indictment was faulty. In his decision, the judge conceded that he may have gone counter to the *Bennett* precedent, but, he believed that he had had authority from cases as substantial as the *Bennett* one. On 4 November 1887, grandmother Slenker once again had her freedom.[26]

Elmina's correspondence, for which she risked a prison term, had two main purposes: first, she saw herself as collecting the empirical data to prove the theory of Diana abstinence. She gathered "sexual experience from all classes . . . from the pious prude to the most abandoned prostitute of either sex." "Of course," she wrote, "I received and wrote all that can be imagined in the line of sex; and much that I had never before dreamed of." Most letters that she received were honest and frank confessions, she related, and if they required answers, she replied in the same forthright vein. Most of the enquirers in the correspondence circle agreed among themselves to use the terse and tabooed sexual terms as being more plain and to the point. Elmina recalled her initial shock at seeing such words in print, but she soon came to see that "the words in themselves were clean, strong, and vigorous; and when intelligently used and in their proper place, entirely unobjectionable."[27]

Elmina believed that the letters had value only as private intelligences; any general circulation of them would perhaps cause misunderstanding. Some *Lucifer* readers who supported Harman's publication of the Markland and O'Neill letters saw extracts from the letters, became quite shocked, and raised questions about Elmina's character and the effect of such work. Elmina reminded her critics of the purity both of her philosophy and of her private life: just because Dianaists discussed sexual problems freely "is no proof that we dispense sexual favors freely, or hold ourselves ready to caress or be caressed indiscriminately by others."[28]

If a few Lucifereans questioned Elmina's method of sexual inquiry, even more questioned her solicitations for correspondents which appeared in *Lucifer*. It appeared, in fact, that another purpose of her correspondence efforts was to unite like-minded men and women, perhaps even as she had been united with her mate through an ad in the *Water-Cure Journal*. She received numerous requests from those who wanted to correspond freely on such subjects as religion, sexology, heredity, and equality, but most such requests came from men. "Now I want the name and address of any woman old or young, married or single," wrote Elmina, "who is ready and willing to take up such a correspondence. Women who are willing to talk and ready to face what they say."[29]

Lois Waisbrooker, a sex radical of the same generation as Elmina's, believed that such solicitations invited the exploitation of women by randy men. Though some correspondents were honest investigators with a creditable desire for sexual knowledge, others were "lascivious hunters after excitement." Waisbrooker blamed the Comstock laws for forcing sexual education into the medium of private letters. The intimacy of this method increased the temptations of prurience. She also criticized Elmina's "ring" correspondence, which designated the identity of letter writers only be a number. Such clandestine communication had the effect of "surreptitious knowledge gained by children . . . [it] opens the way for much evil."

Voltairine de Cleyre, a young anarchist heroine whose star was on the rise, offered concrete reasons why women should shun Elmina's solicitations: "Don't answer unless you are ready to receive all kinds of illiterate, disgusting, and insulting compositions." Elmina's advanced age, de Cleyre hinted, probably kept her from receiving many concupiscent letters; de Cleyre, however, had received them in quantity during her five years as a public anarchist lecturer.[30]

Undaunted by this criticism, Elmina's call for correspondents became more blatant. Her previous appeals had failed to attract the group that was most in demand—single women. "There are liberal men all over the land who do not want to marry creed-bound women and do not know how to get in touch with such women as they would like," she exclaimed in reviewing her invitation for the names of women who sought such men for correspondents, or perhaps, she added, for "nearer and closer friends."

Although her technique may have been naïve, Elmina hoped to promote the cause of women by helping them to find suitably emancipated male companions. She had none of respectable society's qualms about marriage bureaus, and like other Lucifereans, she believed in the virtue of absolute directness. She scoffed that Waisbrooker should imply that women somehow needed protection against lascivious letters, whereas men did not. In this era of the struggle for equality, Slenker announced, "women are strong, sensible and self-reliant" and could accept the exigencies of a correspondence situation. After all, no one was compelled to continue a correspondence. From her experience, Elmina noted that the few lewd letters that did appear often came from those who most strongly repressed their sexual feelings—generally pious women churchgoers. She concluded that "the starved love element impels to abnormal ways and means for temporary satisfaction."[31]

Elmina's efforts for sexual enlightenment were part of a larger philosophy which involved certain ideas about motherhood, heredity, and woman's superiority. In her case, the belief in woman's superiority represented a logical outgrowth of the mother-centered notions of the pre-Galtonian eugenicists. In *Love, Marriage and Divorce* (1853), Stephen Pearl Andrews proposed the idea of woman's superiority and connected it to her role in perpetuating the race:

Suppose, again, that woman, when free, should exhibit an inherent, God-given tendency to accept only the noblest and most highly endowed of the opposite sex to be the recipients of her choicest favors and the sires of her offspring, rejecting the males of a lower degree, as the females of somes species of the lower animals (who enjoy the freedom that woman does not) are known to do; and that the grand societary fact should appear in the result that by this means Nature has provided for an infinitely higher development of the race. Suppose . . . that, generally, God and nature have evidently delegated to woman the supremacy in the whole affectional realm of human affairs, as they have consigned it to man in the intellectual,—a function she could never begin rightly to perform until first freed herself from the trammels of conventionalism, the false sanctities of superstition and custom.

The freed female, a more noble and spiritual being than the male, could elevate man not only by this "natural selection" in breeding, but by inspiring the development of man's own lesser spirituality, argued Andrews in an unpublished manuscript of the 1840s, "Love, Marriage and the Condition of Women." This idea had particular appeal to Ezra Heywood, who in *Uncivil Liberty* (1873) maintained that woman should be enfranchised so that her superior morality could have a direct influence in the realm of politics.[32]

Henry C. Wright, in *The Empire of the Mother over the Character and Destiny of the Race* (1863), considered the prenatal state as the most important stage of human development: "What is *organized* into us in our pre-natal state, is of more consequence . . . than what is *educated* into us, after we are born." Since woman, as mother, served as the prenatal educator of man, Wright exclaimed: "MAN! Behold the organism of woman! Look upon it tenderly and reverently, for within it God has hidden the scroll of destiny to individuals, families, states and nations. There God has laid away the book of his laws for the government of the race." The woman, he repeated "legislates not only for individuals . . . but also for the race." As early as 1858, at the Tenth Anniversary Woman's Rights Convention, both Wright and Eliza Farnham submitted declarations on woman's superiority; Stephen Pearl Andrews, meanwhile, proposed a free-love resolution.[33]

Lester Frank Ward, the pioneer American sociologist, is commonly credited with originating the idea that "woman is the race" when he formulated his gynecocentric theory in the 1880s. Obviously, however, he only gave new voice to an idea that had been developed in print, in those very terms, for at least two decades. Although Ward did not originate the basic thesis, he did develop it into a more elegant and scientific theory which proved to have considerable influence on the sex radicals. Elmina Slenker, who grew up in the aura of Henry C. Wright and who avidly read Darwin, Spencer, and Weissman, could be expected to welcome into her feminist philosophy the whole of Ward's mature theory. This belief in female superiority became, in fact, the capstone of her ideology, and she advocated the theory with such energy that later commentators and journalists sometimes identified her as its originator.[34]

The outlines of Ward's theory appeared in *Dynamic Sociology* (1883) and in concise form in an 1888 article in *Forum*. He claimed the female sex to be the primary one both in origin and in its importance to evolutionary development. Man, the secondary sex, now appeared to be superior in physical strength and intelligence, traits that Darwin termed "secondary sexual characters," because females had consistently selected mates with these secondary characteristics. (Ward considered Darwin's discovery of female sexual selection to be as important as the larger theory of natural selection.) These selected characteristics of the male were "those that tended to insure success in rivalry for mates" within the species rather than those that would protect and nurture offspring and thus the race. "Brains were also transmitted," Ward wrote on another occasion, "and they predominated in male heads according to the law that confined antlers, tusks and spurs to that sex."

As woman began to value sagacity over brute force in her mates, man's brain became his predominant sexual characteristic. With the ascendance of the cunning male came the subjugation of woman, and man took over her prerogative of sexual selection. In this reversal of natural order, woman began to be selected for and characterized by *her* secondary, ornamental characteristics.

Ward debunked the argument from nature that held that the male of the species was generally superior to the female. Considerable evidence existed in both plants and animals to prove the opposite to be the case; but in any event, he disliked the terms of the argument itself, since it assumed that whatever existed in nature must be the ideal. Man should discover nature's general laws, but he should not assume "that whatever can be shown to be *natural* must be the best possible condition." Nature herself was fallible: "The truth comes clearly forth that the relations of the sexes among higher animals are widely abnormal, warped, and strained by a long line of curious influences, chiefly psychic, which are incident to the development of animal organisms under the competitive principle that prevails throughout nature." He believed all social progress to be artificial in the sense that it sought to mitigate the "rude, wasteful, and heartless dominion of Nature."

If man need not be bound by such absurdities as "what is, is right," he could nevertheless appreciate certain comprehensive principles of nature and use them as a basis for improvement. A primary principle was that the female served as the "type form" of the breed, and the male simply as an impregnator, "after performing which function the male form is useless and a mere cumberer of the ground." Characterized by permanence of type, the female contrasted to the variability and adaptability that defined the male. Ward saw the female as the matrix through which the forces of evolution and heredity formed mankind's destiny. Because of this, he believed that "it must be from the steady advance of woman rather than from the uncertain fluctuations of man that the sure and solid progress of the future is to come."

Ward explicitly presented his gynecocentric theory in order to lend scientific credence to the feminist cause. It was at once an affirmation of woman's worth and a call for an end to her degradation. "Woman is the unchanging trunk of the great genealogic tree," he concluded, "while man, with all his vaunted superiority, is but a branch, a grafted scion, as it were, whose acquired qualities die with the individual, while those of woman are handed on to futurity. Woman *is* the race, and the race can be raised up only as she is raised up."[35]

Ward's theory had obvious faults. In overstressing "woman is the race," he seemed to imply, contrary to his own beliefs, that only maternal qualities were inherited. He disclaimed the argument from nature, yet he consistently appealed to biological example and to "natural order" when it aided his case. He unhesitatingly assumed the present intellectual inferiority of woman, and he credited man with the development of all civilization and progress. Yet much of Ward's work echoed the articles of faith of the sex radicals, lending credence to the speculation that he had been influenced by Stephen Pearl Andrews.

He urged an equality for women that not only included politics, but also education, employment, dress, and social deportment as well. A still greater liberty that society withheld from women, Ward pointed out, was woman's right to control her own body. In language that free lovers particularly understood, Ward argued that with the onset of male sexual selection, woman became property, and marriage became man's title deed to her body and her labor. Thus the female surrendered her fundamental virtue, which he defined as her power "over men, over society, over her own interests." Female virtue did not mean sexual continence but meant free choice of the terms of coition. As Stephen Pearl Andrews saw "the trammels of conventionalism" impeding woman's particular superiority, so Ward saw in "the power of the conventional code" an explanation for the "inferiority" of woman's contributions to civilization:

All that women have accomplished, let it be distinctly understood, they have done *in violation of the conventional code*, which requires them to keep aloof from all active pursuits, and devote themselves solely to the pleasing of the male sex and the rearing of offspring. Yet who does not know the power, nay the tyranny, of the conventional code? The real wonder is, that women have ever done the little that they have.[36]

In exploring the concept of woman's superiority, Elmina Slenker found interesting possibilities as well as paradox. She granted, of course, that every healthy woman had a natural right to have a mate and to become a mother. But since nature always strove to produce the feminine, the nurturing element, she reasoned that females would eventually outnumber males. The trend, in fact, had already begun on a wide scale, and she produced statistics showing the predominance of females. The social dogma that enforced monogamy then plainly discriminated against women who were left without mates. Ironically, some members of the superior sex would have to sacrifice sexual satisfaction of any kind except for brotherly association, she noted. But the surplus of females distressed her for other reasons, as she cited figures that showed the economic destitution of husbandless women in New York City. Slenker believed that this course would continue until women were radically deprived of men for either companionship or impregnation.

Despite apparent problems, Elmina held out hope for the future: "If there be a higher and better life yet to come, that race will no doubt be mainly of the feminine sex." She seized on news of biological experiments with virgin reproduction, and she postulated that the female society to come might be able to utilize this parthenogenesis. She admitted that women could be sterilized like bee drones in order to produce fewer females, but such an act seemed to be unthinkable in human terms.[37]

Elmina did not discuss the lesbian implications of a mostly female society, which in light of the present-day consciousness of woman's liberation would seem to have been an obvious subject. It appears likely that such a consideration never seriously crossed her mind. From the more sophisticated viewpoint of the late twentieth century, the naïveté of even avant-garde reformers such as the *Lucifer* sex radicals may appear striking, yet the difference in consciousness emphasizes the great gulf between the sexual mind of the present time and that of the nineteenth century. Lois Waisbrooker, for example, long a worker in free-love and radical feminist causes, claimed that she had reached the age of forty-eight before she discovered the existence of such a thing as oro-genital sexual relations: "I shall never forget the horror I felt when I first learned . . . that such a thing was possible. For years I could never bring myself to put the diabolical perversion into words." The word commonly used by *Lucifer* correspondents to describe participants in such acts was "suckers." Waisbrooker reached the age of sixty-one before she heard a woman refer to a man as a "French taster."

"What is that?" Waisbrooker asked; and then for the first time, she recalled, "I learned that there were men who earned their living in that manner."[38]

Although Elmina proclaimed that women felt sexual passion and were subject to the same intemperance as men, she could not condone such "lust" in either sex; to the Victorians, homosexual intercourse had no such justification as "natural attraction" or procreation, which might make heterosexual lust at least understandable. Most spokesmen of the time considered homosexuality to be a physical disease or, at best, a psychic and moral perversion. Moses Harman printed the O'Neill letter in order to expose a dark vice.

A tragic lesbian scandal in 1892 sent shock waves through the ranks of the sex radicals and provided some indications of their feelings toward homosexuality. Two prominent and wealthy young Memphis ladies, Alice Mitchell and Freda Ward, planned to marry one another and to move away to St. Louis to live. Ward, who had been ardently courted by Mitchell, eventually attempted to call off the wedding, and in a fury, Mitchell slashed Ward's throat in broad daylight in front of the Memphis Custom House. The ensuing trial brought to light the correspondence of the two, the occurrence of transvestism, and the involvement of another girl. The court found Mitchell insane and sent her to an asylum.[39]

In a speech before the New York State Eclectic Medical Society, *Lucifer*'s valued supporter, Dr. Edward Bliss Foote, commented on Mitchell's "unnatural erotic impulse." He believed the homosexual urge to be amenable to medical treatment if treated in the early stages. Mitchell's "timely use of certain sedatives would have saved the life of her young friend, Freda Ward," said Foote, "while the further use of alteratives and uterine regulators would have placed her in both a physical and mental condition to resist such a peculiarly insane impulse."

Oscar Wilde's trial in 1895 and his subsequent imprisonment for homosexual offenses prompted other comments in *Lucifer* with regard to homosexuality. The scholarly anarchist C. L. James took a historical glance at the subject—which was heavily weighted toward Greece and the military arts—and emphasized the cultural relativity of the practice. He disagreed with those who judged homosexuality as insanity, and he hesitated, himself, to call it unnatural; he did believe it to be a vice, however. It was ironic, he wrote, that the Chautauqua Society, under the auspices of leading Comstockians, should publish a textbook discussing Greek homosexuality, while such exposers of present-day sex abuses as Harman and Slenker should be imprisoned.

Lucifer reprinted portions of Wilde's work both before and after the scandal. In an 1895 editorial, Lillian Harman assailed the treatment of Wilde by respectable society, particularly the wholesale quarantine of his literature by those who were afraid of becoming contaminated. She hardly approved of homosexuality, but she believed that there was slight danger of contacting it from his work.[40]

If Elmina's feminism appeared to be sexist, she did not consider herself antimale. She had never wished to be a man, she wrote, and felt proud to belong to the superior sex; "because I respect true womanhood more, is no proof that I respect true manhood less." She saw the sexes as inherently different but complementary; women and men should not seek similarity, but each sex should strive for its highest development with equal opportunities for education, elevation, and station. She believed that every woman needed "a loving kind man to complete her happiness" and that every man needed a woman for the same reason. "I don't believe there is a real man-hater among women, or woman-hater among men. . . . Everything that uplifts woman aids, helps, and uplifts man. There should be no jealousy of sex as regards equality of rights."[41]

In later years, as Ward's gynecocentric theory became popularized by such famous figures as Charlotte Perkins Gilman, Slenker kept her speculative vigil for feminine superiority. In 1901 she added S. L. Schenk's studies on fetal sex prediction to her arsenal of proof. The studies of the Viennese biologist indicated to her that the male sex, as compared to the female, represented an arrested stage of fetal development. The twentieth century had come; and behaviorialists, analysts, and test-tube watchers would replace the loose, if learned, speculations of the nineteenth century, whether they were from accepted thinkers such as Lester Ward or from more unrespectable ones such as Stephen Pearl

Andrews and Elmina Slenker. Elmina's attempt to span the gap between the sensibility of sexual purity—a theological proposition—and the realities of human sexuality was also an attempt to bridge the consciousness of two centuries. That she and other advocates of "feminine superiority" should receive vindication, at least at the biological level, by twentieth-century scientists is a bonus that they, no doubt, expected.

13/ Handmaidens of Diana: From the Horse Penis Affair to Modernity

WHEN Moses Harman once polled *Lucifer*'s friends about their choices for a woman coeditor, the author of the "Markland letter" answered with a warning against the danger of creeping respectability, an ailment peculiar to reform papers. W. G. Markland's earlier letter had proved that a journal could live on publicity and little else and that its impact could depend less on subscription lists than on the degree to which it outraged society. About the matter of a woman coeditor, Markland advised: "I regard pugnacity as a desideratum and Lois Waisbrooker has it. . . . Don't call a 'respectable' woman to your aid."[1]

Markland's feel for the strategy of sexual journalism seemed to match his eye for personality—indeed few women were more indifferent to the approval of respectable society than was Lois Nichols Waisbrooker. In 1891–1892, as Moses Harman moved in and out of prison, the sixty-six-year-old woman served as editor of *Lucifer*; in a short time she succeeded in getting the journal barred from the mails for pointing up the contradictions in the Horse Penis Affair.

In 1892 the Department of Agriculture was mailing, to those who applied for it, a book entitled *Special Report on Diseases of the Horse*. The book contained descriptions, said Waisbrooker in an editorial, which, if applied to human organs, would send Comstock and his pharisees into spasms. At the same time, she knew, Comstock's allies in Congress had presented a new bill to further strengthen the Comstock Act. The proposed revision would add "filthy" to the list of undefined adjectives that now determined what material was prohibited ("obscene," "lewd," "lascivious"), and it specifically added letters to the classes of publications covered by the statute; it would also prohibit any material that was devoted to or principally concerned with "criminal news, police reports, or accounts of criminal deeds, or pictures and stories of immoral deeds, lust or crime," and would ban advertisements for medications or apparatus "for the cure of private or venereal diseases, whether sealed as first-class matter or not." But the bombshell in the proposal was the clause that expressly authorized censoring power for the postmaster general. This power would not only extend to the prohibition from the mails of separate issues of a publication, but also would exclude the publication itself, including future issues, from the mails.[2]

The postmaster general, as the sex radicals pointed out, already had the power of nonjudicial censorship. Since the initiation of the Comstock Act, the Post Office Department had gradually assumed autonomous censoring authority separate from the criminal enforcement of the Comstock law. And in the early years of the Harrison administration, the attorney general had confirmed this power in a case involving Tolstoy's *Kreutzer Sonata*. Sex radicals, then, were extremely concerned about the possibility of even tougher strictures.[3]

Benjamin O. Flower alerted the readers of *Arena* to the fact that the book on horse diseases that was being sent out by the government could earn the secretary of agriculture a jail sentence under the proposed revisions of the Comstock Act. Although Flower meant to embarrass the Comstockians by such speculation, Lois Waisbrooker thought that she knew a better way to dramatize the inconsistencies of official prudery.

She took one paragraph from the horse book, certainly not the most graphic one in the book, she said, and printed it in her editorial in *Lucifer*:

As the result of kicks or blows, or of forcible striking of the yard on the thighs of the mare which it has failed to enter, the [horse's] penis may become the seat of effusion of blood from one or more ruptured blood-vessels. This gives rise to more or less extensive swelling on one or more sides, followed by some heat and inflammation, and on recovery a serious curving of the organ. . . . The penis should be suspended in a sling.

Underneath this excerpt Waisbrooker printed the crucial passage of the Markland letter, in which the mention of "penis" had caused Moses Harman's imprisonment. She urged readers to compare the two passages. Why is it, she asked, that Secretary of Agriculture James Rusk and his department could distribute and broadcast every fact concerning horse generation, whereas the government tabooed knowledge about human generation?

The postmaster at Topeka, alerted by the zealous prosecutor of Moses Harman, United States district attorney J. W. Ady, and by a United States postal inspector, barred the horse-penis issue of *Lucifer* from the mails. The Post Office Department censored *Lucifer* not only because of Waisbrooker's editorial, but also because it considered three advertisements in the issue to be obscene, namely those for *Cupid's Yokes*, Annie Besant's *The Law of Population*, and a book about free love by Juliet Severance, *A Discussion of the Social Question*. In the issues of *Lucifer* after the suppression, Waisbrooker ran a streamer in ornate type across the front page: "Published under Government Censorship."[4]

Her qualifications for the job of editing *Lucifer* were above question; in fact, in 1927 the editor of the English birth-control journal the *New Generation* characterized Waisbrooker as "the strongest personality among American feminists." Born in 1826 into the "lower strata of life," as she put it, she began her working life as a domestic servant. "I have worked in people's kitchens year in and year out when I never knew what it was to be rested," she recalled at the age of eighty; "finally I added enough to the little schooling I received in childhood to enable me to meet the [teaching] requirements of a country school." She taught in black schools in the years preceding the Civil War, a task whose disreputability she once compared to that of sex reform.

After the Civil War she forsook schoolteaching for public lecturing on women's rights, free love, and spiritualism. These were not three separate topics, but the integrated program of an "untrammeled Spiritualist speaker," as she billed herself in *Woodhull & Claflin's Weekly*. Her activities before the advent of *Lucifer* can be traced in *Hull's Crucible, The Word,* and the Claflin sisters' paper. Her direct style and lack of concern for convention did not endear her to general audiences. "I never was popular," she remembered. "When I first began to act as an itinerant speaker my work was mostly done in back neighborhoods in school houses among people who could gather my life force but could give me very little in exchange." When the Claflin sisters deserted the free-love cause, it fell to Moses Hull, Waisbrooker, and others who were active in the Boston area in the mid 1870s to fill the gap in leadership.[5]

She professed to be sickly, but nevertheless she had undaunted energy. When *To-Morrow Magazine* commemorated her eightieth birthday with a biographical sketch, the accompanying photograph showed her as a tiny woman of flinty mien. Ezra Heywood recalled meeting her for the first time at a spiritualist convention in Boston in 1875:

I . . . met what seemed to be a Roman Sibyl, Scott's Meg Merrilies, enacted by Charlotte Cushman, Margaret Fuller, and Sojourner Truth rolled into one. I sat in a pew looking into her eyes and listening to what seemed to be her talking, awhile, when she rose, went up the aisle, mounted the platform, and the tall, angular, weird, quaint kind of a she Abraham Lincoln was introduced to the audience as "Lois Waisbrooker."

She wrote passable poetry, but didactic prose was her forte. In the three-year period between 1869 and 1871 she published *Suffrage for Women: The Reasons Why*; *Alice Vale: A Story for the Times*; *Helen Harlow's Vow: or Self Justice*; and *Mayweed Blossoms*. In the 1890s she brought out several more pamphlets and books, among them *The Fountain of Life: or the Threefold Power of Sex*, *A Sex Revolution*, and *The Occult Forces of Sex*. She also published a journal during the eighties and nineties, *Foundation Principles*, from Clinton, Iowa, from Antioch, California, and from Topeka, Kansas. Although it was dedicated to "Humanitarian Spiritualism," the journal stressed a variety of radical positions, including the abolition of rent and profit. In addition, she contributed to Moses Harman's journals for twenty-five years.[6]

In the year 1900 she began publishing a paper called *Clothed with the Sun*, first from San Francisco and later from the anarchist colony of Home, Washington. She was arrested at the colony in 1902 for violations of the Comstock law.

It was not her first arrest on such a charge. In 1894 in Topeka,

Vice Society agent R. W. McAfee caused her to be arrested for obscenity in *Foundation Principles*. The agent had taken offense at Waisbrooker's answer to a male correspondent in which she suggested that the man divorce his wife and marry the woman he loved as a way to escape from an unhappy marriage. Waisbrooker's vaunted, if misunderstood, reputation as a free lover and as a freethinker did not sit well with the respectable Republican establishment in Kansas, which was in the midst of a successful attempt to regain political hegemony after a brief Populist onslaught. She noted that it seemed strange that she should be arrested "the next issue after my paper came out for the Populist party. Or rather . . . for some of their principles." Ben Henderson, a Populist champion of women's rights, took Waisbrooker's defense in the courts.[7]

Edward W. Chamberlain wrote an article about the seventy-year-old reformer's plight for *Arena*. "Like Moses Harman Mrs. Waisbrooker has advocated the freest and most ample discussion of vital subjects, and it is for this she is attacked." He quoted at length from a circular that Waisbrooker had issued about her arrest, which explained that her sex-education efforts were eugenic in purpose and required the full and open discussion of sex. Her case dragged on in court for months, and ill health caused her to cease publication of *Foundation Principles*. In 1896 Waisbrooker finally won an arrest of judgment.[8]

Her 1902 arrest and trial came as part of the official harassment of the anarchist community of Home, Washington. As members of one of the few anarchist communities in existence at the time of President McKinley's assassination, the residents of the settlement weathered an extended attack by Tacoma newspapers and by local, state, and national governments, which all vowed to stamp out the anarchist menace.

Officials first brought obscenity charges against three of the colonists for articles about free love in the Home newspaper, *Discontent*; but a federal circuit judge in Tacoma found the articles not obscene and freed the three men who had been charged. Meanwhile a grand jury had returned indictments against Lois Waisbrooker for an obscene article in her paper, *Clothed with the Sun*, and also against the postmistress at Home, Mattie D. Penhallow, for mailing the paper. At Waisbrooker's trial in July 1902, the jury deliberated several hours before finding her article "The

Awful Fate of Fallen Women" to be obscene. She was fined the minimum amount, one hundred dollars, by a reluctant judge. The jury acquitted postmistress Penhallow, but the federal grand jury that had launched the charges against the anarchists submitted a recommendation to Washington to close the Home post office as a punitive action against the "settlement of avowed anarchists and free lovers, the members of which society on numerous instances, with the apparent sanction of the entire community, have abused the privilege of the post office establishment and department." The jury specified that the community had repeatedly mailed non-mailable matter and "matter calculated to corrupt and injure the body politic." In April 1902 the postmaster general ordered that the Home post office be closed permanently.[9]

Waisbrooker died in 1909, a few months after Elmina Slenker's death and a few months before Moses Harman's. Fittingly, her last article appeared in the final issue of Harman's magazine, *American Journal of Eugenics*. The text was traditional for Waisbrooker: "The Curse of Christian Morality." Another age would not so readily see the relationship between "Christian morality" and a eugenics journal, nor would it grasp the connections between feminism, free love, and spiritualism that combined so remarkably in the person of Lois Waisbrooker.

Like Elmina Slenker, her comrade-in-arms, Lois Waisbrooker believed in woman's superiority to man, but she attributed her ideas in part to Eliza Farnham, a gynecocentric forerunner to Lester Ward. Farnham's 1864 work, *Woman and Her Era* (New York, 2 vols.), argued that the greater complexity and development of woman—her extra reproductive apparatus, her lack of rudimentary organs (man had rudimentary breasts), her "finer" brain, and her greater proportion of nerve tissue—made her superior to man. Woman produced babies, which to Farnham was the "paramount interest, aim, and office" of feminine life, the "Ideal State of Womanhood," and, in fact, the "highest *function* of life." Woman experienced phenomena which man could not—menstruation and change-of-life—and Farnham's prose extolled these experiences as additional evidences of female superiority. Farnham advanced a theory that woman's ovum contained the total germ of life; male sperm only played an adjunct role in procreation by providing some initial nourishment for the cell.

Farnham had studied medicine and knew that textbooks treated the clitoris as a rudimentary penis. Why adopt this male point of view, she asked; why not view the female organ as a refinement of the male organ? "May not the purpose of the structure in question, be the wider diffusion of nerves, whose more concentrated presence would scarce consist with the functional economies and health of adjacent parts?" Woman's greater complement of nerves did not suggest to Farnham that woman should enjoy the physical senses more than man, in fact she considered sensuality as a particularly masculine trait. Instead, she took a near-masochistic pride in woman's role as the sublime sufferer: "Exclusiveness in suffering," she wrote, "is exclusiveness in power." Her arguments against judging woman by male standards seemed progressive enough, but her work actually glorified Victorian notions of woman's place, and her prescription for more "honor" and chivalry toward woman could not be construed as liberation.[10]

Those who sought to upgrade the place of woman in society could not shrug off the question of menstruation, since many viewed the periodic function as woman's curse, a badge of her inferiority. Waisbrooker agreed with the writings of a sister feminist pamphleteer on the subject, Rachel Campbell. Menstruation refined and purified the female body, creating a vessel that was finer than man's. When a girl came of age, she took a course that her male counterpart could not take; as the menstrual flow began to distill her blood, woman assumed the softness, delicacy, and roundness of form that was characteristic of her sex. "The menstrual flow is just as truly a secretion and excretion by the womb as the urine is by the kidneys," wrote Campbell, "and in this dissolving and evolving current is carried away the dross and scoria discarded in life's refining process, eliminating the grosser particles, giving flexibility and elasticity of tissue." The purified material built "new bodies, cleaner, finer and better fitted to endure the greater tension necessary to manifest a higher grade of life and a superior order of humanity."

This poetic explanation of menstruation had further implications. Since woman played the key role in human evolution, the refinement of her blood by menstruation aided the genetic progress of the race, furnishing women with "a higher grade of matter out of which to build the next generation of babies." Acquisitions of culture and education must first pass through the woman before they might "possibly become fixed and organic": the blood of offspring was an extract of the mother's continually purifying blood.

Not surprisingly, such lay speculations on physiology for political purposes contained certain contradictions. While praising menstruation as a function of superiority, Rachel Campbell also wrote of it as a regular, depleting infirmity. Through this line of argument she hoped to win support for the notion that women should be guaranteed economic support through some sort of social-welfare scheme. After all, as the evolutional laboratory of the race and as the payer of the "monthly physical tax," woman deserved no less.[11]

Nineteenth-century men and women, including specialists, knew little about menstruation and said still less, at least directly, about the function. Most references to menstruation were veiled in the frequent allusions to feminine "weakness" or "delicate nature" which infused the discussion of the woman question. Apparent widespread dysmenorrhoea, or painful menstruation, which seemed to affirm the myth of female debility, especially troubled those feminists who sought thorough equality with the male as well as the destruction of notions of a separate woman's sphere. Other feminists, and even antifeminists who sought chivalric compensations for woman's unequal treatment, tended to embrace the idea of reproductive and sexual pain as part of woman's saintly role.

One may speculate that the chief problem with woman's "curse" was not so much the degree of pain inflicted upon some women, but that, painful or not, virtually every unpregnant or non-lactating member of an entire sex, for thirty-five years of her life, "bled" for several days of every month. George Drysdale, in *Elements of Social Science*, wrote that "disordered menstruation attended by more or less pain is so common, that women look upon it as a natural and inevitable evil, and unless it be severe, pay little heed to it." Other available evidence suggests that most women who had to, took the "monthlies" in stride, without incapacitation.[12] It was the blood taboo, and not the presence (or supposed presence) of pain, that indicated woman's debility.

Consequently, those few writers with feminist leanings who wrote about menstruation for the popular audience advanced several theories to rationalize away the blood taboo. Their knowledge of reproduction, advanced for the time but crudely elemental nevertheless, included a familiarity with the discovery by Polish physician Adam Raciborski of the spontaneous ejection of the ovum; formerly it had been believed that the egg was produced as a consequence of sexual intercourse. Drysdale sought to put menstruation in a positive light by claiming that menstruation was in fact ovulation. This notion had such popularity that, in 1870, Dr. Edward Bliss Foote, author of popular home medical books, took pains to disagree in specific terms: "The only relation that menstruation sustains to ovulation is that the excessive presence of blood in the female generative organs, once in about twenty-eight days, stimulates the generation of female germs." In homey language the doctor claimed menstruation to be nature's washday:

The ovaries above the womb carry on a pretty extensive manufacturing establishment, and throw off the ova and the waste matters, or chips, through the fallopian tubes into the cavity of the uterus. While this work of generation is going on, nature has a wash-day once in about four weeks, and pouring the blood into the womb's cavity, washes its walls, and empties all outside.

His theory came closer than most to the modern recognition that menstruation is the sloughing off of the uterine lining which has been prepared to nourish the early embryo; most of this lining, mixed with blood, is discharged about every twenty-seven days, thus ending one menstrual cycle.[13]

Some believed, with George Drysdale, that painful menstruation signaled the degenerated state to which civilized woman had fallen, a theory that appealed to free lovers who charged that the repression of conventional monogamy caused dysgenic effects. No good could come from pampering women because of her periodic function, wrote Lillie D. White, an interim editor of *Lucifer*. She believed that menstruation that made an invalid of woman for three to seven days each month was "a disease that ought to be cured, not humored or coddled, and any women who spends her whole time in the recovering process ought to be ashamed of herself." Clarence Lee Swartz, who also edited *Lucifer* for a time, agreed with White. He addressed the blood taboo with the most idealistic speculation: "Menstruation accompanied by pain and a colored discharge is a disease, either inherited from the perverted sexual functions of progenitors, or acquired. The maturation and deposit of the ova in the womb need not cause an overflow of the genitalia."

Both sexes demonstrated sexual degeneration, according to Henry M. Parkhurst in *Diana*. In the case of woman, "the production of ova . . . attended with an abnormal loss of blood in menstruation" denoted "an unnatural state" which corresponded in man to the excessive production of sperm—a fact that caused such abuses in the male as masturbation and nocturnal emission. Elizabeth Blackwell, the first woman physician of the modern era, held somewhat the same notion. She believed menstruation to be analogous to nocturnal emission in man, but she saw these phenomena as natural adjustments of the libido, which, moreover, she believed to be equal in both sexes.

A more professional inquiry by Dr. Mary Jacobi, *The Question of Rest for Women during Menstruation*, which won the Boylston Prize at Harvard in 1876, found that although about half the women she surveyed suffered some pain at menstruation, no physiological condition connected with the menstrual process necessarily caused the suffering. She concluded that lack of physical education and poor muscular nutrition in girlhood accounted for most of the pain. Her scientific analysis of menstruation, which was much needed but not widely popularized, outdated old theories about the function, and its conclusion that menstruation did not "imply the necessity or even the desirability, of rest, for women whose nutrition is really normal," provided justification for woman to attempt many forms of work that had previously been closed to her.[14]

The idea that woman should be pensioned because of her special physiology caused hot debate among sex radicals, some of whom felt that only pregnant women deserved this kind of support, while others, such as anarchists, felt that support for women, if any, should be an individualized matter between sexual partners. The idea of a government subsidy for motherhood had an early voice in Henry C. Wright, who asked, "Why should not governments look after the health, the beauty, the perfection and the power" of the "Maternal Organism?" All citizens, he argued, derived their existence, and the state derived its prosperity, protection, and glory, from the mother.[15]

Waisbrooker came out in support of a proposal made by Rachel Campbell in *The Prodigal Daughter* that at age eighteen every woman should receive from the public treasury an ample monthly stipend for her support. Such a payment would not only recognize her evolutional role, but would also be a concrete way to free womanhood from her degrading dependency upon the male sex. Waisbrooker, who compromised her identification with anarchism by supporting the scheme, saw the plan as an ideal, something that a just society, if not the present government, would contribute to woman.

Another Luciferean, Lillie D. White, took Waisbrooker to task, criticizing the efforts of Waisbrooker and others to make of woman a "consecrated priestess" of childbearing and a ward of the state. White urged revolution and a redistribution of wealth, so that both women and men would have the opportunity of self-support and independence through available and rewarding work. Women must seek fulfillment in other ways than breeding, she believed. Voicing an opinion shared by feminists such as Lillian Harman and Voltairine de Cleyre, White wrote that every area of industry that had been opened to woman had become a stepping stone toward her freedom: "She has shown ability to enter every domain of science and art, why should she be above all a childbearing machine?"

As an anarchist, White decried the coercive possibilities of Campbell's plan and foresaw the dangers of state eugenics: "Government carefully supervises what we shall drink, eat, read, write, look at, with whom we live, etc., what could be more proper than for government to superintend the birth of babies." She warned that "none can hope that the State will pension women and stop there. . . . We need not be surprised to see examining boards and various committees to decide upon the fitness of women to be mothers, the adaptability of parents, etc." The basis of the dispute lay not so much in economic differences between anarchism and socialism, but in a differing ideology of feminism; Waisbrooker,

Campbell, and Elmina Slenker, for instance, believed that woman had a separate, superior sphere from that of man and she should not seek her fulfillment, or her "triumph," in man's sphere nor through man's methods. White, in contrast, could see only continued exploitation in such a theory of separate spheres.[16]

Since Waisbrooker and Slenker held that motherhood was the key to woman's superiority, the question of contraception rather confounded them. Both, in fact, vacillated in their stands on the matter, no doubt realizing that if woman systematically denied her motherhood function through contraception, she denied the very element of her nature that made her superior. Elmina Slenker had for many years promoted Heywood's "Comstock syringe," a douching instrument for contraception, but had finally become convinced that contraceptives encouraged lust. Thereafter she advocated Dianaist abstinence and the teaching of scientific sexual facts, presumably about the "safe" period.[17]

Waisbrooker summed up her lukewarm stand on birth control in 1893. She supported the right of the individual woman to use contraceptive methods, but she saw danger in viewing birth control as a social panacea: "I hardly think the work of sex reformers is teaching how to so limit propagation among the working people that there will be just enough of them to furnish servants for the rich, and to produce what these same rich people want." Although she conceded that contraceptives might be the lesser of evils in some cases, with Slenker she believed that coitus only for the sake of pleasure—which was possible with contraceptives—was likely to bring more ill than good effects. This countered one of the basic texts of the sex radicals, George Drysdale's *Elements of Social Science*, which argued that sex without penalty would increase the amount of love in the world. Waisbrooker also countered Drysdale on another point: Why is it, she wondered, that among those who practiced contraception it was always the woman who had to take the preventive steps? To men she wrote: "Throw the responsibility on your own sex, not upon ours. If there must be care upon either side let the men assume it." Drysdale had rather crassly argued that "any preventive means, to be satisfactory, must be used by the *woman*, as it spoils the passion and impulsiveness of the venereal act, if the man have to think of them."[18]

Waisbrooker's spiritualist beliefs colored her principal reform interests with regard to feminism and free love. She personified the sort of "advanced thinker" that nineteenth-century spiritualism seemed to attract. The idea of liberation from physical and material restraints through spirit guidance attracted many who believed in freer love relations. In Waisbrooker's thought the spiritual or "occult" forces in the sexual experience had equal importance with the physical forces. Her references to spiritual "auras" and "magnetisms" showed the influence of mid-century spiritualist writers; she believed that an individual felt attraction for another according to the needs of his inner spirit as revealed in the magnetic aura that surrounded his body. In *The Fountain of Life: or the Threefold Power of Sex* (1893), she asserted that sexuality was the foundation for all dimensions of life—the spiritual and intellectual as well as the physical—and she discussed the relationship between male and female concepts of love.

The desire for intercourse with a variety of persons, or "varietism," she believed to be a lower, characteristically male ideal of free love. Although she defended the rights of "varietistic" free love, she believed exclusivity to be the most satisfactory form of sexual relation, particularly for women, since their special sensitivity allowed them to reach the plane of spiritual love more easily than men could. In sexual intercourse, she explained, individual magnetisms mingled and interchanged; a man who had an aura that was permeated with having sex with one woman would bring this alloyed aura to the next women he fucked. The "adulterated element" (she could not resist the phrase) of his aura would pass into the subsequent female partner and cause her to be disturbed and unhappy. Since such mixed sex magnetisms always produced discord, she advised that women have "unmixed relations" with monogamous men.

Although the spiritualists' "soul love" represented the apex of love's development, such love was still dependent upon basic physical sensation. Unlike some conservative free lovers, Waisbrooker did not decry the physical aspect of sex, but only urged that it be integrated with intellectual and spiritual aspects of sexual interaction. Her view that sex underlay the life of the mind, the spirit, and the body was part of a new element in the nineteenth-century climate of opinion, which stretched from Freud to Walt Whitman to Moses Harman, but which generated hostility in the traditionalists. One reviewer in *Arena* called Waisbrooker's sexualism "antagonistic to the views of perhaps the majority of minds, and to the religious teaching of Christendom."[19]

Her spiritualist analysis of woman in a capitalist society had an equal ring of unpopularity. In "The Sex Question and the Money Power" (1873) Waisbrooker argued that the present "ruling love" of male-dominated society was the love of money. Man, the more acquisitive sex, controlled the avenues of wealth and ownership, including marriage, and thereby controlled woman economically. This dependency on and obedience to the money god had made woman mercenary in her love and sexuality. She shared responsibility for the materialist state of affairs, however, since she provided the necessary spiritual sustenance for the greedy element in man's nature: the "money love" which characterized man's spiritual aura could not thrive unless it "mingle[d] with women whose ruling love is also money." Woman could only be redeemed when the basis of life, namely sex, was taken out of the marketplace and when man's dominion over woman was erased: "Woman must be free to use her sex functions only at the promptings of her love, and then the material of which the throne of the money god is built and sustained will no longer be manufactured." Sexuality and society would then no longer be governed by wealth, but by woman's natural ruling love—maternal love. A utopian vision appeared: the excesses of wealth and the wretchedness of poverty would be erased when woman, guided by her maternal heart, established a merciful and just order. Hers was a holy crusade: "We are rebels in the fullest sense of that word. We are determined to overthrow the ruling power [of money], to dethrone it and to place the Christ of love—existing in woman's soul—upon the throne."[20]

As man's acquisitive nature had perverted the economic sphere, his lust for power had corrupted the political arena, most obviously in his propensity for warfare. In *A Sex Revolution* (1893) Waisbrooker fictionalized her notions of the pacifist nature of woman. As in *Lysistrata*, women staged a strike against man's wars: "Who of you are willing to yield up your sons to fight the sons of other mothers?" asked Lovella, the protagonist. But Waisbrooker's women sought more than an end to war; they demanded the right to their own bodies: "Man's method must be reversed

... love guided by wisdom shall take the place of brute force." Refusing to allow man to continue foolish wars that were based on ideas of patriotism and religion, woman herself prepared to take up arms against the male in order to end wars for all time. Faced with the prospect of a unified female militant force, man agreed to exchange social positions with woman, allowing woman to rule society for fifty years as an experiment. The book ended on a tentative note as women set out alone and in groups to devote the first five years of the new dispensation to investigating methods of bringing about a new, just order of society.

Edward W. Chamberlain, the lawyer who defended several sex radicals in court, praised *A Sex Revolution* in his review in *Lucifer* and called Waisbrooker "the female Abraham Lincoln." Mary Elizabeth Lease, the fiery Populist, responded to the book with a personal letter to its author. "I wish every woman in the land could read your little book," she wrote. "You gave expression to my thoughts so clearly that it almost startled me. I have been organizing the women to war for peace, paradoxical as this may seem; now that I have your help in this most helpful book of yours I shall work with more certainty of success." The present social crises, Lease believed, could be met only by mothers. She called the little book a "revelation . . . to many a weary mother, of the vastness and magnitude of her power if she but use it rightly." As historian James C. Malin pointed out in referring to Lease's spotty record on women's rights, it seemed that Lease did not much take the gist of the book to heart. In any case, it appeared that Lease did not know the free-love context of the book or that she did not see it in the same terms as Chamberlain, who called the book a cogent and irresistible argument against enforced morality.[21]

During much of her career, Waisbrooker often justified her sex-reform efforts in terms of creating an improved human stock—a favored argument, taken from Stephen Pearl Andrews, of that group of free lovers which bloomed in the early 1870s and included Waisbrooker, Ezra Heywood, and Moses Hull. She believed that rigorous investigation could uncover a body of "sex law" regarding procreation which, if followed, would lead to the elimination of virtually all human defects, from blindness and idiocy to certain *"real* crimes" such as murder. Borrowing theological rhetoric, she spoke of "redemption of our bodies" and wrote: "None of us are a tithe of what we might have been . . . had there been such a reverence for the creative act that soul forces had entered into the blending as a positive, controlling factor. Because of this lack, because physical pleasure was the dominating factor, we are all born under the dominion of the flesh instead of the spirit."

She claimed that the "moral inspectors" of present society blocked genetic progress; they "will not let us turn our light upon the great, filthy moral cellar that underlies the structure called society." In another call to redeem the "creative act" so that it would "become a blessing to those engaged therein, and to the new baby, should there be such a result," she explained that the study of sexual generation required discussion of the sex act; "but when we attempt this in print we are arrested for sending obscene literature through the U.S. mails. Which is of most importance, the welfare of future generations, or the U.S. mail sacks?"

In the last years of her life, Waisbrooker witnessed the rise of Progressive eugenics and raised her old libertarian voice against it; in fact she became critical of the prenatal assumptions of anarchist eugenics. In a speech to the Social Science League of Chicago in 1907 she seemed to reject much of her earlier hereditarianism, possibly as a reaction to Progressive eugenics; she suggested to the audience that if mothers concerned themselves with their own development, guarded their sexual autonomy, and loved the coming child at every stage of growth, one could forget eugenics and leave the outcome to nature.[22]

In 1905, at the age of seventy-nine, Waisbrooker brought out an enlarged and revised edition of her *Woman's Source of Power*. Although, like Elmina Slenker, Waisbrooker ended her life destitute and a ward of her children and grandchildren, her own life might have served as an example of the feminine energy that she extolled in the pamphlet. She reiterated her near-mystical feminism, which held that the essential good things—love and creativity—represented the feminine principle in nature. The old woman who in *Woodhull & Claflin's Weekly* had once pronounced present society to be illegitimate because it was the product of "bond-woman," and who had argued that only sexual equality could redeem marriage, reaffirmed her faith that Science would finally justify the demands of sex radicals for the freedom of woman and the freedom of love.

"Love, the feminine principle—Love, the builder—the creator, has been so enslaved and abused, that when we talk of love in freedom, all sorts of degradation are imagined," she wrote in the last paragraph of *Woman's Source of Power*. It was an acknowledgment of an irony of sex radicalism that had dogged every step of her reform career: purity, perceived as degradation.[23]

Waisbrooker served several months as *Lucifer*'s interim editor during 1891 and 1892. Her health suffered, however; and Moses Harman, from prison, convinced Lillie D. White to take over. White had once been a member of the Berlin Heights, Ohio, free-love community, which the humorist Artemus Ward visited and kidded in his article "Among the Free Lovers." She came from a remarkable family of feminists: her mother, Hannah J. Hunt, her sister Lizzie M. Holmes, and her brother C. F. Hunt often wrote in *Lucifer*. White, who was secretary of the Kansas Freethinkers Association, a strong feminist, and a radical antifusionist Populist, brought to *Lucifer* one of the keenest minds of the time on the woman question.[24]

In an early editorial she declared that the Church was woman's enemy, "which we all know is responsible for her greatest suffering and degradation," but that womankind also suffered in the hands of its friends, especially "those friends who believe that woman's pre-eminent duty is to be a wife, mother and housekeeper." She assailed "ladies' book" writers who criticized woman's attempts to engage in so-called men's professions, and she attacked those suffragists who saw woman's first duty as her domestic obligation. Woman, she announced, "has a right to follow whatever vocation in life she please, and if she is unfitted thereby for wife and mother, or chooses to ignore wifely and maternal ties and burdens, who shall deny her that right? Whose business is it but her own?"

To those feminists, including Harman, who held that motherhood was the highest function of woman, she explained that such delusion was "but a repetition of that curse placed upon woman in the garden of Eden as a punishment for seeking knowledge. . . . Above all things, woman must unlearn that she owes duties of any kind to gods, men or communities."[25]

In a January 1893 article called "Housekeeping" she went to the heart of the emancipation problem:

Woman has always been taught that her highest happiness lies in a correct step to the music of pots and kettles, a mastery over the ingredients and process of making palatable bread, butter, pies and pickles, and a general devotion to the loves and duties of home; and my protest is that she has learned the lesson so well.... The teaching of domesticity as her principal virtue confines woman strictly and entirely to the material plane of life. She administers to the physical wants and comforts, gratifies the senses and appetites of the family, and inevitably comes to think, talk of, and handle only material things. The world of thought, philosophy, science, literature and art, loses its charms for her, and she finally has no ability or desire to enter in.

White addressed, in fundamental terms, the question of woman and housework. She believed that technology would one day make housework obsolete. In the meantime she advised women to make housework of secondary importance. "For one thing in my life I am truly thankful," she confided, "I have never been guilty of being a good housekeeper." Continuing to repudiate such concepts as "woman's sphere, natural vocation, and duty," she was led by her logic to ask: "Why is it necessarily any more a woman's place to wash dishes, scrub floors, make beds, etc., than it is a man's? Why not teach our boys to do all these as well as our girls?" She concluded that "woman's work, her place, and sphere so entirely separated from man's special fields of action is a mumbo jumbo that has been revered too long and must be dethroned." The debate that ensued in *Lucifer* attested to the novelty of such statements, even among radicals.[26]

White noted that a good friend of hers, a young housewife, boasted that her housework so filled her day that she had no time to read, write, or even do needlework. Moreover, her friend "assumed quite an air of superiority over me from the fact that she was satisfied with that life and wished for nothing different." Such attitudes, she believed, showed the enormous task that lay ahead for feminism. White characterized wifehood with three words—"duty, submission, self-repression"—but she needed more to describe motherhood. "Motherhood brings pain, suffering, unappreciative devotion and unresponsive affection. To be the 'queen of home' means drudgery and imprisonment. It is to be a galley slave to the appetites and needs of her family," wrote White, a mother herself. She advised mothers to discard the myth that a child's best welfare demanded her constant presence; in many cases, she remarked, children were better off in the care of others.[27]

White did not categorically oppose the idea of home and family, only the existent domesticity which, she felt, dehumanized the wife, the husband, and the children. She asked, "Can affection and parental responsibility, and love of home and family only develop and grow when surrounded by legal restrictions, authority and obedience?" No, she believed; free love would destroy nothing but artificial bonds and falsely-based relationships. Too many people, scientists and radicals included, she wrote, believed that civilization pivoted "on a marriage license and dutiful wives."

White thought that it was fruitless to seek happy homes or feminine fulfillment within domestic institutions that were based upon enforced suffering, legal subjugation, and the tradition of submissiveness. Only a pathological sort of "fulfillment," she believed, required such denigration. "When women learn that their best and highest object in life is to be independent and free, instead of living to make some man comfortable; when she finds that she must first be happy herself before she can make others happy, we shall have loving, harmonious families and happy homes."[28]

By flatly rejecting the mystique of motherhood, she rejected the favorite nineteenth-century basis for the belief in woman's superiority. Consequently she dealt more seriously with the problem of feminism and the male than did those who put woman on a pedestal. While sex radicals professed the need for sexual freedom for both sexes, most of them saw woman as the victim of man and aimed their efforts toward liberating woman from man. It was not quite so simple to Lillie White, who considered man's special problems.

White recognized the plight of husbands who led nightmarish lives because of selfish, tyrannical wives. Consciously or not, a woman became a virago, she believed, in protest against centuries of oppression which had "narrowed her nature to petty spite and fretful bickerings as her only weapons of defense." She regretted that some innocent husbands had to suffer for the sins of others, but in 1891, she saw no other solution in this inevitable balancing of accounts.[29]

In 1899 she wrote about the need to emancipate men from the tyranny of the "little" woman, the sort whose "selfish, greedy, monopolistic, devouring, tigerish maternal feeling is often mistaken for an excess of mother love." By claiming superiority through motherhood, such women not only tyrannized men, but they also often deprived fathers and children of their rights to one another. She saw future possibilities for a journal that would be dedicated to freeing fathers and children from the monopoly of conventional motherhood and to cultivating the parental instinct in man, which had long been discouraged and ignored. Her ideas had a logical symmetry: if woman had no special sphere, even as a mother, then neither did man. She saw no reason why he should not develop his sensibilities to include the possibility of being the househusband and the nurturing parent.[30]

Free lovers had been forced to deal in new ways with the rights of children and the responsibilities of parents. Stephen Pearl Andrews early set an innovative pace by proposing that conventional child rearing be replaced by nurseries of from fifty to one hundred babies under the charge of professional nurses, physiologists, and loving matrons. In the socializing atmosphere of their peers, children would be freed from the burdens and mistakes of child rearing. Before reaching puberty, children would be taught "a perfect understanding of the whole sexual system, its construction, functions, and uses, and its capacity for abuses." Instruction would be in mixed classes, so that false modesty would not develop. Since intercourse was the natural use of the genitals, it would not be discouraged among the youth: "The only obscenity there is, is the unnatural uses to which natural capacities are compelled by the denial of their natural use. Thus self-abuse is obscene, and all its effects horrible; but sexual intercourse, where there is legitimate natural desires, is not obscene and no pure-minded person can ever conceive it to be so."

Andrews sought the radical restructuring of domestic life in order to dissolve the prevailing social bonds, so that pure and voluntary links, namely love and natural attraction, could replace arbitrary ones. He believed that such radical freedom would ensure the love relationships against the degradation of coercion.

Free-love papers, from *Woodhull & Claflin's Weekly* and *Hull's Crucible* in the 1870s to *Lucifer* in the 1900s, at times devoted serious attention to child rearing within free-love arrangements. There was a tendency among free lovers to assume that radical individualism and the replacement of conventional marriage by "natural selection" of sex partners would solve most problems of child rearing. The fate of freely born children with presumed eugenic advantages could be decided by enlightened parents and, of course, by the children themselves. On the disposition of children when parents separated, Lillie White wrote:

From the moment a child recognizes the tender solicitude and affection of its mother or the interest and hearty comradeship of its father or the absence of either, there is no person living more competent to decide the matter of association than the child itself. A fair acquaintance with both parents, freedom of choice, liberty to come and go, to visit or stay, will always be found most convenient and effective in adjusting these relations.

Moses Hull once proposed that a tax be "levied on all property of the nation in order to educate and take care of all the children in the nation, whether born in or out of wedlock." Unlike Rachel Campbell, who believed that the revenue should be paid to individual women and mothers, Hull proposed that the money go to support a network of nurseries. Lillian Harman opposed government payments of any kind for housewives and mothers, but she did propose that couples make private contracts so that the housewife would be paid a salary for her housework. She also believed that a couple should have a certain minimum amount of material wealth before entering parenthood. This property qualification, decided upon by the mother and not by the state, applied only to parentage and not to marriage.

As in society at large, free lovers believed children to be the special responsibility of women. In the autonomous marriage of Lillian Harman and Edwin Walker, Walker affirmed the "paramount right" of the mother to any children that the union might bring forth. Although this arrangement might appear today as subtle exploitation of woman, nineteenth-century feminists felt differently as they battled against the head-of-household laws that prevailed in most states, which gave fathers dominating rights in the family, including jurisdiction over the children. Most free lovers, by assuming the right of contraception and by promoting the notion of bachelor motherhood, only offered women more choices about motherhood; they did not free her from motherhood.[31]

White's career as editor of *Lucifer* lasted seven months. Perhaps if White had stayed on after Harman returned from prison, *Lucifer* could have become a journal of direct, national importance to more than a few. As it was, the journal lapsed into the free-lovers free-for-all that it had always been under Harman. Not all who followed *Lucifer*, however, were impressed by White. One of Benjamin Tucker's favored contributors to *Liberty*, a Russian-born pedant named Victor Yarros, disagreed with White's favorable review of *Government Analyzed*, a book by John R. Kelso, which White had reviewed in the New York journal *Solidarity*. In carrying the argument on in *Liberty*, Yarros called White stupid and dishonest, and remarked in his article "Taming a Shrew" that "the chatter of the weak-minded, especially of the female division, cannot profitably be made the subject of comment; but there are some amusing features in the case of Lillie D. White, who imagines herself an editor of a paper because her stuff happens to appear in print without corrections and in large type." Yarros's venom had the approval of Tucker, who also dismissed White as "stupid."[32]

Such remarks, which were aimed at the most outstanding editor that *Lucifer* ever had and were published in the midst of her series of extraordinary editorials debunking sex roles, motherhood, and housekeeping, seemed to justify Ezra Heywood's claim that *Liberty* had become a reactionary force in the struggle for sexual expression. Once, in support of Heywood's right to publish Walt Whitman, Tucker had openly defied the Vice Society's ban on *Leaves of Grass* by urging readers of *Liberty* to order the book directly from him, daring Comstock to touch him. But by 1890, Tucker and Yarros had backed off from the free-speech issue, urging that there be no more defiance of Comstock. Saddened by the defection, Heywood tagged Tucker and Yarros "mental eunuchs who call themselves 'Anarchists.'"

Heywood considered an 1890 statement by Yarros in *Liberty*, "A Declaration of Independence," to be a literal "proclamation of evasion and cowardice, an unconditional surrender to Comstock." In the article, which was seconded by Tucker, Yarros characterized as "imbeciles" those who believed that blunt language had crucial importance to the "cause of liberty." Those who urged that radicals defend Heywood and Harman on grounds of principle he called fools. "It is possible to forcibly express the most radical views without giving the authorities the slightest pretext for interference," Tucker had written, arguing that libertarian efforts should not center on the discussion of taboo subjects in blunt language. These statements caused *Liberty* some embarrassment when, a few weeks later, the Post Office Department found Tolstoy's *Kreutzer Sonata* to be obscene and banned Tucker's translation of it from the mails.

The forces of prudery, it appeared, had leveled the attack, with Tucker already in retreat. Tucker admitted that his first concern in offering the *Kreutzer Sonata* to the public had been for the response of the Vice Society. Such a patently moral book as Tolstoy's would not be attacked, Tucker felt, and if it were attacked, it could be easily vindicated. In any case, he wrote, he wished "to avoid endangering that partial liberty of speech which I now enjoy and which is my only weapon of warfare upon existing evils." Although several important newspapers criticized the Post Office Department for banning the *Kreutzer Sonata*, the episode seemed to increase Tucker's intimidation. The next year he issued a translation of Émile Zola's *Money*, but in expurgated form, causing Heywood to charge that Tucker "expurgate[d], mutilate[d], the book lest Comstock may pounce on him!" Heywood, Harman, and Lillie White knew by this time, of course, that Tucker and Yarros favored the arena of theoretical anarchism, where they never had to admit defeat nor concede a point in debate. The two did not like the practical, sometimes foolhardy, tactics of the sex radicals nor the sticky questions that their actions raised.[33]

Besides Lillian Harman, who mothered both *Lucifer* and her father far beyond the call of familial duty, perhaps the last in the line of outstanding women to be connected with *Lucifer* was Dora Forster. She and her husband, R. B. Kerr, were British epigones of Harman who later helped to direct the Neo-Malthusian efforts in Britain. Forster wrote a treatise called *Sex Radicalism* for publication in *Lucifer*. It appeared serially in 1904 and, with other items, helped to land Harman in jail for a final time. Early in the series she called for a thoroughgoing empirical report on the sociology of sex. The questions that she propounded foreshadowed the Kinsey Reports a half-century later. On childhood sexuality she observed that

> sexual play is natural to children, and when arising naturally, and not stimulated by bad nurses very early, is usually not injurious, especially when there is plenty of healthy social play. The excess of it in highly nervous children is a symptom not a cause of nervousness. It is quite unscientific to call the excitement of the sex nerves, "solitary vice"; and it is mere cruelty to tell any child or adult that this habit is low and wicked. . . . The child should be given enough knowledge to show him that the habit may become selfish, and, especially in the case of boys, exhausting, and to encourage him in moderation. . . . All these sexual phenomena are observable in domesticated animals of nervous nature, and do not appear to increase their nervousness, though they might if animals were infected with our ideas of sin.[34]

She proposed to abolish the three great evils of the present sex system—celibacy, bond marriage, and prostitution—by theoretical and practical sex education for the young. The practical exercise would be done by the age of sixteen with a partner chosen from good friends of the family, and girls would be prepared by a hymenotomy. Prostitutes would be out of business, Forster wrote, if women freely gave of themselves within their social station and circle of friends; the worst prostitution of all, motherhood in conventional marriage, would be replaced by honored free motherhood.

With as keen an eye as Lillie White's, Forster examined conventional marriage, an institution that she characterized as "this mix up of love and cookery." Woman's legal status was not presently the crucial problem of marriage, she wrote, since only in its worst failures did the legal bonds chafe. The unwritten social laws—custom and convention—cossetted woman far more rigorously than did statutes. The most glaring restriction forbade honest attention to woman's sexual response, which was a critical mistake since, she believed, physical intimacy "is no doubt the crux of married life." Convention allowed "enjoyment to the man, because this is obviously inevitable," but it denied sensual enjoyment to the woman, and taught her rather to use her body for economic and social advantages for herself and her children. With regard to orgasm, she estimated that "married men almost always obtain satisfaction of a kind sufficient for health, a great many married women, probably more than half, fail to do so."

Her arguments recognized that Western society had complex reasons for its defense of monogamy, and she took no dogmatic stance against the practice. She believed, however, that those who seriously pursued the question would agree that sexual intercourse should not be "wholly and rigidly restricted" to one partnership: "Little as we know of the exact nature of sex 'magnetism,' all experience goes to show that at least occasional variety is very beneficial, both mentally and physically." In any case, she advised, the conventional bond should be made lighter in order to encourage those qualities of relationship that were more long-lived than passion—sexual kindness, affection, and courtesy.[35]

14/ The Last Chapter

LUCIFER's ties with England involved more than publishing the works of writers such as Dora Forster. In 1893 the journal began printing correspondence from the Legitimation League, a new English organization whose headquarters near Leeds had been named Harman Villa in honor of the American sex radicals. The league sought to legitimize nonmarital sexual relationships, so that partners and offspring might enjoy the same rights of property and inheritance as those enjoyed under the state-sanctioned form of marriage.

The league proposed a legal alternative to marriage: couples could simply and inexpensively register with a Prothonotary of a Licit Alliance League, which would ensure that any children or the surviving partner of the union had the same rights accorded in conventional marriage. Although the league sought the same goals of sexual liberation as the American sex radicals did, it hoped to attract respectable but socially independent types by avoiding economic, political, or antireligious radicalism in order to focus solely on sex.

Oswald Dawson, founder of the league, wrote to Moses Harman: "I should not be surprised to find that . . . you would consider that 'Legitimation' was a rather tame sort of banner to flaunt . . . and that what we ought to do would be to make a more stalwart response to our friends in America and go boldly in for 'Free Love.'" "I am not sure," he continued, "that I quite understand the meaning of that term as you use it in America, but here it stands for 'indiscriminate adultery' or something else with a very bad odour." The English had no laws forbidding free-love alliances, as did most American states, and English proximity to Continental culture seemed to make them more tolerant of sexual liaisons. One British correspondent to *Lucifer* explained: "For many years, the poets and novelists of England have dealt so freely with sex that all thinking people [in England] clearly perceive the existence of a sex question, and are inclined to discuss it." The Legitimation League wanted to capitalize on this interest in sex in order to change public opinion and existing laws that, in practice at least, discouraged free liaisons.[1]

The league grew swiftly. Although it avoided getting involved in politics, it professed a libertarian or individualist bias. A prominent member was the English anarchist Henry Seymour, who published the *Anarchist* and helped to promote *Lucifer* in England. The league attracted the participation of literary figures such as Richard Le Gallienne and Grant Allen and reformers such as the Neo-Malthusians Alice Vickery Drysdale and her husband, Dr. Charles R. Drysdale. In 1898, upwards of two hundred people attended the meetings of the league.[2]

An 1895 event dramatized the issue of "free love" in Britain. Edith Lanchester, a well-educated young woman from a respectable London family, became a Socialist, moved to the workers' district of Battersea, and began a career as a Socialist politician. There she fell in love with another Socialist, a mechanic named James Sullivan, and the two planned to live together without benefit of matrimony. Her outraged father and brother kidnapped her and, on the authority of a physician named Blandford, committed her on an urgency order to an insane asylum. Dr. Blandford, who judged the woman insane after "about half an hour's conversation," did so because he believed her opposition to conventional matrimony made her unfit to take care of herself.

When James Sullivan finally discovered where Lanchester had been taken, he and the labor leader John Burns, M.P., prevailed upon the Lunacy Commission to visit Lanchester in the asylum. Pronounced sane and freed, she returned to Battersea and to her alliance with Sullivan. The case received a great deal of publicity in the penny press of London and even in the United States; the *New York Times* correspondent reported that the case inspired another rush on Grant Allen's tendentious book *The Woman Who Did*. Lanchester's incarceration outraged not only Socialists and libertarians, but others who were concerned with the abuse of mental-health practices.[3]

The travail of Edith Lanchester attracted the energies of George Bedborough, who was a young university-educated journalist and a member of the Legitimation League. Upon his suggestion, the league took up the Lanchester cause and helped to bring it wide attention. Bedborough, with two others, took the case a step further by presenting a case for Dr. Blandford's censure before the Royal Commission of Lunacy. From the Lanchester case onward, Bedborough played a leading role in the Legitimation League.

In 1897 the league assumed a more radical tone, subordinating its legal-reform work to the new principal goal: "To educate public opinion in the direction of freedom in sexual relationships." This development caused the resignation of the league's president, Wordsworth Donisthorpe, "who, in the new departure," said a magazine report, "saw a Free Love propaganda, which impression, no doubt, was correct." Confirming this free-love direction, the league unanimously elected their American heroine, Lillian Harman, as the new president, while electing George Bedborough as executive secretary. The league also voted to move its headquarters from Leeds to London.

Shortly after the election, the league began monthly publication of the *Adult*, a "Journal for the Advancement of Freedom in Sex Relationships," which was edited by Bedborough. Its lead editorial in the first issue paid tribute to the Harmans, to *Lucifer*, and to Harman's new magazine venture, *Our New Humanity*; the *Adult* also vowed to emulate the Lucifereans' "whole-heartedness in the cause of sex reform." From the beginning, Lillian and Edwin Walker were prominent American contributors. The magazine boasted a varied list of contributors, by no means all of whom agreed on the issue of sexual freedom. Letters appeared from Grant Allen and George Bernard Shaw; and Lady Cook (nee Tennessee Claflin) even contributed an article on Malthus. The Legitimationists argued that free love already existed in England in the form of adulterous alliances and that they sought to end the deceit surrounding the practice. The journal reflected the old-boyish humor of Bedborough; to a reader who wondered if free love might not be illegal, the editor replied: "Oh dear no; free love is not illegal,—the illegality consists in discussing its merits, that is all." England finally had its own version of *Lucifer*.⁴

The man whose presses actually printed both the *Adult* and at least one other pro-sex radical periodical, the *University Magazine and Free Review*, was a strange personage known as Dr. Roland de Villiers. Quite innocently, the sexologist Havelock Ellis in 1897 contracted with de Villiers's "Watford University Press" (no university existed, however, at Watford) to publish the first English edition of *Studies in the Psychology of Sex: Sexual Inversion*, a descriptive study of the "inborn constitutional" predisposition to homosexuality on which Ellis had received help from the late John Addington Symonds. The book had already appeared in a German translation in 1896. De Villiers's press brought out *Sexual Inversion* inobtrusively in November 1897, as Havelock Ellis desired. Review copies were sent to a few professional journals; Lillian Harman received a copy autographed by Ellis early in 1898. For a few months it appeared that the publication of *Sexual Inversion* would be a modest landmark in Victorian publishing.

In a reminiscence in 1936, Ellis remembered Lillian Harman as the "daughter of Moses Harman of Chicago, a famous pioneer of sexual enlightenment in America." To the Legitimationists of London, Lillian herself was a famous pioneer. In 1898 Lillian voyaged to England to meet her admiring comrades, stopping in New York for press interviews and an address before the Manhattan Liberal Club.⁵

"A New Woman came out of the West last night and preached her new ideas to a New York audience," wrote the *New York World*'s reporter. The paper explained the antimarriage stance of the Lucifereans and recorded at length her Liberal Club address. When asked about her free marriage to Walker, Lillian called it "a common-sense arrangement: 'I love you, but will not be tied to you.'" The next morning, a Saturday in early April 1898, Lillian boarded the steamer *Massachusetts* and sailed to England with her message of common sense, a trip that was paid for, quite probably, by leaders of the Legitimation League.⁶

When Lillian presided over the annual meeting of the Legitimation League in London later that month, four-hundred-eleven people attended the meeting and heard congratulatory letters from sex radicals Grant Allen, Edward Carpenter, and Mona Caird, as well as a dissenting view from W. T. Stead, editor of *Review of Reviews*. Lillian Harman and George Bedborough were reelected president and secretary, and Lillian addressed the gathering on "Some Problems of Social Freedom," dealing with the impact of liberated love on marriage, the family, children, and the social relationships between the sexes. She replied to the question constantly asked of her: What arrangement do you prescribe to replace marriage? "It would be quite as reasonable to ask me what size I would make the shoes if I had a monopoly on shoe-making for the entire human race," she told the audience, predicting that free conditions would stimulate "many varied modes of living," including individual, cooperative, and communistic homes:

I consider uniformity in mode of sexual relations as undesirable and impracticable as enforced uniformity in anything else. For myself, I want the right to profit by my mistakes . . . and why should I be unwilling for others to enjoy the same liberty? If I should be able to bring the entire world to live exactly as I live at present, what would that avail me in ten years, when, as I hope, I shall have a broader knowledge of life, and my life therefore probably changed? I do not want to spend my life in converting the world to my method of existence. I want the world to have reason of its own and use it.

Concerning the publicity attending her English reception, Lillian wrote: "The London and provincial papers appear to find me almost as great a curiosity as Edith Lanchester was to American papers. They *will* have it that I have come over here on a propagandistic mission to drag women out of marriage and murder the babies and do all sorts of dreadful things." Actually the British press gave her cause reasonably fair coverage, but the headlines of course played to sensation: "Apostle of Free Love—Mrs. Lillian Harman to Preach Strange Ideas in London," headlined the *Daily Mail*; "A Woman Who Does—She Crusades for Freedom of Her Sex—Has Been in Prison for Her Principles," proclaimed the London *Star*. Notices from *Reynolds's Newspaper*, the *Mail*, *Society*, and the *Daily Record* (Glasgow) were sent home and reprinted in *Lucifer*.[7]

Lillian visited Paris and went on a speaking trip to Leeds, Edinburgh, and Glasgow. Back in London on May 31, on the way to visit the Crystal Palace with George Bedborough and the American anarchist poet William Francis Bernard, Lillian suddenly found herself facing detective John Sweeney, an undercover agent for Scotland Yard's antianarchist section.

The agent produced a warrant and arrested Bedborough for selling an obscene book, *Sexual Inversion*, by Havelock Ellis. Sweeney had infiltrated the Legitimation League to watch its anarchist members, and a few days before he had purchased a copy of the book from Bedborough in the offices of the *Adult*. The connection between *Sexual Inversion* and the *Adult* was not only that de Villiers's press published both, but that the *Adult* shared the same offices as the "Watford University Press." Lillian telegraphed Havelock Ellis at Carbis Bay and obtained a lawyer for Bedborough.

In a celebrated case, Bedborough was thrust into the role of a hero of free expression and of scientific sexual enlightenment in Britain. A Defence Committee led by Henry Seymour prepared the legal fight and attracted support from a glittering roster— Frank Harris of *Saturday Review*, W. T. Stead of *Review of Reviews* (who was not a member of the committee but was a supporter nevertheless), W. M. Thompson of *Reynolds's Newspaper*, George Bernard Shaw, Mona Caird, Grant Allen, Frank Podmore, Edith Lanchester, William Sharp, G. J. Holyoake, Walter Crane, Robert Buchanan, and others. At least thirteen journals, from the popular to the radical, publicized and supported the effort.[8]

"The prosecution of Mr. Bedborough for selling Mr. Havelock Ellis's book is a masterpiece of police stupidity and magisterial ignorance," George Bernard Shaw wrote to Seymour, "I have read the book carefully; and I have no hesitation in saying that its publication was more urgently needed in England than any other recent treatise with which I am acquainted." Shaw referred to homosexuality in England and to the Criminal Law Amendment Act of 1885, which made a crime of private consensual homosexual acts—behavior that *Sexual Inversion* sought to understand. "Englishmen and Englishwomen," wrote Shaw, "are paying rates and taxes for the enforcement of the most abominably superstitious penal laws directed against the morbid idiosyncrasy with which the book deals." W. T. Stead, whose exposés of white slavery had been influential in the passage of the Criminal Law Amendment Act, wrote to the same point as Shaw in his *Review of Reviews*:

It may be alleged that such questions should not be discussed, and that the whole question [of homosexuality] should be buried in impenetrable silence. The answer to this is that if the legislator makes one theory of the Psychology of Sex the basis for passing a law which sends citizens to penal servitude, it is impossible to shut out such a theory from public discussion. Dr. Ellis' inquiry goes to the very root of the theory upon which one section of the Criminal Law Amendment Act is based, and if the conclusions at which he arrives are sound the principle of that legislation is unsound, and will have to be modified, for the same reason that capital punishment is never enforced upon persons of disordered minds.[9]

The indictment against Bedborough, which was delivered in late summer, revealed that Scotland Yard was less concerned with suppressing Ellis's book than with suppressing the free-love agitation in England. Officials had believed that Bedborough was the key man not only in the Legitimation League and the *Adult* but in the publication of *Sexual Inversion* as well. Of the eleven counts in the indictment, the first dealt with *Sexual Inversion*, the second with Oswald Dawson's pamphlet "The Outcome of Legitimation," and the remaining nine with matter from the *Adult*, including Moses Harman's "A Free Man's Creed" and "every line" of Lillian Harman's "Some Problems of Social Freedom."[10]

To the disappointment of his supporters, although it was unknown to them at the time, Bedborough—at a crucial moment in the proceedings—negotiated with the court and admitted his guilt. The prosecution agreed that in exchange for his admission of guilt on the first three counts, they would ask a suspension of judgment in the case, provided that Bedborough disassociated himself from the sex-reform movement in England. They were no doubt moved in this direction by Bedborough's voluntary offer of compromise, by his promise to sever his ties to sex reform, and by his identification of the "real" villain in the case as Dr. Roland de Villiers, the head of Watford University Press. Members of the Defence Committee were not the only ones who were unaware of Bedborough's capitulation until it had occurred; so was Havelock Ellis, who waited in court to testify about the book but was never called.

The pioneer sexual work stood judged in a high court of law as "filthy and obscene." In his decision, Sir Charles Hall, Recorder of London, wrote that "it is impossible for anybody with a head on his shoulders to open the book without seeing that it is a pretence and a sham, and that it is merely entered into for the purpose of selling this obscene publication." Bedborough agreed, to quote the judge, to cease to "touch this filthy work" of the Legitimation League and sex reform. "So long as you lead a respectable life, you will hear no more of this," warned the judge, "but if you choose to go back to your evil ways . . . it will be my duty to send you to prison for a very long time."[11]

Bedborough's action astonished those who had involved themselves in his defense, most of whom felt confident that his case could have been won. The police had calculated Bedborough's character well, wrote one biographer of Havelock Ellis; some browbeating and a short stint in jail had thrown a fright into him. The outcome of the Ellis case effectively ended the Legitimation League—for its work had officially been judged obscene—and staggered the *Lucifer*-inspired movement for greater sexual freedom in Britain. Continued investigation uncovered de Villiers as a scoundrel of dramatic proportions who had been involved in forgery and fraudulent investment schemes and who had enough phony identities to require a filing system to keep them in order. In reality he was Georg Ferdinand Springmuhl von Weissenfield, a scion of a respectable German family. He eluded capture until 1901, when police closed in on him at his Cambridge home. They seized him in a secret passageway, where he abruptly died either of taking poison from a finger ring or because of a fit of apoplexy. Police confiscated the press run of *Sexual Inversion* and then destroyed it. Havelock Ellis did not seem to be able or willing to stop the book burning.[12]

American sex radicals at the turn of the century faced a confusing prospect. The popular press and the professional people increasingly discussed marriage, divorce, and sex education, topics that for a long time had been the monopoly of the sex radicals. The sexual libertarians welcomed the widening discussion; nevertheless they felt chagrined at the persistence of puritanism in American society—a puritanism that was all the more frustrating for being two-faced: despite the widening discussion, the crackdown on sex radicals continued apace. Articles that were accepted as interesting reading in large newspapers, professional journals, and even women's journals were cause for censorship when published in *Lucifer* or by those with no certain connections to respectability or to the professions.

In 1898 a federal court in Wisconsin fined Emil Ruedebusch $1,200 for distributing his reasoned defense of sexual varietism, *The Old and the New Ideal*. *Lucifer*'s promotion of the book had helped to sell two thousand copies before the ban, however. Ida C. Craddock, an ascetic sex reformer from New York who corresponded with *Lucifer*, was repeatedly arrested by Comstock for such pamphlets as "The Wedding Night" and "Right Marital Living." Shortly after she had been released from prison for an obscenity conviction in 1902, Comstock again arrested her and won a conviction on a new charge. She committed suicide rather than face prison once more. The suicide letter that she left behind began: "I am taking my life because a judge, at the instigation of Anthony Comstock, has decreed me guilty of a crime I did not commit—the circulation of obscene literature." Alice B. Stockham, Harman's fellow Chicagoan whose book of obstetrical advice, *Tokology: A Book for Every Woman*, reached circulation of half a million and won her the acquaintance of Count Tolstoy, was arrested by McAfee of the Vice Society and eventually fined $250 and court costs for distributing her "obscene" leaflet, which was also entitled "The Wedding Night." The court exacted a $500 fine from Stockham's business manager, and in a related move, the Post Office Department censored *Lucifer* when it attempted to publish portions of *Tokology* in its pages.[13]

On the other hand, the sociologist Elsie Clews Parsons could discuss in very open language such a delicate topic as the religious uses of sexuality; her article "The Religious Dedication of Women," which appeared in a 1906 issue of the *American Journal of Sociology*, dealt historically with sexual sacrifice, phallicism, and "holy" forms of intercourse but contained specific reference to contemporary religious practices. And one of the editors of the journal, the feminist sociologist Charles Zueblin, would in 1910 tell Vassar faculty and the Poughkeepsie clergy that women who desired to bear children without the legality of the marriage ceremony were perfectly justified in doing so. The National Congress of Mothers, the forerunner of the P.T.A., passed a resolution at its first meeting in 1897 in favor not only of children's education but also of what a P.T.A. historian called "sex adjustment in successful marriage." The mothers heard such addresses as "Reproduction and Natural Law" and "Moral Responsibility of Women in Heredity," which spoke favorably of birth control and suggested eugenics. In 1897 Stanford education professor Earl Barnes wrote a review article on sex-education materials, noting the recent appearance in America of "a considerable body of people who advocate giving children some sort of sex-information." As early as 1892, in fact, the National Education Association had held a seminar on childhood sex education, which Barnes had chaired. Even the National Purity Federation, an organization that for years had been Comstock-oriented, listened with some approval in 1906 to Theodore Schroeder's libertarian views on sexual purity. Anthony Comstock, who was scheduled to reply to Schroeder's assertion that more liberty of the press was needed for the discussion of sex problems, did not appear. Not only did the purity delegates generally favor sexual instruction in schools, but they also unanimously went on record for a clearer judicial definition of obscenity, one that could not be construed to suppress "any scientific and educational purity literature." Commenting on the conference, the *New York Sun* editorialized: "The truth is that a new school of purity has sprung up in the world, and for the present Mr. Comstock must be content to pass as an old fogy, out-of-date, mid-Victorian, unfashionable, or whatever the stronger party chooses." But of course the "new" school of purity was not new, and the death of Comstockery was greatly exaggerated.[14]

In 1905 officials again arrested Moses Harman for using obscenity in *Lucifer*. For two years, the Post Office Department had been increasingly pressuring *Lucifer*. On orders from Washington, *Lucifer* was repeatedly seized in Chicago by the censor, the official in charge of second-class mails; and with no due process, the Post Office Department not only had refused *Lucifer* the use of the mails, but also had confiscated and destroyed the issues that had been submitted for mailing. For several months, in fact, *Lucifer* was denied second-class mailing privileges and was forced to pay a mailing rate of twenty-one cents per pound instead of the one-cent-per-pound rate for second-class mail; the exclusion came after a Post Office Department inquiry had fully revealed the marginal financial status of *Lucifer*. This administrative censorship extended to an advertisement for William Sanger's *The History of Prostitution* (its very title was offensive) and a reprinted editorial from Alice Stone Blackwell's *Woman's Journal*, even though the article in Miss Blackwell's magazine had never been questioned. Peeved at the suppression of the *Woman's Journal* article in *Lucifer*, Blackwell later wrote: "We submitted that editorial to Mrs. Julia Ward Howe, Jane Addams and several prominent clergymen, and all agreed that they could not see the faintest impropriety in it."

The federal grand jury apparently picked two articles at random from *Lucifer* for the 1905 charges against Harman, although the initial arrest warrant was against the publication of Dora Forster's *Sex Radicalism*. In June, Judge Kenesaw Mountain Landis, who would gain fame in 1907 by exacting the "big fine" against Standard Oil for accepting rebates, sentenced the seventy-five-year-old Harman to a year at hard labor at Joliet. Unsuccessful in an appeal attempt, Harman went to Joliet in 1906; for a portion of his sentence the old man broke rocks for eight and one-half hours a day out in the Illinois winter. Harman's health suffered seriously, and intervention by friends won him transfer to the federal prison in Leavenworth, Kansas. He was immediately hospitalized there for bronchitis and spent much of the rest of his sentence in the hospital.[15]

George Bernard Shaw spoke of Harman's plight in a front-page *New York Times* interview in 1905, in which he coined the term "Comstockery" and protested the New York Public Library's move to restrict some of his works. Shaw went on to say:

The one refuge left in the world for unbridled license is the married state. That is the shameful explanation of the fact that a journal has just been confiscated and its editor imprisoned in America for urging that a married woman should be protected from domestic molestation when childbearing. Had that man filled his paper with aphrodisiac pictures and aphrodisiac stories of duly engaged couples, he would now be a prosperous, respected citizen.

In 1907 Shaw answered a question from the London journalist James Douglas about why he had never paid a visit to America. Douglas subsequently reprinted the letter in a 1909 piece in

London Opinion, "Shaw v. America." "The reason I do not go to America is that I am afraid of being arrested by Mr. Anthony Comstock and imprisoned like Mr. Moses Harman," began Shaw. Further on in the letter he wrote:

> If the brigands can, without any remonstrance from public opinion, seize a man of Mr. Harman's advanced age, and imprison him for a year under conditions which amount to an indirect attempt to kill him, simply because he shares the opinion expressed in my *Man and Superman* that "marriage is the most licentious of human institutions," what chance should I have of escaping?
>
> No, thank you; no trips to America for me.

Referring not only to the 1905 attempt by the United States government to forbid Maxim Gorki's entrance into the United States, but also to the 1907 performance of Richard Strauss' "Salome" at the Metropolitan Opera, which was closed after one performance, Shaw wrote: "After the Gorki and Strauss episodes it is clear that no European author of any distinction is safe in the United States, which is now infested by moral brigands, who have turned the Post Office into a most Unholy Inquisition, and are apparently in supreme command of the police."[16]

In 1908 Shaw sent *Lucifer* a £20 draft and wrote:

> 10 Adelphi Terrace, London, W.C.
> Argot, June 11, 1908
>
> Dear Mr. Moses Harman:
>
> I am quite conscious of my obligation to you for sending me Lucifer and the Journal of Eugenics (not to mention those public obligations which I share with the world in general) and though I am too much preoccupied with my work to undertake to help you with special contributions or even with regular subscriptions, I take this opportunity of sending you a cheque to cover the actual out-of-pocket expenses of postage and paper and printing which the addition of my name to your free list put upon you.
>
> Your imprisonment was quite the most monstrous achievement of "the Nation of Villagers" within recent years. Unfortunately there is one subject on which Americans seem invincibly ignorant; and that one subject is America. They never know of anything that happens in their own country until an Englishman writes a book calling their attention to it. Nothing else can penetrate their chronic ecstacy [*sic*] of self-satisfaction in which they tolerate the welter of official de-

spotism and unofficial anarchy which so revolts foreigners who know what really happens in the United States of Arcadia.

Yours faithfully,
G. Bernard Shaw[17]

Shaw mentioned Harman in a pedantic letter to the Better Citizenship Association of Portland, Oregon, in 1910; and the same year, on the occasion of Moses Harman's death, he wrote to Lillian:

Dear Lillian Harman:

It seems nothing short of a miracle that your father should have succeeded in living for seventy-nine years in a country so extremely dangerous for men who have both enlightened opinions and the courage of them as the United States of America. It is certainly no fault of the Americans that he did not die before; that last imprisonment of his was really an outrage to political decency.

I am glad to gather from your letter that he escaped the illness and pain that often trouble a good man's end; and I hope that now that he is dead, and can no longer shock Mr. Comstock and the rest of the American idols, some little sense of shame at the way he was treated may find expression in America.

Yours faithfully,
G. Bernard Shaw[18]

Many influential people, upon learning of the continued harassment of *Lucifer*, were drawn to protest the government's action publicly. In its later years Harman's magazine was filled with reprinted articles and personal letters of support from such people as Louis F. Post of the *Public*, Alice Stone Blackwell of *Woman's Journal*, B. O. Flower of *Arena*, Hugh O. Pentecost of *Twentieth Century*, Elbert Hubbard of the *Philistine*, Leonard D. Abbott of *Literary Digest*, James H. Barry of the *San Francisco Star*, Parker H. Sercombe of *To-Morrow*, Horace Traubel of *Conservator*, various writers in *Physical Culture*, and Bolton Hall, Gilbert Roe, Clarence Darrow, Emma Goldman, Eugene Debs, Terence Powderly, Ernest Crosby, Carl Nold, Johann Most, and Alexander Berkman. Abroad, Harman's plight won publicity not only in Britain but also in French and Dutch Neo-Malthusian journals and in the Japanese press.[19]

More than before, *Lucifer* became a touchstone for those who challenged respectable society on matters of sex and marriage. For instance, the Reverend George D. Herron, the Christian Socialist whose anticapitalism caused his dismissal from the faculty of Iowa College, fanned the controversy surrounding his name in 1901 by denouncing marriage, shedding his wife, and taking another one in a civil ceremony—the daughter of the wealthy woman who previously had endowed his chair of Applied Christianity at Iowa College. In response the Congregational Church ousted him from membership. Harman and Herron entered into correspondence in 1901, and the excerpts that were printed in *Lucifer* record Herron's appreciation of Harman's support for and defense of his actions.[20]

In response to the selective harassment it suffered, *Lucifer* changed its name and format; it also attempted to assume a professional image and to exploit the fact that for some twenty years it had been advocating eugenics, the popular reform enthusiasm of the first decade of the twentieth century. Moses and Lillian Harman, in fact, saw the *American Journal of Sociology* and the *North American Review* as models for the format of a new *Lucifer*. Although the Harmans were polemic journalists, not academics or scientists, they seemed aware that the time had passed for the nineteenth-century anti-institutionalism that had so strongly flavored *Lucifer*. Perhaps they saw a chance for their journal to gain credit with a new professional class and to cultivate sophisticated readers rather than village iconoclasts. Above all, the editors realized that such issues as divorce, eugenics, and sex education, simply as topics, no longer distinguished *Lucifer*. Consequently, in 1907 *Lucifer* assumed the appearance of a scholarly journal and took the name of *American Journal of Eugenics*.

The change brought a few new subscribers and some new contributors, notably the English eugenics popularizer C. W. Saleeby. Theodore Schroeder contributed an important article the first year, "Varieties of Official Modesty," which detailed how prudery affected justice; but on the whole the writers and the content varied little from those of *Lucifer* in its late years. Harman's last imprisonment had aged him considerably; old and tired, and without much of a coherent idea of what he wanted the new journal to be, Harman moved *Eugenics* to Los Angeles in 1908. His death, on 30 January 1910, ended the venture. Lillian Harman brought out a last issue, a memorial tribute to her father, which coincided with Easter memorial services for the old reformer in New York and Los Angeles.[21]

Harman and his journal had outlived most of the Lucifereans of his generation—most importantly the Doctors Foote, Elmina Slenker, and Lois Waisbrooker. Lillian Harman, who always loved domesticity though she believed it had enslaved many of her sex, left the public arena after 1910 for home life. She and Edwin Walker had lived separately for many years, and after the turn of the century she quietly and legally married a printer named George O'Brien. Lillie D. White, who once had edited and written brilliantly for *Lucifer*, contributed for the last time in 1907. Edwin C. Walker helped to edit the *Truth Seeker* in New York; served as president of the Manhattan Liberal Club; became a rare-book dealer; founded the Sunrise Club, which gave Emma Goldman her first platform from which to speak on birth control; and presided last at the club in 1930, a few months before his death in February 1931. A short obituary in the *New York Times* called him a "champion of liberal views."[22]

Unique in its role as light bearer of free love and feminism in the high Victorian era, *Lucifer* had united sex radicals from 1883 to 1907—a considerable achievement simply in longevity. In its best moments, *Lucifer* offered a revelation of the outer limits of American social experimentation, but these moments came more by chance than by plan. At its worst, the journal listed in the uneven seas of its readers' whims and prejudices, guided by Moses Harman's personal visions of martyrdom. Harman had little capacity for initiating new editorial directions for his paper; his belief in liberty was virtually unlimited, but the man himself was limited imaginatively and intellectually to a few ideas. He proudly claimed that the readers ran the paper, that *Lucifer* was a free platform—yet this eclecticism limited *Lucifer*'s impact.

Lucifer sought to present the best-informed sex thought of the time. It got no help from the scientific community itself, for most American scientists in the eighties and nineties did not consider sexuality and sexual practice as subjects for research or reform. They thus abandoned the domain of sex to lay people. These same scientists and the conventional society that they represented then complained that cranks dominated the study of sex. There is no scientific justification for this refusal to look at sex; moreover the scientists conveniently rejected the fact that sex radicals and "cranks" were more than willing to be guided by scientific knowledge. *Lucifer*, however, did disseminate important writings like those of the feminist economist Charlotte Perkins Stetson Gilman; it published extracts from the American edition of Friedrich Engels's *The Origin of the Family* before it appeared in book form; and its selections from August Bebel, Grant Allen, and Karl Pearson provided ammunition for its scattered readership. The journal provided a creditable historic basis for sex radicalism, recalling the writings of William Godwin, Mary Wollstonecraft, and Karl Heinzen, while at the same time noting the current work of such men as Lester Frank Ward and Prof. Earl Barnes of Stanford.[23]

But as a woman correspondent wrote in 1891, *Lucifer* was a woman's cry, not a scholarly treatise:

It is the mouthpiece, almost the only mouthpiece in the world, of every poor, suffering, defrauded, subjugated woman. Many know they suffer, and cry out in their misery, though not in the most grammatical of sentences. . . . A simple woman . . . may know nothing of biology, psychology, or of the evolution of the human race, but she knows when she is forced into a relation disagreeable or painful to her. Let her express her pain; the scientists may afterwards tell why she suffers, and what are the remedies,—if they can.[24]

In the hectic years at the turn of the century, *Lucifer* kept up an interest in other reform causes. It supported the antilynch campaign that was led by Ida Wells-Barnett, the black woman leader from Chicago. In the process, *Lucifer* lost some southern readers. The journal protested the Spanish-American War on grounds of racism and imperialism, and it devoted much energy to defending the ideology of anarchism in the face of the Red panic that had been caused by the assassination of President McKinley by the so-called anarchist Leon Czolgosz.[25]

Although *Lucifer* tried to find a place in the mainstream of American reform, and in later years sought an urban, national, and international audience (it moved to Chicago when a cultural renaissance of national importance was under way there), it nevertheless spoke most directly to the provinces: in the best sense the

Lucifereans were provincial. *Lucifer* fell heir to the tradition of nineteenth-century village skepticism which had as its hero Robert Ingersoll. In the eighties and nineties, however, antireligion was no longer a compelling cause, as the *Kansas Liberal* reflected in its transformation to *Lucifer*. Perhaps Harman felt that from the old constituency of provincial atheists he could raise anarchists and sex radicals to storm those other bulwarks of oppression, the family and the state, using that weapon which had helped to deauthorize literalistic religion, namely, science.

When Emma Goldman, who greatly admired Harman, visited the anarchist writer Kate Austen in the back country of Missouri at the end of the century, she saw for the first time the difficulty, drabness, and isolation of life on a small farm in America. Goldman admired Austen's writings in *Free Society* and other radical journals, including *Lucifer,* and she seemed to be surprised that a person who had not known urban life could be a radical. Goldman recorded the early circumstances of Austen's life—being raised in small towns, caring for eight brothers and sisters after her mother's death, receiving only two years of schooling, then marrying and living in Caplinger Mills, Missouri. Goldman wrote:

> I wondered how she had managed to gain so much knowledge as her numerous articles implied.
> "From reading," she informed me.
> Her father had been a constant reader, at first of Ingersoll's works, later of *Lucifer* and other radical publications.

Goldman discovered that provincials, too, had genuine intellectual and political pursuits. Perhaps it was their special circumstances which determined these pursuits. Austen told Goldman: "You have no idea what the sexual practices of these farmers are. But it is the result mostly of their dreary existence . . . no other outlet, no distraction, no colour of any sort in their lives." Unlike the workingman in the city, who had some opportunity for diversion, continued Austen, "the farmer has nothing but long and arduous toil in the summer, and empty days in the winter. Sex is all they have. How should these people understand sex in its finer expressions, or love that cannot be sold or bound?"[26]

The attitudes of the sex radicals toward liberty and government recalled an earlier, agrarian America. The Lucifereans believed the myth of radical individual independence in America when that myth was increasingly at odds with the realities of a centralizing, urbanizing nation. But the main thrust of their individualism—sexual individualism—often found support from those who heralded the trend toward interdependence. George Bernard Shaw, writing of the dogmatic individualist Benjamin Tucker, observed:

> Tucker is a very decent fellow; but he persists, like most intellectuals, in dictating conditions to a world which has to organize itself in obedience to laws of life which he doesn't understand any more than you or I. Individualism is all very well as a study product; *but that is not what is happening.* Society is integrating, not individualizing. . . . The only individualism worth looking at now is breeding the race & getting rid of the promiscuity & profligacy called marriage.[27]

Lucifer appears to be proof of a phenomenon that has been noted by several writers: each generation, it seems, has to fight the struggle for sexual freedom all over again. It is tempting to assume that, although the environment changes, there are few original elements in the perennial battles, only differences, perhaps, regarding style and the depth at which efforts and arguments take place. Was not Shaw's recommendation of "the only individualism worth looking at now" the same one that was made by sex libertarians of the 1850s or of the 1880s? We must believe that foundations have been laid; each generation need not start completely from the beginning. The pre–Civil War movements for women's rights, communitarian reform movements, and Whitmanesque bohemianism did of course pass on something of their substance to later movements. But these emancipations occurred slowly; in the 1890s, Thomas Beer wrote in *The Mauve Decade* that a writer would be thought daring for venturing "w........" for whore. It is easy to say that the sex radicals merely ventured more and were thrown in jail for it.

But this interpretation of sexual history leads to misconceptions. The sex radicals did not agitate for hedonism but for a special sort of purity, a purity that departed from the traditional equating of it with chastity and abstention. The sex-radical movement held out the promise that humanity might realize a marriage of the often-contradictory goals—freedom and happiness; and their definition of happiness depended a great deal on sexual pleasure that was made pure and reciprocal through reason. They equated sexual morality, not with chastity, but with justice and equality, and they did not object to pleasure that could be justified in rational terms.

Although the sex radicals took a more liberal view of sexual pleasure than did their opponents, both libertarians and restrictionists shared a fear of orgasmic sexuality. While Comstockers feared both liberty *and* sex, the sex radicals believed that only by removing arbitrary restrictions could individual reason—the strongest civilizing force—assume control of sexuality. The sex radicals may perhaps be seen as the apotheosis of all the nineteenth-century preachments on *self*-control. It was this belief in self-control that made anarchism seem possible to them and that made state control seem unnecessary as well as abhorrent.

These Victorians, both Comstockers and libertarians, who concerned themselves with sex saw sex as an awesome power that demanded control of one sort or another, particularly since the forces of science and progress were apparently weakening the traditional sanctions on the sexual sphere. Most Victorian scientists, of course, scouted the problem of applying science to sexuality; indeed most took refuge behind a conservative sociosexual ideology. One may well seek the reasons for this scientific wariness in our own century: Why, for instance, was a clinical study of the mechanics of sexuality such as that of Masters and Johnson not attempted until almost the last third of the twentieth century?

The pervasive Victorian fear of sex determined in large part the nature of Victorian sex radicalism. Both men and women feared sex; but women feared it more, probably because in the man's world of the nineteenth century, in which woman stood, to quote Donald Meyer, at "the furthest remove from the basic image of male existence as potency and power, self-sufficiency and will," she was weak and she was possessed, and in practical terms she had the risks and pain of childbirth. Denied liberty, woman sought power; just as she joined and gave characteristic tone to the movements for abolition, temperance, and social purity, she joined the free-love movement, which, in addition to personal power, offered her liberty as well. It may be difficult to engage in coitus on the pedestal, but it is more difficult to engage in sex when a woman is liberated enough to say no. What appears as a heroic tradition in the sex radicals—their individualism, idealism, tenacity—was in many cases a defense against sex by both men and women.[28]

One appeal of free love and free motherhood no doubt lay in the promise of perpetual wooing that such arrangements entailed. The woman's literature of the nineteenth century particularly romanticized the attractions of courtship; these were woman's halcyon days, when she was treated as a queen, valued for being sexually inexperienced, deferred to and pampered. When married, she was "caught," and there was no need for the preferential treatment. Sentimental expectations, overmodesty, and ignorance about sexual functions made the realities of marriage all the more painful for woman. In a syrupy novel, serialized in *Lucifer*, about a high-minded free-love commune, the writer Rosa Graul addressed the question of whether life in a liberated household would cause couples never to fall out of love with their partners. "No! Certainly not. Such changes will and must come," she wrote. "Yet is it not to be expected that where there is *liberty*, in the fullest sense of the word, *life will be a constant wooing*? Is it not the lack of liberty that deals the death blow to many a happy, many a once happy home?"

The unmarried state for woman, particularly for the young woman, allowed the possibility of courtship. Courtship and chivalry did not mean equality for woman; but for those who believed that woman's "innate weakness" required man's protection and that her sacrificial role as mother required man's homage, chivalry appeared as justice for woman. The chivalric attractions of free love, I believe, particularly appealed to conservative sex radicals like Elmina Slenker and Lois Waisbrooker.[29]

The free-love beliefs and the anarchistic predilections of the sex radicals brought them public disapprobation, but blunt language and birth-control efforts sent them to jail. The greatest failure of the sex radicals, who formed virtually the only organized resistance to the Comstock postal law, lay in their inability to alter the obscenity statutes or to obtain a legal definition of obscenity that was uncolored by prudery. Not until the 1930s was the federal obscenity law redefined. Into the 1970s, states still had lingering Comstock legislation on the books in the form of laws prohibiting or restricting birth-control devices.

The unrespectable style of the sex radicals—outrageous journalism, extreme individualism, the penchant for martyrdom and for using the courts to publicize ideologies—insisted that the changing of men's minds required the jarring of society's complacency. The stigma of unrespectability, however, limited the chance that sex radicalism might succeed as a popular cause. But as free love in the 1850s attained some popularity through its identification with spiritualism, late Victorian sex radicalism also sought association with such trends as free thought, anarchism, Social Purity, eugenics, and the emerging social sciences.

The thread of nineteenth-century free love that emerged from the late 1840s and early 1850s finally spun itself out with the passing of *Lucifer, the Light Bearer*. Sex liberation would of course be promoted in the new atmosphere of the twentieth century, but not with the purpose and sense of righteousness of those who considered free love a paramount moral reform.

Appendix

What "Diana" Teaches
(An essay by Leo Tolstoy)

"The Kreutzer Sonata" and the "Postscripts" have brought to me many letters from different places proving that the need of changed views regarding the relations between the sexes is recognized not by me alone but by a great number of thinking people whose voices have been unheard and unheeded simply because they have been cried down by the multitude who obstinately and warmly uphold the accustomed order of things, granting, as it does, free indulgence in their passions. Among the letters which I received in October, 1890, was the following which accompanied a pamphlet entitled "Diana," referred to in it:

New York, Oct. 7th., 1890.

We have the pleasure of transmitting you by mail a copy of a small book, entitled "Diana, a Psycho-Physiological Essay on Sexual Relations for Married Men and Women," which we hope will reach you safely.

Since the circulation, in America, of your work the "Kreutzer Sonata," many, *so many,* persons have said "Diana carries out, explains and makes practicable Count Tolstoy's theories." We therefore take the liberty of sending you a copy, that you may judge for yourself.

Praying for the fulfillment of your heart's dearest wish, we are, dear Sir, Sincerely yours,

Burnz & Co.

Shortly before this I had received from France a letter from Angele Françoise together with her brochure.

In her letter Madame Angele informed me of the existence of two Societies whose object was the encouragement of purity in sexual life—one in England and the other in France, *"Societe d' Amour Pur."*

In Madame Angele's essay were expressed very much the same thoughts as in "Diana," but much less clearly and definitely and with a shade of mysticism. The thoughts expressed in the essay, "Diana," though taken from a point of view that is not Christian but rather Pagan—Platonic,—are both novel and interesting, and they give such a clear exposition of the folly of wantonness (licentiousness), not only among the unmarried but also among the married in our modern society that I feel a desire to give my readers the benefit of these thoughts.

The fundamental thesis of the essay which had for a motto the text, "And they two shall be one flesh," is as follows:

The difference in organization between man and woman is not only physiological but extends also into other and moral characteristics, such as go to make manhood in man and womanhood (or femininity) in woman. The attraction between the sexes is based not merely upon the yearning for physical union but likewise upon that reciprocal attraction, exerted by the contrasting qualities of the sexes, each upon the other, manhood upon womanhood and womanhood upon manhood. The one sex endeavors to complement itself with the other, and therefore the attraction between the sexes demands a union of spirit precisely identical with the physical union.

The tendency towards physical and spiritual union forms two phases or manifestations of one and the same fountain-head of desire, and they bear such intimate relations to each other that the gratification of the one inclination inevitably weakens the other. So far as the yearning for spiritual union is satisfied, to that extent the yearning for physical union is diminished or entirely destroyed; and, *vice versa,* the gratification of the physical desire weakens or destroys the spiritual. And consequently the attraction between the sexes is not only a physical affinity leading to procreation but is also the attraction of opposites for one another, capable of assuming the form of the most spiritual union in thought only, or of the most animal union, causing the procreation of children and all those varied degrees of relationship between the one and the other.

The question on which footing the connection between the sexes is to be established is settled by deciding what method of union is regarded at any given time, or for all time, as good, proper and therefore desirable.

(A remarkable illustration of the degree to which the relationship between the sexes may be made conformable to what is considered good, proper and therefore desirable, is afforded by the astonishing custom of zheni-khanya or "little marriage" among the Malo-Russians, which allows young fellows for years to sleep with the girls to whom they are betrothed without even impeaching their virginity.)

Perfect satisfaction for different persons united together constitutes the relationship which these individuals consider good, proper and consequently desirable, and depends on their special point of view.

But independently of this, *per se* and, objectively, one relationship must give every person a higher satisfaction than the other. Which mode of union gives this maximum of satisfaction, *per se*, for all, independently of the individual view of those who make the union? That which nearest approaches the spiritual, or that which nearest approaches the physical?

The reply to this question is clear and indubitable, although it is diametrically opposed to all the habitual modes of thought held by society, and is to this effect; that the nearer the form of union approaches the extreme physical boundary the more it kindles the passions (desire) and the less satisfaction it gets; the nearer it approaches the opposite extreme spiritual boundary, the less new passions are excited and the greater is the satisfaction. The nearer it comes to the first, the more destructive it is to animal energy; the nearer it approaches the second, the spiritual, the more serene, the more enjoyable and forceful is the general condition.

The union of man and woman "in one flesh," in the form of an indissoluble, monogamous marriage, the author considers a necessary condition for the superior development of mankind. Marriage, therefore, in the author's opinion, since it constitutes the natural and desirable condition for all men who attain years of maturity, is not necessarily a physical union but may also be a spiritual one. Taking into consideration conditions and temperament, and above all what the contracting parties regard as good, proper and desirable, marriage for some will approach the spiritual union, for others the physical, but the nearer the union approaches the spiritual the more complete will be the satisfaction.

Since the author avows that the same sexual tendencies may lead to a spiritual union, affection,—and to the physical union,—reproductiveness, procreation—and that the one activity passes into the other, conscience being a determining cause, it stands to reason that he does not recognize any impossibility in self-restraint, but considers it a natural and indispensable condition of a reasonable system of sexual hygiene both in married life and outside of it.

The whole essay forms a rich collection of examples and illustrations of the argument which it contains, and physiological data regarding the processes of the sexual relations, their effects upon the organism and the possibility of a conscious directing of them in one way or the other,—affection or reproductiveness.

In support of this theory the author quotes the words of Herbert Spencer: "If any law," says Spencer, "works to the advantage of the human race, then human nature infallibly submits to it, since obedience to it becomes a pleasure to a man."

"And, consequently," says the author, "we ought not to place too much reliance on the established customs and conditions about us; but we ought rather to consider what man should be and may be in the brilliant future which is before us.["]

The substance of all that has been said, the author thus explains. The fundamental theory of "Diana" is that the relations between the sexes have two functions: reproductive and affectional; and that the sexual energy, if only it have no conscious desire to beget children, must be always directed in the way of affection, (love). The manifestation which this energy assumes, depends on reason and custom; in consequence of which there is a gradual bringing of the reason into agreement with the principles here expounded, and a gradual reorganization of customs consonant with them, thus saving men from many of their passions and giving them satisfaction for their sexual desires.

At the end of the essay is a remarkable "Letter to Parents and Teachers" from the pen of Eliza B. Burnz. This letter, notwithstanding the fact that it treats of subjects generally considered improper, (calling things by their names as indeed it is impossible to avoid doing) ought to have such a beneficent influence on unfortunate young men suffering from excesses and irregularities, that its wide circulation among grown men who have thrown away their best energies and ruined their happiness, and especially among the poor who are destroying themselves simply through ignorance, among boys in families, academies, high schools (gymnasiums) and above all in military establishments and private institutions, would be a genuine blessing.

Notes

Only in the case of scholarly journals are volume numbers given in periodical citations. Many of the journals frequently cited, such as *Lucifer* or *The Word*, usually ran four pages in length and were often unpaginated, hence no page numbers are given in these citations. In citing large newspapers, such as the *New York Times*, the last number of the citation is the page number. In general, notes are collected at the end of a paragraph or passage. Books that are cited again in subsequent chapters are identified by author's last name and short title.

Chapter 1
Love Worketh No Ill: Free Love and Spiritualism

1. The more important works included John Humphrey Noyes's *The Bible Argument* (Oneida, N.Y., 1848), M. Edgeworth Lazarus's *Love vs. Marriage* (New York, 1852), vol. 14 of Andrew Jackson Davis's *The Great Harmonia* (Boston, 1855), Stephen Pearl Andrews's *Love, Marriage, and Divorce, and the Sovereignty of the Individual* (New York, 1853), Thomas L. Nichols's *Esoteric Anthropology* (New York, 1853), George Drysdale's *The Elements of Social Science* (London, 1854), Austin Kent's *Free Love* (Hopkinton, N.Y., 1857), and Henry C. Wright's *Marriage and Parentage* (Boston, 1855). The subject of sex relations also prompted books by the phrenologists Lorenzo N. and Orson S. Fowler, the German-American Karl Heinzen, and the elder Henry James. Letter from Noyes published in William H. Dixon, *Spiritual Wives* (London, 1868), pp. 347–53.
2. For the Nicholses' career in reform movements, see Bertha-Monica Stearns, "Two Forgotten New England Reformers," *New England Quarterly* 6:59–84 (March 1933), and "Memnonia: The Launching of a Utopia," ibid., 15:280–95 (June 1942); Philip Gleason, "From Free-Love to Catholicism: Dr. and Mrs. Thomas L. Nichols at Yellow Springs," *Ohio Historical Quarterly* 70:283–307 (October 1961). Davis, *Great Harmonia*, 4:267 ff. Hal D. Sears, "The Sex Radicals in High Victorian America," *Virginia Quarterly Review* 48:377–92 (Summer, 1972).

3. Ronald G. Walters, "Antislavery and Sexuality," a paper presented at the Organization of American Historians, New Orleans (15 April 1971), pp. 7, 14.
4. Warren, *Practical Details* . . . (New York, 1852), p. 13, quoted in James J. Martin, *Men against the State* (Colorado Springs, 1970 ed.), p. 14.
5. Thomas L. Nichols, *Forty Years of American Life* (2 vols.; London, 1864), 2:261, 334, 44–45; Stephen W. Nissenbaum, "Careful Love: Sylvester Graham and the Emergence of Victorian Sexual Theory in America, 1830–1840" (Ph.D. diss., University of Wisconsin, 1968), pp. 266–67, who pointed out Cominos's apparent oversight; see Peter T. Cominos, "Late Victorian Sexual Respectability and the Social System," *International Review of Social History* 8:18–48, 216–50 (1963). In England, Dr. Nichols reissued a version of his *Esoteric Anthropology*, with the "free love" passages expurgated.
6. Nichols, *Forty Years*, pp. 44–45; Andrews, *Love, Marriage, and Divorce*, p. 70. Also see Charles A. Shively, "The Thought of Stephen Pearl Andrews (1812–1886)" (Master's thesis, University of Wisconsin, 1960), pp. 81, 82.
7. Stearns, "Memnonia," pp. 282–83; John Humphrey Noyes, *History of American Socialisms* (Philadelphia, 1870), pp. 93–94.
8. W. M. Leftwich, *Martyrdom in Missouri* (2 vols.; St. Louis, Mo., 1870), 1:40.
9. Nichols, *Forty Years*, p. 65; Emma Hardinge, *Modern American Spiritualism* (New York, 1870), pp. 367, 261, 22; see also Alice Felt Tyler on spiritualism as an American faith, *Freedom's Ferment* (Minneapolis, Minn., 1944), pp. 78–85. Although Hardinge tried to "prove" spiritualism by anecdotes, her book is nevertheless valuable for the selection and abundance of newspaper and document sources it contains, and is itself a primary document on the spiritualist mind. John Humphrey Noyes, "Battle-Axe Letter" (first published in 1837), in Robert A. Parker, *A Yankee Saint: John Humphrey Noyes and the Oneida Community* (New York, 1935), p. 44.
10. Leftwich, *Martyrdom in Missouri*, pp. 37–38; *New York Times*, 8 September 1855, p. 2; Nichols, *Forty Years*, pp. 48–49, 67; on the numbers attracted to spiritualism see Geoffrey K. Nelson, *Spiritualism and Society* (New York, 1969), p. 24. Emma Hardinge, *Modern American Spiritualism*, p. 258, used the figure of five to seven million to estimate the number of spiritualists in 1860, and she was fond of quoting the exaggerated figure of eleven million issued in 1867 by a Roman Catholic convention in Baltimore.

11. *New York Times*, 20 August 1852, p. 2.
12. Davis, *Great Harmonia*, pp. 277–307. Davis believed only in perfected monogamy, however, and did not countenance the multifarious delights of Fourier's "philansteries." William H. Dixon, *Spiritual Wives* (London, 1868), pp. 396–97; Kent, *Free Love*, pp. 109–16; Frank L. Manuel, *The Prophets of Paris* (New York, 1962), pp. 197–248. Popular theories of individual atmospheres can be traced back further than Davis, of course; see discussion of the mesmerist Jean-Louis Carra in Robert Darnton, *Mesmerism and the End of the Enlightenment in France* (Cambridge, Mass., 1968), passim. Goethe's concept of "elective affinities" may also have had some influence on the spiritualist doctrine.
13. *New York Times*, 17 August 1855, p. 2; 8 September 1855, p. 2; 10 October 1855, pp. 1–2, and throughout the week of 17–24 October 1855. On Berlin Heights, see, for instance, *New York Times*, 1 May 1858, p. 5, and 25 June 1858, p. 2. On prurience of the spirits, *New York Times*, 18 February 1859, p. 4. For the conflict between the *Times* and the *Tribune* precipitated by the free love exposé, see also Earl W. Fornell, *The Unhappy Medium: Spiritualism and the Life of Margaret Fox* (Austin, Tex., 1964), pp. 34–37.
14. Isaiah Berlin on alienation, in *Karl Marx: His Life and Environment* (Oxford, Eng., 1968 ed.), p. 142. This discussion and the quotes from Emerson follow Leo Marx, *The Machine in the Garden* (New York, 1964), pp. 177–78.
15. W. W. Rostow, *The Stages of Economic Growth* (Cambridge, Mass., 1960), pp. 4–10, 36–40; Leo Marx, *Machine in the Garden*, pp. 26–27; Samuel Butler, *Erewhon* (London, 1872), in *Erewhon and Erewhon Revisited* (New York, 1927 ed.), p. 253.
16. Leo Marx, *Machine in the Garden*, p. 206; Hardinge, *Modern American Spiritualism*, p. 58. Geoffrey Nelson's work, *Spiritualism and Society*, cited above, a British study that devotes two chapters to the causes of American spiritualism, sees the movement essentially as "one of the unconventional religious methods of solving the problems of individuals confused by the social chaos of the period," yet has problems explaining why nonreligious persons were attracted to the "religion" of spiritualism, see pp. 71, 73, 78. Although he does not see spiritualism as a clear reflection of technology and does not discuss the related social radicalisms, his point that confusing social conditions invoked a spiritualist response is borne out by the present study. On the anxieties caused by in-

dustrialism, see Douglas T. Miller, *The Birth of Modern America, 1820–1850* (New York, 1970), pp. 86–90.
17. Calhoun in a reported remark to the editor of *American Polytechnic Journal* (Washington, D.C.), vol. 1 (January 1853), quoted in Hugo A. Meier, "Technology and Democracy, 1800–1860," *Mississippi Valley Historical Review* 43:634 (March 1957).
18. Johann Jung-Stilling, *Theorie der Geisterkunde* (Stuttgart, 1832), quoted in J. Arthur Hill, *Spiritualism: Its History, Phenomenon and Doctrine* (New York, 1919), p. 57.
19. Charles F. Briggs and Augustus Maverick, *The Story of the Telegraph and a History of the Great Atlantic Cable* (New York, 1858), pp. 13, 21.
20. Carleton Mabee, *The American Leonardo: A Life of Samuel F. B. Morse* (New York, 1943), p. 294; Alvin F. Harlow, *Old Wires and New Waves* (New York, 1936), pp. 156–58.
21. Hardinge, *Modern American Spiritualism*, p. 29.
22. Ibid., pp. 29, 36, 56, 82, 92, 145. The *New York Tribune*, 7 June 1852, p. 7, contained an account of a group séance in which a telegrapher received answers to his mental questions in telegraph code; the code was intelligible only to the telegrapher, reported the paper.
23. *Congressional Globe* (12), 27th Cong., 3d sess., p. 323; see also Harlow, *Old Wires*, pp. 84–85, and Mabee, *American Leonardo*, p. 257. A short while later, Cave Johnson became a fan of the telegraph, and in 1845, as postmaster general, he administered the pioneer telegraph line. The government got out of the telegraph business in 1847.
24. Hardinge, *Modern American Spiritualism*, pp. 65–133; also Paul A. Carter, *The Spiritual Crisis of the Gilded Age* (De Kalb, Ill., 1971), pp. 99–107; *Buffalo Commercial Advertiser* and *Boston Courier*, both in Hardinge, *Modern American Spiritualism*, pp. 153–54, 187; also *New York Times*, 3 July 1857, p. 2. English scientists seemed to be less wary of spiritualism than American ones; when the movement spread to England in the 1850s, it attracted such important mathematicians, physicists, and scientists as Augustus De Morgan, Sir William Crookes, and Alfred Russel Wallace. Michael Faraday took the "table-turners" seriously enough to construct a testing apparatus and perform experiments before opposing spiritualist claims; see his letter to the *Times* (London), 30 June 1853, p. 8. For a detailed discussion of science and spiritualism see R. Laurence Moore, "Spiritualism and Science: Reflections on the

First Decade of the Spirit Rappings," *American Quarterly* 24:474–500 (October 1972).
25. Moses Hull, *Encyclopedia of Biblical Spiritualism* (Chicago, 1895), pp. ii–iii; Adin Ballou, *An Exposition . . . on Spirit Manifestations* (Boston, 1866); Leftwich, *Martyrdom in Missouri*, pp. 37–38; George E. Macdonald, *Fifty Years of Freethought* (2 vols.; New York, 1929), 1:361; Nelson, *Spiritualism and Society*, pp. 80–81.
26. The quotes on the Bible are characterizations of Moses' opinions by his brother Daniel, in Daniel Hull, *Moses Hull* (Wellesley, Mass., 1907), pp. 27, 56, 33–34, 40–41.
27. Hardinge, *Modern American Spiritualism*, pp. 51–52, 84, 296; Madeleine B. Stern, *Heads & Headlines: The Phrenological Fowlers* (Norman, Okla., 1971), pp. 147–50.
28. This account of Spear and the New Motor is based on 1854 accounts from the laudatory *New Era* and from the more objective *Spiritual Telegraph* (New York), and from other documents contained in Hardinge, *Modern American Spiritualism*, pp. 217–29; see also *New York Tribune*, 11 August 1854, p. 3; and *New York Times*, 1 January 1853, p. 8, and 4 January 1853, p. 3.
29. Hardinge, *Modern American Spiritualism*, p. 234. Even the *New York Times* saw the Kiantone Community as an emulation of earlier experiments: "It is manifestly their purpose to repeat the experiment at Berlin Heights," said the *Times* in an editorial on Kiantone, 14 October 1858, p. 4.
30. Arthur W. Calhoun, *A Social History of the American Family* (3 vols.; Cleveland, Ohio, 1918), 2:32; E. Lynn Linton, "The Revolt Against Matrimony," *Forum*, January 1891, p. 594.
31. Philippe Ariès, *Centuries of Childhood* (New York, 1962), pp. 10, 406. Ariès shows that the concept of the family is a modern one dating from about the seventeenth century. See also William L. O'Neill, *Divorce in the Progressive Era* (New Haven, Conn., 1967), pp. 33–88; David M. Kennedy, *Birth Control in America: The Career of Margaret Sanger* (New Haven, Conn., 1970), pp. 36–41; on the constriction of familism, see Oscar Handlin, *Race and Nationality in American Life* (Boston, 1948), pp. 154–63.
32. "Towler's Confession," in Dixon, *Spiritual Wives*, pp. 400–401; Dyer D. Lum, *The "Spiritual" Delusion: Its Methods, Teachings, and Effects* (Philadelphia, 1873).
33. Dixon, *Spiritual Wives*, pp. 400–401; Leftwich, *Martyrdom in Missouri*, pp. 38–39; on the connection of free love to spiritualism see also Nichols, *Forty Years*, p. 66; Noyes, *History of American Socialisms*, pp. 93–94, 638; Adin Ballou, in *New York Times*, 29

September 1854, p. 6, and a representative editorial in the *Times*, 18 February 1859, p. 4. Emanie Sachs, *"The Terrible Siren": Victoria Woodhull (1838–1927)* (New York, 1928), pp. 236, 275. For a critique of the principal free-love theorists by a "varietist" see Austin Kent, *Free Love*.

34. Leftwich, *Martyrdom in Missouri*, pp. 38–39; Shively, "Thought of Stephen Pearl Andrews," p. 85. In a recent study, cited above, which notably does not discuss the connection of free love and spiritualism, R. Laurence Moore, "Spiritualism and Science," writes that "much of the vigorous opposition to spiritualism looks in retrospect very foolish" and "the intensity of the opposition is somewhat surprising, especially since many opponents accepted the reported phenomena as real occurrences," pp. 489–90.
35. On divorce and Victorian attitudes, see O'Neill, *Divorce*.
36. Two recent important British works both refer to American sex radicalism as the "left wing" of the women's movement: Constance Rover, *Love, Morals and the Feminists* (London, 1970), and J. A. Banks and Olive Banks, *Feminism and Family Planning in Victorian England* (Liverpool, Eng., 1964). William L. O'Neill takes a similiar view: what the present essay terms "sex radicalism," he perhaps would call "extreme feminism." O'Neill's analysis is best enunciated in *Dissent: Explorations in the History of American Radicalism* (De Kalb, Ill., 1968). Also see Sidney Ditzion, *Marriage, Morals and Sex in America* (New York, 1969 ed.).
37. "The Pioneers of Sex Reform," by "Fidei Defensor," *Lucifer*, 12 October 1905; this essay referred to Mary Wollstonecraft's *A Vindication of the Rights of Women* (London, 1792), William Godwin's *An Enquiry Concerning Political Justice and Its Influence on General Virtue and Happiness* (London, 1793), and Percy B. Shelley's *Epipsychidion* (London, 1821). Thompson, who has recently been rediscovered by scholars, is quoted from Banks, *Feminism*, p. 19.
38. Important essays by Noyes are collected in *The Berean, Male Continence: Essays on Scientific Propagation* (New York, 1969); *Bible Argument* was reprinted in *Male Continence* (Oneida, N.Y., 1872). For Drysdale, see Peter Fryer, *The Birth Controllers* (New York, 1966), pp. 110–12.
39. Moses Harman believed that Heinzen influenced the later writings of August Bebel and Grant Allen; see *Lucifer*, 23 January 1902. Wendell Phillips also believed that Karl Peter Heinzen influenced several prominent men with his *The Rights of Women and the Sexual Relations* (Chicago, 1898), p. vi. Heinzen's biographer,

Carl Wittke, *Against the Current* (Chicago, 1945), played down his sex-reform ideas, perhaps because Heinzen strongly disapproved of sex outside of marriage; as shown, however, Heinzen advocated "free marriage," an idea that was not far removed from free love; see Heinzen, *Rights of Women,* pp. 98–99. For Mill, see *The Subjection of Women* (London, 1869) and a recent book, John Stuart Mill and Harriet Taylor Mill, *Essays on Sex Equality* (Chicago, 1970), ed. Alice S. Rossi. Croly, an immigrant from England, used the pen name "Jenny June"; for attribution of *The Truth about Love* to her, see *Lucifer,* 10 November 1904, 12 October 1905, and *New Generation* (London), 27 January 1927, p. 6. Carl Bode, in "Columbia's Carnal Bed," *American Quarterly* 15:56–60 (Spring, 1963), discusses *The Truth about Love* and attributes authorship to David Goodman Croly, the husband of Jane ("Jenny June") Croly.

40. For the Social Puritans, see David J. Pivar, "The New Abolitionism: The Quest for Social Purity, 1876–1900" (Ph.D. diss., University of Pennsylvania, 1965).
41. Gamaliel Bailey, in Walters, "Antislavery and Sexuality," p. 12; Andrews, *Love, Marriage, and Divorce,* p. 64; Shively, "Thought of Stephen Pearl Andrews," pp. 75–78.
42. Dora Forster, "Sex Radicalism," *Lucifer,* 24 November 1904.

Chapter 2
Moses Harman

1. Biographical data on Moses Harman is available throughout *Lucifer,* although details about his pre-Kansas years are scarce. Standard county histories and census data on Crawford County for 1850, 1860, and 1870 provide basic facts, but of more value is John S. McCormick, *History of Forest Hill and Vicinity* (Pacific, Mo., 1970), pp. 80–97. A modest number of his personal papers are collected in the Labadie Collection, University of Michigan, although many of his papers remain in the hands of his descendants. Harman planned to publish an autobiography in 1900, but it never materialized. The several obituaries and memorials of Harman's death that appeared in the national press are generally unhelpful for early years; even one written by his son in the *Valley Falls* (Kans.) *New Era,* 10 February 1910, contains errors.

  His life and work are mentioned, with varying degrees of accuracy, in many of the more thorough cultural or social treatments of the period as well as in special studies; see, for instance, Ditzion, *Marriage, Morals and Sex;* Fryer, *Birth Controllers;* David Pickens,

Eugenics and the Progressives (Nashville, Tenn., 1968); James C. Malin, *A Concern about Humanity* (Lawrence, Kans., 1964), and Martin, *Men against the State*. He has been mostly known to scholars who deal with the question of obscenity, for instance: Morris Ernst and Alexander Lindey, *The Censor Marches On* (New York, 1940); James Paul and Murrary Schwartz, *Federal Censorship: Obscenity in the Mail* (New York, 1961); Theodore Schroeder, *Free Press Anthology* (New York, 1909); Frederick Siebert, *The Rights and Privileges of the Press* (New York, 1934); and John Thomas, *Lotteries, Frauds and Obscenity in the Mails* (Columbia, Mo., 1900). A biographical sketch of Harman's life appeared as this chapter was being completed, "The Moses Harman Story," by William West, in *Kansas Historical Quarterly* 37:41–63 (Spring, 1971). The article is a concise treatment, but it is limited to Kansas sources and to Harman's experiences in Kansas. Unfortunately, it contained no new data for the present study.
2. *Mother Earth,* March 1910, pp. 10–15; Joseph Harman, in *Lucifer,* 22 July 1892; Arcadia College, founded as a Methodist high school in 1847, had 150 students in 1858; see W. S. Woodard, *Annals of Methodism in Missouri* (Columbia, Mo., 1893), p. 343. Woodard's work is retrospective and does not include records of Methodist ministers, such as Harman, who became apostates. For Harman in Indiana, see *Lucifer,* 5 June 1891 and 4 March 1892; for Harman in St. Louis, see *Lucifer,* 28 July 1893.
3. Missouri's population in 1860 was 1,182,012, including 114,931 slaves and 3,572 free blacks; see Eugene M. Violette, *A History of Missouri* (Boston, 1918). This slave population was mostly concentrated in a central band along the Missouri River. For local secessionist conflict, compare issues of the *Rolla Express,* 13 and 27 August 1860 with issues of 17 and 24 June 1861. *Weekly Missouri Democrat* (St. Louis), 7 May 1871, p. 1, recounts the Crawford County struggle.
4. *Lucifer,* 8 June 1888. In 1868 Briggs joined Alcander Longley's Reunion Community in western Missouri; see Hal D. Sears, "Alcander Longley: Missouri Communist," *Bulletin of the Missouri Historical Society* 25:129–31 (January 1969).
5. McCormick, *History of Forest Hill,* pp. 80–97.
6. *New Era,* 12 June and 24 July 1880; *Lucifer,* 31 August 1901. The Free Religious Society had grown out of a local "truth-seeking" society, the Philomathic club. S. R. Shepherd, a pioneer Kansas reformer, founded the club in 1872; see *Freethought Ideal and Health Vindicator* (Ottawa, Kans.), 21 December 1901.

Notes to Pages 34–38   289

Chapter 3
Organized Free Thought: The National Liberal League

1. Alexis de Tocqueville, *Democracy in America* (2 vols.; New York, 1945 ed.), 1:275; Albert Post, *Popular Freethought in America, 1825–1850* (New York, 1943), pp. 216–18. Toward 1850, German rationalists from the "Forty-Eighter" immigration published about a third of the free-thought papers, according to Post, *Popular Freethought,* pp. 34, 72.
2. Post, *Popular Freethought,* pp. 32, 75, 187; Sidney Warren, *American Freethought, 1860–1914* (New York, 1943), p. 31; Tocqueville, *Democracy in America,* 2:142–43.
3. *Index* (Boston), 1 and 15 January 1870.
4. For Darwin and Abbot see Stow Persons, *Free Religion: An American Faith* (New Haven, Conn., 1947), pp. 112, 113. See also Carter, *Spiritual Crisis,* pp. 1–42, for the confrontation of faith and Darwinism. See *Oxford English Dictionary,* s.v. "science," senses 4 and 5b.
5. Macdonald, *Fifty Years of Freethought,* 1:181–82, gives freethinkers, particularly Stephen Pearl Andrews, the credit for originating Grant's proposal. For history of the National Liberal League, see Samuel P. Putnam, *Four Hundred Years of Freethought* (New York, 1894), pp. 528–34. On the definition of "Liberal," see *Index,* 14 October 1875.
6. Warren, *American Freethought,* p. 164; *Index,* 6 July 1876, 8 November 1877. Freethinkers often referred to the 1797 Tripoli treaty signed by George Washington, which assured the Muslim nation that the United States was in no sense founded upon the Christian religion.
7. Comstock Act (Birth Control) of 3 March 1873, in *Statutes at Large of the United States of America, 1789–1873* (Boston, 1850–1873), 17:598–600. Comstock treated freethinkers in *Frauds Exposed* (New York, 1880), and in *Traps for the Young* (New York, 1883).
8. Theodore Schroeder, comp., *Edward Bond Foote: Biographical Notes and Appreciatives* (New York, 1913), pp. 12–14; *Index,* 6 and 20 December 1877.
9. Macdonald, *Fifty Years of Freethought,* 1:231, and Putnam, *Four Hundred Years of Freethought,* pp. 528–29, claimed that the petition had 70,000 names: in introducing the petition, Butler mentioned that it contained "over fifty thousand names," *Congressional Record,* 45th Cong., 2d sess., p. 1340; see also pp. 3473, 3960. Orvin

Larson, *American Infidel: Robert G. Ingersoll* (New York, 1962), p. 144; Schroeder, *Edward Bond Foote*, p. 12; Paul and Schwartz, *Federal Censorship*, pp. 29, 252.

10. Larson, *American Infidel*, pp. 144–53; Warren, *American Freethought*, p. 166.
11. *Truth Seeker*, 12 July 1884; *Lucifer, the Light Bearer*, 8 August 1884; Warren, *American Freethought*, p. 166. On the league's general stultification, see Walker in *Lucifer*, 28 August, 19 September, and 17 October 1884.
12. For the impact of professionalization, see George M. Frederickson, *The Inner Civil War: Northern Intellectuals and the Crisis of the Union* (New York, 1965), pp. 199–216. Ward founded the National Reform League and published the *Iconoclast* in Washington, D.C., in 1870–1871.
13. Macdonald, *Fifty Years of Freethought*, 1:361.
14. *Liberty*, 17 July 1886; Macdonald, *Fifty Years of Freethought*, 1:388, 400, 431, and 2:187–88; E. C. Walker, *Practical Co-operation* (Valley Falls, Kans., 1885).
15. *Index*, 28 October 1875; Macdonald, *Fifty Years of Freethought*, 2:90–91; Walker as "Woptia," in *Lucifer*, 16 February 1894; Putnam, *Four Hundred Years of Freethought*, p. 820; *Index*, 1 January 1870; *Truth Seeker*, 27 September 1879.
16. In the late 1880s the *Truth Seeker* began to feature front-page cartoons by "Watson Heston." For Twain, see Macdonald, *Fifty Years of Freethought*, 2:361; for *Investigator*, see Macdonald, *Fifty Years of Freethought*, pp. 494, 535. Macdonald's first volume gives yearly listings of free-thought journals; see also Frank L. Mott, *A History of American Magazines, 1885–1905* (Cambridge, Mass., 1957), p. 278.
17. *Kansas Liberal*, 29 December 1882; Warren, *American Freethought*, p. 177.
18. Elmina Slenker, in *Lucifer*, 2 May 1884; Warren, *American Freethought*, p. 169.
19. Malin, *Concern about Humanity*, pp. 65–66; J. E. Remsburg, "Noted Kansas Liberals," in *Freethought Ideal* (Ottawa, Kans.), 1 February 1899, lists numerous public figures in Kansas who were connected with the free-thought movement.
20. Malin, *Concern about Humanity*, pp. 76, 77. The national political intent of such widespread organizing should be noted; H. L. Green, chairman of the National Liberal League's executive committee, viewed such a grass-roots strategy as basic to the league's plan to run candidates for president and vice-president in 1880.

21. Malin, *Concern about Humanity*, pp. 82, 77, 35.
22. *Topeka State Journal*, 22 August 1891, p. 5; *Lucifer*, 21 and 28 August, 18 September 1891.
23. Malin, *Concern about Humanity*, pp. 123–24; *Topeka Daily Capital*, 9 September 1894.
24. *Kansas Liberal*, 13 April and 20 July 1882. Diggs's part in the Populist movement is discussed in O. Gene Clanton, *Kansas Populism: Ideas and Men* (Lawrence, Kans., 1969), pp. 78–80 and passim. Diggs unfortunately did not include herself in her article "The Women in the Alliance Movement," *Arena*, July 1892, pp. 161–92. On her silk-culture manual, see *Lucifer*, 3 May 1883.
25. *Kansas Liberal*, 29 December 1882.
26. Macdonald, *Fifty Years of Freethought*, 1:188, also notes the cheapness of printing. Harman to Denton, 16 March 1881, Harman Papers, Labadie Collection.
27. *New Era*, 24 February 1883.
28. *Kansas Liberal*, 26 January, 2 and 16 March 1883; *Christian Statesman*, 8 March 1883, quoted in *New Era*, 7 April 1883.
29. The account of the camp meeting is from *Kansas Liberal*, 14 September 1883; *New Era*, 6 September 1883.
30. Former Governor Robinson wrote "God in the Constitution" in response to a theocratic "God in the Constitution Convention" held at Leavenworth in 1875; the text is in Charles and Sara T. D. Robinson Papers, roll 12, Kansas State Historical Society.

Chapter 4
Lucifer, the Light Bearer

1. *Kansas Liberal*, 1 and 29 December 1882; *New Era*, 9 December 1882; Macdonald, *Fifty Years of Freethought*, 1:280, 281, 189, 257, 312, 313; Putnam, *Four Hundred Years of Freethought*, p. 820; *Atchison Globe*, 13 December 1882, p. 2.
2. *Kansas Liberal*, 1 December 1882.
3. Among the sympathetic, Walker's reputation in Kansas quickly grew to that of a "fearless thinker," *Osage County Democrat*, in *Kansas Liberal*, 12 January 1883. Lecture topics listed in *Lucifer*, 28 December 1883.
4. *Liberty*, 6 October 1883.
5. For individualist anarchism see Martin, *Men against the State*, and Eunice M. Schuster, *Native American Anarchism: A Study of Left-Wing American Individualism*, Smith College Studies in History, vol. 17 (October 1931–July 1932). For comparison of types of anarchism, see Irving Louis Horowitz, ed., *The Anarchists* (New

York, 1964), pp. 28–55. The articles by Victor S. Yarros are useful for the peculiarities of the individualists: "Anarchism: What It Is, and What It Is Not," *Arena*, April 1893, pp. 595–600; "Philosophical Anarchism (1880–1910)," *Journal of Social Philosophy* 6:254–62 (April 1941); "Philosophical Anarchism: Its Rise, Decline, and Eclipse," *American Journal of Sociology* 41:470–83 (January 1936). On the anarchist/socialist confusion and the effect of the Haymarket Affair on anarchism, see Henry David, *The History of the Haymarket Affair* (New York, 1963 ed.), pp. 98, 436. The attempt to reconcile the forms of social revolution is recorded by Charles McA. Destler, "Shall Red and Black Unite? An American Revolutionary Document of 1883," *Pacific Historical Review* 14:434–51 (December 1945).

6. In the main, the terms "state" and "government" were practically interchangeable to individualist anarchists such as Walker and Benjamin Tucker. Government was defined as the imposition of an external will upon an individual; its essence was invasion. The state was seen as the physical embodiment of this principle of invasion. Tucker, *Instead of a Book* (New York, 1897), pp. 23, 70.
7. *Lucifer*, 9 March 1888.
8. The Walker-Tucker debate and Walker's portrait of rural life appeared in *Liberty*, 26 July and 6 September 1884. Walker's *Practical Co-operation* detailed his ideas on cooperatives; see also Martin, *Men against the State*, p. 247. For the later debate on the Malthusian question see *Liberty*, 17 April, 22 May, and 31 July 1886; the marriage debate is treated in chap. 6 of this book.
9. *Kansas Liberal*, 1 December 1882.
10. John Locke, *Second Treatise on Civil Government* (London, 1690), articles 31–37. Harman appeared to have been influenced on the land question not only by Josiah Warren and E. C. Walker, but also by J. K. Ingalls, whose writings often appeared in *Lucifer*; for instance, "Land Labor, and Capital," *Lucifer*, 10 September 1886.
11. *Kansas Liberal*, 22 June 1883. Benjamin Tucker justified the use of dynamite for self-defense at about the same time; see Martin, *Men against the State*, p. 220.
12. *Liberty*, 22 and 8 November 1884, 17 April 1886.
13. See, for instance, E. C. Walker, "War," and "Organization," *Anarchist*, May and July 1885. In the early numbers of this journal, *Lucifer* was the only American radical paper that was advertised or excerpted.
14. *Liberty*, 22 January 1887. *Liberty* never had more than six hun-

dred subscribers, according to Charles A. Madison, "Benjamin R. Tucker: Individualist and Anarchist," *New England Quarterly* 16:48 (September 1943).

Chapter 5
Awful Letters: Part 1

1. *Lucifer*, 25 November 1887.
2. *Lucifer*, 10 April and 16 January 1885.
3. See Kennedy, *Birth Control*, p. 60.
4. Pivar, "The New Abolitionism"; Mark H. Haller, *Eugenics: Hereditarian Attitudes in American Thought* (New Brunswick, N.J., 1963), p. 47; O'Neill, *Divorce*; see topics in the *American Digest, 1658–1896* for legal attitudes towards sexual misconduct.
5. For Comstock's life and activities, see Heywood Broun and Margaret Leech, *Anthony Comstock: Roundsman of the Lord* (New York, 1927). The authors make much use of Comstock's diary. Also Anthony Comstock's *Traps for the Young*, in its lately reissued form, has a concise, informative preface by its editor, Robert Bremner, pp. vii–xxxi. Charles Gallaudet Trumbull's adoring biography, *Anthony Comstock: Fighter* (New York, 1913), is a primary reference on the mind of Comstock's supporters. Polemics from the free-thought press include D. M. Bennett's *Anthony Comstock: His Career of Cruelty and Crime* (New York, 1878) and E. C. Walker's *Who Is the Enemy: Anthony Comstock or You?* (New York, 1903). For the vice societies, see Paul S. Boyer, *Purity in Print* (New York, 1968), pp. 1–52.
6. Paul and Schwartz, *Federal Censorship*, pp. 9–24, 254–56.
7. *Statutes at Large of the United States of America*, 17:598–600.
8. Paul and Schwartz, *Federal Censorship*, pp. 30, 253; *Kreutzer Sonata* decision (29 September 1890), in *Official Opinions of the Attorneys-General*, 19:667–68. Benjamin O. Flower, in *Arena*, October 1890, pp. 540–52, December 1890, pp. 126–28; survey of early press opinion in *Liberty*, 16 August 1890. Although friends of Wanamaker's claimed that he did not personally initiate the censorship, the exclusion came, however, "by order of the Postmaster-General," and B. O. Flower and others held him responsible as the head of the department. See also Lindsay Rogers, *The Postal Power of Congress* (Baltimore, Md., 1916), pp. 97–123, 158.
9. *New York Times*, 14 April 1876, p. 4.
10. Comstock, *Traps for the Young*, pp. 171–72; also Bremner's introduction, pp. xxiv–xxvi.
11. Bremner, in *Traps for the Young*, p. xvi; the 1881 episode is from

police reports published in Lum Smith's *Public Herald* (Philadelphia), reprinted in *Lucifer,* 9 December 1887.
12. For the *Times's* treatment of Comstock in an eventful year, see "The Suppression of Vice: The Good a Society Has Accomplished during the Past Year—A Dangerous Occupation for Its Agent," 1 January 1876, p. 2; "Comstock's Western Raid," 17 November 1876, p. 8; "A Blow to Quack Doctors," 29 March 1876, p. 8.
13. The letters, in order, appeared in *Lucifer,* 18 and 25 June and 23 July 1886, and 14 January 1887. James C. Malin's opinion is that Harman "deliberately constructed a test case that covered most contingencies," *Concern about Humanity,* p. 109.
14. *Lucifer,* 28 May, 4 and 11 June 1886.
15. Andrews, resolution before Union Reform League Convention, 1880. Andrews was president of the league, and Ezra Heywood was secretary. See Heywood, *The Evolutionists* (Princeton, Mass., 1882), excerpted in Ralph E. McCoy, *Freedom of the Press: An Annotated Bibliography* (Carbondale, Ill., 1968), H240. For E. C. Walker on Harman and Andrews, see *Fair Play,* 20 July 1889.
16. *Lucifer,* 9 April 1886.
17. Robinson, in *Jeffersonian* (Topeka), June 1890, reprinted in *Lucifer,* 16 October 1891.
18. *Lucifer,* 18 and 4 June 1886.
19. Moses Harman to Joseph Labadie, 6 July 1905, Harman Papers, Labadie Collection; Heywood, in *Word,* August 1889.
20. *34 Federal Reporter,* p. 872; *Lucifer,* 28 October and 4 November 1887.
21. Reindictment came on 9 April 1888, *50 Fed. Rep.,* p. 922; *Lucifer,* 27 April 1888.

Chapter 6
Children of Progress

1. "R." ("Rustic"), in *Valley Falls Liberal,* September 1880. Moses Harman adopted the pen name Rustic "partly in reference to my lack of experience as a writer for the press," *Lucifer,* 31 August 1901.
2. *Lucifer,* 13 June 1884.
3. *Lucifer,* 17 September 1886.
4. The account of the wedding is in *Lucifer,* 1 October 1886, and in *13 Pacific Reporter,* pp. 279–82.
5. Carrol D. Wright, commissioner of labor, *Report on Marriage and Divorce in the United States, 1867–1886* (Washington, D.C., 1889),

pp. 50–56. An 1871 test case in the Maryland court of appeals upheld the necessity of the religious sanction of marriage in that state, *Dennison* v. *Dennison, 35 Md.,* p. 361.
6. *Lucifer,* 17 September 1886 and 31 August 1901.
7. See, for instance, Macdonald, *Fifty Years of Freethought,* 1:424.
8. Elizabeth C. Stanton et al., *History of Woman Suffrage* (6 vols.; New York City and Rochester, N.Y., 1881–1922), 1:294–95; *American Journal of Eugenics* (Chicago), September–October 1909, pp. 105–6.
9. Henry James, "Is Marriage Holy?" *Atlantic Monthly,* March 1870, p. 364; Lillian Harman, "Marriage and Morality," *Light Bearer Library* (Chicago), February 1900; Moses Harman, "Institutional Marriage," ibid., June 1901.
10. *Lucifer,* 15 October and 24 September 1886.
11. L. L. Bernard and Jessie Bernard, *Origins of American Sociology* (New York, 1943), pp. 334, 321. This study is valuable for its treatment of the Social Science movement and of Stephen Pearl Andrews and others in this context. John R. Kelso, *Autonomistic Marriage as Viewed from the Standpoint of Law, Justice and Morality* (Valley Falls, Kans., 1886), pp. 20–21 and passim.
12. Sachs, "*The Terrible Siren,*" p. 236; Hull, *Moses Hull,* pp. 39–42; *Hull's Crucible* (Boston), 15 and 29 July 1876.
13. *Pioneer Press and Tribune* (St. Paul), in *Crucible,* 1 July, following events in *Crucible,* 8, 15, and 29 July, and 12 August 1876, 3 March 1877; Macdonald, *Fifty Years of Freethought,* 1:383; for Miller's earlier career in spiritualism, see Hardinge, *Modern American Spiritualism,* pp. 93–94.
14. This account of ensuing events is primarily from *Lucifer,* 24 September and 1 October 1886, but incidental information appears throughout October numbers; *Compiled Laws of 1879,* p. 539, cited in *13 Pac. Rep.,* p. 280. Jefferson County attorney W. F. Gilluly, assisted by former state representative L. A. Myers, served as the prosecution .
15. *Lucifer,* 15 October 1886.
16. *Lucifer,* 24 September, 17 and 23 December 1886, 11 February 1887.
17. Trial and sentencing reported in *Lucifer,* 15 and 22 October 1886; a terse account appeared in *Valley Falls New Era,* 21 October 1886. Legal arguments before the Kansas Supreme Court are by W. F. Gilluly (county attorney) and S. B. Bradford (attorney general), *Brief for Appellee, The State of Kansas v. E. C. Walker and Lillian Harman, No. 4312,* and David Overmeyer, *Supplemental Brief for Appellants,* same case.

18. *Star* (London), 15 April 1898, in *Lucifer,* 14 May 1898; prison letters from Lillian and Edwin in *Lucifer,* 5 November 1886.
19. *13 Pac. Rep.,* pp. 279–89; Jerome Harman, commissioner, Supreme Court of Kansas, to author, 30 April 1971; *Lucifer,* 11 March 1887.
20. *26 American Digest 1658–1896,* cols. 2000, 1206, 1217; *33A Federal Digest,* pp. 111, 112; compare to citations in *10 American Digest 1897–1906,* for changes. See also Leo Kanowitz, *Women and the Law* (Albuquerque, N. Mex., 1969), pp. 40, 42, 263.
21. Quoted in *Lucifer,* 17 December 1886.
22. *Lucifer,* 10 December 1886 and 27 February 1887.
23. *Lucifer,* 8 April 1887.

Chapter 7
Public Opinion, the Satan Paper, and the Kansas Free Lovers

1. *Lucifer,* 1 October and 24 September 1886; *Topeka Daily Capital,* 21 September 1886; *New Era* (Valley Falls, Kans.), 30 September 1886 and 11 February 1887. For alarmist views of the state of marriage, see E. H. Bennett, "Marriage Laws," *Forum,* May 1887, pp. 219–29, and E. Lynn Linton, "The Revolt against Matrimony," *Forum,* January 1891, pp. 585–95.
2. *Winchester Argus,* in *Lucifer,* 24 September 1886. A. W. Robinson, editor of *Argus,* was the brother-in-law of Dr. A. M. Cowan, a leader of the Valley Falls efforts against *Lucifer. Lucifer* reprinted many press reports that were critical of the "Lucifer Match" in order to refute them and, perhaps, to give distant subscribers a sense of what was going on. A roundup of typically unfavorable press comment appears in *Lucifer,* 29 October 1886.
3. *Ozawkie Times,* 8 October 1886; *Valley Falls Register, Troy Weekly Kansas Chief,* in *Lucifer,* 29 and 15 October 1886; *Oskaloosa Independent,* in *Lucifer,* 5 November 1886; *New Era,* 3 May 1888.
4. *Lucifer,* 1 October 1886.
5. *Lucifer,* 11 July 1884, 24 September 1886, and 24 February 1887. *45 Fed. Rep.,* p. 418.
6. *Lucifer,* 24 September 1886; the churchman was the physician A. M. Cowan, and the businessman was C. C. Lord.
7. Another extreme denunciation appeared in the Oskaloosa paper on 9 October 1886.
8. *Lucifer,* 15 and 22 October 1886; *Topeka Daily Capital,* 17 and 22 October 1886.
9. Reprinted in *Lucifer,* 8 October 1886.
10. The *Times* article and Harman's subsequent exchange with the

editor are in *Lucifer*, 4 February 1887; later *Times* comment in *Lucifer*, 24 February 1887.
11. *Lucifer*, 15 and 22 October 1886. Benjamin Tucker reprinted more of Pinney's writings on the wedding in *Liberty*, 30 October 1886.
12. *Lucifer*, 28 January 1887. Gifts often took the form of literature that could be sold, such as contributions from the Drs. Foote and from Ezra Heywood in *Lucifer*, 29 October 1886.
13. Hull in *Lucifer*, 12 November and 24 December 1886.
14. *Lucifer*, 14 January 1887. Jay Chaapal, substituting as editor of *Foundation Principles*, strongly supported *Lucifer*'s fight. *Lucifer*, 13 December 1886.
15. See particularly "Not Compromise, but Surrender," *Liberty*, 30 October 1886. For Tucker's views on marriage see *Instead of a Book*, p. 15.
16. *Lucifer*, 26 November 1886; *Liberty*, 30 October 1886.
17. *Liberty*, 20 November and 11 December 1886.
18. *Lucifer*, 24 December 1886.
19. *Lucifer*, 1 July 1887. Harman nicknamed the St. Louisan "Pope Longley." Longley, an unlikely blend of radical and reactionary, pounced upon the Walker-Harman marriage to further publicize the evils of anarchism. In a typical opinion he considered the "Chicago [Haymarket] anarchists got what they bargained for." *Altruist* (St. Louis), November 1887. See also Hal D. Sears, "Alcander Longley," pp. 123–37.
20. In *Lucifer*, 17 December 1886.
21. *Anarchist*, December 1886.
22. *Lucifer*, 28 January 1887.
23. *Lucifer*, 24 September and 8 October 1886. Perhaps Lillian's reference should read "Judge Crozier."
24. *Lucifer*, 12 August 1887.
25. "Moses Harman: An Address Delivered before the Saturday Night Club, Topeka, Ks., by Justice William A. Smith, 1942," manuscript (Kansas State Library, Topeka), pp. 1, 15. I am grateful to Jerome Harman, commissioner, Supreme Court of Kansas, for bringing this paper to my attention.

Chapter 8
Awful Letters: Part 2

1. *Lucifer*, 22 June 1888. For Train, see Broun and Leech, *Anthony Comstock*, pp. 108–14. The Wise case is detailed in *Lucifer*, 17 April 1896; see also Warren, *American Freethought*, 2:82, 142.

One civil-liberties expert held that these cases substantially proved obscenity in the Bible: Schroeder, *Free Press Anthology*, pp. 257–59.
2. *Truth Seeker*, in *Lucifer*, 18 March 1887; *Liberty*, 28 April 1888; *Fair Play*, 20 July and 10 August 1889. Also see Heywood, in *Word*, August 1889, on the Walker-Harman division.
3. *Lucifer*, 4 October and 5 July 1889, 16 December 1887. As an indication of the number of papers published in Kansas, Valley Falls alone had five; more significant was the number of dailies published in Kansas—seventy-two in 1888; see *Annals of Kansas, 1886–1910* (Topeka, n.d.), p. 67.
4. *Word*, August 1889; Patterson, in *Lucifer*, 8 November 1889. Harman reprinted in *Lucifer* these press comments on his work, *Lucifer*, 2 August and 5 July 1889. For Robinson, see C. B. Hoffman to Charles Robinson, 30 March 1888; Harman to Robinson, 11 April 1888; and "Ruth" to Robinson, 3 March 1891, in Charles and Sara T. D. Robinson Papers, roll 4, Kansas State Historical Society.
5. *Lucifer*, 23 August 1889; 28 March, 4 and 11 April 1890.
6. Sydney Barrington Elliot, "Hygiene and Physiology of the Sexual Sphere, and the Physician's Relation to the Laity as Regards This Subject," *Journal of the American Medical Association* 18:784 (18 June 1892); Norman E. Himes, *Medical History of Contraception* (New York, 1970 ed.), pp. 282–83. Although they are not necessarily applicable to the American scene after the Civil War, the attitudes discussed in Steven Marcus, *The Other Victorians* (New York, 1964), are informative on Victorian sexuality.
7. *Lucifer*, 18 April 1890. A detailed account of the trial is in *Fair Play*, 26 April 1890. Edward W. Chamberlain, a New York freethought lawyer, came to Kansas to aid in Harman's defense, but arrived only in time to hear the verdict. According to *Fair Play*, Chamberlain had earlier advised O'Neill to send his letter to Harman and had advised Harman to print it.
8. *State Journal* (Topeka), 1 May 1890, p. 4; *Daily Capital* (Topeka), 1 May 1890, p. 5.
9. *45 Fed. Rep.*, pp. 414–24; *50 Fed. Rep.*, pp. 921–23; *68 Fed. Rep.*, pp. 472–74.
10. *United States v. Harman, 45 Fed. Rep.*, pp. 415–16; *Roth v. United States* and *Alberts v. California*, 354 U.S. 476 (1957); Roth discussion, in Paul and Schwartz, *Federal Censorship*, passim; see also discussion on Roth and references to Harman in James J. Kilpatrick, *The Smut Peddlers* (Garden City, N.Y., 1960), pp. 81–168.
11. *45 Fed. Rep.*, pp. 417–18; *38 Fed. Rep.*, p. 829; *Parmelee v. United*

States, 113 F. 2d, 729 (D.C. Cir. 1940); *United States v. One Book Entitled "Ulysses,"* 5 Fed. Supp. 182 (S.D.N.Y., 1933), 72 F. 2d, 705 (2nd Cir. 1934); Manton twice cited the 1891 Harman decision. See also Ernst and Lindey, *Censor Marches On*, pp. 288–89 and passim.

12. *45 Fed Rep.*, p. 418; *United States v. Bennett*, 24 Fed. Cas., p. 1102; Siebert, *Rights and Privileges*, cites Harman, pp. 230, 233, 235, 237–38; also Theodore Schroeder, *"Obscene" Literature and Constitutional Law* (New York, 1911), pp. 328, 329, 330, 332, 335, 336; also Thomas, *Lotteries*, pp. 275–76.
13. *Twentieth Century*, 29 May 1890, pp. 6–7, 11–13; *Arena*, October 1895, pp. xxiii–xxiv. The editor of *Arena* had previously spoken out against Harman's imprisonment, *Lucifer*, 15 April 1892.
14. *Woman's Tribune*, 11 March 1893, p. 50; *Woman's Journal*, 11 October 1890, reprinted in *Lucifer*, 31 October 1890.
15. *Christian Life*, July–September 1890; Caldwell to Harman in *Lucifer*, 14 November 1890; *Woman's Journal*, 2 May 1891, p. 138.
16. *Dr. Foote's Health Monthly*, October 1890, in *Lucifer*, 17 September 1890.
17. *Word*, March and April 1890; Macdonald, *Fifty Years of Freethought*, 1:530.

Chapter 9
The Prairie Cauldron: Reform and Regeneration, 1885–1895

1. D. W. Wilder, *The Annals of Kansas, 1541–1885* (Topeka, 1886), p. 463. In 1861 Kansas became the second state to grant woman suffrage in school elections, following Kentucky's very early lead in 1838. Territories in the West allowed women unlimited suffrage, and when Wyoming became a state in 1890, it became the first state where women had an equal franchise with men.
2. *New York Times*, 8 April 1889, p. 1. Kansas' experience with prohibition was also being watched closely at the time. Martha B. Caldwell, "The Woman Suffrage Campaign of 1912," *Kansas Historical Quarterly* 12:300 (August 1943); Cecil Howes, "Rise of 'Petticoat' Government Started 50 Years Ago in Kansas," *Kansas City* (Mo.) *Times*, 8 December 1937; *Oskaloosa* (Kans.) *Independent*, 7 April 1888.
3. *New York Times*, 7 April 1887, pp. 1, 4.
4. *New York Times*, 8 April 1889, p. 1.
5. *Lucifer*, 16 December 1887.
6. *Lucifer*, 9 December 1887.
7. *Word*, April 1875.

8. "Prefatory Chapter to the Edition of 1892," in Francis Galton, *Hereditary Genius* (Cleveland, 1962 ed.); Haller, *Eugenics*, p. 10; Andrews, *Love, Marriage and Divorce*; Henry C. Wright, *The Empire of the Mother over the Character and Destiny of the Race* (Boston, 1863).
9. Andrews, *Love, Marriage and Divorce*, p. 70.
10. "Women and Natural Selection in Marriage," an interview with Alfred Russel Wallace in the *Daily Chronicle* (London), reprinted in *Lucifer*, 14 September and 5 October 1894. Wallace repeated his arguments about natural selection in marriage in *Social Environment and Moral Progress* (London, 1913), pp. 144–48. Wallace, "Human Selection," *Popular Science Monthly*, November 1890, pp. 96–99. Wallace specifically referred to two characteristic articles by Grant Allen: "Plain Words on the Woman Question," *Fortnightly Review*, October 1889, and "The Girl of the Future," *Universal Review*, May 1890. Allen's most influential work in America was *The Woman Who Did* (Boston, 1895). Virna Winifred Walker, the daughter of Lillian Harman and Edwin Walker, was born in 1893.
11. Haller, *Eugenics*, p. 23; *Nature*, 24 August 1893. pp. 389–90; Havelock Ellis, *Studies in the Psychology of Sex* (Philadelphia, 1928 ed.), 5:218–27, 6:3. Marie Stopes was one of the most prominent later advocates of prenatal influence; see her *Married Love* (London, 1918) and *Radiant Motherhood* (London, 1921), in which she cites Wallace, Ellis, and others.
12. *Journal of the American Medical Association* 18:784–85 (18 June 1892).
13. For instance, vol. 9 of *Arena*, covering December 1893 through May 1894, had articles on heredity and prenatal influence by A. M. Holmes, Sydney Barrington Elliott, and Helen H. Gardener. Gardener was an important hereditist, an editor of *Arena*, and the wife of its publisher, C. Selden Smart; her efforts in the "sex in brain" controversy of the 1880s helped to dispel the myth that the female brain was structurally different from that of the male. See also B. O. Flower, "Well-Springs of Present-Day Immorality," *Arena*, August 1893, pp. 394–400, and "The Right of the Child Considered in the Light of Heredity and Prenatal Influence," *Arena*, July 1895, pp. 243–62. An early call for prescriptive eugenics in *Arena* was Hiram M. Stanley's "Our Civilization and the Marriage Problem," June 1890, pp. 94–100.
14. The Jukes study was first published as *A Record and Study of the Relations of Crime, Pauperism and Disease*, in Prison Association

Notes to Pages 125–133

of New York, *Thirty-first Annual Report* (1875), pp. 130–83; by 1877, three editions of the study had been published. For present use, see fourth edition (New York, 1910), pp. 67–70.

15. For eugenics and the nature of American hereditarianism, Haller is indispensable; see also Pickens, *Eugenics*. Both works contain almost nothing on pre-Galton eugenics thought and both contain fragmentary and incorrect accounts about Moses Harman.
16. *Lucifer*, 13 April 1888, 13 May and 22 November 1889. In "English Methods of Birth Control," a 1915 pamphlet, Sanger argued that working women should not produce children "who will become slaves to feed, fight and toil for the enemy—Capitalism," in Kennedy, *Birth Control*, p. 110; two years earlier Rosa Luxemburg and Anatole France urged European workers to begin a "birth-strike" for these same reasons.
17. De Cleyre in *Lucifer*, 6 April 1898; Holmes in *Lucifer*, 6 December 1895, 3 July 1896, 29 July and 26 August 1899, 10 November 1900; White in *Lucifer*, 4 January 1901.
18. For Buchanan's influence on Flower and *Arena*, see Benjamin O. Flower, *Progressive Men, Women, and Movements of the Past Twenty-five Years* (Boston, 1914), pp. 210–11; *Lucifer*, 29 November and 20 December 1895, 31 January 1896.
19. Emma Goldman, *Living My Life* (New York, 1934), p. 553; Himes, *Medical History of Contraception*, pp. 224–30; Kennedy, *Birth Control*, pp. 44–45.
20. *Lucifer*, 8 November 1889. The mother's letter appeared originally as a letter to the editor of *Woman's World* and was reprinted thereafter in other feminist and reform journals.
21. Macdonald, *Fifty Years of Freethought*, 1:225–27; *Lucifer*, 7 September 1888; Larson, *American Infidel*, pp. 148–49.
22. *Lucifer*, 28 December 1888, 15 February 1889. Clough was being prosecuted in a New York court at the time by Anthony Comstock "not on a charge of obscenity but on a charge of fraud," not unreasonably, it would appear (correction in *Lucifer*, 11 January 1889). *Lucifer* published the Clough and Colgate circulars side by side and compared the legal treatment of Clough to the preferential treatment given to Samuel Colgate.
23. *Lucifer*, 9 March and 15 June 1888.
24. *Lucifer*, 15 June 1888.
25. *Lucifer*, 26 July 1889.
26. Severance, a cousin of Lucretia Mott's, aided in the formation of the Union Labor party, introducing the woman-suffrage plank at the 1888 convention; sketches of Severance and Chandler are in

Frances Willard and Mary Livermore, *A Woman of the Century* (Detroit, 1967 ed.).
27. *Lucifer*, 13 December 1889.
28. *Lucifer*, 13 April and 9 March 1888. Harman reprinted Stanton's "Christian Church and Women" from the *Index* during the spring and summer of 1886. Another reprint is in *Lucifer*, 19 October 1888.
29. *Lucifer*, 5 April 1889.
30. Hull, *Moses Hull*, passim; Sachs, "*The Terrible Siren*," pp. 156–59.
31. *Lucifer*, 7 and 14 October, 1887.
32. Probably one of Walker's unspoken objections against this Greenback reformism was to its messenger, Moses Hull; as a "Materialist Infidel," Walker had no use at all for Hull's "Biblical Spiritualism," even though its exegete was radical on the marriage question.
33. *Lucifer*, 14 October 1887. Arguments appear in *Lucifer*, 21 and 28 October, 4, 11, and 18 November 1887. The egoistic base of individualist anarchism connotes an elitism, but not a class or collective elitism; conversely, communistic anarchism stresses a collective equalitarianism.
34. Henry David, *History of the Haymarket Affair*, p. 331, pointed out the similar positions of *Liberty* and *Lucifer*. For free-speech aspects of the Haymarket case, see Harman on Johann Most and August Spies, *Lucifer*, 4 June 1886, and Walker on Most, in *Lucifer*, 11 June 1886.
35. *Lucifer*, 21 October 1887.
36. On the state socialism of the Haymarket radicals, see *Lucifer*, 6 August 1886; *Lucifer*, 7 October 1887.
37. *Lucifer*, 4 and 25 November 1887. For Trumbull's background and the veracity of his accounts, see David, *History of the Haymarket Affair*, pp. 339–40; *Lucifer*, 25 November 1887.
38. *Lucifer*, 18 November 1887.
39. *Lucifer*, 8 June and 13 July 1888.
40. *Lucifer*, 26 October 1888. For the revilement of anarchism after the Haymarket riot, see David, *History of the Haymarket Affair*, p. 436.
41. For this affair and its investigation, see *Investigation of Coffeyville Explosion: Proceedings of the Joint Committee of Kansas Legislature, 1891* (Topeka, 1891). Conclusions, such as they were, appear on pp. 608–38. This source is chiefly valuable for its wealth of documentary material, particularly on the Videttes, and for its glimpses into statehouse politics of the time. See also Malin, *Concern about Humanity*, pp. 155–69; *Lucifer*, 26 October 1888.

42. As published, for instance, in *Topeka Capital,* 19 October 1888.
43. Malin, *Concern about Humanity,* p. 159; David, *History of the Haymarket Affair,* p. 444.
44. Kirk Porter and Donald Johnson, *National Party Platforms, 1840–1964* (Urbana, Ill., 1966), pp. 83–85. The United Labor party, which appeared the same year, shared some goals of the Union Labor party, notably the nationalization plank; the United, however, mainly emphasized a single-tax scheme.
45. Malin, *Concern about Humanity,* pp. 14, 34, 35. The 1888 state platform, Malin points out, excluded mention of railroad regulation and monopolies; an emphasis on tactics rather than ideology is suggested.
46. Malin, *Concern about Humanity,* p. 161.
47. *Lucifer,* 19 and 26 October 1888.
48. *Investigation of Coffeyville Explosion,* see note 41 of chap. 9.
49. *Lucifer,* 16 November and 26 October 1888.
50. *Lucifer,* 30 November 1888; *Ottawa Journal and Triumph,* 8 November 1888.
51. For Culverwell, see *Lucifer,* 15 June and 26 October 1888, 12 April 1889.
52. John D. Hicks's *The Populist Revolt* (Minneapolis, Minn., 1931) is the classic historical primer on Populism; for Kansas, see Raymond C. Miller, "The Populist Party in Kansas" (Ph.D. diss., University of Chicago, 1928), and Clanton, *Kansas Populism.*
53. *Lucifer,* 13 January 1893.
54. *State of Kansas Session Laws of 1891* (Topeka, 1891), S. B. no. 346, chap. 161. Although it was introduced by Republicans, the bill had the support of the single Populist senator (passing the senate 29 to 0) and the Populist majority in the house (passing 95 to 1). Of 125 house seats, the Populists had over 90 in 1891; a Republican from Bourbon County cast the one dissenting vote, *House Journal, 1891* (Topeka, 1891), pp. 847–48.
55. See, for instance, the *Sun* for 30 March 1889 and for 9 February 1896; one of its correspondents was the famous Kansas editor Noble L. Prentis; *Daily Capital* (Topeka), 10 May 1891, p. 4. The Swartz case was detailed in *Lucifer* throughout May and June 1891, also 10 July, 16 and 30 October 1891; *in re Banks,* 56 Kan., 242 (1895), upheld the law.
56. *Recorder,* 19 May 1891, quoted in *Lucifer,* 29 May 1891; also *Lucifer,* 5 June 1891; *Liberty,* 2 May and 13 June 1891.
57. *House Journal, 1891,* pp. 526–27, quoted in Clanton, *Kansas Populism,* p. 94.

58. Malin, *Concern about Humanity*, pp. 35, 84; Macdonald, *Fifty Years of Freethought*, 2:82–83, 111. For Overmeyer's early career as a "Resubmission Republican" advocating repeal of prohibition, see Wilder, pp. 1073–76, 1110. Overmeyer ran for governor as a Democrat in 1894. For his reform ideas, see his article "The Future of the Democratic Party," *Arena*, September 1897, pp. 302–18. For Clemens, see Clanton, *Kansas Populism*, passim.
59. *Farmer's Vindicator*, 23 May and 18 July 1891; Malin, *Concern about Humanity*, pp. 111, 116–22, 131; *Lucifer*, 5 May 1893; *Foundation Principles* (Topeka), July 1893, 15 August and 15 September 1894.
60. *Lucifer*, 28 April and 22 September 1893.
61. "Please Publish One Less," *Advocate*, 6 March 1890. With the issue of 20 March 1890, Diggs officially joined the *Advocate* as an editor; she had previously conducted an Alliance column in the *Lawrence Journal*.
62. *Lucifer*, 17 August 1894.

Chapter 10
Comstock's Yokes

1. A valuable, comprehensive account of the Heywoods is Marvin Liebling's "Ezra Heywood: Intransigent Individualist: A Study of a Radical in Post Civil War America" (research paper, Brandeis University, 1970). Martin's *Men against the State*, pp. 105–25, is the most important published work on Heywood and deals with his ideology. Heywood's autobiographical prison letters to Moses Harman (1890–1892), published in *Lucifer*, have provided a rich source of material for this chapter, particularly concerning his early career and his later struggles with Comstock.
2. *Index*, 29 November 1877. Considering his future career, it was appropriate that Heywood chose as a topic of his graduation speech from Brown, "Milton: Advocate of Intellectual Freedom."
3. *Lucifer*, 20 May 1892.
4. *Lucifer*, 26 June 1891. Carleton Mabee's *Black Freedom: The Nonviolent Abolitionists from 1830 through the Civil War* (Toronto, Can., 1970) is instructive throughout on Garrison and his "double standard," especially the chapter "Peace Men Face War," pp. 333–70. For Heywood, see pp. 336, 346, 366.
5. *Lucifer*, 19 December 1890.
6. Merle Curti, *Peace or War: The American Struggle, 1636–1936* (Boston, 1959), p. 58. For examples of Heywood's thought in the *Liberator*, see his speeches "The Present Crisis," 5 July 1861; "The

War Method of Peace," 17 July 1863; and his article "Might versus Right," 6 May 1864.
7. *Index*, 29 November 1877.
8. *Lucifer*, 15 August 1890.
9. Liebling, "Ezra Heywood," pp. 22, 23; *Dictionary of American Biography* (New York, 1928–1936), 4:609–10.
10. *Word*, April 1875, May 1872.
11. For a full discussion of Heywood's economic theories, see Martin, *Men against the State*, pp. 105–25. For Heywood's critique of genteel reformers and Gilded Age capitalism, see "The Great Strike: Its Relations to Labor, Property, and Government," *Radical Review* (New Bedford, Mass.), November 1877.
12. The record of the convention is in *Word*, April 1875.
13. In *Lucifer*, 20 May 1892, Heywood cites 1876 as the first publishing date of *Cupid's Yokes*. The 1879 edition has been used for this chapter. The distribution figures are from *Dictionary of American Biography* (50,000 copies) and Putnam, *Four Hundred Years of Freethought*, p. 537 (200,000 copies).
14. *Index*, 29 November 1877.
15. *Cupid's Yokes* (Princeton, Mass., 1879), p. 19.
16. Ibid., pp. 3, 12.
17. Ibid., p. 23.
18. Ibid., pp. 17, 19, 3. See Noyes, *The Berean*.
19. *Cupid's Yokes*, pp. 16, 20.
20. Ibid., pp. 9, 19.
21. Ibid., p. 18.
22. Ibid., p. 21.
23. Ibid., pp. 5, 6, 10, 11.
24. Ibid., pp. 7, 8.
25. The free-thought publisher J. P. Mendum, of the *Boston Investigator*, published and sold Knowlton's book throughout the period from the 1830s to the 1870s, but few seemed to be aware of it.
26. Heywood quoted from pp. 348–49 of an early edition of the *Elements of Social Science*; cf. the 1886 edition ("twenty-fifth edition, enlarged"), pp. 348–50.
27. *Index*, 29 November 1877.
28. Comstock, *Traps for the Young*, pp. 163–66.
29. *Cupid's Yokes*, p. 12.
30. For Bennett, see George H. Genzmer's sketch in *Dictionary of American Biography*, 1:192–93; the histories of free thought cited in chap. 3; Bennett's own *The World's Sages, Infidels and Thinkers* (New York, 1876); and Larson, *American Infidel*, pp. 144–53.

Bennett reported that there were 70,000 signatures on the anti-Comstock-law petition; Macdonald, *Fifty Years of Freethought,* 1:231.
31. Comstock, *Traps for the Young,* pp. 159, 158; Broun and Leech, *Anthony Comstock,* p. 175.
32. Macdonald, *Fifty Years of Freethought,* p. 192; Putnam, *Four Hundred Years of Freethought,* p. 537; Larson, *American Infidel,* p. 145.
33. Putnam, *Four Hundred Years of Freethought,* p. 539; Warren, *American Freethought,* p. 195; Broun and Leech, *Anthony Comstock,* p. 180.
34. Harry G. Balter, "Some Observations Concerning the Federal Obscenity Statutes," *Southern California Law Review* 8:276, 277 (June 1935); *U.S. v. Bennett,* in *24 Fed. Cas.,* pp. 1093–1107; Paul and Schwartz, *Federal Censorship,* pp. 2, 25.
35. *U.S. v. Bennett,* passim. Paul and Schwartz, *Federal Censorship,* pp. 12–17, 27, 31.
36. *U.S. v. Bennett,* pp. 1097, 1104, 1105; Liebling, "Ezra Heywood," pp. 29, 30; Broun and Leech, *Anthony Comstock,* p. 174.
37. Parker Pillsbury, *"Cupid's Yokes" and the Holy Scriptures Contrasted in a Letter from Parker Pillsbury to Ezra H. Heywood* (Boston, 1878); Liebling, "Ezra Heywood," pp. 30–32; Benjamin Tucker on Kendrick, in *Liberty,* 21 January 1882; Ralph E. McCoy, "Banned in Boston: The Development of Literary Censorship in Massachusetts" (Ph.D. diss., University of Illinois, 1956), p. 78, cited in Liebling, "Ezra Heywood," pp. 32, 65.
38. Broun and Leech, *Anthony Comstock,* pp. 174, 175.
39. Larson, *American Infidel,* pp. 144–53; Putnam, *Four Hundred Years of Freethought,* p. 539.
40. Responding to the attempted suppression of *Leaves of Grass* by the Boston Watch and Ward Society in 1887, Heywood picked what he called "two of the 'worst,' best poems" from the book—"To a Common Prostitute" and "A Woman Waits for Me"—and printed them in *Word* in August 1882; he also published them on a separate sheet for distribution, *Lucifer,* 26 June 1891. Liebling, "Ezra Heywood," pp. 34–38; *Liberty,* 9 June 1883; *Lucifer,* 10 October 1890.
41. *Word,* September 1889.
42. *Lucifer,* 4 July 1890, printed excerpts from the Pinney article; *Word,* June 1890; Liebling, "Ezra Heywood," p. 20.
43. *Word,* April 1881.
44. Angela Heywood, "Natural Modesty," *Word,* March 1889, and

"The Ethics of Sexuality," *Word,* April 1881.
45. *Word,* April 1881.
46. *Lucifer,* 7 November 1890. One of Angela's sisters, Josephine Tilton, took an active part in the Heywoods' work.
47. Maren Lockwood Carden, *Oneida: Utopian Community to Modern Corporation* (Baltimore, Md., 1969), pp. 58–59.
48. Pinney, in *Lucifer,* 4 July 1890.
49. *Lucifer,* 14 August 1891.
50. See chap. 5 for Andrews and free language; Heywood mentioned two others who influenced the free-language policy: "the keen essayist 'Diana'" (Elmina Slenker or Henry M. Parkhurst), and the "Biblical scholar and artist, Prof. S. L. Rawson" (probably Albert L. Rawson), *Lucifer,* 14 August 1891.
51. Angela Heywood, "The Ethics of Touch—Sex-Unity," *Word,* June 1889.
52. *Word,* July, September and October 1889.
53. Apparently through confusion over the obscenity indictment against *Word,* which included one of Angela's articles as well as the "Letter from a Mother," Liebling attributed the anonymous letter to Angela in his essay. She may well have been responsible for its publication, but Ezra Heywood specifically attributed it to a New York mother in a letter to Harman, *Lucifer,* 14 August 1891. It is not likely, moreover, that Angela would disguise either her name or the name and age of a daughter.
54. *Lucifer,* 16 May 1890; Liebling, "Ezra Heywood," p. 40.
55. The jury was ordered to acquit on the O'Neill letter charge because the receiver named in the charges was not the same alias as Comstock used on *Word's* mailing wrapper, Liebling, "Ezra Heywood," pp. 46, 42, 45.
56. Liebling, "Ezra Heywood," pp. 41, 49, 50; *Lucifer,* 16 May 1890.
57. Liebling, "Ezra Heywood," pp. 45–49; *Lucifer,* 21 November 1890.
58. *Lucifer,* 7 November 1890, 31 July 1891, 11 April 1890, 15 August 1890. Heywood noted that he was allowed to send sixteen letters per year from prison; if this allowance was not changed, he sent most of his quota to Harman, who in turn printed them in *Lucifer.*
59. *Lucifer,* 24 April 1891, 27 May 1892.
60. *Lucifer,* 9, 16 and 23 June 1890.

Chapter 11
The Doctors Foote

1. Putnam, *Four Hundred Years of Freethought,* pp. 726–31; *The*

National Cyclopedia of American Biography (New York, 1893), 3:68, Himes, *Medical History of Contraception,* pp. 276–79.
2. Edward Bliss Foote, *Plain Home Talk, Embracing Medical Common Sense* (New York, 1870, 1881, etc.), pp. v, 912, 933–35; Himes, *Medical History of Contraception,* p. 276. Foote's success inspired imitations, for instance the advertised contents of Dr. T. R. Kinget's *Medical Good Sense* (New York, 188?) read like a gloss of Foote and placed similar emphasis on sexual problems. Foote's book, in turn, was presaged by works such as A. M. Mauriceau, *The Married Woman's Private Medical Companion* (New York, 1847).
3. Foote, *Plain Home Talk,* pp. v, vi.
4. *New York Independent,* reprinted in Foote, *Plain Home Talk,* pp. 933–34.
5. Foote, *Plain Home Talk,* pp. iii, 319–21, 273–85.
6. "Philosophy of Sexual Intercourse," in Foote, *Medical Common Sense* (New York, 1862 ed.), pp. 275–83, and in Foote, *Plain Home Talk,* pp. 622–30.
7. Foote, *Plain Home Talk,* pp. 239–40, 138–39, 462, 532. Foote's prescriptions on equal rights for women as well as his concern for sex education seem to have been inspired by suggestions in Davis, *Great Harmonia,* 4:225–57. His notions about the ill effects of masturbation were common Victorian ones; see, for instance, Robert H. MacDonald, "The Frightful Consequences of Onanism: Notes on the History of a Delusion," *Journal of the History of Ideas* 28:423–31 (July–September 1967).
8. Foote, *Plain Home Talk,* p. 462.
9. Ibid., pp. 905, 863–64, 906–7.
10. Foote, *Medical Common Sense,* pp. 308–9; Foote, *Plain Home Talk,* pp. 646–747, 772–74, 830–41.
11. Ditzion, *Marriage, Morals and Sex,* pp. 351–52, 382; Robert Riegel, *American Women: A Story of Social Change* (Cranbury, N.J., 1970), 129–30; Foote, "The Physical Improvement of Humanity" (New York, 1876); *Dr. Foote's Health Monthly,* August 1877, p. 4, and July 1891, pp. 2, 5; Foote, *Plain Home Talk,* pp. 220–21. Himes, *Medical History of Contraception,* p. 279, wrote that "Foote seems to have been early in expressing the opinion that a decrease of numbers resulting from contraception would be compensated by an improvement in quality. This view has been much stressed in recent decades by those associated with the English Malthusian League and the American Birth Control League. The proposition needs to be carefully stated to avoid fallacy. It is true only up to a certain point."

12. *Health Monthly,* August 1877, p. 4; Fryer, *Birth Controllers,* p. 70.
13. *Lucifer,* 9 September and 28 October 1892.
14. Sydney Barrington Elliott, "Hygiene and Physiology of the Sexual Sphere, and the Physician's Relation to the Laity as Regards This Subject," *Journal of the American Medical Association* 18:784 (18 June 1892). Also see the section in Himes, *Medical History of Contraception,* pp. 282–85, entitled "Lack of Leadership of the Medical Schools and Early Condemnation of Birth Control."
15. "Importance of Contraceptics," in *Health Monthly,* September 1892, and in *Lucifer,* 28 October 1892.
16. *New York Times,* 29 March 1876, p. 8. In a letter to the editor (*Times,* 14 April 1876), Foote responded to the above article.
17. Putnam, *Four Hundred Years of Freethought,* pp. 728–29.
18. *Health Monthly,* August 1877, p. 7; Foote, *Medical Common Sense,* pp. 335–39, 378–80.
19. *U.S. v. Foote,* in 25 Fed. Cas., pp. 1140–41; *New York Times,* 12 July 1876, p. 3; Foote, *Plain Home Talk,* pp. 876, 880.
20. Foote, *Medical Common Sense,* pp. 378–80. Himes, *Medical History of Contraception,* p. 279, apparently overlooked the "Preventions" section of early editions of *Medical Common Sense;* he noted, however, that he knew of no evidence to doubt that the elder Foote invented the cervical cap.
21. Foote, *Medical Common Sense,* pp. 335–37.
22. *Health Monthly,* July 1891, August 1877; Himes, *Medical History of Contraception,* p. 278; Putnam, *Four Hundred Years of Freethought,* p. 730.
23. Putnam, *Four Hundred Years of Freethought,* p. 730; Schroeder, *Edward Bond Foote,* pp. 62–63.
24. The best source on the younger Foote is Schroeder, *Edward Bond Foote;* also see *The National Cyclopedia,* 3:68, and *Who's Who in America,* 1903–1905 (Chicago); Schroeder, *Edward Bond Foote,* pp. 8–9.
25. Schroeder, *Edward Bond Foote,* pp. 21, 9–11; Putnam, *Four Hundred Years of Freethought,* pp. 731–33.
26. Putnam, *Four Hundred Years of Freethought,* pp. 536–47, contains a history of the National Defense Association; *Liberty,* 21 January 1882.
27. *Lucifer,* 1 and 15 May and 10 July 1902, 26 November and 3 and 17 December 1903; Schroeder, *Edward Bliss Foote,* p. 18; *New York Times,* 12 February 1953, p. 27; Schroeder, *A New Concept of Liberty* (Berkeley Heights, N.J., 1940), p. xxxviii. For a legal expert's opinion of Theodore Schroeder, see Harry G. Balter,

"Some Observations Concerning the Federal Obscenity Statutes," *Southern California Law Review* 8:269–70 (June 1935); Schroeder became a psychologist in later life.

28. Edward Bond Foote, *The Radical Remedy in Social Science: or, Borning Better Babies through Regulating Reproduction by Controlling Conception* (New York, 1886), extensively reviewed and quoted by E. C. Walker in *Lucifer*, 4 and 11 June 1886.
29. *Medical Critic and Guide*, November 1910, p. 408; Himes, *Medical History of Contraception*, p. 281.
30. *Mother Earth*, November 1912, p. 277. Other journals that published memorials to Foote when he died included *Public, Truth Seeker, New York Herald,* and two British journals, *Malthusian* and *Freethinker*. Schroeder, *Edward Bond Foote*, p. 19. Foote's contributions ranged from an endowment to the Thomas Paine Memorial to aid for the IWW, for Japanese anarchists, and for dozens of humanitarian agencies.

Chapter 12
Handmaidens of Diana: Superwomen vs. "Cumberers of the Ground"

1. *New York Times*, 29 April 1887, p. 5; 30 April 1887, p. 5.
2. *Lucifer*, 6 June 1907. The short biography of Slenker in the *National Cyclopedia of American Biography* (New York, 1897), 7:448, is somewhat garbled. *Lucifer*, 29 October 1886.
3. *Allibone's Dictionary of English Literature and British and American Authors, Supplement* (Philadelphia, 1896), 2:1353; *Lucifer*, 9 August 1889, 28 March 1890, 26 August 1892; see Slenker's "Sexual Facts Compiled from Darwin," *Lucifer*, 27 July 1894. *Liberty*, 7 May 1887, noted Slenker's literary output.
4. "Sexual Intemperance," extracted in *Diana*, pp. 43–44; Slenker on natural desire, in *Lucifer*, 20 January 1893. The successful edition of Tissot's diatribe against masturbation appeared as *L'Onanisme* (Lausanne, 1760); it came to be regarded as the standard work on masturbation throughout Europe, according to Nissenbaum in his work on Sylvester Graham, "Careful Love," p. 162. Tissot's work appeared in the English language as early as 1776, translated by A. Hume, London; the American translation appeared in 1832, *A Discourse on Onanism* (New York). For a discussion of orgasmic theories in Sylvester Graham's *A Lecture to Young Men on Chastity* (Providence, 1834) and in Nichol's *Esoteric Anthropology*, see Nissenbaum, "Careful Love," pp. 162–65, 251–53. Also valuable is MacDonald, "Frightful Consequences of Onanism," pp. 426–28. The idea of will over "natural desire" and natural functions in

Slenker's work may have owed something to William Acton, *The Functions and Disorders of the Reproductive Organs* (London, 1857), which is discussed at length by Steven Marcus in *The Other Victorians,* pp. 1–33.

5. *Lucifer,* 28 May 1886, 16 October 1891, 1 February 1895.
6. Pivar, "New Abolitionism," pp. 8, 34, 74–101.
7. Lillian Harman, "Marriage and Morality" (an address before the Ohio Liberal Society, 1899), reprinted in *Light Bearer Library,* February 1900, p. 17. A list of Purity Alliance executives for 1895 is in Pivar, "New Abolitionism," p. 328.
8. The authorship of *Diana* was a well-kept secret, particularly since Slenker encouraged the belief that she wrote it; see letter by Annie Parkhurst in *American Journal of Eugenics,* September–October 1908, p. 279. The copy of *Diana* used for this chapter is the second edition, 1882, published by Burnz & Co., New York; phonetic spelling has been changed to standard for purposes of quotation.
9. Carden, *Oneida,* pp. 57–58; Ellis, *Studies in the Psychology of Sex,* 6:553. "How the sexual function is to be redeemed and true relations between the sexes are to be restored" was the chapter of *The Bible Argument* that dealt with male continence; Noyes reprinted it in *Male Continence* (Oneida, N.Y., 1872). Himes, *Medical History of Contraception,* pp. 269–72, contains a good discussion of male continence, also called *coitus reservatus* and *amplexus reservatus.* Although Noyes probably did not originate the method, he did invest it with doctrine.
10. The journal *Sundaze* (Santa Cruz, Calif.), 4 January 1971, p. 15, described the method of ejaculate retention.
11. Henry M. Parkhurst, *Diana: A Psycho-fyziological Essay on Sexual Relations for Married Men and Women* (2d ed.; New York, 1882), pp. 7, 8, 13.
12. Ibid., pp. 14, 15, 17. *Diana* used the term "equilibration" much as we use the term "sublimation."
13. Ibid., pp. 20, 21, 39, 22.
14. Ibid., pp. 10, 11, 13, 47, 12.
15. Ibid., pp. 29, 31, 43, 17.
16. Ibid., pp. 44, 34–37.
17. Ibid., p. 34.
18. Ibid., pp. 28, 37, 33.
19. *Lucifer,* 15 May 1891, printed the essay in "simplified" spelling. It is reprinted here in the appendix in standard orthography.
20. For Dianaist sexual contact, see letter from "Elmina's correspondent," *Lucifer,* 14 January 1887; *Lucifer,* 24 September 1886.

21. *Lucifer,* 24 September and 13 August 1886.
22. *Diana,* pp. 40, 41; *Lucifer,* 22 June 1883, 13 March 1885.
23. *New York Times,* 29 April 1887, p. 5; 30 April 1887, p. 5.
24. *U.S.* v. *Foote,* in 25 Fed. Cas., pp. 1140–41.
25. *New York Times,* 30 April 1887, p. 5.
26. *U.S.* v. *Bennett,* in *24 Fed. Cas.,* p. 1098; *U.S.* v. *Slenker,* in *32 Fed. Rep.,* pp. 691–95.
27. *Lucifer,* 19 June 1891.
28. *Lucifer,* 13 July 1894.
29. *Lucifer,* 15 June 1894.
30. *Lucifer,* 5 October 1894.
31. *Lucifer,* 7 and 14 September and 19 October 1894.
32. Andrews, *Love, Marriage and Divorce,* pp. 19–20; "Love, Marriage and the Condition of Women" (unpublished manuscript), p. 37, cited in Shively, "Thought of Stephen Pearl Andrews," p. 86.
33. Henry C. Wright, *The Empire of the Mother over the Character and Destiny of the Race* (Boston, 1863), pp. 4, 77, 101; *New York Times,* 14 May 1858, p. 5, and 15 May 1858, p. 4.
34. In a historical sketch of Slenker's life in *To-Morrow Magazine* (Chicago), W. C. Cope claimed that "she it was who first proclaimed the doctrine of female superiority"; reprinted in *Lucifer,* 6 June 1907.
35. Lester Frank Ward, "Our Better Halves," *Forum,* September 1888, pp. 269–75; *Glimpses of the Cosmos* (6 vols.; New York, 1913–1918), 4:127; *Dynamic Sociology* (2 vols.; New York, 1911 ed), 1: 648–49, 654, 658–62, and 2:617–18. See also Samuel Chugerman, *Lester F. Ward: the American Aristotle* (New York, 1965 ed.), pp. 378–95; for a discussion of the gynecocentric theory, see Carl H. Mills, "Shaw's Debt to Lester Ward in 'Man and Superman,'" *Shaw Review* 14:2–13 (January 1971).
36. On the possibility of Andrews influence on Ward, see Bernard and Bernard, *Origins of American Sociology,* pp. 315, 331, 332; Ward, *Dynamic Sociology,* 1:654, 648, and 2:616; Chugerman, *Lester F. Ward,* p. 384.
37. *Lucifer,* 14 September 1894, 3 July 1891.
38. *Lucifer,* 11 April 1890, 5 August 1892.
39. For the Mitchell-Ward affair see *New York Times* for 26, 29, and 31 January, 2, 16, and 28 February, and 31 July 1892.
40. Foote's speech in *Lucifer,* 23 September 1892; *Lucifer,* 6 January 1893, 2 August and 13 December 1895. James was referring to the

Notes to Pages 227–232   313

Chautauqua Press's *College Greek Course in English* (New York, 1884), by William C. Wilkinson.
41. *Lucifer*, 25 May 1894.

Chapter 13
Handmaidens of Diana: From the Horse Penis Affair to Modernity

1. *Lucifer*, 13 December 1889. The *Library of Congress Catalog* lists Waisbrooker's original name as Adeline Eliza Nichols.
2. H.R. 120, to amend Section 3893 of *Revised Statutes of the United States,* presented by Republican Congressman David B. Henderson (Iowa), 52d Cong., 1st sess. (5 January 1892); the bill was subsequently referred to the Committee on the Post-Office and Post-Roads. Amendments to strengthen the Comstock Act were periodically proposed, but the implications of this 1892 bill particularly frightened the sex radicals.
3. Paul and Schwartz, *Federal Censorship*, pp. 29–30; *Official Opinions of the Attorneys-General*, 19:667–68.
4. Flower, in *Arena*, quoted in *Lucifer*, 15 April 1892; *Lucifer*, 15 and 22 April and 13 May 1892. Waisbrooker, quoted from James Law, "Diseases of the Generative Organs," in D. E. Salmon, comp., *Special Report on Diseases of the Horse* (Washington, 1890), p. 138.
5. R. B. Kerr, in *The New Generation* (London), January 1927, p. 2; *To-Morrow Magazine* (Chicago), October 1906, pp. 6–7; *Foundation Principles*, 15 August 1894; *Woodhull & Claflin's Weekly*, 12 April 1873; *Lucifer*, 16 April 1896; Sachs, "*The Terrible Siren*," p. 275; see accounts from the 1875 Social Freedom Convention (Boston), in *Word*, April 1875, and Hull's speech at the 1876 meeting of the Free Love League (Boston), in *Hull's Crucible*, 17 June 1876; also see discussion in Ditzion, *Marriage, Morals and Sex*, pp. 188–89.
6. Heywood on Waisbrooker, in *Lucifer*, 25 September 1891; *To-Morrow Magazine*, October 1906, pp. 6–7; *Lucifer*, 25 September 1891; Lois Waisbrooker, *Suffrage for Women: The Reasons Why* (St. Louis, 1869); *Alice Vale: A Story for the Times* (Boston, 1869); *Helen Harlow's Vow: or Self Justice* (Boston, 1870); *Mayweed Blossoms* (Boston, 1871); *The Fountain of Life: or The Threefold Power of Sex* (Topeka, 1893); *A Sex Revolution* (Chicago, 1893); *The Occult Forces of Sex* (Chicago, 1893). Also included in *Library of Congress Catalog* are *From Generation to Regeneration* (Los Angeles, 1879) and *Nothing Like It: or, Steps to the Kingdom* (Boston, 1875). Other works known to have been written by Waisbrooker but unlisted by *Allibone's Dictionary* or

by the Library of Congress include *Woman's Source of Power, Perfect Motherhood,* and *My Century Plant.* An advertisement for *Foundation Principles* first appeared in *Lucifer,* 19 December 1884.
7. *Lucifer,* 22 December 1900, 7 August 1902; *Foundation Principles,* 15 August and 15 September 1894; Malin, *Concern about Humanity,* pp. 116–32, contains a valuable account of Waisbrooker which has been useful to the present study.
8. Edward W. Chamberlain, "In the Midst of Wolves," *Arena,* November 1894, p. 836; Malin, *Concern about Humanity,* pp. 126–28, 130–31; copy of "Agreed Statement of Facts" in Waisbrooker case, in *Lucifer,* 8 May 1896.
9. Charles P. Le Warne, "The Anarchist Colony at Home, Washington, 1901–1902," *Arizona and the West* 14:163–66 (Summer, 1972); *Tacoma Daily Ledger,* 8 March 1902, quoted in Le Warne, "Anarchist Colony," p. 166; *Discontent,* 15 January 1902; *Lucifer,* 16 February, 8 and 29 May, and 7 August 1902.
10. One wonders how Farnham would have reacted to the present-day feminist assertion that the clitoris is the only human organ whose function is solely and simply sensual. Farnham, *Woman and Her Era* (New York, 1864) 1:26–27, 101, 74–75, 64, 44, 54, 42–44, 58, 51–53, 102, 78. See also Eric Dingwall's flippant account about Farnham in *The American Woman: A Historical Study* (London, 1956), pp. 98–100. *Lucifer,* 10 July 1891, for Waisbrooker's reference to Farnham.
11. Rachel Campbell's leaflet, *The Prodigal Daughter,* excerpted and discussed by Waisbrooker in *Lucifer,* 10 July 1891. For more information on the life and ideas of Rachel Campbell (1834–1892), see Mary Florence Johnson, "Pioneer Chips: From the Private Correspondence of Rachel Campbell," *Our New Humanity,* December 1895, pp. 32–37.
12. Drysdale, *Elements of Social Science* (1854), quoted from the 1886 edition, p. 188. See Elaine Showalter and English Showalter, "Victorian Women and Menstruation," *Victorian Studies* 14:86–88 (September 1970), on evidence that menstruation did not necessarily curtail woman's activities.
13. Drysdale, *Elements of Social Science,* p. 66; Foote, *Plain Home Talk . . . Embracing Medical Common Sense* (1870), p. 456.
14. Drysdale, *Elements of Social Science,* p. 189; *Lucifer,* 31 July and 21 August 1891; Parkhurst, *Diana,* p. 13; Elizabeth Blackwell, *The Human Element in Sex* (London, 1884), p. 30, cited in Pivar, "New Abolitionism," p. 142; Mary Jacobi, *The Question of Rest*

for Women during Menstruation (New York, 1877), pp. 225, 227, and passim.
15. See, for instance, *Lucifer,* 31 July, 14 and 21 August 1891; Wright, *Empire of the Mother,* p. 78.
16. *Lucifer,* 31 July, 14 and 21 August 1891. Ezra Heywood in *Lucifer,* 25 September 1891, decried Waisbrooker's apparent embrace of "the greatest of extant frauds,—governmentalism"; Heywood continued: "Greenbackism, state nurseries, taxation,—these are swindles sufficiently humiliating to men to advocate, but women should know better."
17. *Lucifer,* 28 May 1886, 16 October 1891. Slenker's change of position confused not a few, and she noted in *Lucifer,* 5 August 1892, that she still received a steady flow of "imploring letters from burdened wives who crave surcease from unwelcome motherhood."
18. *Lucifer,* 3 February and 12 May, 1893, 18 August 1904, 12 May 1897; Drysdale, *Elements of Social Science,* p. 350.
19. Waisbrooker, *Fountain of Life,* pp. 39, 42–47, 131–33, reviewed by Lucinda B. Chandler in *Arena,* January 1894, pp. xiii–xiv.
20. Lois Waisbrooker, "The Sex Question and the Money Power," pp. 74, 81, passim; this essay was first published as a lecture at Jackson, Michigan, 14 December 1873, and subsequently published in *The Occult Forces of Sex.*
21. Malin, *Concern about Humanity,* pp. 118–20; *Lucifer,* 17 March 1893; Lease letter in *Lucifer,* 5 May 1893, and in *Foundation Principles,* July 1893.
22. Waisbrooker, quoted in Chamberlain, *Arena,* November 1894, pp. 836–37; for Stephen Pearl Andrews's influence on Waisbrooker, see his *Love, Marriage and Divorce,* p. 70; excerpts from *Fountain of Life,* in Lucinda Chandler's review in *Arena,* January 1894, p. xiv; *Foundation Principles,* November 1894, in Malin, *Concern about Humanity,* p. 128; Waisbrooker, "Eugenics, or Human-Culture," speech reported by Lillie D. White in *Lucifer,* 9 May 1907.
23. Extracts from *Woman's Source of Power,* in *Lucifer,* 5 January 1905; *Woodhull & Claflin's Weekly,* 22 March 1873.
24. *Lucifer,* 23 September 1892, 31 December 1903; *Word,* November 1892; Artemus Ward, *Artemus Ward: His Book* (New York, 1862), pp. 86–90.
25. *Lucifer,* 7 and 14 October 1892.
26. *Lucifer,* 20 and 27 January, 3 and 24 February 1893.
27. *Lucifer,* 24 February 1893; 17 July 1891.
28. *Lucifer,* 19 June 1891.
29. *Lucifer,* 5 June 1891.

30. *Lucifer*, 21 October 1899.
31. See discussion of Andrews's ideas on child-rearing contained in "Love, Marriage, and the Condition of Women," in *Love, Marriage and Divorce,* and in articles in *Woodhull & Claflin's Weekly,* in Shively, "Thought of Stephen Pearl Andrews," pp. 75–79; Andrews, quoted in Shively from *Woodhull & Claflin's Weekly,* 26 April 1873. For other examples of concern with child-rearing, see *Hull's Crucible,* 17 June 1876, and *Lucifer,* 16 June and 4 August 1900, 7 September 1901; White, in *Lucifer,* 21 October 1899; Hull, in *Word,* April 1875; Lillian Harman, in *Lucifer,* 5 August 1899; Lillian Harman, "The Regeneration of Society" (an address before the Manhattan Liberal Club, New York, 31 March 1898) (Chicago, 1900), p. 17; Calhoun, *Social History of the American Family,* 3: 108–12.
32. *Liberty,* 25 February and 18 March 1893. In *Lucifer,* 3 February 1893, White had twitted *Liberty* for its eagerness to reduce people and ideas to labels, a criticism that apparently made Tucker and Yarros seethe; see also *Lucifer,* 25 February and 3 March 1893.
33. *Lucifer,* 15 May and 26 June 1891; *Liberty,* 21 June, 16 and 30 August 1890. Heywood made the charge against Tucker's translation of Zola's *L'Argent,* in *Lucifer,* 26 June 1891.
34. *Lucifer,* 4 August 1904.
35. *Lucifer,* 24 November and 27 October 1904; *Sex Radicalism* appeared in ten installments in *Lucifer,* from 21 July to 24 November 1904. In the 1920s R. B. Kerr edited the Malthusian League's *The New Generation* and served as an officer in the league, see Kerr and Forster on the sex radicals, in *New Generation,* January 1927, pp. 1, 2, 6, iii.

Chapter 14
The Last Chapter

1. *Lucifer,* 13 October 1893, 1 June 1894; R. B. Kerr, in *Lucifer,* 2 March 1898.
2. Accounts of the league's meetings were printed regularly in *Lucifer* throughout 1897 and 1898.
3. *Lucifer,* 8 November and 6 December 1895; *New York Times,* 3 November 1895, p. 1; letter of Edith Lanchester's father to *Times* (London), 31 October 1895, p. 10.
4. *Lucifer,* 25 June 1895, 28 April, 9 and 16 June 1897; *University Magazine and Free Review,* excerpted in *Lucifer,* 16 June 1897; *Adult,* February, March, and September 1898; *Adult,* August 1898, quoted in Rover, *Love, Morals and the Feminists,* p. 134. The

University of Michigan Library has a nearly complete microfilm file of *Adult*.
5. Havelock Ellis, *My Life* (Boston, 1939), pp. 350–55; *Lucifer*, 6 April 1898; Ellis on the Harmans, in "Studies in Sex: A History," *American Mercury*, January 1936, p. 17, and in *My Life*, p. 356.
6. *New York World*, 2 April 1898, quoted in *Lucifer*, 20 April 1898.
7. *Lucifer*, 4, 14, 21, and 28 May and 5 June 1898; *Adult*, June 1898.
8. The Bedborough case is given much discussion in all standard biographies of Havelock Ellis; see also Ellis, *A Note on the Bedborough Trial* (London, 1898), and the *Times* (London) chronicle of the case, 1, 3, 8, 14, and 22 June and 1 November 1898.
9. W. T. Stead, in *Review of Reviews*, 15 August 1898, quoted in Ellis, *Note on the Bedborough Trial*, p. 7; Shaw, in *Adult*, September 1898. The homosexuality clause was not part of the original Criminal Law Amendment Act bill, but was tacked on before final passage by Henry Labouchere; see H. Montgomery Hyde, *The Love That Dared Not Speak Its Name* (Boston, 1970), pp. 134–37.
10. *Lucifer*, 17 September 1898.
11. Arthur Calder-Marshall, *The Sage of Sex: A Life of Havelock Ellis* (New York, 1959), p. 167. Although this book is not very carefully written, it is in many ways more insightful about Havelock Ellis's life than more adulatory biographies. Houston Peterson, *Havelock Ellis: Philosopher of Love* (Boston, 1928), contains a verbatim account of the trial, pp. 249–56.
12. Calder-Marshall, *Sage of Sex*, pp. 165–67; for Bedborough's side of the affair, see his statement in Isaac Goldberg, *Havelock Ellis: A Biographical and Critical Survey* (New York, 1926), pp. 163–67. Bedborough was roundly condemned as a coward in the *Adult*, December 1898; immediately after the affair, Bedborough fled in shame to Germany, where he worked for a time as a college lecturer.
13. See correspondence of Ruedebusch to *Lucifer*, 2 February and 2 March 1898, and E. C. Walker, "The Rapid and Sweeping Advance of the Censorship," *Lucifer*, 16 March 1898. For Craddock see issues of the *Truth Seeker* for October and November 1902; *Lucifer* printed her suicide letter, 13 November 1902. For Stockham see *Lucifer*, 25 May and 8 June 1905.
14. *American Journal of Sociology* 11:610–22 (March 1906); *San Francisco Bulletin*, 6 January 1910, p. 10; *The Parent-Teacher Organization: Its Origins and Development* (Chicago, 1944), pp. 155–56; Earl Barnes, "Books and Pamphlets Intended to Give Sex-

Information," *Studies in Education*, 1:301–8 (February 1897). On the Purity Federation, see *Arena*, December 1906, pp. 657–58; *Arena* also reprinted the editorial from the *New York Sun* of 13 October 1906.

15. *Lucifer*, 31 December 1903, 3 March 1904, 16 February, 2 March 8 June, 6 and 20 July, 28 September, and 29 October 1905, 21 June, 5 and 19 July, and 30 August 1906. Moses Harman's letters to Joseph Labadie, Harman Papers, Labadie Collection, have also been helpful for the 1905–1906 phase of *Lucifer's* problems. *Woman's Journal*, February 1910, p. 28.
16. *New York Times*, 26 September 1905, p. 1; see also George Bernard Shaw, *Bernard Shaw: Collected Letters, 1898–1910*, ed. Dan H. Laurence (London, 1972), pp. 559–62. Shaw apparently referred to the Markland-letter case, which initiated Harman's legal problems. Gaylord Wilshire, editor of *Wilshire's Magazine*, was one of the Americans who informed Shaw of Harman's plight, *Lucifer*, 9 November 1905. *London Opinion*, 30 January 1909, p. 202; also in Shaw, *Collected Letters*, pp. 683–84.
17. Letter printed in *American Journal of Eugenics*, July 1908, p. 154.
18. Shaw, *Collected Letters*, p. 928; Shaw to Lillian Harman (no date), in *Memorial of Moses Harman*, ed. Lillian Harman (Chicago, 1910), p. 11.
19. Press and personal opinions about Harman are collected in Schroeder, *Free Press Anthology*, pp. 210–15; in *The Persecution and the Appreciation: Brief Account of the Trials and Imprisonment of Moses Harman . . .*, ed. Moses Harman (Chicago, c. 1907), pp. 12–33; and in *Memorial of Moses Harman*. Especially notable was Louis F. Post's defense of Harman, see the *Public*, 22 July 1905, p. 242; 12 August 1905, pp. 290–95; 3 March 1906, p. 806; 10 March 1906, pp. 815–20; 12 January 1907, p. 963. For Harman's case in the foreign press see *Lucifer*, 13 and 27 April and 21 December 1905, 12 April and 27 September 1906. The letters of Eugene V. Debs to the Harmans appeared in *Lucifer*, 2 August 1895, August "extra" issue, 1905, 10 May 1906, 3 January 1907, 25 April 1907, and in *American Journal of Eugenics*, September–October 1908, p. 250, and in *Memorial of Moses Harman*, pp. 29–30, which also included Debs's obituary for Harman for the *Appeal to Reason*.
20. *Lucifer*, 6 and 13 July 1901.
21. *American Journal of Eugenics*, September 1907, p. 166; Schroeder's article in *AJE*, December 1907, was later reprinted in his *"Obscene" Literature and Constitutional Law*, pp. 302–26; see reports of the memorial services for Harman in *New York Times*, 28 March 1910,

p. 4, and *Los Angeles Times,* 28 March 1910, p. 1. For representative obituaries of Harman, see the two in *Mother Earth,* March 1910, pp. 10–15; *Boston Globe,* 29 March 1910 (reprinted in *Memorial of Moses Harman,* p. 49); Alice Stone Blackwell's tribute in *Woman's Journal,* February 1910, p. 28; and that by Lillian Harman in the *Malthusian* (London), 15 March 1910, pp. 22–23.

22. Interview by author with George Harman O'Brien, son of Lillian Harman and George O'Brien, 22 June 1971, San Francisco, California. For Walker, see *Lucifer,* 16 February 1894, 3 November 1900; Macdonald, *Fifty Years of Freethought,* 2:77–79; Goldman, *Living My Life,* p. 553; *New York Times,* 5 February 1931, p. 23.
23. For example, *Lucifer,* 24 June and 5 August 1899, 4 May 1900, 11 and 18 September 1902, 27 July 1901, 23 January 1902, 31 March and 14 April 1893.
24. Lizzie Holmes, in *Lucifer,* 28 August 1891.
25. *Lucifer,* 24 June and 7 October 1899; 28 September, 14 and 21 November 1901.
26. For Goldman's opinion of Harman and the Lucifereans, see *Living My Life,* pp. 216, 219–20, 553; for her visit to Kate Austen, see pp. 240–43.
27. Shaw to James Huneker, in Shaw, *Collected Letters,* pp. 415–16.
28. Donald Meyer, *The Positive Thinkers* (New York, 1965), pp. 47, 57; chapters 3 and 4 of Meyer's work are valuable on the sources of woman's fear of sex; also suggestive is Bryan Strong, "Sex, Character, and Reform in America, 1830–1920" (Ph.D. diss., Stanford University, 1972), pp. 56–57, 89–90.
29. Final installment of Rose Graul, *Hilda's Home,* in *Lucifer,* 1 December 1897; R. B. Kerr on chivalry, in *Lucifer,* 10 December 1898.

Bibliographic Essay

Since books that deal with reforming ideas are themselves bibliographical, this essay will focus on literature that was most helpful to the author in writing this book, and on those sources that seem to offer promise for further scholarship. For the primary literature that influenced the sex radicals, see the discussion in chapter 1; later sources and influences are treated in part 3, "The Sex-Radical Circle." Chapter notes contain a more detailed selection of sources and discussions of technical points.

The best living record of sex radicalism after the Civil War is periodicals. *Lucifer, the Light Bearer, Our New Humanity,* and *American Journal of Eugenics,* all edited by Moses Harman, cover the period 1883–1910. The important predecessors of these journals are *Woodhull & Claflin's Weekly* and the Heywoods' *Word.* More obscure but useful are such journals as *Hull's Crucible* and *Dr. Foote's Health Monthly.* Benjamin Tucker's *Liberty* is an anarchist journal that contains a rich lode of sex-reform materials. Emma Goldman's *Mother Earth,* Edwin C. Walker and Lillian Harman's *Fair Play,* and the journal *Discontent* (Home, Washington) are other anarchist papers that were helpful in this study. Sex reformers may be traced in the freethought journals *The Index, Investigator,* and *Truth Seeker.* Journals of a genteel image have not been lacking in sex-reform materials and data, particularly B. O. Flower's *Arena,* Hugh Pentecost's *Twentieth Century,* and the Blackwell's *Woman's Journal.* For spiritualist journals, consult Emma Hardinge, *Modern American Spiritualism* (New York, 1870), and Frank Podmore, *Modern Spiritualism,* 2 vols. (London, 1902). The *Adult* has an important place as an English sex-radical journal; for others see Constance Rover, *Love, Morals and the Feminists* (London, 1970). Since sex history is largely hidden history, Frank L. Mott's exhaustive *A History of American Magazines,* 4 vols. (Cambridge, Mass., 1930) is useful in ferreting out sources.

Those interested in free expression and questions of sex, which are frequently interrelated matters, have a valuable tool in Ralph Edward McCoy's massive *Freedom of the Press: An Annotated Bibliography* (Carbondale, Ill., 1968); it is quite detailed in scope and also contains notes on the materials. McCoy's doctoral dissertation, "Banned in Boston: The Development of Literary Censorship in Massachusetts" (University of Illinois, 1956), is helpful on sex radicalism in that important location. Not as recent but still of benefit in the study of obscenity are the works of Theodore Schroeder; see his *"Obscene" Literature and Constitutional Law* (New York, 1911) and the collection *Free Press Anthology* (New York, 1909). Paul S. Boyer, *Purity in Print: Book Censorship in America* (New York, 1968), contains a history of the vice societies. For British problems, see Donald Thomas, *A Long Time Burning: A History of Literary Censorship in England* (New York, 1969).

The real story of law and sex in America is to be found in the law libraries, in their runs of the *Federal Reporter* and regional reporters; the topics in the *American Digest 1658–1896* are generally revealing of legal attitudes towards sexual misconduct. For those who prefer their legal research at one remove, there is a growing body of literature by competent legal publicists. James Paul and Murray L. Schwartz, *Federal Censorship: Obscenity in the Mail* (New York, 1961), is first rate. C. Thomas Dienes, *Law, Politics and Birth Control* (Urbana, Ill., 1972), is a close study of law as a socially responsive institution from the time of Comstock to the present era of publicly supported birth control. See also Morris L. Ernst and Alexander Lindey, *The Censor Marches On* (New York, 1940); Ernst Schwartz and Alan Schwartz, *Censorship: The Search for the Obscene* (New York, 1964); Lindsay Rogers, *The Postal Power of Congress: A Study in Constitutional Expansion* (Baltimore, Md., 1916), and John L. Thomas, *Lotteries, Frauds and Obscenity in the Mails* (Columbia, Mo., 1900). James J. Kilpatrick, *The Smut Peddlers* (Garden City, N.Y., 1960), is informative if quite slanted. Frederick S. Siebert, *The Rights and Privileges of the Press* (New York, 1934), covers many important but unsung cases and has been reprinted in a 1970 edition. Also pertinent are two books by Norman St. John-Stevas, *Obscenity and the Law* (London, 1956) and *Life, Death and the Law* (Bloomington, Ind., 1961); the latter study contains appendices on state sterilization laws as well as a chapter on the history of birth control. Leo Kanowitz has rendered a service with *Women and the Law* (Albuquerque, N.Mex., 1969), a study of the myriad legal discriminations against women, and *Sex Roles in Law and Society: Cases and Materials* (Albuquerque, N.Mex., 1973). Dorothy Smith, *Justice Is a Woman* (Philadelphia, 1966), argues that women have preferential treatment under law in most states. The persistence of chivalry in our thinking and institutions needs a thoughtful evaluation.

For some suggestive reading on marriage and the family, a good place to begin is with the concept of the family itself and the unparalleled study of Philippe Ariès, the American translation of which is *Centuries of Childhood: A Social History of Family Life* (New York, 1962). Arthur W. Calhoun, *A Social History of the American Family*, 3 vols. (Cleveland, Ohio, 1918), is rich in ideas as well as directions for further research. L. L. Bernard and Jessie Bernard, *Origins of American Sociology* (New York, 1943), treats subjects that are not often dealt with, such as the Social Science movement, Stephen Pearl Andrews, and family and marriage reform. Sidney Ditzion, *Marriage, Morals and Sex in America* (New York, 1953), is a general work covering much territory, but it offers little formal documentation. Had the book been better annotated it might have been more effective in helping scholars find their way into Victorian sex radicalism. Ditzion's work nevertheless shows the breadth of research that is necessary for such an enormous topic. William L. O'Neill, *Divorce in the Progressive Era* (New Haven, Conn., 1967), has discovered a topic that is an indicator of an age. In addition, see Roy Lubove, "The Progressives and the Prostitute," *Historian* (May 1962), and John C. Burnham, "The Progressive Era Revolution in American Attitudes Toward Sex," *Journal of American History* (March 1973). Burnham sees as revolutionary the voices that were raised against the Victorian conspiracy of silence and the double standard. Of significance to our present appreciation of sexual politics is Rover, *Love, Morals and the Feminists*.

A primary source on Victorian marriage is Carrol D. Wright, commissioner of labor, *Report on Marriage and Divorce in the United States, 1867–1886* (Washington, D.C., 1889). Anthony Comstock's books, such as *Traps for the Young* (New York, 1883), reveal the concerns of social conservatives. Robert Bremner's preface to a new edition (Cambridge, Mass., 1967) provides insight into Comstock's personality. For organized Victorian social purity, see David J. Pivar's doctoral dissertation, "The New Abolitionism: The Quest for Social Purity, 1876–1900" (University of Pennsylvania, 1965). Important groundwork for the assessment of Victorian sexual thought has been laid by Stephen W. Nissenbaum in his doctoral dissertation, "Careful Love: Sylvester Graham and the Emergence of Victorian Sexual Theory in America, 1830–1840" (University of Wisconsin, 1968).

The categories of respectability and unrespectability as they relate to late-nineteenth-century America deserve more study; on this topic see Peter T. Cominos, "Late Victorian Sexual Respectability and the Social System," *International Review of Social History*, vol. 8 (1963), and Walter M. Gallichan (pseud., Geoffrey Mortimer), *The Blight of Re-*

spectability (London, 1897). For what the term "Victorian" has come to mean and why it has come to mean it, see Thomas Beer, *The Mauve Decade* (New York, 1926); Steven Marcus, *The Other Victorians: A Study of Sexuality and Pornography in Mid-Nineteenth-Century England* (New York, 1964); Gertrude Himmelfarb, *Victorian Minds* (London, 1968); Walter Houghton, *The Victorian Frame of Mind* (New Haven, Conn., 1957); Van Wyck Brooks, *The Confident Years, 1885–1915* (New York, 1955). Robert Shaplen, *Free Love and Heavenly Sinners* (New York, 1954), covers the Beecher-Tilton Affair. The journals *American Quarterly, Feminist Studies,* and *Victorian Studies* are all fruitful sources on sexual topics.

An example of Charlotte Perkins Gilman's prophetic work on woman and her relationship to family and society is *Women and Economics* (Boston, 1898); a 1966 reprint of an 1899 edition with an introduction by Carl Degler is available. As scholarship proliferates, so does the novelty of topics. On the taboo of masturbation, see Robert H. MacDonald, "The Frightful Consequences of Onanism: Notes on the History of a Delusion," *Journal of the History of Ideas,* vol. 28 (1967). Ben Barker-Benfield, "The Spermatic Economy: A Nineteenth Century View of Sexuality," *Feminist Studies* (Summer, 1972), deals with the masturbation phobia and the development of gynecology, and relates these to the subject of "maleness." Finally, Page Smith's study, *Daughters of the Promised Land: Women in American History* (Boston, 1970), offers both a historical survey and a reasoned exploration of the values in the traditional view of marriage and the family.

The topic of birth control is as intimately linked with medicine and eugenics as it is to social attitudes and economics. Norman E. Himes, *Medical History of Contraception* (Baltimore, Md., 1936), though it is not a social history, is written with an awareness of the contributions of the Victorian sex radicals. A recent and excellent all-around history of the topic is Peter Fryer, *The Birth Controllers* (New York, 1966). An important biography, as well as a study of the social-movement aspects of birth control that followed the Victorians, is David M. Kennedy, *Birth Control in America: The Career of Margaret Sanger* (New Haven, Conn., 1970). Dienes, *Law, Politics and Birth Control,* is invaluable on legal aspects; it also contains an appendix of state laws relating to birth control. Victor Robinson, *Pioneers of Birth Control in England and America* (New York, 1919), is a small tribute to the early sex reformers; it contains rare photographs of Ezra Heywood and Moses Harman. Like Victor Robinson, Marie Stopes was a transition figure between the Victorians and the modern birth-control movement; see her *Early Days of Birth Control* (London, 1922).

Bibliographic Essay 325

Two influential studies of the sociological determinants of the birth rate are J. A. Banks, *Prosperity and Parenthood: A Study of Family Planning among the Victorian Middle Classes* (London, 1954), and J. A. Banks and Olive Banks, *Feminism and Family Planning in Victorian England* (Liverpool, Eng., 1964). For illumination of present-day disputes concerning genetics, see Mark H. Haller, *Eugenics: Hereditarian Attitudes in American Thought* (New Brunswick, N.J., 1963). David Pickens, *Eugenics and the Progressives* (Nashville, Tenn., 1968), attempts to deal with the impulse to apply Progressive reforms to human genetics, not a task for one who doesn't relish irony. Neither Haller nor Pickens engages pre-Galton eugenics thought in America, and both contain misleading and fragmentary information on Moses Harman. A recent article that makes use of some source materials that I have used in this book is Linda Gordon, "Voluntary Motherhood: The Beginnings of Feminist Birth Control Ideas in the United States," *Feminist Studies* (Winter–Spring, 1973).

Studies of the women's movement which help put the sex radicals in context are William L. O'Neill, *The Woman Movement* (New York, 1969), *Everyone Was Brave* (Chicago, 1969), and "Feminism as a Radical Ideology," in Alfred Young, ed., *Dissent: Explorations in the History of American Radicalism* (De Kalb, Ill., 1968); two studies by Robert Riegel, *American Feminists* (Lawrence, Kans., 1963) and *American Women: A Story of Social Change* (Rutherford, N.J., 1970); and Carl Degler's essay "Revolution Without Ideology: The Changing Place of Women in America," in Robert Jay Lifton, ed., *The Woman in America* (Boston, 1964). An essay that looks at the historical definition of women in feminist terms is "Women in American Society: An Historical Contribution," by Ann D. Gordon, Mari Jo Buhle, and Nancy E. Schrom, in *Radical America* (July–August 1971).

Of the standard biographies of figures who were important to Victorian sexuality, three books written in the 1920s stand out: Heywood Broun and Margaret Leech, *Anthony Comstock: Roundsman of the Lord* (New York, 1927); Houston Peterson, *Havelock Ellis: Philosopher of Love* (Boston, 1928); and Emanie Sachs, *"The Terrible Siren": Victoria Woodhull (1838–1927)* (New York, 1928). Havelock Ellis's *My Life* (Boston, 1939) is helpful on the Bedborough affair, as is his short *A Note on the Bedborough Trial* (London, 1898). Madeleine Stern's biography of Stephen Pearl Andrews, *The Pantarch* (Austin, Tex., 1968), while a needed narrative of his life, doesn't treat the most important aspect of Andrews—his thought. It would take an uncommon biographer not to be discouraged or intimidated by the volume of Andrews's prose, much of which is arcane. Charles Shively,

"The Thought of Stephen Pearl Andrews (1812–1886)" (Master's thesis, University of Wisconsin, 1960), deals with Andrews's important ideas on sex, marriage, and the family; it aided my understanding of the reformer. Also see "Stephen Pearl Andrews: American Pioneer Sociologist," by Harvey Wish, in *Social Forces* (May 1941).

I am sure that graduate students or their teachers are toiling away on new biographies of John Humphrey Noyes, Victoria Woodhull, Anthony Comstock, and others, but no thorough studies have been published about Ezra and Angela Heywood, Andrew Jackson Davis, Thomas and Mary Gove Nichols, or Voltairine de Cleyre, to name a few of the more interesting personalities. A recent book that centers on the workings of J. H. Noyes's community is Maren Lockwood Carden, *Oneida: Utopian Community to Modern Corporation* (Baltimore, Md., 1969). Carden deals clearly with sexual topics. Marvin E. Liebling's unpublished research paper "Ezra Heywood: Intransigent Individualist: A Study of a Radical in Post Civil War America" (Directed Research 201, Dr. Leonard Levy, Brandeis University, 1970), is an invaluable aid on the Heywoods; my work is indebted to his.

Biographical sketches, portraits, chronologies, and information on obscure disputes of lesser-known reformers of many causes appear in Samuel P. Putnam, *400 Years of Freethought* (New York, 1894), and George E. Macdonald, *Fifty Years of Freethought*, 2 vols. (New York, 1929). Also helpful is B. O. Flower, *Progressive Men, Women, and Movements of the Past Fifty Years* (Boston, 1914), and D. M. Bennett, *The World's Sages, Thinkers and Reformers* (New York, 1876). Theodore Schroeder's compilation *Edward Bond Foote: Biographical Notes and Appreciatives* (New York, 1913) includes information on New York social radicals. Recent published sources on Moses Harman include William L. West, "The Moses Harman Story," *Kansas Historical Quarterly* (Spring, 1971); and Hal D. Sears, "The Sex Radicals in High Victorian America," *Virginia Quarterly Review* (Summer, 1972). For Harman's early life, see the genealogical history by John Steele McCormick, *History of Forest Hill and Vicinity* (Pacific, Mo., 1970). A short biography of Moses Hull by Daniel Hull, his brother, is *Moses Hull* (Wellesley, Mass., 1907). Emma Goldman's autobiography, *Living My Life*, 2 vols. (New York, 1931), illuminates her sex-reform attitudes and her relations with the Lucifereans.

Some sex radicals can be traced in anarchist literature as well. James J. Martin, *Men against the State* (New York, 1957), is the primary work on individualist anarchism; it liberally treats Ezra Heywood and Stephen Pearl Andrews. Also valuable is Rudolf Rocker, *Pioneers of American Freedom* (Los Angeles, 1949). Carleton Mabee, *Black Free-*

dom (New York, 1970), deals with nonviolent abolitionists and treats Adin Ballou, Heywood, Moncure D. Conway, and others.

There is not much secondary historical literature about spiritualism; Hardinge's *Modern American Spiritualism* and Podmore's *Modern Spiritualism* are the early starting points. Geoffrey K. Nelson's recent *Spiritualism and Society* (New York, 1969), though not a thorough history, is helpful as an approach; the literary impact of spiritualism is the subject of Howard Kerr, *Mediums, and Spirit-Rappers, and Roaring Radicals: Spiritualism in American Literature, 1850–1900* (Urbana, Ill., 1972). On the materialist frame of reference of the spiritualists, see R. Laurence Moore, "Spiritualism and Science: Reflections on the First Decade of the Spirit Rappings," *American Quarterly* (October 1972). Alice Felt Tyler's social history, *Freedom's Ferment* (Minneapolis, Minn., 1944), contains a chapter on spiritualism. Standard works on freethought are Albert Post, *Popular Freethought in America, 1825–1850* (New York, 1943), Sidney Warren, *American Freethought, 1860–1914* (New York, 1943), and Stow Persons, *Free Religion: An American Faith* (New Haven, Conn., 1947). In Orvin Larson, *American Infidel: Robert G. Ingersoll* (New York, 1962), one may follow this important figure in his Liberal League activities and in his relationships to some of the sex radicals. Arthur H. Nethercot, *The First Five Lives of Annie Besant* (Chicago, 1960), reveals the day-to-day life of a pioneer liberated Englishwoman and free-thought campaigner.

Helpful in gathering a perspective on late-nineteenth-century America are these analyses: George M. Frederickson, *The Inner Civil War: Northern Intellectuals and the Crisis of the Union* (New York, 1965); Frederick C. Jaher, *Doubters and Dissenters: Cataclysmic Thought in America, 1880–1918* (New York, 1964); R. Jackson Wilson, *In Quest of Community* (New York, 1968); Robert Wiebe, *The Search for Order, 1877–1920* (New York, 1967); Christopher Lasch, *The New Radicalism in America (1889–1963): The Intellectual as a Social Type* (New York, 1965), and Gabriel Kolko, *The Triumph of Conservatism: A Reinterpretation of American History* (New York, 1963).

W. I. Susman's article "The Persistence of American Reform," in Daniel Walden, ed., *American Reform: The Ambiguous Legacy* (Yellow Springs, Ohio, 1967), is particularly applicable to the recurrence of the sex-reform impetus. Henry J. Silverman, "American Social Reformers in the Late Nineteenth and Early Twentieth Century" (Ph.D. diss., University of Pennsylvania, 1963), is a study of W. D. P. Bliss's *Encyclopedia of Social Reform* in light of theses of reform that have been put forth by Richard Hofstadter, Otis Pease, Eric Goldman, and others. Arthur Mann, *Yankee Reformers in the Urban Age: Social Reform in Boston, 1880–1900* (Cambridge, Mass., 1954), takes a look at values and actions of reform intellectuals. A recent work on genteel reform that provides contrasts to the free-love radicals is John Sproat, *"The Best Men": Liberal Reformers in the Gilded Age* (New York, 1968). An earlier intellectual history that recognizes sex reformers is Oscar Cargill, *Intellectual America: Ideas on the March* (New York, 1941).

The impact of Darwin's *Origin of the Species* on American religious thought is treated in Paul W. Carter, *The Spiritual Crisis of the Gilded Age* (De Kalb, Ill., 1971). Henry May, *End of American Innocence* (New York, 1959), a cultural history of much value, notes the passing of provincial culture, which I found to be such a reality in my work. A slim volume by Samuel Haber, *Efficiency and Uplift: Scientific Management in the Progressive Era, 1890–1920* (Chicago, 1964), documents the rationale of turning men into machines and shows the ruthless potential of Progressive social engineering. Oscar Handlin, *Race and Nationality in American Life* (Boston, 1957), should be seen for his thoughts on nineteenth-century attitudes on sex and the family.

Many sex radicals, particularly those who reached California, were inclined toward "mind power" and "New Thought"; for definitions of these terms and for another phase of American reform, see the work of Donald Meyer, *The Positive Thinkers* (Garden City, N.Y., 1965), and Richard Weiss, *The American Myth of Success* (New York, 1969). Martin Gardner's scientism gets in the way of much understanding of his subjects in *Fads and Fallacies in the Name of Science* (New York, 1957), but he deals with some interesting eccentrics and their schemes; where else can one find a discussion of Koreshanity?

One of the things that led me on in my research was the discovery that the Midwest in the last century was a hotbed of cranks, radicals, and eccentrics. Some useful sources on midwestern life are Russel B. Nye, *Midwestern Progressive Politics* (East Lansing, Mich., 1959), and Edgar W. Howe's watershed novel, *The Story of a Country Town* (Atchison, Kans., 1883). John D. Hicks's classic study on Populism, *The Populist Revolt* (Minneapolis, Minn., 1931), is enhanced by O. Gene Clanton's *Kansas Populism: Ideas and Men* (Lawrence, Kans., 1969), which also includes Populist women. James C. Malin, *A Concern about Humanity: Notes on Reform, 1872–1912 at the National and Kansas Level of Thought* (Lawrence, Kans., 1964), aided my understanding of freethought, Kansas agitation, Lois Waisbrooker, and Elmina Slenker.

Moses Harman, Lillian Harman, and Edwin Walker

The Labadie Collection, University of Michigan, Ann Arbor, has a modest collection of letters and papers of Moses Harman and Edwin C. Walker in its rich collection on social radicalism. The Kansas State Historical Society, Topeka, has nearly complete runs of the various periodicals of the Kansas free lovers, as well as several fugitive pieces. The Charles and Sara T. D. Robinson Papers there also proved valuable for the study of the Lucifer group. The State Library in the State House, Topeka, also contains items on Harman. The New York Public Library has numerous pieces of Harman and Walker literature. An interview with George Harman O'Brien, San Francisco, proved helpful to my work, as did the use of some literature in the family's possession. To my knowledge the bulk of the Harman letters and papers are still in possession of the family. The Edwin C. Walker papers came to rest at the Paterson Museum, Paterson, New Jersey; they are part of the James F. Morton, Jr., papers. The following is a list of publications, mostly pamphlets, from the *Lucifer* principals.

Lillian Harman:
Marriage and Morality. Chicago, 1900.
Memorial of Moses Harman: Tributes by George Bernard Shaw, Bolton Hall, . . . Chicago, 1910.
The Regeneration of Society. Chicago, 1900.
Some Problems of Social Freedom, etc. London, 1898.

Moses Harman:
Digging for Bedrock. Valley Falls, Kans., 1890.
A Free Man's Creed: Discussion of Love in Freedom as Opposed to Institutional Marriage. Los Angeles, 1908.
Free Press: Arguments in Support of Demurrer to the Indictment of M. Harman, E. C. Walker, and Geo. Harman. Valley Falls, Kans., 1889.
Institutional Marriage. Chicago, 1901.
The Kansas Fight for Free Press: The Four Indicted Articles. Valley Falls, Kans., 1889.
Love in Freedom. Chicago, 1900.
The Next Revolution: or Woman's Emancipation from Sex Slavery. Four Pamphlets. Valley Falls, Kans., 1890-91.
The Persecution and the Appreciation: Brief Account of the Trials and Imprisonment of Moses Harman. . . . Chicago, 1907.
The Right to Be Born Well. Chicago, 1905.

Edwin C. Walker:
  Bible Temperance: Liquor Drinking Commended, Defended and Enjoined by the Bible. Valley Falls, Kans., 1884.
  Communism and Conscience, Pentecost and Paradox, Also Crimes and Criminals. New York, 1904.
  E. C. Walker's Third Letter from Jail. Valley Falls, Kans., 188–.
  The Ethics of Freedom: You and the Other Man in the Covenant of Liberty. New York, 1913.
  The Future of Secularism: When Will the Cause of Justice Triumph? New York, 1889.
  Kansas Liberty and Justice. Valley Falls, Kans., 188–.
  Liberty vs. Assassination: Terrorism Has No Standing in the Court of Reason. . . . New York, 1907.
  Love and the Law: An Exposure of the Basic Principles of Social Relations. Valley Falls, Kans., 1882.
  Marriage and Prostitution. New York, 1913.
  The Nine Demands. Valley Falls, Kans., 188–.
  The One Issue—Secularism. Los Angeles, 1910.
  Our Worship of Primitive Social Guesses. New York, 1899.
  Practical Co-operation. Valley Falls, Kans., 1884.
  Prohibition and Self-Government: Their Irreconcilable Antagonisms. Valley Falls, Kans., 1883.
  Religion and Rationalism: The Relation of Each to Human Liberty. New York, 1897.
  The Revival of Puritanism. New York, 1903.
  The Sexual Enslavement of Woman. Valley Falls, Kans., 1883.
  A Sketch and an Appreciation of Moncure Daniel Conway. New York, 1908.
  Variety vs. Monogamy. Chicago, 1897.
  Vice: Its Friends and Its Foes. N.p., 1901.
  What the Young Need to Know: A Primer of Sex Rationalism. New York, 1905.
  Who is the Enemy: Anthony Comstock or You? New York, 1903.

Index

Abbot, Francis: as leader of Free Religious movement, 35–38; loses presidency of Liberal League over obscenity issue, 38

Abolition: and free love, 5; unpopularity of, in Moses Harman's early career, 30; and the Republican party, 67. *See also* Heywood, Ezra

Abortion, used as smear term for birth-control efforts, 129, 192–93

Adult, The (English equivalent of *Lucifer*), 256–57

Ady, J. W. (prosecutor of sex radicals), 231

Agrarianism, and anarchism, 60–61. *See also* Provincialism

Allen, Grant: eugenics ideas of, 122; mentioned, 255, 256

Alphaism, sexual theory and principles of, 132, 207–9

American Journal of Eugenics, Lucifer becomes the, 267

American Protective Association, and anti-Catholicism and the Liberal League, 42

American Woman Suffrage Association, 115

Anarchism: and spiritualism, 21; Liberal, Mo., experiment, 42; communist, 58–59; individualist, 58–60; practical dilemmas of, 68; and woman suffrage, 119; and gradual reform, 136; individualist, and Haymarket radicals, 138; and violence in Kansas, 139; and Home, Wash., community, 233–34; and social support of women, 238–39; and *Lucifer* and McKinley assassination, 269; mentioned, 274, 292 n, 302 n. *See also* Individualism; Tucker, Benjamin; Warren, Josiah

Andrews, Stephen Pearl: justifies free love, 6; and New York Free Love League, 9–10; free-language ideas of, 77, 177; and science of government, 87–89; hereditarian ideas of, 121–22; and Equal Rights party and Victoria Woodhull, 135; on the Heywoods, 173; and National Defense Association, 200; his influence on Lester Ward, 224; on restructuring family life, 248; mentioned, 199, 227, 228, 243

Anthony, Susan B., campaigns for her brother, 119

Austen, Kate, and Emma Goldman, 270

Ballou, Adin, 15, 154

Barclay, W. A. (post-office inspector), 216–17

Barnes, Earl, 263, 269

Bedborough, George: edits *Adult*, 256; and "Lanchester Affair," 256; and "Bedborough Affair" and Havelock Ellis, 256, 259–61; indictment against, 260; and aftermath of "Bedborough Affair," 317 n; mentioned, 258–59

Beecher scandal, 23, 24

Beer, Thomas, 271

Bennett, De Robigne Mortimer: as free-thought publisher, 37–38, 40; his influence on *Lucifer* editors, 54; and Comstock laws, 166–68; and *Cupid's Yokes* case, 171; Bennett case precedent in trial of Elmina Slenker, 218; mentioned, 40, 41, 74, 129, 170

Benson, Helen (wife of William Lloyd Garrison), 154

Berlin Heights, Ohio, community, practices spiritualist free love, 19

Besant, Annie, 164

Bible, earthy stories in, 107

Birth control: information about and methods of, 126–29; Ezra Heywood and, 164–65; Edward Bliss Foote and, 191–98; Edward Bond Foote and, 201–2; Elmina Slenker and, 205; and male continence, 209; and

Dianaism, 215–16; criticized by Lois Waisbrooker, 240. See also Comstock Postal Act; Knowlton, Charles; Owen, Robert Dale
Birth-control devices, promoted by Edward Bliss Foote, 195–97
Blacks: in Kansas, 118; mentioned, 5, 156, 181. See also Abolition
Blackwell, Alice Stone, and Moses Harman, 264
Blackwell, Henry: nativism of, 42; marriage of, 86
Blatchford, Judge Samuel, makes decision in *Cupid's Yokes* case, 168–69
Bradlaugh, Charles, 168
Briggs, Stephan S. (abolitionist colleague of Moses Harman's), 30
Buchanan, Joseph Rodes: hereditarian ideas of, 126–27; mentioned, 109
"Burned-over district": sex radicalism from, 3–4; technology, impact of, 11, 13
Burnz, Eliza B., writes to Tolstoy, 275, 278
Butler, Ben, 38

Campbell, Rachel: menstruation notions of, 235, 236; and social support of women, 239
Celibacy, 162
Censorship: and *Lucifer*, 231; and Post Office Department, 264. See also Comstock, Anthony; Comstock Postal Act; Post Office Department
Chamberlain, Edward W.: opposes woman coeditor for *Lucifer*, 133–34; defends Elmina Slenker in court, 218; his article on Lois Waisbrooker, 233; mentioned, 243
Chandler, Lucinda: nominated to edit *Lucifer*, 133; mentioned, 209
Chicago, Ill.: *Lucifer* moves to, 114; cultural renaissance in, 269
Children: born under protest, 78; free love and, 248–50; sexuality of, recognized in *Sex Radicalism*, 252
Chivalry, 273
Christianity: theology applied to "New Motor," 17–18; its early influence on Moses Harman, 29; and obscenity, 79; and marriage, 83; its theology and women, 131, 134–35; and party platforms, 147; and free love, 158; "purity" forces of, 171; criticism of, by Lillie D. White, 245; mentioned, 1, 234. See also Protestantism
Civil War: its influence on postwar sex radicalism, 27; its influence on Moses Harman, 29–31; and theocratic movement, 43; and pacifism, 154–55
Claflin, Tennessee (also known as Tennie C. Claflin), 256
Clemens, Gaspar C.: as attorney for *Lucifer*, 80, 90, 91; Populism and socialism of, 147
Cleyre, Voltairine de: on Elmina Slenker's "ring correspondence," 220; mentioned, 45, 126
Clitoris, 314 n
Clough Circular, contraception theory in, 129–30
Coffeyville, Kans., bombing. See Red scare
Coitus interruptus, 197, 209
Colby, Clara Bewick, gives editorial support to Moses Harman, 115
Colgate, Samuel, and vaseline contraceptive affair, 129
Communitarianism, its influences on marriage reform, 3
Comstock, Anthony: troubles the Liberal League, 37–38; and First Amendment, 72; power of, 73; strategies of, 73–74; as social reformer, 73, 208; criticized in *Revolutionary Review*, 109; and Ezra Heywood, 116–17; and conservative editor of *Christian Life*, 116; arrests Ezra Heywood, 165; writes about the Heywoods, 165–66; arrests D. M. Bennett, 167–68; on presidential pardon of Ezra Heywood, 170–71; foils presidential pardon of D. M. Bennett, 171; pursues Ezra Heywood, 172; dared by Ezra Heywood, 179; strategy of, against Ezra Heywood, 180; and medical profession, 192–93; and Edward Bliss Foote, 193; losing favor of "purity" advocates, 263; George Bernard Shaw's comments on, 264–66; mentioned, 153
Comstock Postal Act: and sex radicals, 23; origins of, 69–74; and obscenity, 71; and state laws, 72, 74; constitutionality of, 72, 112, 169; opposed by sex radicals, 74; and First Amendment, in O'Neill letter case, 112; criticized by press, 115; and

birth control, 128, 129, 191, 192; and sex education, 163; and first-class mail, 194; and expurgation of published sex information, 197; and Elmina Slenker, 204, 216–19; and censoring power of Post Office Department, 230; and arrests of Lois Waisbrooker, 232–33; legacy of, 273
Comte, Auguste, his influence in America, 40
Condom. See Birth-control devices
Contraception. See Birth control
Courtship, attractions of, versus marriage, 273
Craddock, Ida C., death of, and Anthony Comstock, 200, 262
Cridge, Alfred: attacks sexual asceticism, 132; mentioned, 101
Croly, Jane Cunningham, influences sex radicals, 26, 287 n
Crozier, Judge Robert, 91–93
Culverwell, James (agrarian radical), 144
Cupid's Yokes: discussion of free-love theories of, 159–65; and obscenity laws, 168; legal trials of, 169, 170; mentioned, 154
Curti, Merle, on Ezra Heywood's pacifism, 156

Darwin, Charles: his theory of natural selection, 121; his influence on free-thought movement, 135; and female selection, 222
Davis, Andrew Jackson: publicizes free-love ideas, 4; spiritual-affinity doctrine of, 8–9; his ideas on sex education, influences of, 188
Dawson, Oswald (founder of Legitimation League), 254
Death, and spiritualism, 7, 15–16, 20
Devins, Charles (U.S. attorney general), declares *Cupid's Yokes* not to be obscene, 170
Diana, and sexual desire, 211
Dianaism (theory of sublimation of sexual energy), 162, 209, 211–17
Diggs, Annie L.: assists Moses Harman on *Kansas Liberal*, 46–47; and sex radicalism, 148; mentioned, 44, 146
Divorce, reform of laws concerning, 23
Domesticity, Lillie D. White on, 245–46
Donisthorpe, Wordsworth, 256
Doster, Frank, 44

Dr. Foote's Health Monthly, its significance as a reform journal, 198
Drysdale, Alice Vickery, 255
Drysdale, Charles R., 255
Drysdale, George: influence of, on sex radicals, 25; particular influence of, on Ezra Heywood, 164–65; his theories about menstruation, 236, 237; his birth-control theories criticized by Lois Waisbrooker, 240
Dugdale, Richard (author of *The Jukes*), 124–25
Dynamite, 142

Economics: and social change, 10–11; and money power and sex, 242. See also Anarchism
Electricity, and spiritualism, 11–20
Eliot, George (Mary Ann Evans), marriage of, 87
Elliott, Sydney Barrington, birth control, and American Medical Association, 123, 192
Ellis, Havelock: his ideas on prenatal influence, 123; in "Bedborough Affair," 257–61 passim
Emerson, Ralph Waldo: his view of materialism, 10; and Free Religion, 35
England: Walker-Harman marriage publicity in, 92; *Lucifer*'s ties with, 254; and America compared, 254–55
Eugenics: anarchistic, 120–21; prescriptive, 121; anarchistic and Progressive, 124; and Edward Bliss Foote, 191, 197–98, 308 n; and Edward Bond Foote, 201–3; coercion, 239; Lois Waisbrooker and, 243–44; pre-Galtonion, 301 n; mentioned, 274. See also Hereditarianism

Fair Play, 108, 133, 138
Family: free-love critique of, 20–21; and Victorian social theory, 26–27; Moses Harman and Victorian social theory of, 87; Lillie D. White on, 247, 249. See also Children; Domesticity; Free love; Marriage
Farnham, Eliza: her influence on Lois Waisbrooker, 234; feminist theories of, 234–35
Feminism: origins of, in America, 6, 8; and free love, 8; and sex radicalism, 24, 286 n; and Edward Bliss Foote, 188–91; and Lester Frank Ward, 222–24; and complementariness of

sexes, 227; criticism of some aspects of, by Lillie D. White, 248. *See also* Women

Flower, Benjamin O.: supports Moses Harman in *Arena*, 115; and eugenics, 123–24; as purity reformer, 208

Foote, Edward Bliss: compares himself with Comstock, 73; advises Moses Harman, 111; as Populist, 147; aids D. M. Bennett, 167–69; biography of, 183–98; obscenity trial of, 194; invents cervical cap, 196–97; supports social reformers and radicals, 198; and paired sleeping, 213; on homosexuality, 226; on menstruation, 237; mentioned, 103

Foote, Edward Bond (also known as E. B. Foote, Jr., and Ned Foote): his efforts against Comstock Act, 38; as secretary of National Defense Association, 116; and contraception, 128; biography of, 198–203; mentioned, 183

Forster, Dora (Mrs. R. B. Kerr): British epigone of Moses Harman, 251; advanced sexual ideas of, in her booklet *Sex Radicalism*, 251–53; mentioned, 178–79

Foster, Abby Kelly, 204

Foster, Judge Caius G.: petition of women to, 109; relations of Moses Harman with, 109–10; Markland letter decision of, 112; mentioned, 107

Fourier, Charles, and doctrine of spiritual affinity, 8–9. *See also* Communitarianism

Franklin, Benjamin, as a spiritualist symbol, 16

Free love: ethical justification of, 4; early principles of, 5; historical origins of, 7-8; combines with spiritualism, 8; and feminist movement, 8; anarchistic origins of, 20–21; theory of, 22–23; and freedom from sexual intercourse, 27, 208, 272–73; and Kansas free thinkers, 44–45; and free marriage, 87; and eugenics, 120; and Ezra and Angela Heywood, 158–82 passim; and marriage, 177; and purity reformers, 208-9; in Home, Wash., 233; and "varietism," 241; and children, 248–50; in England, 254–61; and insanity, 255; and Bedborough case, 260, 261; commune, novel about, 273; mentioned, 274

Free press: and freedom of tongue and pen, 96; issue in Markland letter case, 108–9. *See also* Journalism

Free Religious Association, origins of, 35

Free speech: as issue in Markland letter case, 76–77, 79; its precedence over other causes for *Lucifer* radicals, 96; and free love, 97; Elmina Slenker on, 219. *See also* Obscenity

Free Speech League: founded, 200; and John Turner affair, 201

Free thought: antebellum origins of movement, 34; post–Civil War development of movement, 35; its appeal to radicals and spiritualists, 40; and scientists and intellectuals, 40–41; press of, 43, 47–49, 54; in Kansas, 44–52; camp meeting, 49–50; and Elmina Slenker, 204–5; and politics, 209 n; mentioned, 274. *See also* Liberal League

Freud, Sigmund, 241

Fruits of Philosophy (a birth-control pamphlet). *See* Knowlton, Charles

"Fuck," use of the word by the Heywoods, 177, 178

Galton, Francis: influence of, on hereditarian thought, 120–21; and Progressive eugenics, 124

Gardener, Helen H., and "sex in brain" controversy, 300 n

Garrison, William Lloyd: his influence on Ezra Heywood, 154; his pacifism and change in pacifist principles, 155–56

Gilman, Charlotte Perkins Stetson: gynecocentric theory of, 227; mentioned, 269

Goldman, Emma: on birth-control pioneers in America, 128; aided by the Drs. Foote, 203; and birth control, 268; and Kate Austen, 270

Graham, Sylvester, sexual theories of, 207

Graul, Rosa, 273

Greeley, Horace: opposes free love, 9–10; mentioned, 199

Greenback party, 135-36

Greer, Edwin, publishes exposés of Videttes, 140

Hagaman, James M., and factions in Kansas Liberal League, 51
Harman, George: working at *Lucifer*, 64; as Populist editor, 147; mentioned, 80, 96–97
Harman, Lillian: working at *Lucifer*, 64; free marriage of, to Edwin C. Walker, 81–96; jailed for marriage, 90–91, 92–93; refuses to pay court costs, 95–96; writes of her marriage, 105; as bachelor mother, 122; begins *Fair Play*, 133; on free love and morality, 208; comments on homosexuality, 228; on children, 249; elected president of Legitimation League in England, 256; and Havelock Ellis, 257; publicity about, 257–58; visits England, 257–58; retires from sexual journalism, 268
Harman, Moses: biographical sketch of, 28–33; as Methodist minister, 29; arrives in Valley Falls, Kans., 32; begins career as journalist, 33; as free-thought editor of *Valley Falls Liberal* and *Kansas Liberal*, 46–48; and individual sovereignty, 59; as individualist anarchist, 62; and dynamite rhetoric, 63; discovers sex question, 68; on Markland letter and free-speech issue, 74–78, 107, 109; free-speech philosophy of, 77, 79; hereditarian theories of, 78, 121–22; his strategies of reform, 78–79; and Ezra Heywood, 79, 109, 111, 156, 181; his criticism of marriage, 81–82; and Walker-Harman marriage, 81–86 passim; prints O'Neill letter, 110–11; and Markland letter trial, 111–14; his imprisonments, 112; obscenity cases of, set legal precedents, 113–14; and feminism, 119, 125–26, 130; eugenics ideas of, 125–26; and birth control, 126; and Populism, 145, 149; and Julian Hawthorne's pamphlet on Heywood, 181–82; arrest of, in 1905, 263; sentenced to Joliet prison, 264; George Bernard Shaw on, 264–66; gains support from influential people, 266; memorial services for, in New York and Los Angeles, 268
Harman, Noah: as Populist publisher, 147; mentioned, 32, 89

Hawthorne, Julian, protests imprisonment of Ezra Heywood, 181
Hayes, Rutherford B. (president): pardons Ezra Heywood, 170, mentioned, 129
Haymarket Affair: violence and anarchism in, 58; and public opinion, 97; *Lucifer* reports on, 137–38; and Union Labor party, 140
Heinzen, Karl: as theorist of free marriage, 25–26; mentioned, 286–87 n
Henderson, Ben, 233
Henrie, C. A., 142
Hereditarianism, 122–25. See also Eugenics
Herron, George D., corresponds with Moses Harman, 267
Heywood, Angela Tilton: and *The Word*, 153; and *Uncivil Liberty*, 157; her influence on Ezra Heywood, 159; biographical sketch of, 172–74; her writings in *The Word*, 172–79; her daring use of language, 172–79; her relationship with husband, 173, 176–77; on free love and marriage, 174–75, 176; her satire on Comstock's power, 179
Heywood, Ezra Hervey: influenced by George Drysdale, 25; and obscenity laws, 37–38; and Kansas Liberal League, 52; as individualist anarchist, 59–60; compares Moses Harman to William Lloyd Garrison, 79; champions Moses Harman, 109; advises Moses Harman, 111; and anarchist eugenics, 120; publishes *The Word*, 153; biographical sketch of, 153–82; and abolition, 154–56, 181; writes letters to Moses Harman, 155; and pacifism, 155–56; economic theories of, 157–58, 163; legal trials of, 169–70; pardoned by President Hayes, 170; his prison letters to Moses Harman, 181, 307 n; death of, 182; describes meeting Lois Waisbrooker, 232; publishes poems by Walt Whitman, 306 n; criticizes socialist schemes, 315 n; mentioned, 74, 104, 146, 250–51. See also *Cupid's Yokes*
Hicklin standard: defines obscenity, 168–69; and Ezra Heywood's final trial, 180; mentioned, 114, 166, 168–69, 218
Himes, Norman E., on Edward Bliss Foote, 184

Hiser, W. F.: as complainant in Walker-Harman marriage case, 86; testifies in Walker-Harman case, 91
Holmes, Lizzie M., 126, 245
Homosexuality: and Victorian sex radicals, 225–26; treated in Chautauqua Society publication, 227, 312–13 n; and *Sexual Inversion*, 257–60
Horton, Chief Justice, and marriage decision of Kansas Supreme Court in Walker-Harman marriage case, 93, 95
Housework, 176, 245–46. *See also* Domesticity
Howe, Edgar: describes small-town life, 33; characterizes Edwin C. Walker, 54
Hull, Moses: bridges Christianity and spiritualism, 16; and spiritualist factions, 21–22; free marriage of, 88–89; Greenbacker ideas of, influence Moses Harman, 135; agitates for Union Labor party, 136–37; calls Social Freedom Convention, 158; and Lois Waisbrooker, 231–32; and children, 249; mentioned, 101, 146
Hunt, C. F., 245
Hunt, Hannah J., 245

Index (influential free-thought journal of the Free Religious Association), 36
Individualism: and dissolution of family, 20, 21; George Bernard Shaw on, 271. *See also* Anarchism
Industrialism: and spiritualism, 7; and humanistic machine, 17–19
Infidel. *See* Free thought
Infidelisms, 6–7
Ingersoll, Robert: as influential agnostic, 37–39; and obscenity issue, 38, 39; popularity of, 43; on the influence of *Boston Investigator*, 43; asks President Hayes to pardon D. M. Bennett, 170, 171; mentioned, 129, 167
Insanity: Moses Harman's legal defense on grounds of, 111; in Mitchell-Ward case, 226; of free love and socio/sexual deviation, 255
International Women's Council, eugenics ideas presented at, 125

Jackson, Andrew (president), attempts to censor mails, 70

Jackson, Phebe, introduces Ezra Heywood to radical thought, 154
Jacksonian democracy, 19, 34
Jacobi, Mary, on menstruation, 238
James, C. L., on homosexuality, 226–27
James, Henry, quoted, 87
Jewett, John P., 199
Jews, participation of, in Liberal League, 42
Johnson, Judge, and decision on Walker-Harman marriage by Supreme Court of Kansas, 93
Journalism: Moses Harman's philosophy of, 98–99; strategies of sexual, 229. *See also* Free speech
Juke family, influence of study of, 124
Jung-Stilling, Johann, 12

Kansas: free thought in, 44–52; Supreme Court of, and decision on Walker-Harman marriage, 93–95; public opinion in, 97–106 passim; status of women in, 118; reform tradition in, 118; conditions in, in 1887–1888, 139; election of 1888 in, 143–44
Kansas Liberal, 46–49
"Karezza" (name for male-continence technique), 210
Kelso, John R. (author of pamphlet on Walker-Harman marriage), 88
Kendrick, Laura Cuppy: obtains pardon for Ezra Heywood from President Hayes, 200; mentioned, 170
Kent, Austin (free-love theorist), 160
Kiantone, N.Y., where free love and spiritualism combined, 19, 285 n
Kneeland, Abner: tried for blasphemy, 34; founds *Boston Investigator*, 43
Knowlton, Charles: contraceptive pamphlet by, 128, 305 n; and Bradlaugh-Besant trial, 164
Kreutzer Sonata, banned from mails, 72, 251

Lanchester, Edith, and marriage affair in England, 255–56
Landis, Judge Kenesaw Mountain, sentences Moses Harman to Joliet Prison, 264
Laws regulating sexual conduct, 69. *See also* Comstock Postal Act; Obscenity
Lease, Mary Elizabeth: praises Lois Waisbrooker's *A Sex Revolution*, 147–48; corresponds with Lois

Waisbrooker concerning *A Sex Revolution*, 243
Le Gallienne, Richard, 255
Legitimation League: origins of, 254–55; demise of, caused by Bedborough Affair, 261
Lesbianism, and Victorian sex radicals, 225–26
Lewes, George Henry, marriage of, 87
Lewis, Diocletian, 164
Liberal League: origins of, 36; votes for repeal of Comstock laws, 38; doctrines of, 39–40. See also Free thought
Libertarianism. See Anarchism; Individualism
Liberty, antifeminism of, 250
Lindsey, Ben, 190
Lohman, Ann, suicide of, and Anthony Comstock, 72
London Star, on Walker-Harman marriage, 92
Longley, Alcander (St. Louis communist), on *Lucifer* radicals, 104
Love: belief that marriage contravened, 21; interrelation with sexuality, 175, 176; and sexual intercourse, 207; called by Lois Waisbrooker "the feminine principle," 245. See also Free love
Lucifer, the Light Bearer: as journal of sexual radicalism, 28; significance of its name, 55–58; as anarchist journal, 63–64; compared to other journals, 64; indictments against, 76, 79–80; moves to Topeka, Kans., 114; its policy toward women contributors, 133; women editors of, 134; and *The Word*, 153; aided by the Drs. Foote, 203; changes to *American Journal of Eugenics*, 267; assessed as to its place and influence, 268–71; as mouthpiece of suffering womanhood, 269; and provincialism, 270
Lum, Dyer D., 21
Luxemburg, Rosa, 126
Lysistrata, theme of, in *A Sex Revolution*, by Lois Waisbrooker, 242

McAfee, R. W.: as agent for Society for Suppression of Vice, 79; arrests Christian editor, 116; and arrest of Elmina Slenker, 204, 216–17; and arrest of Lois Waisbrooker, 233
Macdonald, George: as editor of *Truth Seeker*, on free speech and Moses Harman and Ezra Heywood, 117; opposes coercive eugenics from libertarian point of view, 127
McKinley, William (president), and anarchist scare, 233
Mail, sealed, and Comstock Act, 217. See also Post Office Department
Male continence, 209–10
Males, and feminism, 247, 248
Malin, James C., 243
Malthus, Thomas, *Essay on the Principle of Population*, 191
Malthusianism, 191, 201. See also Birth control
Manhattan Liberal Club, important members of, 199
Markland, W. G.: and Miller-Strickland marriage, 89; on Walker-Harman marriage, 103–4; favors woman to coedit *Lucifer*, 133; assesses Lois Waisbrooker, 229
Markland letter: text of, 75–76; and "sexual vileness" of marriage, 87; mentioned, 96, 107, 179
Marriage: experimentation in, 3–6; of Moses Harman, 78; of Lillian Harman and Edwin C. Walker, 81–106 passim; laws pertaining to, 83; reform ceremonies, 86, 205; and morality, 87; Kansas laws on, 90, 92; legal trial of Walker-Harman marriage, 91–96; and childbearing, 132; as plural unity, 176; reform ideas of Edward Bliss Foote on, 190–91; manuals on, 210; Tolstoy on Russian customs of, 277–79. See also Free love
Married Women's Property Acts, 94
Marx, Karl, on concept of alienation, 10
Masturbation: Edward Bliss Foote's notions about, 188; male and female, 188–89; Stephen Pearl Andrews on, 248; mentioned, 158, 162, 197, 310–11 n. See also O'Neill letter
Medical profession: and Edward Bliss Foote, 184–85, 186–87, 192–93; and Edward Bond Foote, 202–3. See also Elliott, Sydney Barrington
Memnonia, Ohio, free-love community, principles of, 4
Menstruation: theories on, 235–40; and blood taboo, 237, 238
Mesmerism, 12
Midwest, reform schemes in, 135

338 Index

Mill, John Stuart, his marriage to Harriet Taylor, 26, 87
Miller, George Noyes, describes male-continence technique, 209, 210
Miller, Leo, his free marriage and the law, 88–89
Miller, Sol, 98
Modern Times community, its influence on social radicalism, 6, 40
Morality, and free love, 87, 274
Moral Physiology. See Owen, Robert Dale
Most, Johann (communist anarchist), 58
Motherhood: as key to "woman's superiority," 239–40; criticism of, by Lillie D. White, 245–47; and head-of-household laws, 249–50; mentioned, 120

National Defense Association, its origin and works, 170, 199–200
National Order of Videttes, exposés of, by Kansas press, 140–43
Neo-Malthusianism, 191. *See also* Malthusianism
New England Free Love League, 157
New England Labor Reform League, 157
New York Liberal Club, 199
New York Times: on spiritualist movement, 8–9; its concern about free love, 9–10; and Vice Society, 74; reporting on Elmina Slenker, 216, 217
Nichols, Mary Gove: and Memnonia community, 4; her free-love novel assailed in *New York Times*, 9
Nichols, Thomas Low: and Memnonia community, 4; on causes of free love in America, 5–6; sexual theories of, 207; mentioned, 164
Noyes, John Humphrey: and religious and sexual love, 3–4; on propagative and amative functions of sex organs, 25; and eugenics, 125; theories of, and Ezra Heywood, 161; male-continence doctrine of, 209–10, 211; his influence on *Diana*, 278
Nudity: Anthony Comstock on, 73; and Dianaism, 212, 216

O'Brien, George, 268
Obscene Publications Act (England), 69–70
Obscenity: and Robert Ingersoll and Liberal League, 38, 39; as origin of the Comstock Act, 69–71; and *Hicklin* standard, 71–72; and Post Office Department, 71–72; and art, notions of Anthony Comstock on, 73; arrests of George and Moses Harman on charges of, 96; and free speech and Moses Harman, 112–14; laws on, shaped by *Cupid's Yokes* decision, 168. *See also* Comstock Postal Act; Free speech
Oneida Community: doctrines of, 3–4; couples fell in love in, 175–76; and male continence, 209
O'Neill, Richard V., 110
O'Neill letter: published in *Lucifer*, 110–11; Ezra Heywood vows to reprint, 116, 179; mentioned, 226
Orgasm: pleasure of, and "dominion of the flesh," 244; incidence of, in married men and women compared, 253; fear of, related to control, 272; mentioned, 213–14
Oro-genitalism, in O'Neill letter, 110–11
Oskaloosa, Kans., 90
Overmeyer, David: as attorney for *Lucifer*, 80, 90, 91; in *Topeka Capital*, 102–3; and Markland letter case, 112; as a Populist and "fusion" Democrat, 147; mentioned, 304 n
Owen, Robert Dale: marriage of, 86; contraceptive pamphlet by, 128, 164

Paine, Thomas, and free thought, 167
Parent Teachers Association, 262–63
Parker, Theodore, has influence on Ezra Heywood, 153
Parkhurst, Henry M.: and theory of Dianism, 162; his ideas on sex in *Diana*, 211–16; on menstruation, 238
Parmelee v. *U.S.* (obscenity law), 113
Parsons, Elsie Clew, 262
Patterson, E. C., 109
Paul, Judge J., and trial of Elmina Slenker, 218
Paul, Saint, and Christian sexual teachings, 131
Penhallow, Mattie D. (postmistress at anarchist community), charged with obscenity, 233
Penis: as word used in Markland letter, 75, 79; as word used by Angela

Heywood, 173; Department of Agriculture and Horse Penis Affair, 229–31

Pentecost, Hugh O., gives editorial support to Moses Harman, 115, 116

People's party: in Kansas, 144–49; criticism of, by sex radicals, 145–47; mentioned, 233, 203 n. *See also* Populism

Philips, Judge, on First Amendment and O'Neill letter case, 112–13

Phillips, Wendell, 25, 155

Pillsbury, Parker, 154, 170, 204

Pinney, Lucien V.: on the Heywoods, 173; mentioned, 47, 101

Pleasure, as separate function of the genitals, 210–11

Pomeroy, M. M. ("Brick"): defends Moses Harman, 109; his interview with President Harrison and Attorney General Miller on Moses Harman's behalf, 116

Populism: and free thought, 46; and unrest in Kansas, 139; Videttes exposé of, 142–43; criticism of *Lucifer* in its press, 148–49. *See also* People's party

Post Office Department: and Elmina Slenker, 216–17; closes Home, Wash., post office in reprisal, 234. *See also* Comstock Postal Act; Obscenity

Professionalization, and free-thought intellectuals, 40–41

Prohibition: laws on, and personal liberty, 47, 48, 53; related to alcohol and sex, 206–7

Prostitution, 162–63

Protestantism, 39–40. *See also* Christianity

Provincialism: and Protestantism, 44; and *Lucifer*, 270. *See also* Agrarianism

Public opinion: on *Lucifer* free lovers, 97–107; and Markland letter, 107–9; and petition to Justice Department for Moses Harman's release from prison, 116; and harassment of *Lucifer*, 266–67

Puritanism: and free love at turn of century, 261–68

Purity, and sex radicalism, 271–72

Putnam, Samuel, 46

Quakers, marriage ceremonies of, 86, 205

Index 339

Raciborski, Adam, on menstruation, 237

Rawson, Albert, 199

Raymond, Henry. See *New York Times*

Reason, and free love, 161, 162

Red scare: Haymarket Affair, 97; in Kansas, 139–45

Replogle, Georgia, and Replogle, Henry, as free lovers divide communitarian experiment, 42

Republican administration, and Ezra Heywood's first trial, 179–80

Republican party: in Kansas, 142–43; and sex radicals in Kansas, 233

Richard, Henry, on Ezra Heywood, 156

Robinson, A. W., 98

Robinson, Charles: and free thought, 44, 51; as Anti-Monopolist candidate, 67; and Victorian womanhood, 78; supports Moses Harman, 109

Robinson, Mary, marriage of, 86

Rose, Ernestine: and radical feminism, 24; her acquaintance with Elmina Slenker, 204

Rosen v. United States, sustains Comstock Act, 72

Roth-Alberts case, and precedent of O'Neill letter case, 113

Ruedebusch, Emil (author of free-love book), fined, 262

Sanger, Margaret: Emma Goldman on, 128; mentioned, 126

Sawyer, Mattie: free marriage of, 88–89; calls Social Freedom Convention, 158

Schenk, S. L., his fetal studies and gynecocentrism, 227

Schroeder, Theodore: free-speech work of, 201; contributes to *American Journal of Eugenics*, 267; mentioned, 198, 263

Science: and spiritualism, 11–20; and free thought, 40–41

Searl, A. J., helps found *Kansas Liberal*, 46

Semple, Etta, 45

Severance, Juliet: as candidate to co-edit *Lucifer*, 133; mentioned, 301 n

Sex, power of, and control, 272

Sex education: and Ezra Heywood, 163–64; and Edward Bliss Foote, 184–86, 189; and Andrew Jackson Davis, 188; and sexual intemperance, 216; mentioned, 126–27, 278–79

Sex radicalism: as separate movement from feminism, 24–25; and historians, 24; early theorists of, 24–25; as title of book by Dora Forster, 252–53, 264
Sex radicals, influences on, 24–25
Sexual-advice books, 308 n
Sexual intercourse: described by Angela Heywood, 173–74; theory of Edward Bliss Foote about, 187–88
Sexualism, and nineteenth-century climate of opinion, 241–42
Sexual passion, and women, 226
Sexual satisfaction, 277
Seymour, Henry, 255
Shaw, George Bernard: on prosecution of George Bedborough, 259; on Criminal Law Amendment Act, 259; on "Comstockery" and Anthony Comstock, 264, 265; his letters to and about Moses Harman, 264–66; his opinion about America, 265–66; his observation on Benjamin Tucker, 271; mentioned, 256
Shockley, William, 125
Simpson, R. D., 89–90
Slenker, Elmina (Elizabeth Drake): and Dianaism, 162; humorously used by Ezra Heywood, 178; *New York Times* reports of, 204; biographical sketch of, 204–9, 215–28; literary output of, 205–6; and Alphaism theory of sexual abstinence, 207–8; her influence reflected in *Diana*, 213; identified with *Diana*, 215; and sexual inquiry through correspondence, 218–19; and chivalry, 273; mentioned, 74, 133
Smith, William A., reminisces about Moses Harman in Valley Falls, 106
Socialism, and anarchism, 135
Social Purity movement: relation of free love to, 26–27; and Alphaism, 207; mentioned, 116
Social science, and social reform, 87
Society for Prevention of Vice. See Comstock, Anthony
Spear, John M., and New Motor experiments, 17–19
Spencer, Herbert: his influences on American anarchism, 58; quoted, 278
Spiritual affinity, doctrine of, 4, 6, 8–9, 283 n. *See also* Spiritualism
Spiritual aspect of sex, 214–15

Spiritualism: origins and growth of, 7; as idea of progress, 11, 20; and technology, electricity, and the telegraph, 12–20; and Congress, 14; prominent persons involved with, 14–15; and Christianity, 15; and science, 15, 283–84 n, 286 n; and John M. Spear, 17–19; and scientific knowledge, 19–20; and democracy, 20; historians puzzled by, 22, 286 n; and free thought, 41; and Lois Waisbrooker, 240–41; causes of American, 283 n; mentioned, 274, 282 n
Spiritualists, as free lovers, 21
Spiritual union of sexes, 277–78
Spooner, Lysander, 59, 103
Stanton, Elizabeth Cady: as radical feminist, 24; mentioned, 134
Stead, W. T., 259–60
Steffens, Lincoln, 201
Stockham, Alice B.: career and arrest of, 262; mentioned, 210
Stone, Lucy, marriage of, 86
Stopes, Marie, 210
Strickland, Mattie, free marriage of, 88–89
Suffrage, woman, in states and territories, 299 n
Sumner, William Graham, 155, 156
Swartz, Clarence Lee: as *Lucifer* editor, 145–46; on menstruation, 238

Tariff Act of 1842, and origins of obscenity law, 70
Taylor, Harriet, marriage of, 87
Technology. *See* Science
Telegraph, spiritual implications of, 12–14
Temperance, and sex, 206, 207, 215. See also *Diana*
Theocratic organizations, 43, 44, 50. *See also* Christianity
Thompson, William, as early critic of marriage, 25
Tilton, Lucy M., teaches children about sex, 174
Tissot, Samuel, seminal theory of, 207
Tocqueville, Alexis de, on free thought, 34
Tolstoy, Count Leo, his essay on *Diana* teachings, 215, 273–79
Train, George Francis, 107
Truelove, Edward, supported by Edward Bliss Foote, 198
Trumbull, General M. M., reports trial

of Haymarket radicals in *Lucifer*, 138
Truth Seeker, The (free-thought periodical), 40–43 passim
Tucker, Benjamin: as publisher of *Liberty*, 53; as individualist anarchist theorist, 59–60; praises *Lucifer*, 63–64; on concept of free marriage, 102–3; his influence on Edwin C. Walker, 108; intimidated by Comsock, 250, 251; mentioned, 146

Ulysses case, and obscenity law, 113
Union Labor party: origins of, 140–41; mentioned, 135–36, 303 n
United States Department of Agriculture, and mailing of "horse penis" book, 229–31

Valentine, Judge, and Kansas Supreme Court decision in Walker-Harman marriage case, 94
Valley Falls, Kans.: free-thought activity in, 46–50; public opinion in, 97–99, 104–6; businessmen of, vouch for Moses Harman's moral character, 116; and *Lucifer* radicals, 139; mentioned, 81, 86, 90, 130
Valley Falls Liberal, 46
Van Meter, R. E., 97
"Varietism," sexual, 253
Venereal disease, 162
Victorian sexual attitudes, 68–69, 78
Victorian social code, and style of sex radicals, 274. *See also* Comstock, Anthony
Villiers, Roland de, 257, 259, 260
Vincent brothers (radical Kansas editors), 140–41
Virginia (state), 28, 218

Waisbrooker, Lois Nichols: Populism and her arrest on obscenity charges, 148; on Elmina Slenker's "ring correspondence," 219–20; her reaction to concept of oro-genitalism, 225–26; unrespectability of, 229; edits *Lucifer*, 229–31; and "horse penis" affair, 229–31; biographical sketch of, 231–34; literary output of, 232; arrested at Home, Wash., 233–34; and menstruation, 235–36; and sexualism, 242; and chivalry, 273; mentioned, 45, 74, 102, 157
Wakeman, Thaddeus B.: organizes Liberal League, 37; as Populist, 147
Walker, Edwin Cox: as radical in Liberal League, 39; anti-Protestantism of, 42; as free-thought organizer, 53; characterized by Edgar Howe, 54; joins Moses Harman, 54–55; anarchism of, 58; on agrarian life, 60–61; on rural women, 61; communal ideas of, 61; his discussions with Benjamin Tucker, 61–62; free marriage of, to Lillian Harman, 81–96; imprisoned for marriage, 81, 90–91, 92–93; his marriage debate with Benjamin Tucker, 102–3; begins *Fair Play*, 133; anarchism of, influences Moses Harman, 135; has dispute with Moses Harman over voting, 136–37; writes obituary for Ezra Heywood, 182; and Free Speech League, 200–201; on children, 249; mentioned, 50, 51, 146, 268
Walker, Virna Winifred, 300 n
Wallace, Alfred Russel: on eugenics and female selection in marriage, 122; on prenatal influences, 123; on natural selection in marriage, 300 n
Walser, G. H., founds town of Liberal, Mo., 41
Ward, Lester Frank: as free-thought journalist, 41; his development of gynecocentric theory, 222–24; possibly influenced by Stephen Pearl Andrews, 224; his gynecocentric theory popularized, 227; mentioned, 269
Warfare, and sex, 242, 243
Warren, Josiah: his theory of individual sovereignty, 5; his influence on Ezra Heywood, 156, 157; mentioned, 59. *See also* Anarchism
Weaver, James B. (Greenback Democrat), 136
Weissenfield, Georg F. S. von (Roland de Villiers), identity of, and Bedborough case, 261
Weissman, August, hereditarian theories of, 122
Wells-Barnett, Ida, 269
White, Lillie D.: criticizes feminist eugenics, 126; radicalism of, 148; edits *Lucifer*, 148, 245–50; on menstruation, 237–38; criticizes ideas of state support of mothers, 239; background of, 245; has dispute

with *Liberty* editors, 250; mentioned, 45, 268. *See also* Domesticity
Whitehead, Celia B., 133
Whitlock, Brand, and Free Speech League, 201
Whitman, Walt, 109, 199, 200, 241
Whitney, Anne, questions Bible on free love, 154
Wilde, Oscar, 226–27
Wise, J. B., 107
Wollstonecraft, Mary, 25
Woman's Christian Temperance Union, and Christian feminism, 135, 171
Woman's Journal: supports Moses Harman, 115; and Anthony Comstock, 116
Women: leadership of, in free-love movement, 22; and leadership among spiritualists, 22; and the law, 94; in the government of Kansas, 118–19; suffrage, dilemma to *Lucifer*, 119; and economics, 189–90; outnumber males, 216, 225; theory of superiority of, 221, 222, 224–25, 227–28. *See also* Feminism; Marriage
Woodhull, Victoria: as first woman candidate for president, 3; proclaims herself free lover, 3; and free-love factions, 22; on love and prostitution, 23; influenced by Stephen Pearl Andrews, 23; as free-love agitator, 23; her Equal Rights party, 135; and the Heywoods, 157
Woodhull & Claflin's Weekly, 88, 231–32, 244
Word, The: as precursor of *Lucifer*, 28; begins publication, 156
"Words in Pearl" (birth-control information pamphlet), 194–95
Wright, Elizur, 170, 200
Wright, Frances, urges marriage reform in public speeches, 3
Wright, Henry C.: and principles of free love, 4; and Elmina Slenker, 204; promotherhood ideas of, 239

Yarros, Victor, 250–51
Yogic systems, and sexual energy, 210
Young Men's Christian Association, 166

Zueblin, Charles, 262
"Zugassent's Discovery" (male continence), 210

www.ingramcontent.com/pod-product-compliance
Lightning Source LLC
Chambersburg PA
CBHW070232240426
43673CB00044B/1765